Contributing Citizens

Contributing Citizens

Modern Charitable Fundraising and the Making of the Welfare State, 1920-66

Shirley Tillotson

UBCPress · Vancouver · Toronto

15 14 13 12 11 10 09 08   5 4 3 2 1

Printed in Canada with vegetable-based inks on FSC-certified ancient-forest-free paper (100% post-consumer recycled) that is processed chlorine- and acid-free.

Library and Archives Canada Cataloguing in Publication

Tillotson, Shirley Maye, 1956-
Contributing citizens : modern charitable fundraising and the making of the welfare state, 1920-66 / Shirley Tillotson.

Includes bibliographical references and index.
ISBN 978-0-7748-1473-7 (bound); ISBN 978-0-7748-1474-4 (pbk.)

1. Charities – Political aspects – Canada. 2. Public welfare – Canada – History – 20th century. 3. Welfare state – Canada – History. I. Title.

HV41.9.C3T54 2008   361.70971'09041   C2008-902294-7

Canada

UBC Press gratefully acknowledges the financial support for our publishing program of the Government of Canada through the Book Publishing Industry Development Program (BPIDP), and of the Canada Council for the Arts, and the British Columbia Arts Council.

This book has been published with the help of a grant from the Canadian Federation for the Humanities and Social Sciences, through the Aid to Scholarly Publications Programme, using funds provided by the Social Sciences and Humanities Research Council of Canada.

UBC Press
The University of British Columbia
2029 West Mall
Vancouver, BC V6T 1Z2
604-822-5959 / Fax: 604-822-6083
www.ubcpress.ca

Contents

Illustrations

Tables

Acknowledgments

To thank those who contribute is essential in organizing any collective enterprise. Writing a book may be an individual activity, but it is impossible without a large community of readers, funders, assistants, records managers, and supporters of various sorts. So, like the fundraisers I have studied, I end this intellectual campaign with appreciations.

At a difficult moment in my life, Judith Fingard and Janet Guildford pushed me to keep going with this project, and their interest in my work, their high standards, and their deep knowledge of Halifax were invaluable. Suzanne Morton is also an important part of the Halifax history crew, and she read the whole manuscript with a helpfully sharp eye. Colleagues in Vancouver and Ottawa contributed either to my local knowledge or to my thinking about social work or both: in Vancouver, Bob MacDonald, Mark Leier, and Todd McCallum; in Ottawa, John H. Taylor and Allan Moscovitch. Raymond B. Blake and Jane Jenson gave me wonderful opportunities to present the material at enormously interesting interdisciplinary conferences. One of the best readers of the work-in-progress was Jim Struthers, whose comments on my conference papers were hugely important to me.

I have also been fortunate in my Dalhousie and King's colleagues, who contributed in many ways, especially through their challenging questions and supportive encouragement in the history department's weekly seminar, where most of this material was first presented. While I was writing this book, I supervised two excellent graduate students, Renée Lafferty and Jessica Squires, in related projects; their contributions can be found in my endnotes and were much appreciated. Michael Cross's comments on the introduction got me off to a great start. Jerry Bannister read the whole manuscript in its penultimate form and helped me to see the manuscript in a fresh light. Conversations about ethical theory with members of the Dalhousie Department of Philosophy and the Women's Studies program, Richmond Campbell, Sue Campbell, and Susan Sherwin, played an important part in the making of Chapter 7.

Historians depend on archives. It is no exaggeration to say that this book would have been impossible without the helpful co-operation of the United Way of Ottawa-Carleton (in particular Valerie Parker and Bill Zimmerman) and the United Way of the Lower Mainland (especially Bruce Levens). They gave me and (in Ottawa) my research assistant not only access to records but also research space. Their openness to an historian's interest in their organization exemplifies the community mindedness of the United Way and represents an admirable faith in research-based knowledge as a part of social leadership. The book took much longer to appear than they could ever have expected, but I kept my promise. Two men who appear as historical actors in these pages also talked with me, and, although this research is archival rather than interview based, it was a pleasure to meet in person or by e-mail former Community Chest directors Howard Naphtali and George Hart. Archives staff at Library and Archives Canada, City of Vancouver Archives, UBC Special Collections, Ottawa City Archives, Dalhousie University Archives, British Columbia Archives and Records Services, and Nova Scotia Archives and Records Management helped me to navigate the complex tangle of private and public records on which I drew. I especially appreciate the confidence placed in me by the Ottawa City Archives in giving me access to some essential, but at the time unprocessed, records. All of these archives struggle with inadequate funding to manage an essential cultural resource, and I was uniformly impressed with the enthusiasm and diligence of the staff in the support they gave my research.

The Canadian taxpayer, through the Social Sciences and Humanities Research Council of Canada, provided most of the financing for the research on which this book is based. SSHRCC's anonymous reviewers saw the project's potential, and their comments shaped the project from its beginning. The SSHRCC funding paid the salaries of three excellent research assistants – Chris Dummitt, Paul Jackson, and Russell Johnston – who made it possible for a Halifax-based historian to write Canadian history. To their intelligence, organizational skills, and reliability, I owe a considerable debt.

Finally, the patience and competence of the editors and other staff at UBC Press have made the final stages of producing this book a pleasure. The anonymous reviewers and the copy editor, Dallas Harrison, helped the manuscript to put on its best, final face. Of course, any errors and eccentricities that remain are my responsibility. The book's readers will be the next participants in its making, and for their contributions to the life of the book, through critique, discussion, and the use of it in their own projects, I offer my thanks now, in advance.

Contributing Citizens

Introduction: Public and Private in Welfare History

Now that I know what I know about the history of charitable fundraising, I find it difficult to take seriously the view that the welfare state was to blame for a decline in charitable giving. But I understand why that idea is plausible to us as potential donors. There is an effort and an emotional strain entailed in truly thinking about need and in deciding how much to give and to whom. If we imagined that adequate state programs existed, then we might think ourselves relieved of that effort. As an explanation of how public provision affected giving, however, this overlooks a major phenomenon of twentieth-century fundraising: its modernization. Many of the innovations that made fundraising modern were designed to free donors from exactly the work of feeling and choosing that charity supposedly entailed. Several decades before Canada's welfare state was well established, modern fundraisers tried to make efficiency and impersonality the basis for giving. They failed – but only after making modern charity look like the welfare state in waiting.

The development of the Community Chests is the defining story of how charity became modern in twentieth-century Canada. When Charles Darrow created the board game Monopoly in 1934, the Community Chest (featured as the good luck square) was as well known as the street names on the board. In almost 400 American cities, there was a Community Chest that annually made an appeal for funds on behalf of the cities' charities. In Canada, too, all of the major cities had similar organizations, as did several smaller centres. These organizations (sometimes called "federations" or "united appeals") were a new expression of the rationalizing impulse that, in the nineteenth century, had produced associated charities groups such as the Charities Organization Society. In the 1920s and 1930s, the federations represented what was innovative in charitable fundraising. The first welfare federations in the United States had begun just before the First World War. In Canada, they emerged in the war's immediate aftermath.[1] By 1958, the number of

FIGURE 1

GNP, Canada, 1931-58

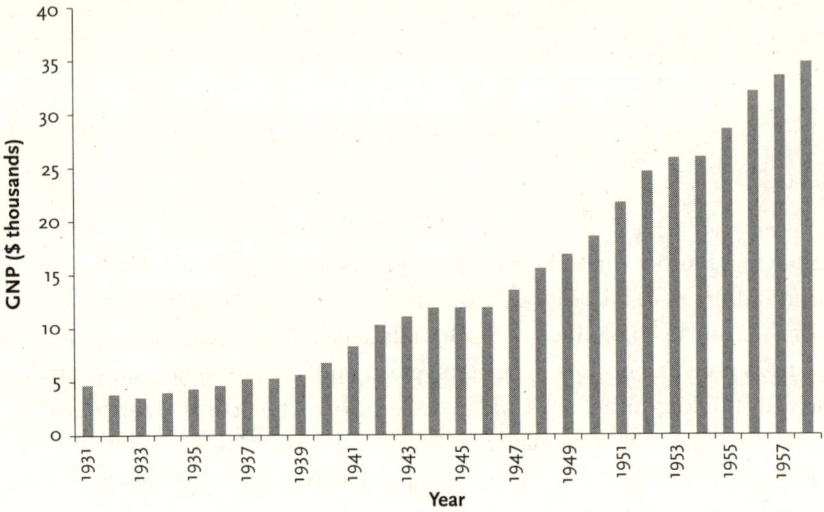

SOURCE: F.H. Leacy, ed., *Historical Statistics of Canada*, 2nd ed. (Ottawa: Statistics Canada, 1983), Table F13.

welfare federations in Canada had grown to seventy-four from eight in 1934. They had become a normal element of the system of welfare provision in Canada. Although not yet present in Newfoundland, they were increasingly found in rural centres such as Truro, Nova Scotia, and Joliette, Quebec.[2] And, rather than shrinking as the welfare state grew, the donations they collected grew as the economy grew (see Figures 1 to 4).

The "chest idea" was that all the charities making public appeals in any given city would unite to make one common appeal each year and that the amount asked would be the precise amount required to meet the needs of efficiently organized welfare agencies.[3] A single appeal combined with competent spending would efficiently use the publicity dollars and volunteer energies that were available to charity. Central oversight of services would prevent duplication and unnecessary spending. Businessmen sitting on management boards and the male and female office workers in the various agencies would be saved the work of planning, managing, and record keeping for many separate, smaller fundraising campaigns. Door-to-door canvassers, mainly women, would make the circuit once a year rather than repeatedly.

FIGURE 2

Community Chest donations, Canada, 1931-58

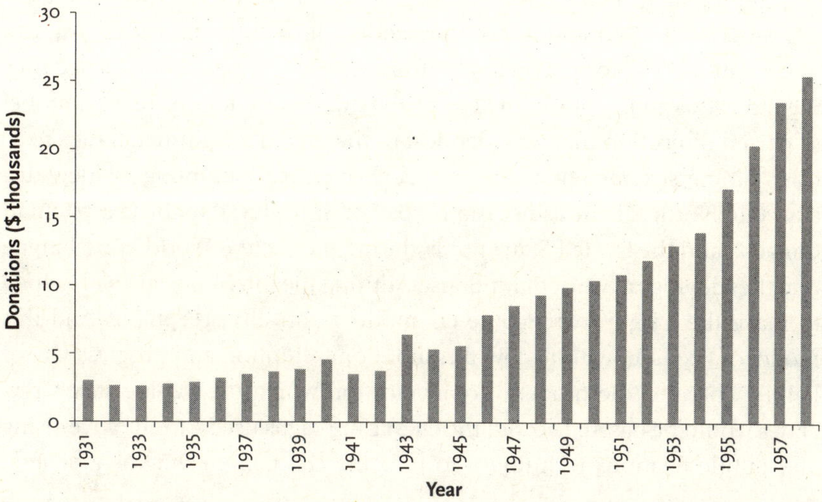

SOURCE: *Canadian Welfare*, various issues.

As a result of these efficiencies, charities would be able to give up on risky and irritating fundraising methods. No longer would social work have to take the risk of relying on events such as teas, dances, and fairs, which required lots of effort but produced unreliable, often small, returns. And the chest promoters promised that their fundraising would be less irritating than, for example, the infestation of store foyers and downtown streets with "taggers": people soliciting donations for charity, giving out little lapel labels to each donor. Retail merchants thought that having shoppers run a gauntlet of taggers was bad for business. They hoped the annual appeal would eliminate this nuisance. Finally, the annual appeal of a federation of charities was supposed to increase charitable giving. A welfare federation, larger than any of its single member agencies, would command greater and better fundraising resources. It would be able to mount a modern sales campaign. Systematic record keeping, co-ordinated publicity, team organization, and a military-style chain of command would provide fundraisers with data for strategic planning and the means to motivate and support canvassers. Moral suasion, frail on its own, would be empowered by the tools of modern business.

This new method of charitable fundraising, as I will show, helped to make the welfare state possible. Some people intended to use fundraising for private welfare services to make tax-funded services unnecessary; however, even though federated appeals funded more and more charities over the decades between 1920 and 1960, they ended up helping in several ways to make public provision increasingly attractive. First, the chests succeeded during the 1920s and 1930s in increasing the number of donors, using a model of citizen obligation that was identical to the one that legitimated the cross-class, progressive income tax. This model of obligation, though widely discussed in North America since the 1890s, was introduced in the tax system in Canada (and the United States) only during the Second World War.[4] I argue that the ideological work of fundraisers during the interwar years had helped to make the progressive income tax model politically acceptable. And this model of taxation, with its low threshold of exemption and progressivity of liability, became the model of obligation on which the welfare state's revenues would be based. Second, the chest campaigns used various advertising and public relations techniques to redefine charitable giving as a general

FIGURE 3

Personal income tax, Canada, 1931-58

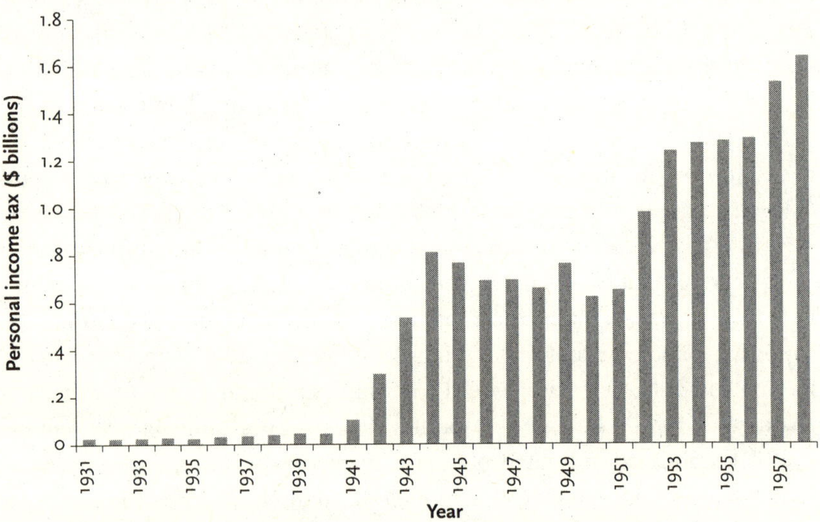

SOURCE: Canada, Department of National Revenue, *Taxation Statistics* (1961), 20.

civic duty rather than a more specific gender, religious, ethnic, or fraternal obligation. In this way, they promoted conceptions of private duties that appeared increasingly similar to public ones. Third, their fundraising methods generated a particular kind of awareness of welfare needs, a kind that, paradoxically, made it logical to meet those needs through tax-funded programs rather than donation-funded ones. This was especially important during the war years and the 1950s, when better economic conditions seemed to make the needs of the poor less pressing. Fourth, these fundraising organizations built a network of social leaders, from business, labour, religious organizations, and professional social work, who, by the 1950s, became an influential policy community with a broad social base. Their influence was substantially derived from their record of fundraising success. As fundraisers, their purpose was to support private charity, but one of their means of protecting private charity's viability was to advocate for the expansion of particular tax-funded social programs. By the 1950s, the united appeals had become part of the new welfare regime. The charities they helped to finance were complements and not alternatives to public programs.

FIGURE 4

Government health and welfare spending, Canada, 1931-58

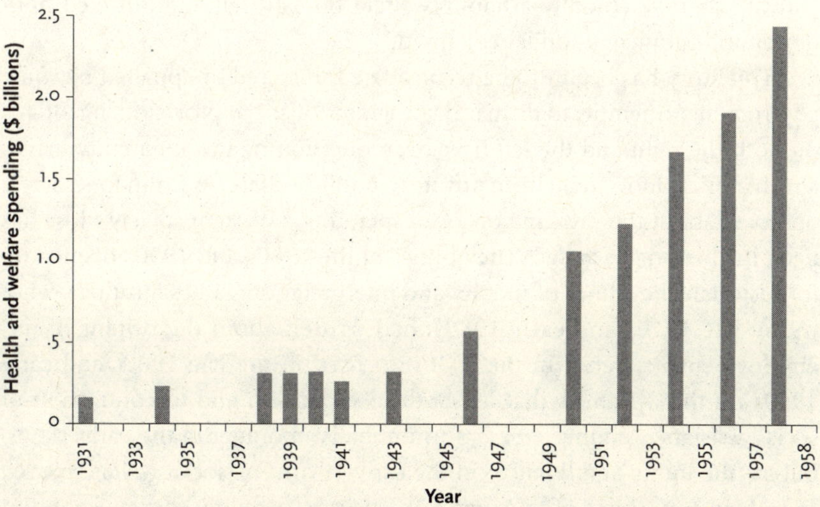

SOURCE: Dennis Guest, *The Emergence of Social Security in Canada*, 3rd ed. (Vancouver: UBC Press, 1997), 305.

Our present historical knowledge of the development of welfare in Canada does not prepare us to understand the coexistence of increasing charitable giving and a growing welfare state. The headline news of twentieth-century welfare history was, rightly, tax-funded programs. In the decades from 1920 to 1960, while the Community Chest movement was surging ahead, public programs of welfare provision also grew dramatically. Beginning with workmen's compensation, veterans' pensions, and mothers' allowances, and proceeding to old age pensions, unemployment insurance, family allowances, and unemployment assistance, the provision of relief to the needy was radically transformed. In the same period, tax funds also became increasingly the sole or fundamental support for social services such as hospitals, public health nursing, child protection, recreation, and housing for the elderly. The beginnings of all of these developments together can, in short form, be called "the origins of the welfare state." And as the diversity of these developments indicates, the welfare state is not a single thing with a common underlying causality. But in the various histories written of its component parts, there has typically been a theme of these new phenomena replacing older, inadequate agencies, usually ones that relied substantially on private funding: in a word, charities. Thus has grown up in historical writing, as well as in journalistic history and popular memory, a common-sense story in which the welfare state (its agencies at first called "public charities") took over when "private charity" (usually a family welfare bureau that administered both donor and municipal funds) collapsed.[5]

This story has begun to be reconsidered. Inspired or appalled by some governments' attempts to dismantle programs of social provision, historians on both the right and the left have been questioning the apparently inevitable historical movement from private to public welfare. As Colin Jones wryly observed about the savaging of social spending, "Western society's loss has been the historian's gain."[6] The politics of the 1980s and 1990s opened up for historians new lines of inquiry and interpretation. James Struthers, who, in the late 1970s and early 1980s, had written about the origins of unemployment insurance in the 1930s, focused in the late 1980s and early 1990s on the dynamics that led both to expansion and to contraction of social assistance, ending, not at a triumphalist moment in the early 1960s, but at "the limits of affluence" in the early 1970s.[7] As social welfare moved from being an object of apparent consensus to a central focus of political controversy, researchers began to analyze which crucial contingencies made the welfare state's expansion in the twentieth century possible. Economists, philosophers, and sociologists have all made contributions in this area.[8] Historians have been particularly interested in revisiting the 1930s to understand the conditions that made state expansion politically viable.[9] One set of conditions that has emerged as significant has to do with the role of private welfare agencies. Were private agencies no more or no less able than public ones to respond to the crisis of the 1930s? Did they lose ground only when government agencies, for ideological reasons, took over? Or were reluctant governments pressed into relief provision (and other forms of social work) only because no system of donations or private insurance could meet the manifest and socially accepted needs? If, metaphorically speaking, private welfare in the 1930s took a dive off a tall building, did it jump, or was it pushed?[10]

Some of the newer studies echo the older common sense on this question. Lizabeth Cohen, for example, shows that, for Chicago's working class, it was the failure of private charities and mutual aid in the face of structural economic change that destroyed the old ways of dealing with need and made the intercession of the state, with its resources of taxation and borrowing, necessary to finance the response to new and larger-scale kinds of need. She regrets the loss of some of the older forms of security provision, emblematic as they were of working-class cultural norms. But, from Cohen's perspective, the eclipse of, for example, mutual aid societies was inevitable. These privately funded welfare agencies were part of a cultural response to insecurity that ceased to be effective in the face of the Depression's sweeping structural unemployment. Working-class collective response to insecurity took newer, more relevant forms in campaigns for state-managed, tax-funded social provision.[11]

In other interpretations of the change from private to public provision, the phenomenon was not an inevitable response to the magnitude of need (at least for male workers) but a deliberate enactment in law of ill-advised state-collectivist ideologies. For example, David Beito argues that fraternal societies would have continued to be viable means of providing institutional care for orphaned children and the elderly had not governments provided competing programs such as old age pensions and mothers' allowances. Faced with this kind of competition, some fraternal orders closed their homes, and most had reorganized by the 1940s as social clubs or life insurance businesses. In losing the practical programs of fraternal societies, Beito argues, the United States lost relationships of "voluntary reciprocity and autonomy" and relegated its poorest citizens to the standing of disparaged dependents.[12]

While he acknowledges that there were many contributing factors in fraternalism's decline, including structural change in the workforce and market competition from commercial insurance, Beito emphasizes the primary causal weight of government intervention in the security business. His is a "crowding out" argument that owes its basic logic to libertarian macroeconomics. In an interview with Manitoba's Frontier Centre for Public Policy, he made clear his belief that his argument also applies to Canada.[13]

Canada's most recent treatment of the Depression's role in state formation is Nancy Christie's. In *Engendering the State: Family, Work, and Welfare in Canada,* Christie acknowledges both the charities' struggles and the ideological critique of private welfare. But a welfare state ideology did not necessarily and directly lead to government takeover. Charities that served women workers begged for help but were left to private funding auspices. Men's income needs, inadequately met by private organizations, attracted the attention of governments, however, and the ideology of support and discipline for male breadwinners justified unemployment insurance and family allowances.[14] In this view, public programs were the result of private charity's inadequacies, to be sure, but the ideological push came from gender politics more than class.

Along with debates about the value of the shift from private to public provision and its causes has come a literature that questions whether the public/private division ever existed in the pure form that political ideologies assume. In 1995, Mariana Valverde made the beginnings of a case for Canada having had, not a purely private welfare regime, but a "mixed social economy," with significant participation by government, since at least the mid-nineteenth century.[15] Others have followed in developing this thesis.[16] In this view, governments have always participated in welfare provision, whether through subsidy, regulation, licensing, criminal law, or direct service. What has changed over time, and what is therefore a subject for historical inquiry, is the actual blend of state and private citizen direction and financing. Thus, historians can study what figuratively has been called the boundary or the frontier between the public and the private provision of welfare.[17]

The most fully developed historical empirical study of a mixed social economy is Geoffrey Finlayson's 1994 publication *Citizen, State, and Social Welfare in Britain, 1830-1990.* Part of what is admirable about Finlayson's survey is its rich description of the private side of welfare. Following British social policy vocabulary, Finlayson calls this the "voluntary" sector and distinguishes it from the "statutory" sector. Voluntarist welfare includes not only agencies that fund their work through collecting donations but also a range of non-profit economic organizations such as fraternal mutual benefit societies, unions and co-operatives, and penny savings banks. From the two ends of an altruism scale of welfare work, Finlayson also includes, at one extreme, profit-making insurance companies (because of their risk-pooling and educational aspects) and, at the other limit, informal mutual aid, especially the poor helping the poor. The general picture that emerges from this rich description is one of diversity, multiplicity, and patchiness of provision, especially in the voluntary sector but also in statutory programs throughout much of the nineteenth century. Commercial insurance ventures and fee-charging services, meanwhile, ebbed and flowed with demographic and other market forces.[18] The varied picture of private agencies that Finlayson offers, even though it is specific to Britain, informs my efforts in this book to depict federated fundraising within an encompassing world of diverse private and public provision.

In addition to scholarship that reveals the diversity of the private side of the public-private relationship, there has been valuable work on the many mechanisms by which the state has taken a hand in voluntary enterprises. Here some examples will suggest that there are common patterns in the North Atlantic anglophone world but also some significant national variations. In Britain, for example, an early-nineteenth-century crisis surrounding the use of charitable endowments led to the creation of a reformed and permanent Charity Commission, a national state agency that oversaw these matters.[19] However, in Canada, the constitutional location of welfare agencies made any such national regulation impossible. Some provinces incorporated particular charitable societies and conferred quasi-police powers on certain ones.[20] But no province appears to have erected an overarching regulatory framework for all charities; Quebec's Public Charities Act of 1921 and Ontario's Charities Aid Act of 1874 did exercise some kind of control over the subset of agencies that received provincial grants. In Valverde's depiction, the Ontario legislation effectively enforced modern administrative practices. The comparable American regulatory apparatus, state welfare boards, were, according to Robert Bremner, much less effective, unable to do more than exercise "shadowy supervision" and to advise legislatures.[21] The existence in the United States of legal precedent that protected voluntary associations from state intervention set real limits on the extent of government regulation. The same body of precedent made legal incorporation the basis of charities' autonomy.[22] Thus, in the United States, federated fundraising's national body was, in the 1920s and 1930s, the Association of Community Chests and Councils, Incorporated. In Canada, national co-ordination began not with a legally incorporated enterprise but with the community organization division of the voluntary Canadian Welfare Council.[23] Differences in tax law also regulated philanthropy distinctively in Canada: for example, the 1930 amendment that allowed Canadians to deduct charitable contributions from up to 10 percent of their taxable income came thirteen years after its more generous (15 percent) equivalent in American tax law.[24] The federated fundraising movement was both American and Canadian, to be sure, and much that I will say about the Canadian case may be true also of the American case. But, as the examples above begin to suggest, the constraints and possibilities set by the legal, institutional, and political contexts of each country were significantly different.

A final dimension of the public and private relation in welfare is the role of the familial private sphere. In this respect, the Canadian urban experience approximates the American and British ones closely enough to make work done elsewhere on women, welfare, and social work relevant to this study. This well-established literature shows that both public and private agencies relied on and helped to reinforce a breadwinner/housewife division of labour in family welfare.[25] In the social work profession, it has become equally clear, masculine and feminine roles were differentiated and hierarchical. A field dominated by women in the 1910s became, by the 1950s, a mixed-sex one, with a pattern of male administrators and female staff emerging as the norm in all three countries.[26] Less well studied is the question of how gender figured in changes in the organization of fundraising. Frank Prochaska argues, for the British case, that nineteenth-century charity canvassing was utterly dependent on women's labour, whether as volunteers or as commission-paid collectors.[27] Evidence from Canadian research, especially in the history of religion, supports in large measure his depiction.[28] Wives and widows of wealthy men also played a part in large-scale philanthropy, as Kathleen D. McCarthy and Ruth Crocker have shown in American case studies.[29] And Laura Tuennerman-Kaplan's superb study of popular charitable practices in Cleveland argues persuasively that charitable giving formed an avenue to power for women as well as for racial and ethnic communities.[30]

It is remarkable, then, that women as fundraisers and donors do not appear in the most recent Canadian study of this aspect of social work. In *A Marriage of Convenience: Business and Social Work in Toronto, 1918-1957*, Gale Wills has applied a gender analysis to the relationship of fundraisers and service providers. In her interpretation, this relationship became a clash of gender cultures, with a male-dominated business class championing business efficiency in fundraising and spending against the feminine culture of the social work side, which valued social efficiency and emphasized planning and justice. Hers is a provocative and important thesis that contributes a persuasive account of how the chest movement helped to create an apolitical, feminized, social work profession in the 1950s. But in telling that story, Wills leaves the impression that chest fundraising was simply anti-statist, masculine, and business dominated.[31] In so doing, she overlooks some of the positions and powers available to women in the financing side, as distinct from the service delivery side, of private charity. The questions of women's citizenship that were still so controversial in the period of the chests' origins made the gender politics of the welfare federations more complex, I will argue, than a social worker/businessman binary can capture. Moreover, the mixture of forces that shaped the relation of masculinity to fundraising for charity also needs to be explored if we are to understand the gender politics in this aspect of private welfare and the relation of private welfare to government, high politics, and the growth of the welfare state.

If we consider the welfare federations as fundraising mechanisms and not primarily in light of their goals of service, then they become very useful means of viewing the multiple links between public and private welfare in the period of the welfare state's formation. As I will show in Chapter 1, these organizations were created by people who hoped that the application of business methods to fundraising would both relieve pressure on existing donors and increase the funds available to existing charities, all the while making the most efficient use of the time and effort of the social agencies' staff and volunteers. In this hope, the promoters of federation often spoke in both their private charity and their public charity roles – that is, both as donors and as taxpayers. Efficient charity, they anticipated, would help to reduce and keep to a minimum the calls on tax-funded services of income assistance, child welfare, and health care. Some key figures also spoke both as fundraisers and as past, present, or aspiring politicians and civil servants. In these and other ways, the work of fundraising mixed commercial motives, power brokerage, policy activism, associational loyalties, and partisan networks. The federated appeals both used and were used by elements of the state, whether civil servants, police and hospital administrators, or politicians. They built on and sometimes challenged the private sphere social relations on which much public policy was based. In short, the federated fundraising organizations formed a thick tissue of connections between private and public welfare worlds. And these connections worked more often in favour of state expansion than against it.

If the federated charities were so much a part of the making of the welfare state, why is it that they have not been more centrally featured in the Canadian or the international welfare literature? The first reason may be that historians have been satisfied with early interpretations of the chests as conservative forces necessarily left behind in the progress toward public provision. This is certainly how they figure in Robert Bremner's 1960 *American Philanthropy.* But Bremner describes them only briefly, as he does for most of the topics in his short survey of a long subject.[32] A fuller and more analytical treatment of federation in its first decades is the one Roy Lubove offers in his 1965 history of American social work. He presents the chests as the high point of the bureaucratization and professionalization of social work and argues that, despite their early co-operative democracy rhetoric, they were a force that militated against voluntarism of the individualist sort and that regimented both canvassers and donors.[33] Walter Trattner's 1974 history of social welfare in the United States situates the federation movement in an explanation of why social work became more conservative in the 1920s, adding the sin of impeding reform to the federations' fault in contributing to impersonal, bureaucratic social work.[34] Daniel Walkowitz's study of social work and middle-class identity focuses, like Wills' Toronto study, on the conflicts between social workers' professional culture and the sometimes competing priorities of the businessmen who dominated the chests.[35] In spite of the consensus in this American historiography, however, I am not convinced that the welfare federations were an unambiguously conservative force, at least not in Canada.

Canadian historians have had less to say about the chests (and charitable fundraising more generally) than have American historians. Dennis Guest's survey *The Emergence of Social Security in Canada,* which takes as its focus the description of the progressive increase of statutory programs and the recent threats to those developments, describes private philanthropy only in schematic terms, making it a mere cartoon figure of what progress left behind.

With his focus thus firmly on the system that apparently replaced private charity, Guest does not describe developments in fundraising, and its role in the explanation of statutory change goes unexamined. More inexplicably, given what the research for this book has uncovered, the federations are absent from Allan Irving and Patricia Daenzer's article-length survey of the social work profession's relation to unemployment policy. Focusing as they do on the Canadian Association of Social Workers (CASW), they might seem to be justified in their conclusion that "social workers moved out of the 1950s having made no significant contribution to policy direction."[36] But "social workers" were a larger group than the professionals in CASW. Other organizations, namely the fundraising federations and their associated welfare councils, seem to better represent social work, defined more broadly to include not only social workers from member agencies but also fundraisers, volunteers, and donors. Closer attention to the work of these organizations brings to light considerable and effective policy activism by social work in the 1950s.

But the Canadian welfare history in which charitable fundraising does appear takes it up without considering it as an intrinsic factor in state formation. Social work scholar Gale Wills investigates the conflict between the chests and social workers and, like the American historiography, depicts the business element in the Toronto federation as a constraint on social workers' projects. She sees the policy impact of the chest as largely conservative.[37] Others who have worked with chest archives have had even less interest in the relation of this private charity work to public policy. Historian Anne MacLennan's history of Montreal's anglophone federations in the period before their merger in 1972 with their francophone counterparts serves mainly to preserve a positive memory of one of the city's anglophone institutions. Similarly, Stephen Speisman treats Toronto's Federation of Jewish Philanthropies as an element in the formation of that city's Jewish community. For James Struthers, Toronto's Federation for Community Service forms a relatively small part of the background of social assistance politics.[38] On fundraising beyond the chests, Desmond Morton's study of the Canadian Patriotic Fund (CPF) describes an immediate precursor of the chests. Unlike them, the CPF was a service agency. Its fundraising rhetoric was in one sense distinctive to the wartime emergency: the appeal was "fight or pay," thus framing the donation as an exchange of money for freedom from a specific guilt or debt. Nonetheless, the CPF resembled the chests in targeting a mass public as prospective donors and in functioning as an alternative to increased taxation.[39]

But this relative neglect of fundraising in the history of twentieth-century state formation should not be taken to mean that it was insignificant in the key years of social policy innovation. Two sociological studies from the 1950s indicate that contemporaries understood the chests' importance for the post-war period. The University of Toronto's John R. Seeley studied the Indianapolis Community Chest, and McGill University's Aileen D. Ross examined the fundraising federations in a pseudonymous city that was identifiably Montreal, albeit a Montreal perceived wholly as an anglophone community.[40] These studies treat the chest phenomenon as an intriguing innovation that marked important social currents: Ross notes that large-scale, organized philanthropy was distinctively North American and barely forty years old. The changes that she found socially significant were "the change from giving as a sporadic individual affair to giving through the carrying out of highly organized campaigns; from giving by the pious and wealthy to giving by all sections of the community; from giving as a means of securing reward in heaven to giving as a means of establishing good relations with the public; from giving where the stress was on need, to giving where it is on the efficiency of the agencies involved; and from giving as a monopoly of the church to giving as a monopoly of business." She also notes, as changes less significant to her analysis, a shift from enthusiasm to "apathy and weariness," from amateur to professional social work, from individual choice to group pressure, and from a private matter to a matter of social status.[41] Her purpose was to describe the development of "organized philanthropy," to analyze its place in the social structure, and to identify its social function. She was not interested in state formation.

One notable feature of welfare studies has made it easy for Canadian welfare historians to overlook the importance of the financial federations. International comparison is methodologically central to welfare research, and most of the countries to which Canadians compare themselves – Britain, Scandinavia, Australia, Germany, and France – did not take up the federated fundraising system. The only real point of comparison is to the United States. In Lubove's account of the movement's American origins, the associated charities, when transplanted to the New World, were rendered into a new hybrid by means of a distinctively American voluntarist graft, found only on this side of the Atlantic.[42] If the organizers of federated fundraising were progressives of a sort, they were not, however, those importers of European ideas that Daniel T. Rodgers has described.[43] They seem, in fact, to have been exceptions to the European trend when they created the welfare federations, even if the logic of rationalization they embraced was part of the larger progressive culture shared across the Atlantic. A distinctively American element of anti-statism marked the chests at their origins. The extent of that element in the whole of the American federated fundraising movement is beyond the scope of this study to determine. But a Canadian study can help to illuminate the subject. After all, American influence was always present in twentieth-century Canadian welfare history. Social workers, volunteer and professional, participated in conferences and associations and labour markets in which the Canada-US border was largely invisible. To study the chests in Canada allows us to see how the range of available policy ideas was produced in a country that was part of the American social work sphere, even while not being politically, institutionally, or culturally exactly like the United States. The history of the federated fundraising movement draws our attention not to Atlantic crossings, then, but to border crossings at the forty-ninth parallel.

Perhaps the most fundamental and important reason for scholarly neglect of the fundraising federations has to do with definitions of the welfare state and the political priorities of welfare historians. Not only in Canada, but also in welfare history generally, the focus on income assistance, and in particular on unemployment relief, helped to make the chests invisible to the generations of historians formed politically and intellectually in the 1960s and later. In the 1960s and 1970s, the New Left made a compelling critique of the helping services as mechanisms by which the dominant classes imposed their values on others and sought to preserve their wealth and privilege.[44] In this critique, the path to a better welfare state (if such a path existed other than through revolution) seemed to lie straightforwardly in programs that redistributed wealth to the working class. In the short term, this meant that struggles to improve income assistance were politically central. From this viewpoint, the united appeal federations of the 1960s were at best irrelevant. Although the chests had helped to fund relief-giving agencies in the 1920s and 1930s, the united appeals of the 1950s tried to get away from funding income support. By the 1960s and 1970s, they had largely succeeded in doing so.[45] Their member agencies provided counselling, advocacy, recreation, health education, crisis intervention, and a diverse array of other services. It is easy to see how they might thus have seemed of little interest to those interested in the politics of income. In recent years, however, social agencies have returned to the centre of welfare planning as we discuss the financing of and need for services such as home care, transition houses, suicide prevention, foster care for children, addiction treatment, child day care, and community integration of people with disabilities. Once the importance of this aspect of welfare work comes into focus, the chests and their successor organization, the United Way, re-emerge as part of the main story of the welfare state. And understanding the historical relations of the welfare federations and the state then becomes a means of thinking anew, and less dismissively, about the relationships, actual and theoretical, between social services and income assistance, care and money.

If studying modern charitable fundraising can help to improve our explanation of how and why public provision changed, it is because the relationship between voluntary associations and government is not as distinct as American-influenced political ideology would have us think.[46] In making this observation, I am drawing on various bodies of Foucauldian, Gramscian, and feminist social and political theory that consider the complicated relationships between state and society.[47] In different specialized vocabularies, each of these bodies of theory offers tools for analyzing a complex problem: how do we describe, so as to explain, changes in freedom and constraint, oppression and liberation, if we no longer believe liberal simplicities? Moreover, if state and civil society interpenetrate and neither is uniquely the source of tyranny or the guarantor of security, how do we understand the complicated nets of limitation and possibility made by the intersection of public and private powers?

In *Contributing Citizens*, I tell a story that shows how some significantly situated Canadians encountered this problem and addressed it. Fundraisers faced both toward civil society – the economy, popular culture, family, and associational life – and toward the state. In relation to each of these fields of reference and sets of social relations, they found obstacles to and opportunities for their project. Taking their material from these fields, they shaped notions of need, authority, obligation, and resources. These notions in turn became available to other social actors, including politicians and other policy makers. Different sets of conceptual tools and terms served as vehicles for this traffic between fundraisers, the state, and other elements of civil society. These vehicles included religions, social sciences, political ideologies, and managerial models. While such vocabularies have native habitats, so to speak, they can also be redeployed in other discursive contexts as metaphor. Consequently, actors can carry them across the boundary between society and the state, between public and private life, or between market relations and personal ones. For example, references to family obligations can be brought into political life, to be used as models for proper order, and images from politics can be used to underpin authority in families. Similarly, images of efficiency in organizing industrial production may provide useful analogies to advance a project of change in social organization. Because of this metaphorical capacity for translating experience between supposedly distinct fields of life, terms that are drawn from various large conceptual systems help to organize the interactions among their native fields and others.[48] Fundraising as a project required of its performers that they operate effectively in relation to a wide array of social fields and interact legibly with multiple layers of the state. To do so, they became adept at translating their project into multiple languages: religious, commercial, familial, social scientific, and political. To trace how a major charitable fundraising movement framed its project and pursued it over four decades, then, is to watch from the front bench the development of the relations between the state and multiple dimensions of society. Narrative makes it possible to explain the interaction and relations of determination among different kinds of human organization – economic, cultural, political – in networks of various sizes – interpersonal, urban, national, and international.

In fashioning these narratives, I have drawn on a conception of power relations based mostly in materialist traditions, such as neo-Marxism, although there is a Foucauldian element to my analysis as well.[49] I have investigated the use by fundraisers, donors, and others of appeals to common cultural terms, in tandem with the coercive tools available – police, economic leverage, and control of access to material and social resources – to co-ordinate collective action for the purpose of wielding power. This investigation is materialist, insofar as I see the tools of coercion as distributed differentially among classes or class fractions defined by their relations to the means of production, and I see this distribution of "tools" as tending to determine all power relations. But I have also been attentive to the power resources and interests of other categories of people: for example, racialized groups (as such rather than as class fractions) or women and men as gendered beings (and not only in reproductive labour). These non-class interests and resources for power are sometimes economic in a narrow sense and sometimes not. Combined with a focus on economic interests and economic resources for exercising power, this view of power has enabled me to explain most of the changes that charitable fundraisers made in their own methods and, over time, the consequences of fundraising activity in building support for tax-based programs.

But I have not always found the relations of determination between the ideological or cultural work and the interests and powers of the parties involved to be analyzable solely in material terms or illuminated by taking interests and resources as given by social position. While this is common, there are also aspects of the story that seem more Foucauldian in their logic. That is, the story here includes not just the use of available tools for power, whether discursive or coercive, in the pursuit of interest but also the consequences of changes in the tools themselves. It seems that changes in the tools of power can alter the definition of the problems (including interests worth pursuing) to which the exercise of power is addressed. In other words, some of my questions are about whether and how tools alter strategies. The tools I consider are mainly the social technologies: the routine practices of publicity, organization, and representation and management of data.

In this sort of analysis, cultural and material realities are related in ways that can only be seen by means of both local micro-history and broad-brush cultural, economic, and political description. The design of the research and of the book thus reflects my general interest in analyzing the interactions among levels of social and political organization.[50] I have studied, in local history terms, the politics and personalities, conditions and circumstances, of the federated fundraising movement in three Canadian cities: Vancouver, Ottawa, and Halifax. In each of these cases, I was fortunate to be able to build on the work of two scholarly generations of urban historians interested in welfare, elites, gender, and labour.[51] In this study, Vancouver represents the top tier of Canadian cities, whose fundraising history shows what was possible and impossible for large, wealthy, and nationally significant community elites. Vancouver as a case study also had the advantage of a well-studied and politically engaged labour movement, which made more easily visible the competing and converging class ideologies of charity. I chose Ottawa from among other central Canadian cities for its combination of francophone and anglophone communities, a key element of Canadian political culture in the formative years of the welfare state. Ottawa was also simply a more manageable size than the other "bicultural" city, Montreal. For studying the Ottawa chest, there was the additional advantage of Charlotte Whitton's presence as a player during its organizing years and, later, her more peripheral involvement as mayor. This leading Canadian social worker was a prolific, thorough, and frank correspondent on all sorts of welfare questions, and her papers provide detailed descriptions of the chests' organizational strategies. Halifax, the city where I have lived during my research for this book, had the advantages of proximity but more importantly the benefits of a small scale: here, more easily than in Ottawa or Vancouver, I could decipher the politics of elite networks. In regional terms, an equally adequate (and equally inadequate) approach might have used Montreal, Hamilton, and Winnipeg. It may be that Canada cannot be truly represented by any partial sample of its various regions and that a complete sample of every important regional variation may be impossible in one volume. In that sense, Canada may not be a manageable object of generalization. But the sample I have used is based on the belief that, for the history of charity and the welfare state, to have considered only Montreal or Toronto would have entailed mistaking local politics for national ones.

The detail and texture that local history methods offer to this study are complemented by the efforts I have made to see the events in particular cities in relation to national and international developments. It was not difficult to see the effects of these larger systems in each of my cities. Whether through the field workers of the Canadian Welfare Council or through the movement of professional social workers among these cities for their own career reasons, social workers acted as transmission vectors for national and international ideas. Another source of broader influences was the impact in each of these cities of controversies about fundraising or other welfare questions that erupted in Toronto or Montreal, New York or Detroit. These controversies were reported in the national mass-circulation press and broadcast media and were taken up at conferences and in social work and business publications. Other national networks also reflected and influenced the strategies of specific welfare federations. Fundraisers in each of these cities, while responding to local conditions, were also influenced by the nationally or internationally devised projects of the labour movement, the service clubs, the first wave women's movement, social scientists, and political parties, to name some of the most central I have identified. By combining the methods of local and national history, I have tried to bridge a gap that has troubled those of us who, though trained as social historians, regret the limitations of history with the politics left out.

In analyzing the cultural world in which all of these groups operated, I have borrowed the methods of intertextual analysis from scholars of literature.[52] Intertextual analysis is based on a theory about how cultural products are made and have their effects. This theory posits that we understand any particular text only in relation to our experience of other similar kinds of speech and writing in its contemporary world or its generic tradition. On this assumption, to understand fundraising rhetoric, we need to look at other kinds of persuasive texts and, in particular, texts whose purpose was to induce audiences to exchange dollars in return for a mix of personal and social benefits. The method of intertextual analysis is primarily useful for understanding how local strategies were affected by national and international currents in the methods of advertising (especially for insurance), public relations, and electoral politics. Borrowings among and allusions to these different textual worlds help to explain what cultural producers thought would be effective in each. Whether or not they were right was measurable in funds raised, market share captured, and votes won. Among fundraisers, as among advertisers and politicians, no one could ever be sure that these effects were solely the results of their efforts or entirely within their control. But in each of these fields, men and women relied on their intuitive (and later social scientific) readings of what would work and were admired as successful when the results confirmed they had read well the anxieties, hopes, and needs of their publics. What was successful in one realm was certain to be appealing to practitioners of other, related genres.

I conclude that the tools modernizing fundraisers developed had the effect of increasing charitable giving, as they had hoped. But they also, unintentionally, helped to make the financing, the administrative methods, and the justice standards of the welfare state more acceptable. Pointing to this unintended effect is not merely an exercise in making bitter fun of shortsighted businessmen and their middle-class wives, widows, and daughters. Rather, I want to show how politically fertile the federated fundraisers' project was. It attempted to combine in a common action a diverse array of social groups, all of whom exercised some degree of real material power and who cherished conflicting ideologies.[53] In orchestrating common action, the fundraisers were forced into a search for common ground. They found that common ground but developed it only by promoting double-barrelled, seemingly paradoxical ideals – sentiment and reason, particularity and universality, altruism and self-interest, personal care and abstract rights, communitarianism and individual freedom. Once the fundraisers fashioned and purveyed such a complex and ambiguous discourse, and tested it in the field for its power to extract dollars from donors, it is only a small wonder that their enterprise fed other, and (to some of them) unwelcome, innovations in state formation.

Contributing Citizens is, then, a story of a project, its struggles, and its transformation. Chapters 1 and 2 describe the project, its proponents, and the circumstances from which it grew. In these two chapters, I establish the common moral and conceptual framework that links taxation and charity: the culture of contribution. I also present examples of the sort of people who could be found promoting both Community Chests and tax reform. In Chapter 1, Halifax represents the beginning of the chest movement. Chapter 2 maps the common ground between the conceptual worlds of taxation and charitable fundraising. The development of the chest idea into a movement is the subject of Chapters 3 and 4. The concepts of fair contribution and efficient management were sold and promoted by means of intense political and cultural work in the highly charged circumstances of the 1930s. In Chapter 3, Vancouver serves as the focus for my discussion of the cultural politics entailed in selling the chest idea, and Ottawa, in Chapter 4, illustrates the deployment of the sharp and dirty tools of local politics in the service of this ideal of welfare provision. By the end of Chapter 4, the Community Chests, having been created in a world where reformed charity had seemed to have a chance of forestalling the welfare state, are established and appear as both an alternative to the welfare state and its prototype.

In Chapter 5, the strategic circumstances of fundraising shift. The chests felt themselves to be on the defensive as they faced competition from war charities, the new unemployment insurance and family allowances, and the apparent promise of a more systematic welfare state for Canada. While local stories continue to feature in my narrative, and to have counted in the past, the scale of the remainder of the book is national. So, too, by this time, was the emerging welfare system. In Chapter 5, I look back to the national debate in the 1930s over the role of private charity and show how challenges of the war years, such as rising social work salaries, exceptional demands from the member agencies, and flat-out refusals to donate, made a fundamental reframing of the public-private relationship necessary in the 1940s.

After the war, as I show in Chapter 6, it remained to be established whether this new form of the relationship could be made to work. I explain how it was that the chests neither collapsed in the face of reconstruction crises nor found themselves reduced to insignificance by an aggressive state. I show that they were essential players in postwar state formation and, in particular, in the creation of the federal Unemployment Assistance Act in 1956 and the Canada Assistance Program in 1966. Finally, in Chapter 7, I return to the cultural dimension of the public-private relationship to discuss the working out in the 1950s of the relationship between principles of justice and practices of care. Against the dichotomous thinking that associated the former with statutory entitlement and the latter with charity, I argue that the postwar chests managed to contribute to a welfare state culture of universal entitlements and inclusive citizenship – a culture of justice – while also attempting to preserve for charity a role in promoting care. Faced with postwar donor fatigue, they invented more coercive pressures, increased their conceptual borrowing from consumerism, and devised ever more abstract images of need. In all of these cultural tactics, the fundraisers again demonstrated that private means of legitimating contribution were not very different from public ones.

Overall, what I hope to show in this book is that the welfare federations became an institution through which a modern common sense about social obligation and its appropriate expression emerged. By means of the fundraisers' work, a modern citizenship of contribution was constructed in tandem with the period's growing citizenship of entitlement.[54] The chests operated within a local framework but were also positioned on the national social and political stage, increasingly so in the 1950s. Ideas about social obligation flowed into the chest movement not only from intellectuals in universities but also from international service clubs and business organizations, from international unions, from churches and synagogues, and from chest canvassers meeting individual Canadians and reporting back on this experience. The mechanisms of reporting and strategic analysis that framed the canvassers' work produced a flow of information into the planning processes of the chests and out again into the community in the form of fundraising rhetoric. The result was significant innovations in ways of both knowing and shaping what a community could afford to give and what images of need would incite increased donations.

In their increasing but never entirely successful efforts to be inclusively representative and publicly accountable, the welfare federations resembled a kind of democratic government.[55] More inclusive by the 1950s even than any institutional religion, these organizations brought into an interactive relationship Canadians from different classes, genders, ethnicities, and generations.[56] Then as now, they were a training ground or a staging platform for political careers, legitimately so because they provided opportunities for people to demonstrate the kinds of leadership power and community responsibility that were valued in their time.[57] The significance of the welfare federations thus rests on the most general claim this book advances, that the work of governing and the activity of social citizenship were and are shaped by a common cultural framework.

This is more than just a point of theoretical interest. It suggests that, once a spirit of individualism or a family-only model of social obligation takes hold in economic relations, cultural rhetoric, or electoral politics, it cannot easily be confined to its original habitat. It seems that, whatever conception of self and society is current in one of these spheres will be communicated, often by fundraisers or their critics, to the others. This interconnectedness may explain why Swedes are enthusiastic participants in voluntary organizations but also elect welfarist politicians. Similarly, it might suggest why Japanese support neither social spending by their governments nor a large non-profit sector.[58] And the difficulties in Russia of establishing private charitable giving as a norm also make sense in this light. They follow clearly from problems that affect both democratic state formation and the organization of civil society alike – expectations of cheating, suspicion of the needy, fear of coerced contribution.[59] At the least, the connections I demonstrate between public and private modes of contribution should make us wary of assertions that an anti-tax position is necessarily a position in favour of private charitable giving. Which needs require a social response and how each of us as individuals will give of our own money and time are not decided separately in private benevolence and public citizenship. They are the questions we answer through both charity and taxation, from a common culture of contribution.

1

The Citizenship of Contribution: Taxation in the 1920s

Of the three Community Chests studied here, Halifax was the first. It belongs, with Toronto and Montreal, to the small group that took their first steps in the latter years of the First World War, amid concerns about the postwar taxation regime and the crisis in social welfare. During the war, the dominion government had attempted to co-ordinate the soliciting of charitable donations, by means of the War Charities Act of 1917, but after the war it was an open question whether this form of government management of the private sector, like the public regulation of manufacturing, could or should be continued. The wartime experience of co-ordinating charity, with its various frictions and failures, provided an example that might desirably be either emulated or avoided. And it was not entirely clear whether methods adopted to serve the extraordinary needs of war mobilization would be relevant to the peacetime economy or the postwar social imaginary. Fundraising for a great common cause had been celebrated as the expression of collective will. But did Canadians want more collectivism in peacetime?[1]

Soon after the war, a sense of crisis about welfare needs encouraged the renewed discussion of co-operative solutions and not only on the left. High levels of unemployment triggered this crisis mood. Seen in relation to the new threat and promise of communism, masses of men out of work became an incentive for new, if temporary, government support for the unemployed. Charities, too, understood that postwar unemployment required exceptional relief efforts. As important as unemployment was to the sense of crisis, other postwar problems also demanded more from social agencies. Wartime dislocations and disasters meant, in the postwar period, abandoned wives, orphaned children, disabled veterans, the influenza epidemic, and a spike in tuberculosis rates.[2] The scope of the welfare needs Canadians faced in these years was so great as to be difficult to grasp, then as now. Compounding the challenges were the taxation problems of the 1920-23 period. During wartime, new taxes had been introduced by the dominion government. After the war, major decisions had to be made about whether these taxes would be continued and how to organize postwar public finance at all levels of government. The federated fundraising method appeared in this context as a potential co-ordinating but non-governmental solution to two problems: how to respond effectively to the onslaught of welfare needs and how to minimize the increase in tax-funded social services.

In this chapter and the next, I want to anatomize for the interwar period the ways in which charitable fundraising and taxation were related, not just as alternatives (either more charitable giving or more taxation), but also as overlapping projects. In the first of these two chapters, I outline the taxation debates of the 1920s, focusing especially on 1920-23, also the period in which federated fundraising was first proposed in Vancouver, Ottawa, and Halifax.[3] In my discussion of this period, I seek to show that taxation debates were not only about the defence of particular economic interests (although they were that) but also about the morality of citizenship. The central moral questions in these debates were what constituted fairness of contribution and what relation should exist between financial contribution and a voice in public questions. Particular answers to these questions were also central to the claims that fundraisers made for the superiority of the federated appeal method. Common underlying concerns about moral citizenship, then, were one kind of link between innovations in charities and taxation. Another was overlapping leadership. In the course of discussing the taxation debates, I draw attention to the connections between the leaders in those debates and the leadership of and participants in the instigation of the federated fundraising movement. Among the members of these connected groups, parallel solutions to the problems of social contribution and social need were being proposed.

In my discussion of taxation problems and fundraising leadership, I draw on information about all three of my cities and from national sources. In this chapter, to give a richer description of taxation and charity networks and issues than the national viewpoint will allow, I focus in greatest detail on Halifax. I chose Halifax because, of the three cities, it was the only one able to quickly and successfully move from a proposal in the early 1920s to a functioning campaign organization in 1925.

War finance had introduced significant innovations in Canadian taxation. The central government's revenue-raising methods had multiplied, with war income taxes and the business profits war tax added to the earlier mix of customs and excise duties and bond sales. Of these new taxes, the income taxes on personal and corporate incomes were the most important new departure because of their great potential as a revenue source. Previous dominion governments had avoided income tax for three reasons. One reason was that its collection would require the creation of a whole new mechanism of federal tax collection. Unless rates were high, its cost would initially outweigh its benefit. A second reason was that there were already some provincial and municipal income taxes; to introduce a dominion one would strain relations with those governments and with taxpayers in those jurisdictions. And the third and most important reason was that Canada risked losing citizens and businesses to the United States if it levied income taxes before the United States did. Not until the imposition of the US national personal income tax of 1913 did income tax become a practical possibility in Canada, and even then the US tax was so low and the levels of income it affected so high that, for Canada, the revenue of a comparable tax would scarcely have covered the cost of its implementation and enforcement. Only in 1917, after the US tax was set at higher rates on a broader base of incidence, were Canadian authorities convinced that it would be a good source of revenue and free of the risk of driving Canadians and capital out of Canada. That risk was also low because, even after 1917, the vast majority of Canadians were exempt from paying income tax: ordinary levels of salaries and wages fell below the level at which the war income tax was targeted. Only 1 or 2 percent of the population paid this tax in its early years.[4] Income tax was a particular responsibility of some, not a universal obligation of all, income earners.

The taxation innovations of wartime were not simply reversed after the armistice. Before the war, there had been agitation for tax reform, and in the debate about the fate of the war taxes the pre-war issues persisted. In the difficult economic conditions that continued in 1919 and 1920, questions of economic justice and social need fed into a continuing debate about fair taxation. In 1920, the dominion government appointed a commission of inquiry to consider "how the country's fiscal policy was affecting the people of Canada" and to hear public opinion on whether the revenue from the tariff should be replaced or supplemented by other forms of taxation.[5] In nation-wide public hearings during the fall of 1920, Canadians discussed public finance, with an emphasis on the taxation side of the question. The farm lobby called for elimination of protective tariffs and argued that any revenue thus lost to the dominion government could be replaced by direct taxes on income, estates, and undeveloped land and natural resource properties.[6] Labour kept alive the single tax idea, which emphasized a property tax on land that would return to social purposes wealth that was socially created and unearned by individual effort.[7] Businesses protested the continuation of direct taxes such as the federal business profits tax, and retailers complained of the harmful effects of both the luxury and the sales taxes.[8] As the United States and Britain lowered income tax rates after 1920, a chorus of Canadian business commentators clamoured for Canada to do so also.[9]

Thus, in the 1920s, the politics of taxation involved a broad array of competing interests. A sign of the times was the convoking in 1923 of the first public meeting of self-defined Canadian tax experts, the Canadian Tax Conference.[10] This event, which took place annually until at least the late 1940s, was organized by the newly formed Citizens' Research Institute of Canada (CRIC). Founded in 1919, CRIC was financed by memberships and by fees for its services, such as its newsletter, *Effective Government*, and municipal finance studies. The organization's stated purpose was to collect, interpret, and publish facts, "with the aim of promoting effective government at every level."[11] Its board of trustees included prominent insurance executives, major newspaper publishers, wealthy industrialists, and notable professional men.[12] Modelling itself on similar American organizations (notably the Bureau of Municipal Research), CRIC became a key transmitter of tax ideology in Canada. It publicized its views through pamphlets sent to boards of trade, city administrators, and newspapers, providing them with facts and figures pertinent to taxation debates. It remained an important voice for the efficiency in government discourse into the 1950s.[13] The public face of CRIC was its director from 1914 to 1947, Horace L. Brittain. Notably, Brittain also played an active role in the creation of Toronto's Federation for Community Service. As Wills points out, Brittain was also a hospital board member and a Rotary Club activist. He thus embodied the connections between taxation and charitable fundraising, being an expert on both mechanisms.[14]

In the early 1920s, the connections that Brittain represented were evident when, in the business and professional circles from which the federated fundraising project came, reflections on taxation questions led to strong assertions of crisis. Nationally, Nellie McClung (known as a suffragist, novelist, and prohibitionist but also the wife of a small business owner) expressed the fear that the new taxes would be an unfair exaction on the already heavily burdened "salaried and professional people": "To them [these taxes] will mean a further lowering of the standards of living, and they become more than ever the new poor."[15] In Vancouver, lawyer and Board of Trade member P.G. Shallcross linked the expenses of paying down the war debt to the need for increased donations to charities, so as to prevent the takeover of charities by governments and the consequent shifting of that burden, too, to the "comparatively few direct [i.e., income] taxpayers."[16]

In the early 1920s, some Vancouver taxpayers were also chafing under the continued existence of another direct tax – the personal property tax. This tax, which does not now exist anywhere in Canada, was based on an assessment not of real estate but of household effects. Assessors did not peer through the jewellery boxes, closets, and garages of the well-to-do. They simply estimated, no doubt conservatively in the case of the rich, the likely value of the household's goods, based on "the appearance of the exterior of the house and the supposed wealth of the owner."[17] Halifax had eliminated this tax in 1916, but the Vancouver Board of Trade in 1923 was still railing against it. They called it "purely class legislation" and "vicious in its operation," perhaps because of the looseness of the assessment practices it entailed.[18] Some could hide their wealth: investment income was notably difficult for assessors to see. Others – retail merchants (deemed to own their inventories as personal property) and the salaried middle class (whose taxes could be deducted at source) – had particular reasons to dislike the personal property tax.[19]

Although taxation concerns were voiced in general terms, provincial and municipal jurisdictions varied considerably in the kinds of direct taxes they sought to collect. The BC provincial personal property tax, for example, remained an issue for Vancouver's businessmen until it was repealed in 1927. In Ottawa, the tax problems were different: Ontario had eliminated the personal property tax in 1897. But Ottawa continued to assess a municipal income tax. Reluctance to pay that tax had prompted many of the city's wealthiest citizens to move outside the city, to nearby Rockliffe Park Village. Profiting from the Rockliffe tax assessor's deliberate disregard of income as part of taxable property, the residents of Rockliffe formed one of the tax-dodging "colonies of persons with large incomes" well known to tax experts in the 1920s.[20] Further evidence of tax concerns in Ottawa in the early years of the chest was the enthusiastic welcome afforded to CRIC's director, Horace L. Brittain, when he attacked excessive taxation and spending at a Board of Trade event attended by many municipal politicians.[21] In Ottawa, as in Halifax, there was a concentration of tax-exempt government and religious real estate in Ottawa that limited the revenue generated by the tax on real property.[22] Charitable institutions run by churches thus had an interest in the tax system, as property owners, and the residents of Rockliffe involved in the Community Chest leadership brought particular tax interests into the question of how social needs should be met.[23]

In Halifax, the moment of crisis between 1920 and 1923 revealed not only the obvious importance of the Board of Trade in leading the taxation debate but also the active participation of religious leaders, women's organizations, labour, and men's service clubs. In November and December 1919, committees were struck by several of these groups to discuss changes to the city's tax system. The Local Council of Women created its taxation committee in December, following the Board of Trade's initiative.[24] "Until women understand taxation," the committee's chair, journalist Ella Murray, claimed, "they are not in a position to undertake public life."[25] But the women's committee was not included in a joint group consisting of a City Council delegation, Board of Trade representatives, and men from the Trades and Labour Council. And only later would the city's leading men's service club, the Rotary, strike its own taxation committee. The city's clergy, in the Halifax Ministerial Association, added their voices to the taxation discussion in 1923.[26] But the joint committee, even though limited in its membership, represented in its ranks the key differences of opinion on civic taxation. Its report in April 1920 was discussed in the City Council's January 1921 meeting and again in March, with no prospect of agreement in sight. The reasons for their disagreements had to do with the specifics of Halifax's tax situation.

Halifax's tax problems after the war were in some respects shared with other nation-wide constituencies and in others distinctively local. Like other government centres (notably Ottawa and Victoria), Halifax had much valuable real estate that belonged to governments – imperial as well as dominion and provincial. In Halifax, however, expropriations during the First World War and property destruction in the 1917 explosion had worsened this situation. So, too, had the new port facilities, which converted a large tract of the city's south end from private to government property. This meant a smaller real property base in relation to population than in other cities. In addition to the shrinking assessable property base, the city had to deal with some exceptional costs. In 1918, the city engineering department estimated at $1.7 million the cost of the city-owned buildings and infrastructure (schools, streets, etc.) that had been destroyed in the explosion. There was, in 1919, no certainty that any of the money donated for disaster relief would flow into the city's capital spending coffers.[27] And the unemployment problems in 1921 that hit Canadians everywhere also exacerbated the relief needs of Haligonians.[28] In the Board of Trade, the reality of Halifax's small taxable property base and extraordinary spending needs translated into claims about "heavily burdened real estate."[29]

To this distinctive dimension of Halifax's tax situation was added in the early 1920s the Board of Trade's concern about the proposed re-enactment of the wartime business profits tax. A delegation to the dominion finance minister, Sir Henry Drayton, claimed that one Halifax firm paid thirteen different kinds of tax and protested the burden on productive capital that such multiple taxation entailed. But Drayton took a similarly tough line with them as he had with the national Retail Merchants Association in 1920: he told them that "he required money to conduct the business of Canada and was obliged to get it in a manner that would be least oppressive to the community at large."[30] In Halifax, the repeal of the personal property tax had served the needs of the city's many large wholesaling firms, which had been obliged to pay tax on the value of their inventories.[31] But relief from that form of taxation seemed only to mean an increase in the rate at which real property was taxed.

On taxation questions, the board was not simply the whinging anti-tax voice of a single class interest. Criticizing tax reform that benefited some sectors or individuals more than others, the Board of Trade's monthly magazine, *Commercial News,* affirmed the importance of paying taxes: "Some revel in the fact they are escaping by paying a little less than their neighbour or competitor, but the fact remains, however, that taxes, and increased taxes, have to be paid, if the City is to be improved in keeping with other Cities of its size and prominence." The improvements in question included basics such as paved streets for the street car routes, oil on the roads to keep the dust down, and new sewer systems. The question was how fairly to finance these uncontroversial needs. When Board of Trade writers pointed out the disadvantages of various methods of taxation, they gave reasons that reached out beyond specific business interests. In relation to the business profits tax, they claimed that "in all cases, it is the consumer that pays." Opposing the municipal income tax, they contended that "it keeps people of moderate incomes out of the city." And against escalating the land tax and its attendant costs for larger residential plots, they asserted that it would punish "the workman who takes pleasure in raising his own vegetables."[32] While business interests certainly can be discerned within or behind these arguments, their use indicates a reasonable attempt to build a cross-class basis for opposition to particular taxes. Although in favour of what it considered fair and necessary taxes, Halifax's voice of organized business nonetheless positioned itself as a critic of large-scale government spending. Support of community responsibility, expressed through support of fair taxation, did not imply enthusiasm about state expansion. And conversely, opposition to particular taxes was not necessarily an indicator of ideological anti-statism.

The view of the taxpayer that makes sense of this Board of Trade position is that the taxpayer is a stockholder in a firm. In this picture, the firm is the city or the province or the country, and the government is the management committee.[33] This perspective was also apparent in the language used by Associated Property Owners Associations and, historically, by Canada's first prime minister.[34] The term "stockholder" was explicitly used by CRIC's Horace L. Brittain in his talks in the early 1920s.[35] Being a responsible stockholder, as Ella Murray of the Local Council of Women had suggested, meant having an informed view of the workings of the public enterprise, especially its finances. Here, then, is one mode of social contribution: the citizen as stockholder. In this view, citizenship is only as inclusive as the tax base.

An example of how CRIC promoted and developed the image of the taxpayer as stockholder is apparent in the way one Halifax business writer used CRIC's pamphlets. In 1921, the editor of Halifax's *Commercial News* quoted extensively and approvingly from the CRIC pamphlet on municipal indebtedness.[36] The news for Halifax was not at all bad: it had the lowest debt per capita of eleven major Canadian cities. However, the Halifax writer did not take this as an argument for increasing the percentage of municipal spending that was financed by bond sales. Rather, he emphasized CRIC's notion that both high indebtedness and high taxation were the result of extravagant public spending. The examples of such spending that were most relevant to charity questions were giving excessive tax exemptions to educational, religious, and other institutions and making "lavish" grants to organizations that governments did not control. Because of this latter practice, accounting for how tax dollars were spent was so lax that money was inevitably wasted. Public borrowing was bad because governments had "artificial" means of making their bonds more attractive to investors than industry's bonds were and so competed unfairly in capital markets. But taxation was also bad if it financed government inefficiency or unnecessary expenditures: taxation always took away money available for productive use by business and industry, and it always reduced personal savings that would otherwise be available for investment in productive enterprise. These were the common-sense views that any good stockholder in the public enterprise should share. And the representatives of the Board of Trade on Halifax's 1920-21 taxation committee certainly seemed to hold such views.

However, the labour members of the taxation committee had a different perspective, and so did some of the members of the Council of Women. In these constituencies, an international movement to use taxation as a means to social justice exerted a powerful appeal. That movement was American social philosopher Henry George's single-tax crusade. From its beginning in 1879, this vision of how to connect the wealth of individuals and the social good recruited many Canadian followers. George argued that the rents on land collected by property owners constituted wealth that had been created entirely by the economic activity of the surrounding community because that activity was what made land valuable. As such, that wealth was owed to the community. If landlords paid to society all of their rents excepting a small fraction (owed to them as collectors), then governments would have to impose no other tax. A single tax on land rents would finance all public spending. Both in its morality and in its simplicity, the Georgite conception of tax appealed hugely and was a serious contender in its time for an alternative to customs duties and income or personal property taxation as a means of converting socially based wealth into resources available for collective use. In Canada, single taxers proposed a variant of this approach, which consisted of making tax on land the main source of municipal revenue, with improvements on land (such as buildings, household effects, and production equipment) taxed separately.[37]

This single-tax solution for a city's revenue problem was the one that the labour council proposed for Halifax.[38] This was not, however, a position so strictly dictated by economic interests that no reasonable businessman could endorse it. The two city aldermen who sided with labour against the Board of Trade were John W. Regan, an investment broker, and G.E. Ritchie, manager of Fleischman's Yeast.[39] Against labour and these allies, the Board of Trade representatives held to a combined real property tax that would reflect the whole value of the land and buildings. Whether for or against the single-tax model, all agreed that modest homes and small businesses should be exempt from the real property tax. But businessmen, especially the downtown merchants, opposed the single taxers for fear that the increasing need for municipal spending would lead to ever higher business taxes on the value of the land that their stores and offices occupied. One member of the board reported that a property on the city's main retail street had had a tax bill (on land alone) of $500 in 1915, which had risen to $900 in the five years since, with a prospect of $1,000 in 1921. He feared that he would soon be unable to pay the taxes and would thus lose the property.[40] For the labour members, such fears no doubt seemed merely to be part of a disproportionate lamenting of their sufferings, apparently a perpetual refrain among "Halifax merchants."[41]

On the joint committee, the labour council representatives were supported in their single-tax views not only by Aldermen Ritchie and Regan but also, in May 1920, by a resolution from the Local Council of Women. In the latter, we can see yet another view of how the tax system should organize the financing of social responsibilities. Their resolution tells its own story:

> WHEREAS one of the most menacing things in the life of this community is the shortage of houses, which leads to extortionate rents, overcrowding, and high mortality; and
> WHEREAS assessing improvements at a fixed lower rate and letting the main burden of taxation fall upon land value has resulted in fencing land, formerly held for speculation, for building sites; and
> WHEREAS the past year has seen an unprecedented increase in building as a result of the separation of land and improvement for purpose of assessment and taxation; and
> WHEREAS such separate assessment works out to the advantage of the small store-owned [sic] and encourages the building of homes, therefore be it
> RESOLVED that the Local Council of Women of Halifax go on record as approving the action of Aldermen Ritchie and Regan and the Labour representatives on the Taxation Committee in opposing sections 2, 3, 4, 5 of the Committee report, which propose reverting to the old method of taxing improvements at the same rate as land; and further
> RESOLVED that a copy of this resolution be sent to the City Council in connection with the question of assessment and taxation shortly to come up before that body when the Taxation Committee presents its final report to the Council.[42]

In this statement of single-tax philosophy, we can see its role as a means of discouraging land speculation (and its morally questionable unearned income) and preventing poverty by keeping rents low.

The resolution came out of the work of the Local Council of Women's committee on taxation, led by journalist Ella Murray, who was part of the editorial staff of the Liberal newspapers, the *Halifax Chronicle* and the *Evening Echo*. Her committee proposed in December 1921 to forward a similar, but even more ideologically explicit, single-tax resolution to the National Council of Women. It opposed all other forms of tax as tending to increase the cost of living. But another prominent member of the council, Agnes Dennis, whose family owned the competing Halifax daily newspapers, the Conservative *Herald* and the *Evening Mail*, balked at endorsing the committee's proposal.[43] While she succeeded in having a vote on the resolution deferred to the next meeting, the tax committee's motion did subsequently pass, in spite of the reservations of Dennis, at that next meeting. However, Dennis took steps to prevent such untoward reverses in the future. She convoked an executive meeting immediately afterward to propose that resolutions on new matters henceforth be vetted first by the executive before being presented to the general membership.[44] Clearly, women, even among the middle-class Local Council of Women, were not united in support of the single-tax solution. But they were united in seeking a voice as taxpayers. Dennis herself was the instigator of a second motion that also went to the City Council's tax committee, seeking to make married women eligible for the civic franchise. Noting that only those assessed for taxes in Halifax could vote there, the Local Council of Women's resolution called for steps to be taken so that, in the case of married couples, the household tax would be assessed in the name of "the partner who is not assessed on real estate, whether it be the husband or the wife."[45] And once the Community Chest was organized, Dennis and others from the Local Council of Women would insist that women be represented as such on the chest's board. The "ladies' organizations" made an important contribution to the chest, they argued, and so were entitled to a voice in its management.[46]

In this claim for voice in the affairs of the chest, as in the clubwomen's taxation resolutions, the conception of the taxpayer (or contributor) as stockholder was clearly present. Those who did not pay taxes in Canada in 1920 – recipients of government support in poorhouses, status Indians, and (for the purposes of Halifax city elections) married women who owned no real estate – were not, in 1920, enfranchised. They were not among the stockholders, with voting rights attached to their figurative investment. But these exclusions were the vestiges of the nineteenth century's property qualification for full political rights, of which little now remained. In the debates on the 1920 Dominion Franchise Act, abhorrence of a property test was a norm affirmed by both parties, though its residue in the disenfranchisement of charity cases and of Indians was defended.[47] Locally, Halifax's political community was also changing. In the mid-nineteenth century, an experiment in a universal male franchise based on a poll tax had elicited elite fears that "those who owned nothing voted the money out of the pockets of those who [had] means."[48] In 1929, in contrast, property owners in the city's mainly working-class and residential north end would organize public meetings in their ward, "with a view of stirring up interest in civic politics among residents."[49] Encouraging political expression in the north end was more than just a neighbourhood aspiration. In 1921, in the midst of the taxation debates, City Solicitor F.H. Bell called for the use of a broadly based occupant's tax, precisely to encourage interest in "civic affairs," even among those without property: "It is desirable to affect directly by taxation as many persons as possible and thus compel them by the most sensitive of nerves, the pocket, to take a personal and direct interest in civic affairs. A tax on real property alone, which only filters down to the non-property owners through an increase in rents, will not arouse the same interest in civic expenditures as a direct demand from the City Collector."[50]

Bell's logic echoed that of the CRIC's Brittain. "Right economy," Brittain argued, "will only become good politics when a sufficient number of the people think it worthwhile to make it good politics ... For [that] one reason, if for no other, there was value in the Federal Income Tax because it had taught many people that they were really paying taxes and were really stockholders of the country. Indirect taxation [such as customs duties] had induced a false security."[51] Across the country, as the franchise and taxation systems took new shapes, there was a rethinking of who were the citizens, who had a voice in the nation's affairs, and who owed a duty of contribution in the form of taxation. Similar questions would also arise in charity.

In the Halifax taxation debate, one figure embodied the connection between contribution in taxes and charitable giving. That individual was a prominent wholesale merchant named A. Handfield Whitman. The Board of Trade's president in 1920, Whitman was also its representative on the joint civic taxation committee. At a key moment in the debate about taxation, Whitman was the chosen leader of Halifax's business community. He was also one of the city's leading social work volunteers. In the first few days after the 1917 explosion, when a small number of the city's "big men" (and women) formed themselves into an executive committee to manage relief and reconstruction, Whitman was one of their number. In 1921, he was president of the Halifax Welfare Bureau, a service co-ordination organization that had been formed in 1914-15. It, too, was a central project of the city's civic-minded elite. In 1921, after his term as president of the Board of Trade, Whitman was fifty-one years old. Perhaps he was looking for new challenges and a project on which he could make his mark. It is not surprising, then, to find him in 1921 as the person who sparked and actively promoted the formation of the Community Chest.[52]

From the first meeting to propose the idea in November 1921 to the end of the chest's first campaign in 1925, Whitman brought to bear on charitable fundraising and financing in Halifax his modernizing business beliefs and resources. He loaned to various charities the services of his own firm's accountant to improve the reporting of revenue in their financial statements. He put the final touches on the chest's constitution. He brought in volunteers through his connections in the Rotary Club and the Gyro Club. No doubt it was also Whitman who arranged to have the Board of Trade supply clerical support and office space for the chest. In the first campaign, he would tell Halifax that "some of the ablest financiers of the city" had given of their time and energy to organize the chest and that the least the public could do was support the welfare agencies' work, "work which MUST BE DONE."[53] Whitman represented, as did Brittain, the sort of business idealism that saw social problems as amenable to repair through efficient use of social resources. Modern fundraising and co-ordinated social service, like proper taxation and modern government, would meet social needs by ensuring that all interests and all citizens contributed their share to the necessary civic work.

Among Halifax's social leadership in the early 1920s, then, a problem in public administration was being defined. An array of pressing needs was being presented as requiring a collective response. As civic minded as Whitman and his element of the business community were, it is also worth remembering that, on the joint taxation committee, he and the labour representatives had agreed to disagree on how taxation would be organized. They differed on which needs were most important. And the system then existing by which government could collect from citizens the funds with which to address such needs was also open to question. Who should be paying, how much, and on what basis were all unsettled matters. In Halifax, as elsewhere in the country, it was clear that a new fiscal regime was being constructed and that the country's solvency, social peace, and prospects for growth would demand innovation in public financing.

Canadian economist W. Irwin Gillespie has argued that the taxpayer in Canada has not been "a hapless, helpless victim of a rapacious government that taxes indiscriminately." Rather, taxpayers' ability to oppose taxation has shaped government's choices about which kinds of taxation to use.[54] Accordingly, as politicians such as dominion finance minister Sir Henry Drayton sought in the early 1920s to build coalitions of support for a new tax regime, they faced a considerable job of ideological work, overcoming such resistance. Building this support entailed more than simply striking a balance between competing economic interests. Politicians and finance officials had also to advance the state's interest in maintaining an adequate revenue. The politicians, moreover, had the electoral interest of appealing to a wide variety of publics. As Martin Daunton has shown in his study of British taxation politics, these publics were defined not only by immediate financial interests but also by viewpoints on the proper sources, uses, and obligations of different kinds of property. In this way, the public was divided along ethical lines as well as economic ones.[55] Figures such as citizens and shirkers, profligates and producers, all appeared in taxation rhetoric, doing the work of organizing consent to taxation. Taxation strategies were understood as a means to manage not only the market economy but also the moral one. Even though, as Daunton acknowledges, "'real' material interests" were important, politicians' tax proposals were also designed to appeal to identities that cut across the boundaries of such interests.

The link between charitable fundraising and shifts in the depiction of the taxpayer is suggested by Daunton's work. Daunton shows that taxpayer identities were moral ones. The same array of moral identities was apparent in the ways that charitable fundraisers addressed their publics. In this sense, then, both the selling of tax policy and the promotion of charitable giving were cultural exercises. Both were exercises in persuading people with money to see the justice of giving some of it over to be administered by others in service of interests that went beyond immediate gain or enjoyment. Such exercises inevitably spoke to broad questions of values and responsibility in relation to property and collective well-being. Both politicians and fundraisers could pose this sort of question – about fairness and sharing, rights and duties – and draw on common cultural reference points to carefully shift common-sense ideas. Thus, at the same time as individuals such as Brittain and

Whitman, Dennis and Murray, went about the ideological work of promoting certain taxation methods and resisting others, they were also and not coincidentally reorganizing the practices and norms of charitable fundraising. In each of these realms, they were both defending their economic positions and promoting a particular morality of citizenship.

In the ideological work of making new standards for fair contribution and new common-sense ideas of how taxation should properly work, the federated fundraisers would make an unintended contribution to politicians who needed to use and expand the dominion income tax. The chest method of fundraising would help to prepare the political ground for the great increase in the 1940s in the number of payers of income tax. By a nation-wide, decades-long campaign of public education, beginning at the moment of fiscal crisis in the early 1920s, the Community Chest movement helped to create a new conception of the taxpayer for a newly expanded state. The "citizen as stockholder" notion inherited from the nineteenth century, and evident in the tax discourse of the early 1920s, would shift subtly but importantly to a "citizen as consumer" position.

2

The Technologies of Contribution: Taxation and Modern Fundraising Methods

In addition to explicit discussions about what constituted fair taxation, and about which needs should be met with tax funds, there was another, less obviously ideological, aspect of the changing culture of contribution. Not only the ideas and activists but also the tools and techniques of taxation and charity overlapped and converged in the interwar years. The federated fundraisers' attempt to change the practices of charitable fundraising and the culture of giving was inspired by and, indeed, was part of larger contemporaneous changes in both business management and public administration. As Paul Pross has shown, the interwar years saw a symbiotic growth of government bureaucracy and private interest groups.[1] As both grew, their work was shaped by a common set of assumptions about what constituted legitimate expertise. Increasingly, both came to require systematic and statistically rendered social data as the basis for policy and planning.[2] While this sort of social science expertise was becoming important in public life, other similar kinds of data management had also become part of expertise in private business, especially in the large enterprises that had emerged in the late nineteenth century and the early twentieth century.[3] In such enterprises, large-scale information gathering and organization had become an important means of achieving co-ordination, planning, and ultimately profitability. These methods became part of a business ideology of efficiency. In social work, elements of this ideology of efficient business matched up with equivalents in the conception of scientific social work. In Toronto's Federation of Community Services, as Gale Wills has shown, agreement on modern methods provided, at first, a basis of co-operation between businessmen and social workers. Later, however, social workers clashed with their business allies about standards and goals. Those ideological differences had tangible consequences for choices about which services were to be provided. When applied to actual social service operations, it turned out that, in spite of their commonalities, the business and social work conceptions of efficiency were incompatible.

But when we shift our attention from service provision to fundraising, and from the relationship between business and social workers to the one between the same businessmen and taxation authorities, a different relationship emerges. In the interwar period, there were points of common beliefs and values between the business-inspired world of charitable fundraising and taxation expertise. This chapter identifies five of these points of connection, areas in which the tools and techniques of taxation and fundraising overlapped. They were (1) cost-effective collection, (2) accounting controls, (3) data collection, (4) use of "ability-to-pay" measures, and (5) base broadening. In the first four, the overlapping of methods bespeaks the existence of shared views on how public business should be managed. In these respects, charity and taxation innovations were growing simultaneously from a common public culture. In base broadening, an area in which the Community Chest had considerable success, charity's innovation came before its equivalent in public administration, and its success could be presented as an argument for a new model of citizenship: the citizen as consumer.

Cost-Effective Collection

A central element in the chest fundraiser's claim to superiority over traditional charities' appeals was that a single appeal was the most cost-effective means of collecting for charity. Reducing costs of collection made for the largest possible net amount of charity dollars available for their intended use. Similarly, governments, when choosing a means for raising revenue, weighed the cost of collection against the amounts that a tax might raise. For instance, one of the arguments advanced in favour of the particular form of the 1920 manufacturer's sales tax, and indeed in favour of sales taxes generally, was the low cost to the public treasury of the administrative methods involved in collecting it. The tax collectors were the manufacturers and wholesalers who handled the taxed goods, and the returns that they submitted required only about three dozen additional inspectors and auditors in the Department of National Revenue.[4] In contrast, the chief argument against the federal income tax before 1917 had been the cost of collection compared with the prospective revenue. And once it was introduced, the cost of administering the federal income tax continued to be a concern, tracked from year to year.[5] Moreover, the changing particulars of income tax policy would continue to be assessed on the ground of administrative cost. For example, employment expenses for the self-employed were allowable deductions but those of employees were not: only the goal of saving administrative costs explains this difference. As increasing numbers of employed Canadians came to pay the income tax, the standard personal deduction was adjusted to cover normal work-related expenses. By this means, the Department of National Revenue in the 1940s and later was saved the work of checking millions of employee tax returns, work that would have required hundreds of additional staff.[6]

Progress in tax reform was judged by Citizens' Research Institute of Canada (CRIC) tax experts in terms remarkably like those by which the chest appeal was justified. In taxation discourse, the equivalent of the fundraisers' worry about multiple social agencies dunning donors was the "chaotic condition" of taxation discussed in the CRIC's 1938 report to the Rowell-Sirois Commission. The CRIC pointed out, for example, that several provinces might seek to collect death duties from one estate. In many provinces, individuals were required to complete two completely separate income tax returns (one provincial, one federal). Taxpayers were irritated and public money was wasted when both federal and provincial governments had to audit the securities transactions on which tax was collected.[7] Such multiple taxes were problematic for some of the same reasons that multiple charitable appeals were. One reason both were considered objectionable was that multiple assessments, like multiple campaigns, were costly.

In a 1937 Vancouver canvasser training pamphlet, the fundraisers made explicit the analogy between the costs of collecting taxes and donations. After giving in proportional terms the costs of the fundraising methods that it wanted to disparage, the Welfare Federation pamphlet noted that

> even the government spends a large amount of money to collect our taxes from us; the exact percentage is unknown, but the costs of the income tax department, assessment offices, finance departments, etc. (The Finance Department is comparable to the Federation) can safely be estimated as costing not very far short of 10% of the total revenue of city or province. In other words, the Federation, in using only 6 cents out of every dollar received and passing on 94 cents direct to service, is operating at a lower cost than any other revenue raising device, not excluding taxation departments of government.[8]

When Community Chest promoters argued for a cheaper cost of collections, then, they were thinking in the same way public administrators did in planning tax collection. And at least some of them thought that federated fundraising was better than taxation because it was cheaper administratively.

Accounting Controls

The call for particular kinds of managerial expertise was another theme that linked discussion of charity fundraising and taxation in the interwar years. In particular, tax experts and the Community Chest managers agreed that, in each of their areas of operation, sound practice required better accounting controls. The leading businessmen active in Boards of Trade and Community Chests readily moved from promoting improved financial controls in the spending of tax revenue to doing the same for spending chest funds.

While the annual appeal was the most obvious innovation that the federated appeal offered, the reform of spending was equally key and every bit as much a part of the system of fundraising as the collecting of dollars. This was so because, to legitimate the use of other people's money, an accurate accounting of that money was required as evidence of its effective use for the purposes its suppliers intended. This connection between controlled expenditure and accounting had developed both in business and in government.[9] Over the course of the nineteenth century, as the British electoral system and methods of public administration underwent a host of reforms, an array of taxation and spending methods was developed that succeeded, by the twentieth century, in securing comparatively high levels of consent to taxation in the United Kingdom.[10] All tax revenue was to go into a general fund, and budget estimates debated and approved in Parliament determined how it would be spent. To ensure that this budgetary approval really mattered, tight accounting for each penny spent was necessary. The system required a strict prohibition on spending any surplus in one budget area to cover shortfalls in the resources allocated to another. Were this sort of flexibility allowed, it was argued, there would be no effectual limit on government spending: it would always rise to the level of the revenue available. Proper budgeting, in contrast, allowed for the possibility of using surplus in some areas to pay off government debt. This system of accounting controls was crucial to the unusual level of acceptance and compliance that the British income tax system, in particular, enjoyed by 1914.[11] For Canadians in the 1920s, the values of the British system were part of their political education. Not all would have agreed that it was the best system or appropriate to Canada, but it provided one influential model of just taxation.

Its influence is apparent in the CRIC's 1937 *Special Study of Taxation,* which analyzed government spending during the 1920s and 1930s. One of the criticisms that the study offered of Canadian taxation was that neither provinces nor municipalities used real revenue-expense accounting. This technical failing had worsened problems in the early 1930s, when municipalities facing a revenue shortage had to "slash rather than prune" public spending because they kept no "real expense records." They lacked the "information necessary for administrative and public control."[12] The study's readers would also have known that poor accounting practices had made it only too easy for municipal officials to steal. In Ottawa in 1930, for example, several such officials were found to have diverted into their own pockets tens of thousands of dollars of taxpayers' money. The city auditor, when called to task by an independent accounting firm, pointed out that, over the 1920s, in spite of his recommendations, he had not been allowed to develop a central accounting office and that political patronage determined how Ottawa's city business was conducted and by whom.[13]

Both to monitor the proper allocation of funds and to prevent their theft, accounting controls were required. Without them, the Ottawa experience and others suggested, governments did not deserve public trust.[14] As Michael Piva and Bruce Curtis have shown, colonial Canadian governments had once relied (not altogether wisely) on the good character of public officials more than on routine audit and control mechanisms.[15] Similarly, in the CRIC's view, some municipalities (and even provinces) in the interwar years of twentieth-century Canada were still operating as though to require expense records was to impugn the character of officials. This attitude could not continue. A similar sense of urgency was expressed in 1939 by a more left-wing expert in public administration, social worker Harry Cassidy. Toward the end of his tenure as director of social welfare in British Columbia's civil service, he became extremely frustrated with the cronyism and wastefulness he saw in the provincial government. He argued that amateurism in public administration only brought democracy into disrepute and gave credence to the anti-government polemics of fascists and communists. For this voice from the social democratic left, professionalism in public administration was essential for the legitimation of taxation.[16]

Charities, like nineteenth-century colonial governments, had relied on the prestige of their boards to produce confidence in their spending. When the Community Chest movement promised a business-like audit of all member agencies' accounts, it was promising as an inducement to charitable giving the same kind of enhancement in administrative control that tax experts were calling for in government as a prerequisite of legitimate taxation. Budget committees on Community Chests queried agency board representatives about particular items in their budgets. Agencies could be removed from the federation if their expense records failed to meet proper standards. That was the fate of several agencies in the early years of the Vancouver Welfare Federation: in 1931, it ousted from its ranks for this reason the Original Great War Veterans Association as well as the Western Association for the Blind and the Tuberculous Veterans.[17] In Ottawa, a Catholic family services agency, the Joan of Arc Institute, had to be instructed that its expense reports could not be unchanging boilerplate but had to show the "actual cost of each item."[18] Business leaders viewed both governments and charities as being in need of business expertise. While this view was not new in the interwar years, its expression in the institutional form of the federated appeals was both new and significant. By way of the chest movement, across the country in major and later in minor cities, charitable fundraising became a widespread means of promulgating to a wide audience the gospel of accounting controls as a necessary part of public spending, whether of charity dollars or of tax dollars.

Data Collection

Both tax collection and modern fundraising depended (and still depend) on lists of names: names of property owners, names on payrolls, and names of area residents are three lists that the two kinds of collection require. Both also need to assess wealth, either in ways that attach assessments of individual wealth to particular names, or in ways that apportion aggregate estimates of wealth to categories of population so as to determine per capita rates of contribution or incidence of particular taxes. One of the conditions of an effective system of taxation is its ability to count accurately the resources its managers wish to tax; the same is true for a system of fundraising. Fundraisers need to know, in effect, where the money is. And when a fundraising method involves pledges and installment payments, effective fundraising, like taxation, also entails monitoring lists of contributors' due dates. To set tax rates, as in setting fundraising targets, planners think not only of spending needs but also of aggregate and sectoral capacities. To organize either fiscal policy or a modern fundraising campaign, then, requires lists of names and obligations and assessments of the population's resources.[19]

We may think of the techniques of producing such lists and assessments as coming from the social sciences. And, in a broad cultural sense, they do. The methods of systematic social observation developed in the eighteenth and nineteenth centuries formed the cultural ground from which the federated fundraisers' tools grew. More immediately, however, the closest models for their record keeping were sales occupations and especially the insurance industry. Lists of prospects and lists of due dates for clients' premiums closely resembled the donor lists that the chests developed. Insurance companies certainly drew on (and had helped to develop) the social science of populations. But on a more minute level, the agent, operating in neighbourhoods, participated in this larger science by performing some of the detailed harvesting of information about particular populations. Insurance men and women brought this expertise to the campaign organizations of the chests.

In each of the three cities studied here, key promoters of the chest method and volunteer campaign leaders were from the insurance industry or closely connected with it.[20] And insurance companies often supplied teams of canvassers for this work.[21] Accustomed to meeting the public and talking about risk and security, agents (usually men) from Metropolitan Life, London Life, Sun Life, and other firms were an ideal sales force for the chest idea. Their industry had an array of economic reasons to support privately funded social services. But in addition to those reasons, enterprising individual agents must also have seen sales opportunities in fundraising conversations. After all, what better way to raise with potential customers the subject of insurance than to talk about charities that helped out people who had lacked such protection?[22] Along with men from service clubs, the insurance company canvassers performed in the business districts the same kind of work that teams of women did in the residential neighbourhoods.

It is hardly surprising, then, that some of the insurance business's list-making methods were used by the chests. Like insurance agents, canvassers for the federated appeals were equipped with client lists whose contents they amended or confirmed when they met the donor public at front doors, on shop floors, and in stores and offices. The first lists were compiled, like an insurance agent's lists, from city directories. The pertinent information was transferred to an index card, one for each prospective donor, and sets of the cards (plus some blanks for new donors) were supplied to canvassers (see

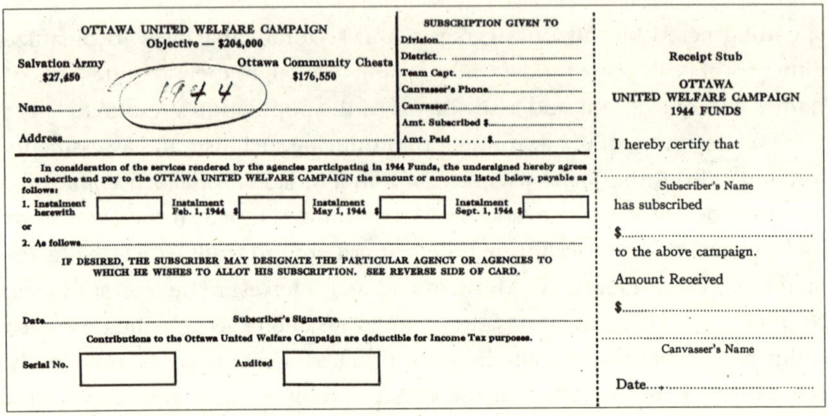
OTTAWA UNITED WELFARE CAMPAIGN
Objective — $204,000
Salvation Army $27,450
Ottawa Community Chests $176,550
1944
Name
Address

SUBSCRIPTION GIVEN TO
Division
District
Team Capt.
Canvasser's Phone
Canvasser
Amt. Subscribed $
Amt. Paid . . . . . $

In consideration of the services rendered by the agencies participating in 1944 Funds, the undersigned hereby agrees to subscribe and pay to the OTTAWA UNITED WELFARE CAMPAIGN the amount or amounts listed below, payable as follows:

1. Instalment herewith — Instalment Feb. 1, 1944 $ — Instalment May 1, 1944 $ — Instalment Sept. 1, 1944 $

or

2. As follows

IF DESIRED, THE SUBSCRIBER MAY DESIGNATE THE PARTICULAR AGENCY OR AGENCIES TO WHICH HE WISHES TO ALLOT HIS SUBSCRIPTION. SEE REVERSE SIDE OF CARD.

Date — Subscriber's Signature

Contributions to the Ottawa United Welfare Campaign are deductible for Income Tax purposes.

Serial No. — Audited

Receipt Stub
OTTAWA
UNITED WELFARE CAMPAIGN
1944 FUNDS
I hereby certify that
Subscriber's Name
has subscribed
$
to the above campaign.
Amount Received
$
Canvasser's Name
Date

FIGURE 5 Welfare campaign subscription card, 1944. Subscription cards were among the modern methods of data management for Community Chest fundraisers. (LAC, CCSD, MG 28 I 10, vol. 240, file 240-2)

Figure 5). If there was information about a donor's circumstances that might be relevant to the canvasser – such as a recent legacy – it would be indicated on the card. The makers of fundraising lists could glean information about donors from newspapers or social networks, just as insurance agents did.[23] The goal was for every household in the city to be canvassed and every place of business to be reached.[24] For each contact, the result was to be recorded on an index card. From these index cards, the comprehensive list of donors would be updated. The cards also provided the basis on which the chest could monitor installment payments of pledges over the year and improve rates of collection. Moreover, this list was to be updated over time with information supplied not only by canvassers but also by block representatives who were to keep "track of and report new residents and removals on their block."[25]

As promoters of the Community Chest repeatedly rejoiced, these were "business-like method[s]."[26] But they were also government methods. Not only were lists necessary for collecting taxes, but also some municipal tax collectors as late as 1938 appear to have used the same source for their lists as the sales agents and the fundraisers did – that is, the city directory.[27] Even the dominion government was not above using local observers as a means of revising electoral lists. In 1937, voters in urban areas were encouraged, apparently for the first time, to help ensure a qualified electorate by reporting to the returning officer any names of people on posted voters lists who were not genuine residents of their neighbourhood.[28] As well as sharing methods, there was some data sharing between governments and fundraisers, at least in one direction. Charitable fundraisers liked to use property tax assessment rolls and income tax collections data to estimate the donor capacity of their communities.[29] They also checked their canvassing lists against the voters list.[30] In the enumeration and assessment methods, fundraisers shared with tax collectors and salespeople some common problems and common methods.

At another level of business-like data management in fundraising, there were the special names lists. These were lists of prospects whose capacity to give and whose past record of giving inspired expectations of a substantial donation. The individuals on these lists were approached personally by people of similar wealth and status. In an analogy to the Canadian taxation system of the 1920s, these prospects were the equivalent in the chest canvass of the federal income tax payers. (They were likely also literally among the wealthy minority who paid the federal income tax.) These "special" donors were told that they had special responsibilities and were called on to provide campaign-launching donations and to make up campaign shortfalls, much as federal income tax payers were targeted for a tax that was justified as meeting emergency fiscal needs from the war.[31] When Charlotte Whitton was researching the donor capacity of Ottawa, she developed lists of leading philanthropists in each of the major religious/linguistic sections of the community. This list making was to ensure that the people who would be expected to give to the new federation would also be personally addressed about the plans for its formation. A failure in data collection at this stage of planning would have meant uncertainty about donor support: these donors, like major taxpayers, would have expected to be able to "call the tune" because they saw themselves as paying the piper.[32]

In contrast to this highly individualized group were Asian residents of Vancouver. In the 1930s, the city directory gave no names at some households, just the word *Orientals.* Vancouver's Chinese Canadians were thus left off the ordinary poll tax lists in the interwar years. Similarly, in the Vancouver Welfare Federation records, one cheque came to the federation from Chinatown via the Chinese Benevolent Association. No individual ascriptions were made of Chinese Canadian donations until the 1935 campaign.[33] Apparently, it was not initially relevant to the Vancouver Welfare Federation's purposes to see Chinese Canadians as individual donors.

Donor data, either individualized or categorical, were essential to the federated charities' claim to be able to plan. Setting a campaign goal involved reviewing economic and demographic data as well as assessing member agencies' needs. Tracking the results of campaigns in concrete terms of donor numbers and donor dollars, analyzed by sector, was a means of testing the effectiveness of particular campaign methods.[34] As I will show in Chapter 4, the categories of data collection could be designed to identify and pressure specific groups of potential donors. As Bruce Curtis has argued about census making, there are in these methods of population counting two tendencies. One is the individualizing process, which treats each resident or donor as equally and alike subject to the intentions of the counters. In the case of fundraising, the aim to reach virtually every resident of the city (excepting preschoolers and babies-in-arms) was the expression of this atomizing and homogenizing impulse. The other was the totalizing effect, in which assignment to a category and disregard of individual distinctions within those categories served the administrative purposes of the data collectors.[35] This aspect of data gathering appeared in the fundraisers' tracking of donations by occupational, religious, and ethnic categories. Fundraisers lacked the coercive powers and resources of census makers and tax collectors. But like such agents of the state, the designers of the federated fundraising methods used lists to see society.[36] By means of methodical data collection, fundraisers hoped to produce social facts that would enable them to meet their goals.

"Ability to Pay": The Link between Income and Obligation

Another distinctive feature of Community Chest fundraising was the means that the chests used to increase the size of donations and the number of donors. More than efficiency in collections and controls in accounting, the techniques adopted to implement this feature of the chest idea prepared the public to contemplate with a degree of acceptance the expanding incidence of personal income taxation, especially in lower income cohorts, in the 1940s. The campaign to induce more people to give to the chests linked income and social obligation in ways that also appeared in discussions of just taxation in the interwar years.

The links between income and obligation in conceptions of tax in the interwar years may be read from the parliamentary debates incited by R.B. Bennett's 1931 federal budget. Participants in taxation debates throughout the interwar years continued to assume, correctly, that less than 2 percent of Canadians paid income tax.[37] In 1931, paying income tax was still clearly an experience of the most highly paid salary earner and the rich.[38] In the period, wage earners rarely, if ever, earned more than the $3,000 that for a married, childless household head was then exempt from federal taxation. Thus, most of Bennett's opponents in the 1931 budget debate focused on the tax reductions Bennett proposed to give to a small number of the fabulously wealthy: either the "25 millionaires" or the 523 individuals whose taxable income was greater than $50,000. These were the happy souls whose reduced tax bills under Bennett's new income tax scale gave the 1931 budget its name as "the rich man's budget." These few plutocrats became the symbol of unjust tax privilege contrasted with the sufferings of "the poor man," whose cup of tea would now cost more in light of a 3 percent increase in the sales tax. In this rhetoric, the income tax payer appeared as a figure of privilege, contrasted with the downtrodden ordinary man or woman, the payer of sales tax.[39]

Bennett's critics were right to deplore his government's reliance on increased consumption taxes, regressive forms of taxation that ate away at the pennies and nickels of the poor. But it is equally clear that the moral and symbolic meaning of taxation informed the debate more than did real information about tax incidence. J.S. Woodsworth's intervention was especially striking in this respect.[40] "We are told this country belongs to the people," he said, clearly about to puncture a myth, "and yet, when we come to matters of taxation we find the taxes are loaded upon only a few people." At this point, it would seem, rather oddly, that Woodsworth, labour's champion, was deploring the burden of income tax carried by the rich. However, with no apparent regard for consistency, he went on to aver in a more usual vein that "this government is nothing more or less than a vast debt collecting agency operating to collect from the poor people or the people of moderate means moneys to be turned over to the wealthy people." While this was sound labourist polemic, it was, as a comment on the income tax, simply wrong. Although the *sales* tax did indeed collect disproportionately from the poor and the middling sort, the *income* tax did not. Woodsworth's remarks were those of a man completely unused to dissecting the impact of income tax. His confusion, and the emotional tone of the debate generally, confirm the image of the income tax as a rich man's tax, outside the obligations and tax-paying experiences of most working-class and many middle-class Canadians.

The fundraising campaigns of the Community Chests would contribute to changing that image, both by imitating the methods of the income tax and by enlarging the scope of their application. The model of charitable giving in the chest idea mimicked in two ways the ability-to-pay model of income taxation. One was the use of a progressive scale of giving, tied to income. Figure 6 shows one such scale.[41]

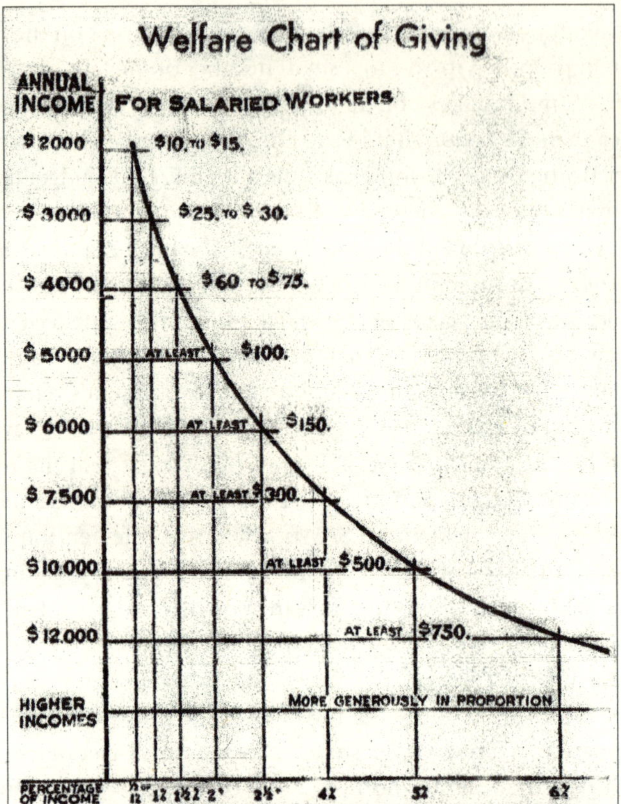

"How much should I give?" is the question which Vancouver Welfare Federation canvassers say is asked most often of them in the campaign now on for a budget of $350,000. The Federation had anticipated this question with the above chart which it prepared to show what it considers a fair donation in each salary bracket.

FIGURE 6 "Welfare Chart of Giving," 1936. This graph illustrates ability to pay as a model of fair contributions to the federated appeal. By using the model of contribution associated with the progressive income tax, the chests endorsed the conception of fairness embedded in the tax, which was still controversial in the 1930s. (*Vancouver Sun*, 16 October 1936, 2)

Worth noting is that the lowest annual income registered on this scale (and other similar scales) was $2,000. This was also the lowest threshold in the income cohorts (based on income above the exempt amount) into which data on income tax were divided.[42] If a worker's income fell below the minimum threshold, however, there was also an "ability-to-pay" measure designed for him or her – a day's pay.[43] In this way, the link between income and obligation to give was maintained. Like the income tax payer, and unlike the sales tax payer, the donor to charity in the chest method was asked deliberately to pay what he or she "owed," knowing that the amount represented something about himself or herself individually. Moreover, the more well-to-do would be expected to carry an appropriate amount of the responsibility. Vancouver's 1937 canvasser pamphlet said the chest model was superior because it funded its services on this progressive model of contribution, unlike tax-funded services where "most taxes, at present anyway, [fell] with equal weight on every individual alike – regardless of ability to pay."[44] The logic of the chest's model of contribution (and a more progressive model of taxation) was that the burden of giving would be both fairly distributed and limited by a clear principle of obligation. If this model were followed, then contributing citizens would not need to fear having to respond to unlimited demands posed by infinite human needs. Nor would they need to worry about being taken advantage of by free riders. Two objections that could arise either to charitable giving or to taxation were thereby removed.[45]

Base Broadening

The Community Chest's main purpose was to increase charitable giving, and its main method of doing so was to increase the number of donors. Figures on increased numbers of donors were a central element in the claims of success that the chest fundraisers used in the 1920s and 1930s. It was a particular point of pride in Ottawa, for example, that they had "introduced into giving to charity some 18,000-19,000 people who never gave to charity before."[46] As Halifax's campaign organizers discovered in the first appeal, to increase the number of donors required enlarging their own common-sense notion of who were responsible citizens, the bearers of the citizenship of contribution. Two weeks into the first appeal, in 1925, it was clear that the new method had failed overwhelmingly to meet its goal. The goal had been $56,000; the revenue from homes, businesses, and special names was only $31,000. Looking for an untapped pool of potential donations, the campaign committee decided to target employees of the city's largest manufacturing firms. This was a somewhat desperate tactic, given what realistically could be expected by way of donations from industrial workers' pay packets. There were not nearly enough industrial wage earners in Halifax to cover the $25,000 shortfall.[47] To generate that amount, every male industrial worker would have had to contribute $17.86 over the year. This was even more than the published scale of giving recommended. The scale suggested one day's pay, which, for a relatively well-paid worker, such as a longshoreman, would have been about $5.41. And as the published names of donors and donations in Halifax suggest, most working-class people gave between one dollar and five dollars.[48] By 1937, 82 percent of Halifax's donors came from this cohort. Realistic or not, the appeal to workers as potential donors had become part of Halifax's base-broadening strategy. The other two cities would follow suit. Their success in increasing the number of donors (if not in making up shortfalls) is indicated by the important percentages of donations in this size range: in Ottawa, donors contributing less than five dollars in 1936 and 1937 were 71 percent of the total donor population, and in Vancouver in 1936 they comprised 62 percent.[49]

In each of these cities, the appeal to workers and the base-broadening strategy took a somewhat distinctive shape. To assess these strategies in the early years of the chests, I examined the 1937 campaigns. I chose that year because, in each of the three cities, I was able to locate not only newspaper advertising and related news and editorial materials but also the campaign's main fundraising pamphlet. That was also an interesting year for fundraising because, as business conditions and employment rates improved, the chests (at least in Ontario and British Columbia) anticipated an upswing in donations.[50] At the same time, the demands on private welfare were increasing in all three cities because of shortfalls and cutbacks in public relief.[51] And 1937 is a good year to compare the three chests because by then they were past the experimental early days and working with a base of at least four years of experience and community response. All believed that it was possible to attract new donors.

New donors might have been expected to come from any social group, so not all of the base-broadening strategies were specifically aimed at working-class people. Even so, lower-income people would have been seen as part of the general audience for these appeals.[52] The fundraisers' interest in tapping the incomes of wage earners was apparent in strategies that spoke specifically to lower-income wage earners or, indeed, to the non-earning poor. Of the campaigns in the three cities, this was clearest in Vancouver. In Halifax, the target was not so much a working-class person as a lower-income "average citizen." And in Ottawa, base broadening was targeted at a working-class population identified not by occupation or income but as francophone Catholics. The origins of Vancouver's and Ottawa's specific strategies of inclusion are the subjects of the following two chapters. Here, however, I want to outline elements of the chests' base-broadening project in all three cities that prefigured a universalist model of income taxation. The vision of a citizenry in which all individuals were equally obliged to join in the financing of collective care was apparent both in the chests' general appeals and in the targeting of potential donors among lower-income groups.

Among the general appeals, religious themes, mainly Christian, figured prominently and served the purpose of a broadly inclusive image of charitable donation through the chests. In Vancouver, the use of religious appeals was relatively slight: there was one mention of a biblical figure, the Good Samaritan, in the back of the campaign pamphlet. (The Samaritan represents someone who acts as a good neighbour even to a stranger, especially someone to whom he has no ethnic or religious ties.)[53] An editorial writer for the *Vancouver Sun* mentioned the historical importance in all religions of helping the needy. But he immediately affirmed that charity was no longer a religious exercise.[54] Halifax, in contrast, gave to a biblical quotation the same prominence in its pamphlet as the main campaign slogan. From the Bible's New Testament came the Halifax campaign's phrase "inasmuch as ye have done it unto one of the least of these." Any graduate of Sunday School in the 1920s, reading this, would have mentally heard Jesus completing the sentence with the words "my brethren, ye have done it unto me."[55] Ottawa's campaign used a religious appeal specifically to argue that giving benefited the giver. In a question-and-answer ad, meant to answer criticisms of the chest, one question was "what do I get [from the chest]?" Of the three answers provided, two were Christian. One echoed the Haligonians' reference to the book of Matthew: "the happiness of rendering aid even 'unto the least of these.'" The other answer was more explicitly Catholic: "the thrill of giving sacrificially in order to show mercy."[56]

While religious duty or benefit would not, of course, become the basis for tax-paying obligations, the use of this appeal to link Canadians from a variety of Christian denominations in a common charitable endeavour represented a departure from denominationally based charitable giving toward a more inclusive citizen identity. Ottawa's anglophone Protestant campaign chairman specially emphasized that, in his city, the project of the chests was a pathbreaking exercise in co-operation between Protestants, Catholics, and Jews.[57] The Vancouver Welfare Federation congratulated itself on its cosmopolitan inclusiveness, implicitly making a contrast to such "backward" places as Montreal and Toronto, where ecumenism came in the 1940s or later.[58] And in the hands of the Vancouver editorialist, the discursive translation of Christian obligation went beyond ecumenism to an even more inclusive term, "moral civilization." A Halifax cleric, Father Burns, speaking during the 1937 drive, was less willing to treat Christianity as a superseded phase in the evolution of moral life. But he, too, emphasized the transcendence of particularistic religious identities in progressive terms: Christian charity united the "whole community" against the danger of becoming "pagan, barbarian."[59]

The Christian rhetoric in these campaigns, then, emphasized an inclusive community in which each had obligations to all rather than only to co-religionists. In so doing, it was also offering a kind of class inclusion. In the interwar years, Catholics were still perceived in these cities as more likely to be labouring men and women with lower incomes and more often in need of welfare services.[60] The ecumenical appeal was thus both to Christian unity and to working-class men and women as donors. Similarly, other appeals meant to be general in their effect also could be framed to speak specifically to the material situations of working people. One was a shaming strategy in which fundraisers reported a small gift given by someone who could ill afford it. These stories alluded to the New Testament story of charity in which Jesus observed both the donations of the rich to the temple and the gift of "a certain poor widow" who gave two tiny coins. Jesus tells his disciples that the widow gave more than the rich did because she actually gave money she needed to live.[61] The effectiveness of this as a fundraising story was that it not only shamed the truly well-to-do but also positioned everyone else as obliged to give, and it represented everyone but the utterly destitute as relatively privileged. Just as the archbishop of Quebec, in a national address for the chests, had called for donations from those who were "less poor than the penniless," so too fundraisers in Halifax told "Mr. Average Citizen" that it was not the few large contributions from the wealthy that made the difference but the many small donations from people like him who should help others who were "less fortunate."[62] It might reasonably be argued that, in the specific context of the Halifax ads in 1937, Mr. Average Citizen was still a somewhat middle-class figure. In another ad, the donor was addressed as "you who live in bright, comfortable, happy homes in more prosperous sections of Halifax."[63] But the story of the moral value of the small donation was capable of being addressed pointedly at working men and women, and in Vancouver it was.

Of the three cities, Vancouver was the most thorough in proposing the image of the working-class donor, tailoring general themes to suit the fundraisers' notion of this sort of person. In Vancouver's 1937 campaign, all but one of the ads in the *Vancouver Sun* were about the agencies and the work they did.[64] This general strategy reflected the campaign chairman's belief that only "ignorance" of the work of the agencies prevented more people from giving.[65] Here is a hint of the "good stockholder" metaphor in which tax-paying and political voice were linked to each other and to the possession of well-informed expertise on public matters. Skepticism about whether working-class people had such expertise was still an element of welfare policy making in the late 1940s and 1950s, but it would by then be contested.[66] As welfare rhetoric, Vancouver's 1937 campaign was pathbreaking in its presentation of working people as knowledgeable about welfare.

This presentation was accomplished by a series of captioned photos published in the *Vancouver Sun* during the ad campaign. Each shows a man or a woman at work, under the heading "Community Chest Supporter" (see Figure 7). They are pictured smiling and holding or using the tools of their trade: a woman cook, a warehouse man, a "business girl" (apparently a photographer), a milkman, and a fireman. One caption echoes the tale of the poor widow's pennies: "It's not much, but we do what we can," the warehouse man says. The milkman's caption affirms working men's membership in moral civilization: "Anyone who believes in helping anyone else should be all for it." He was, according to the ad, "but one of thousands of Vancouver's workers who pledge themselves to support the Federation because they know their neighbors' need." This was a particularly working-class expertise: lower-income donors did not have to be invited to imagine, from their own prosperous homes, the discomfort in which some of their fellow citizens lived. They knew about need and economic insecurity. But, as another ad showed, a working man might also understand in a theoretical way the sociology of juvenile delinquency and the role of children's agencies in its prevention, as did fireman J.E. Shaw. The business girl's caption highlighted her appreciation of business-like methods: she recognized the efficiency of the single drive. Only in the caption under the woman cook were the working-class donor's image and the description of the needy rendered as opposites: the cook and the hungry poor.[67] In this campaign's serialized photo essay, a case was being made that working-class men and women were, like middle-class and well-to-do income tax payers, citizens who understood their obligation to contribute, out of their own income, to the community's collective projects. They or members of their families might be users of welfare services, but they were also among those willing and able to share the burden of collective provision.

Community Chest Supporters

Mr. Gardner-Smith is a milkman. He knows of quarts being left where no quarts were left before. He expressed the spirit of the campaign very simply. "Anyone who believes in helping anyone else should be all for it."

Gerry is but one of thousands of Vancouver's workers who pledge themselves to support the Federation because they know their neighbors' need.

FIGURE 7 "Community Chest Supporters," 1937. This photo emphasizes not only the emotions of obligation but also the knowledge of need that working-class people brought to their assessments of fundraising appeals. (*Vancouver Sun*, 18 October 1937, 3)

While my discussion here of the base-broadening appeals has focused on the 1937 campaigns, an example taken from Vancouver's 1935 campaign underscores the importance of "knowing their neighbors' need" in fundraising rhetoric addressed to working-class donors. In a 1935 solicitation to all of Vancouver's "helping hands," the fundraisers created fictive working-class voices. One was the voice of "tired, unaided domestic hands" who replied, "yes, indeed, I want to do my tiny share, for did not the Welfare help my little girl last year when we were unable to give her the care she needed so badly?" The other was of "tough, calloused, work-thickened hands" that expressed appreciation for the summer playgrounds for the kids and promised "it won't be much, but I'll do me little bit."[68] In these representations, the working-class donors who gave to the chest were represented as not only fulfilling obligations to the community but also helping to pay for social services they themselves or their families would use. In addition to citizen responsibility and personal altruism, working-class men and women were expected to give in anticipation of direct benefit as users of social services.[69]

By presenting working-class donors as both contributors to and users of services, this rhetoric began to recast the class relations of community services. Working-class donors were grouped with the helpers and not the helpless. They were being offered, as an image of their place in a system of collective care, the citizen as consumer, whose responsibility consists of paying part of the price of the services he or she uses. Fundraising that used this model of the citizen would appear in other cities in the 1940s and 1950s. By then, donors in all three cities would be told that "everybody gives, everybody benefits." Frequent representations of the citizen as consumer belong with the triumph of a universalist vision of welfare in the postwar period.[70] But, as the 1935 ad from Vancouver indicated, the notion of charitable giving as mutual aid, where responsibility and benefit were intertwined, was part of the fundraiser's appeal to working-class Canadians even in the 1930s, at least in Vancouver. It would become in the postwar years part of the cultural logic by which working-class participation in paying income tax would be legitimated. The territory that fraternal societies' insurance schemes had occupied, with their fulsome rhetoric of mutual responsibility, would be occupied by the soon-to-be equally celebrated collectivism of social insurance.[71] Giving to federated charities was a stop along the way.

In this chapter, I have pointed to values and practices that were embodied both in Community Chest fundraising and in the conception of a broadly based income tax for a welfare state. I have suggested that some aspects of these common values and practices were cost-effective collections, accounting controls, data collection, obligation based on ability to pay, and breadth of participation. The last aspect, furthermore, was grounded in part on a sense of obligation based on anticipated benefit and not purely on a spirit of altruism. These were parts of an emerging public culture from which would come both increases in a certain kind of charitable giving and legitimation in the 1950s of increased income taxation. Chest fundraising educated the mass of Canadians, not just social elites, in the ways of a modern, rationalized system of funding social services.

It would be difficult to overstate how thoroughgoing were the challenges that faced Canada and other Western societies in the interwar years. The period saw many attempts at a fundamental reframing of the obligations of participants in civil and political society. In Canada, this process of combined cultural and institutional change was under way both in taxation policy and practice and in methods of fundraising. In both, business leaders and their allies in public administration attempted to introduce modern innovations. They hoped thereby not only to protect the profitability of their enterprises but also to legitimate and stabilize the fiscal basis of social provision. In combining these goals, business leaders were like politicians and civil servants, who often came from business circles. They meant to organize charity, like taxation, so that its practice would both facilitate accumulation of capital and legitimate their leadership. In both aspects of fiscal management, their innovations had potential for broad appeal. They offered not just services to business but also genuine public goods such as rationally run government that would keep small homeowners' property taxes low and well-managed charities that would provide accessible social services for all. The work of charitable fundraisers in promoting the value of business-like social administration was part of the larger project of enlisting broad popular support for such goods. The challenge that the federation fundraisers faced, however, after getting launched in the 1920s, was making this project credible in the social, economic, and ideological environment of the 1930s and 1940s. A project that promised to satisfy citizens both as stockholders and as consumers had to contend with ferocious internal tensions. How fundraisers attempted this exercise in political and cultural persuasion is the subject of the next two chapters.

3
Social Advertising and Social Conflict: The Community Chest Method, 1930-35

In the 1920s, Halifax succeeded in organizing a Community Chest, but Vancouver failed. In both Vancouver (where a serious effort to federate fundraising was made in the 1920s) and Ottawa, there were robustly independent charitable communities that turned down the idea of federation. They preferred to manage their own affairs.[1] Even in Halifax, several of the financially stronger institutions stayed out of the Community Chest.[2] However logical the appeal to save effort and rationalize operations appeared to be, loyalty to existing institutions and practices was a barrier to adopting the chest method of fundraising. In this chapter and the next, I examine two kinds of strategies fundraisers used to cajole and coerce competing and hostile social groups and institutions into a combined annual appeal. One strategy was to create new, more inclusive mechanisms of representation, and the other was to build an inclusive vision of society into the chests' advertising.

In this chapter, my focus is advertising. As much a method of modern business as were the data management, accounting, and prospecting techniques covered in the previous chapter, consumer advertising spawned a new variant in this period: social advertising.[3] This was the term given to what has come to be known as public relations. Experts in public relations and publicity work drew on the emerging social sciences, especially psychology, to offer technical means of achieving social goals. Like other public relations and advertising experts, charitable fundraisers tried to avoid the two extremes of nineteenth-century consumer advertising. On the one hand, they were aware that the vaudevillian excesses of patent medicine sales, with their tales of horror and redemption, had fallen into disrepute. On the other hand, consumer advertising that was heavily textual and ploddingly descriptive, offering apparently reasonable accounts of the qualities of the goods for sale, had less psychological force than they wanted to wield. The new techniques pioneered in the 1920s deployed modern psychology to appeal to and manipulate the reader's irrational fears, guilt, and anxieties. Like the mouthwash merchants whose methods they borrowed, fundraisers were selling something whose psychological appeal was weightier than its practical function.[4] While Ottawa's and Halifax's chest ads in the 1920s and 1930s remained heavily textual and largely Victorian in their visual style, the Vancouver Welfare Federation from its first campaign brought modern advertising methods to the work of federated fundraising. The other chests would follow suit in the 1950s.

In pursuing the object of providing dollars for charities, Vancouver fundraisers evoked, as if it were a reality, an image of Vancouver as a cohesive, just community, where neighbour was at peace with neighbour. This social advertising, like its commercial equivalent, depicted a world that was far from a realistic representation of normal experience. Vancouver in the 1930s staggered under the pressures of collapsed commodity markets and large-scale unemployment. A wide array of vigorous left-wing political movements made class conflict common sense in some circles. And, since 1917, British Columbia's largest city had never been short of right-wing stalwarts willing to warn against the dangers of communism.[5] Compounding these tensions in class relations were attacks or the memory of recent attacks, verbal and literal, legal and bodily, on Vancouverites who were immigrants or descendants of immigrants from Asia. In 1900, Tomey Homma, a Japanese-born British Columbian, challenged the ethnic exclusions in the province's electoral law, and in 1903 he lost his case at the Judicial Committee of the Privy Council. In the early 1920s, pressure from white British Columbians played an important role in the closing of Canada's borders to new Chinese immigration.[6] Members of the city's various Asian communities defended their interests as best they could in this climate of racism.[7] Social and partisan politics in the city also made for bitter feelings on matters such as temperance legislation, women's rights, and policing of morals.[8] Similar conflicts could be found in many, probably most, Canadian cities in the 1920s and 1930s. But certainly nowhere in Canada were city dwellers more likely than in Vancouver to know that the vision of a peaceable, just community was an ideal, not a reality.

In this context of politicized social divisions, an advertising campaign that sought to engage everyone in a common charitable project had to frame that project so as to transcend or integrate these differences. Examining how chest fundraisers dealt with this challenge is a way of understanding the place of this movement in the development of welfare state citizenship. Did the fundraisers seek to deny any significance to particular social identities in their presentation of the obligations of citizens? In other words, did they claim that a universal form of social responsibility transcended the city's politicized social differences? Or would they recognize the importance and persistence of subcultural communities and integrate representations of these groups into their image of the larger polity, while defining for each a distinctive kind of obligation? Philosopher Iris Marion Young points out that the former strategy is unrealistic in its wishing away of differences and, in practice, has often worsened hostility to groups that differ from the mainstream; she proposes, therefore, the latter strategy as an ideal for a late-twentieth-century politics of social justice.[9]

But it was not the strategy that Vancouver's chest advertising adopted. Instead, campaign ads offered as a model of moral citizenship a universal, transcendent vision of homogeneous individuals united in a single community. As I will show, the strategy suffered from precisely the problems Young's analysis suggests. But the ideal of an inclusive citizenship of contribution nevertheless served one progressive purpose in Vancouver in the 1930s. The celebration of all classes and categories of citizens as equally able to be competent moral actors was part of the ground on which could be built a more truly inclusive franchise, literally in electoral politics and figuratively in social politics. By the 1950s, a campaign against the property vote in municipal elections had been launched, Asian Canadians would have the franchise, and, in the world of fundraising and social planning, the labour movement would have an established voice, and Asian Canadians would be taking on new roles.[10]

In selling the view that Vancouverites were united in a shared moral project, the chest fundraisers apparently sought to ease certain tensions in social relations. For those Vancouverites who felt threatened by the anger of the disenfranchised, this part of the chest message was undoubtedly an appealing one. However, advertising, whether commercial or social, works not only by offering attractive goods but also by inspiring and exacerbating the needs those goods supposedly will satisfy. Consequently, we can see in the publicity materials of the Vancouver Welfare Federation a strategic use of social tensions. The campaigns engaged with and deployed for fundraising purposes the mistrust among social classes, the elements of envy and anxiety in gender relations, fears among ethnic communities, and religious suspicions.[11]

The result was a series of ironic contradictions, as this exercise in community building evoked, and sometimes inflamed, envy, fear, and resentment among social groups. We may regard these ironies as the mildly tragic fate of well-intentioned efforts or as the predictable consequences of social action by blinkered elites. I tend toward the latter perspective. But even if one is more sympathetic to the biases of the federation's publicity work, it is important for the purposes of historical explanation to note the contradictory features of their fundraising. These contradictions, between evocations of solidarity and indications of anxiety about differences, explain the relationship between the fundraisers' promotional tactics and the responses of their critics. Between 1930 and 1935, this interaction produced a linked pair of opposing discourses of citizen obligation.[12] Each discourse separately offered different proposals for how needs should be met and pooled dollars should be administered. But from the common elements in their logic came the material from which was being built a rationale for the welfare state's citizenship of contribution.

The federation campaigns whose materials I examine in this chapter were designed by a combination of paid and volunteer publicity experts. At the head was the federation's executive director, Howard Falk, whose qualifications included having held the same position in the Montreal and Winnipeg federations. Falk also hired for each campaign a professional publicist. These staff men worked with a volunteer publicity committee, itself headed by men whose paid jobs were in advertising or public relations. Closely connected was the publisher of the *Vancouver Sun*, Robert Cromie. A distinctive contribution was also made by the businessmen and wives of businessmen who, as general chairmen and women's division chairs, made motivational remarks, duly reported in the *Vancouver Sun*. Together these were the people who designed and delivered the federation's publicity. Perhaps because of Falk's guiding hand, each campaign was quite coherent, with a discernible theme. As a team, these men and women saw themselves as engaged in community organization.[13]

The framework for this chapter is supplied by six documents. One is a newspaper story from 1934, reporting on a major attack on the federation. The other five are a selection of the Vancouver Welfare Federation's advertisements printed in one of its main supporters, the *Vancouver Sun*. These ads are from the first campaign in 1931 and two subsequent ones: 1933 and 1935. Each of these documents provides the focus for a discussion on how the federation advertising and publicity machine deployed one particular aspect of the dream of community or the fear of conflict.

The "1931 Budgets" Ad: The Uses of Prestige

The federation's first campaign was the most apparently rational in the nature of its appeal. While efficiency was always a selling point for the federation, only in the first campaign was fiscal competence featured as the centrepiece of the advertising, in ads such as "1931 Budgets of the Agencies in the Welfare Federation" (see Figure 8).[14] This ad is designed to inspire a certain kind of confidence. It is not confidence that suffering people will get sensitive, skilled care. The ad lists the agencies funded but makes no claims about their value or effectiveness. Rather, the ad is meant to inspire a certainty that the expenditures of the charitable agencies in the federation will be confined to the limits of an approved budget. And that budget is all "that will be required from the citizens of Vancouver to enable [these agencies] to balance [their] books." In other words, there will be no further pitiful appeals for funds to make up any of these agencies' deficits. Furthermore, the ad assures the reader that salaries will be kept constant, "in conformity with the policy practiced by business houses at this time." As part of the campaign to solicit donations, both the phrasing and the look of this ad appeal to the practical, rational, business-like potential donor.

The rational argument of this ad spoke to a kind of mistrust that the federation itself had helped to create. The early 1930s saw something of a moral panic about charity fraud, the "exploiting of a charity for selfish purpose."[15] Newspapers carried reports such as "Charity Sport Racket," in which almost all the revenues from a charity benefit, in this case a professional football game, went to the "expenses" of the promoter, leaving little or nothing for the cause that ticket buyers imagined they were supporting.[16] Howard Falk and the federation office staff worked with a city police detective to help track down such "charity racketeers." In 1960, Falk's assistant, Ivor Jackson, recalled enjoying these "lively interludes" of criminal investigation, and he pointed out that they had been "good publicity" for the federation, presumably because catching charity crooks was a public service and because reports of charity fraud made that much more attractive the prospect of giving to so obviously reputable an organization as the federation.[17] Like Falk's anti-racketeering efforts, the "1931 Budgets" ad was designed to represent unquestionable probity. By supplying the names of publicly respectable people such as leading

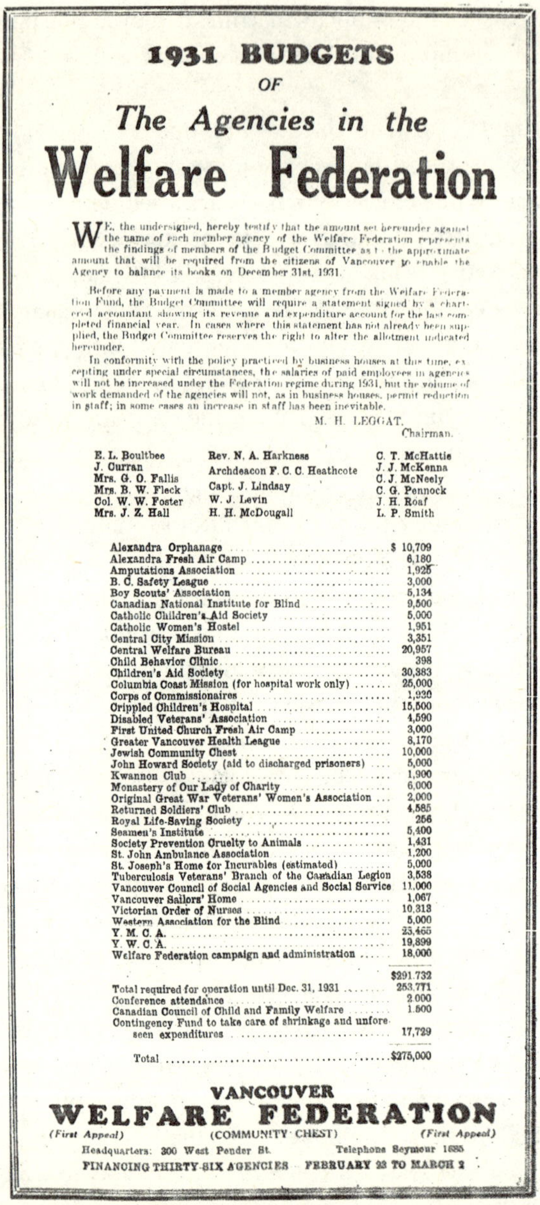

1931 BUDGETS

OF

The Agencies in the

Welfare Federation

WE, the undersigned, hereby testify that the amount set hereunder against the name of each member agency of the Welfare Federation represents the findings of members of the Budget Committee as to the approximate amount that will be required from the citizens of Vancouver to enable the Agency to balance its books on December 31st, 1931.

Before any payment is made to a member agency from the Welfare Federation Fund, the Budget Committee will require a statement signed by a chartered accountant showing its revenue and expenditure account for the last completed financial year. In cases where this statement has not already been supplied, the Budget Committee reserves the right to alter the allotment indicated hereunder.

In conformity with the policy practiced by business houses at this time, excepting under special circumstances, the salaries of paid employees in agencies will not be increased under the Federation regime during 1931, but the volume of work demanded of the agencies will not, as in business houses, permit reduction in staff; in some cases an increase in staff has been inevitable.

M. H. LEGGAT,
Chairman.

E. L. Boultbee
J. Curran
Mrs. G. O. Fallis
Mrs. B. W. Fleck
Col. W. W. Foster
Mrs. J. Z. Hall

Rev. N. A. Harkness
Archdeacon F. C. C. Heathcote
Capt. J. Lindsay
W. J. Levin
H. H. McDougall

C. T. McHattie
J. J. McKenna
C. J. McNeely
C. G. Pennock
J. H. Roaf
L. P. Smith

Alexandra Orphanage	$ 10,709
Alexandra Fresh Air Camp	6,180
Amputations Association	1,925
B. C. Safety League	3,000
Boy Scouts' Association	5,134
Canadian National Institute for Blind	9,500
Catholic Children's Aid Society	5,000
Catholic Women's Hostel	1,951
Central City Mission	3,351
Central Welfare Bureau	20,957
Child Behavior Clinic	398
Children's Aid Society	30,383
Columbia Coast Mission (for hospital work only)	25,000
Corps of Commissionaires	1,930
Crippled Children's Hospital	15,500
Disabled Veterans' Association	4,590
First United Church Fresh Air Camp	3,000
Greater Vancouver Health League	8,170
Jewish Community Chest	10,000
John Howard Society (aid to discharged prisoners)	5,000
Kwannon Club	1,900
Monastery of Our Lady of Charity	6,000
Original Great War Veterans' Women's Association	2,000
Returned Soldiers' Club	4,585
Royal Life-Saving Society	256
Seamen's Institute	5,400
Society Prevention Cruelty to Animals	1,431
St. John Ambulance Association	1,200
St. Joseph's Home for Incurables (estimated)	5,000
Tuberculosis Veterans' Branch of the Canadian Legion	3,538
Vancouver Council of Social Agencies and Social Service	11,000
Vancouver Sailors' Home	1,067
Victorian Order of Nurses	10,313
Western Association for the Blind	5,000
Y. M. C. A.	23,465
Y. W. C. A.	19,899
Welfare Federation campaign and administration	18,000
	$291.732
Total required for operation until Dec. 31, 1931	253.771
Conference attendance	2.000
Canadian Council of Child and Family Welfare	1.500
Contingency Fund to take care of shrinkage and unforeseen expenditures	17,729
Total	$275,000

VANCOUVER

WELFARE FEDERATION

(First Appeal) (COMMUNITY CHEST) *(First Appeal)*

Headquarters: 300 West Pender St. Telephone Seymour 1885

FINANCING THIRTY-SIX AGENCIES FEBRUARY 23 TO MARCH 2

FIGURE 8 "1931 Budgets of the Agencies ..." The first few ads in the history of the Community Chests emphasized fiscal competence, yet, in highlighting the presence on their boards of senior businessmen, the chests also appealed to less rational motivations for giving, such as the wish to be associated with prestigious men. (*Vancouver Sun*, 23 February 1931, 18) clergy, volunteer social workers, and businessmen to guarantee the propriety of the "revenues and expenditures" of each of the member agencies, the ad implicitly promised that those budgets included no inflated expenditures destined to line the pockets of racketeers. Fundraisers spoke of mistrust to evoke the need for their trustworthy services.

The appeal of the "1931 Budgets" ad relied on the reputations of its signatories, and to some extent this appeal was rational. Some of the signatories were indeed people with expertise in the financial management of charities. For example, one of those listed, C.G. Pennock, was an investment dealer, a banker, and the president of the Vancouver Stock Exchange, and he had been on the national executive of the Canadian Patriotic Fund and the Red Cross.[18] His testimony on matters of institutional budgeting might legitimately have inspired confidence. When, for example, the regional president of the Canadian Imperial Bank of Commerce, Mayne D. Hamilton, spoke in 1935 about the sound management techniques of the federation, his detailed and specific remarks convincingly suggested that the federation had its financial house in order.[19] The appeal based on trust of expertise such as Pennock's was featured more prominently in the early years of the federation's publicity, although (as the Hamilton example suggests) it remained a staple.

The value of the signatories to the "1931 Budgets" ad lay, then, in a claim to expertise that was at least sometimes genuine. But prominent names lent the campaign more than just an air of fiscal competence. In the "1931 Budgets" ad and in later campaigns, we can recognize prestige used to make the kind of "snob appeal" familiar from consumer advertising. This kind of appeal was what lay behind the publication of the photos and the lists of names of a glittering gallery of social and business luminaries who occupied the volunteer offices of campaign leadership every year. At campaign lunches and dinners, there were head tables, there was an "A" division of canvassers, and in the usual front-page stories of the campaign's progress the biggest donations of the day were listed in bold type. In another fundraising device, the federation offered a little bit of prestige to the smaller givers too. In these early years of the campaign, a donation of five dollars or more (six dollars after 1933) got a person's name in the paper, in the long, alphabetically arranged lists of donations published toward the end of the campaign. As campaign chairman T.S. Dixon observed in 1933, "the subscription lists now being printed in the newspapers are as interesting reading matter as you will find. I expect most people in Vancouver are daily going over the lists to find out how those they know have come forward." He thought people would find it "thrilling" to see someone being generous and that people would be interested in a different kind of way to see someone whose financial position they knew listed as having given "a very modest amount."[20] Clearly, there were possibilities both for shame and for a small kind of glory in this fundraising tool.

As well, the whole structure of the campaign provided opportunities for business networking and social climbing as canvassers met their team and division captains and competed for the achievement trophies that began to be offered in 1933.[21] The business leaders of the community were, of course, well represented in the federation. In the photo gallery entitled "Who's Who in Welfare Federation" published in 1931 at the launch of the first campaign, six of the twelve presidents of the Board of Trade since 1919 were pictured.[22] Vancouver's political elite was actively involved, too, lending their prestige and, in the process, perhaps cleansing some superficial partisan tarnish from their names. One former Liberal MLA, Victor Odlum, and W.C. Woodward, the son of another, appeared in the "Who's Who" photos and continued to be actively involved in the federation throughout the 1930s. Other leading Liberals, such as former Attorney General J.W.deB. Farris, would join them in prominent campaign roles.[23] Similarly, prominent Conservatives, such as future leader of the opposition, R.L. Maitland, would also appear at federation events.[24] Of the other men in the 1931 campaign team, I have been able to identify seven out of thirty-six as notable Conservatives.[25] Two of them – George Kidd and Austin C. Taylor – served on the Vancouver blue-ribbon business leadership's 1932 inquiry into public finances, the Kidd Commission.[26] The Welfare Federation's supporters were major political figures.

Beyond business and political influence, some of the federation's gallery of leaders, such as BC Tel president Gordon Farrell and mine syndicate financier Austin C. Taylor, owned famously splendid mansions on millionaire's row (South West Marine Drive) or on the tonier blocks of Kerrisdale and Shaughnessy Heights. Taylor, the first campaign chairman, was renowned for his stable of race horses.[27] With such men in their number, the Welfare Federation belonged in the most desirable circles and presented a choice opportunity for anyone who aspired to mingle among the gilded few. Some of the women in the group were wives of such men, but others brought a different sort of credibility to the enterprise. For example, Mrs. R.J. (Anna) Sprott, a businesswoman who would serve as a city councillor in the 1940s and who would run as a Liberal candidate in the 1952 provincial election, was also a member of the IODE, the Business and Professional Women, and the Soroptimists.[28] Drawing on the women leaders' reputation in society and social work circles, and the business and political prominence of its male leadership, the federation, following contemporary community organization advice, based its claim to legitimacy on prestige.[29] It also offered to a broad public some connection to that prestige, whether through daily involvement in the campaign organization or, more indirectly, through its published subscribers lists. The "1931 Budgets" ad hints at the importance of status aspirations in attracting Vancouverites to this new form of charitable giving.

This social and political prestige of the federation project had not been emphasized in the arguments made in the 1920s concerning the benefits of federated fundraising. To the extent that prestige figured in the early expressions of the federation idea, it did so through the reputation of the federation's business directors as sound planners, effective salesmen, and responsible trustees.[30] Indeed, in the 1920s, federation had been proposed in part as an alternative to a kind of charitable giving in which the pursuit of prestige through "wasteful" status display was prominent. There is no mistaking the aversion in the early Board of Trade reports to balls, bazaars, and "fantasies," the kind of capital "E" charity Events at which the opportunity to give was richly coated with occasions for fancy clothing, artistic performance, and personal recognition. When J. Pitcairn Hogg's 1923 Board of Trade committee agreed that "no one" would miss these events, they seem to have misunderstood the ways in which this form of fundraising was a source of sociable pleasure and a certain amount of possibly innocent, possibly repugnant, posturing.

The federation may have intended to alter the status games associated with charity fundraising, but this aspect of their rationalization of charity could not immediately alter existing charity culture. In the wider community, during the early years of the federation campaign, women's organizations persisted in holding status-generating fundraising events outside the purview of rationalized charity. In 1933, for example, the Women's Auxiliary of the Infants' Hospital hosted a benefit dance at the Commodore Ballroom, involving not only an orchestra but also a performance before the supper by the Vancouver Ladies' Pipe Band. Nearly ten column inches of description covered the fashions of the women attending, including the cameo pink lace gown worn by Mrs. Harry Reifel.[31] She and her husband, a wealthy businessman, the son of the opulently rich brewer and distiller (and mainstay of Liberal Party finances), Henry Reifel, donated thousands of dollars to the Welfare Federation. But they also enjoyed the mixed duty and pleasure of the charity ball.[32] Women of more modest circumstances, such as the members of the True Pals Club of Mountain View United Church, raised money for charity by holding events such as a Hallowe'en tea, at which aprons and candy were sold to finance the making of Christmas hampers. Similarly, at a bridge and musical evening, the women of the Duoette Club held a draw for silver flatware, the proceeds of which went to the club's philanthropic fund. Part of their fund was spent on winter clothes for the club's "Little Sisters." Especially in the months leading up to Christmas, the clubwomen of Vancouver continued, in spite of business leaders' campaign for rational charity, to raise money for the needy in forums where the givers enjoyed both the sense of doing good and opportunities to be entertained and to display talent and good taste.[33]

The federation was not immune to the linking of sociable pleasures and good works in charity culture in spite of what some of its founders may have preferred. From the beginning, the campaign's closing ceremonies included the presentation of roses to the women's division "chairman" and the wife of the general campaign chairman.[34] The closing dinners featured the donated services of Calvin Winter and his orchestra, and kick-off rallies included "high class" musical programs in splendid venues such as the Orpheum Theatre.[35] That these were occasions to see and be seen seems likely before 1935, and certain in 1935, when the Welfare Federation women's rally was for the first time featured on the *Vancouver Sun*'s society page. This report was studded with studio portraits of the wealthy women involved and accounts of their various artistic and organizational performances. The effect was to give the earnest Welfare Federation every bit as much, if not more, society glamour as the earlier, allegedly wasteful, charity pursuits the Board of Trade men had deplored. It should be noted, too, that this aspect of the pleasures of charity was recognized as distinctly feminine, with well-to-do men absent or portrayed as reluctant participants.[36]

The glamorizing of the united appeal through society events was not just a concession to supposedly feminine tastes (although it was that). Rather, society events were entirely consistent with a key element in federation fundraisers' tactics for raising funds: that is, promises that charitable giving could enhance social status. The banner headline, "You Are No Bigger than Your Community Chest Contribution," was typical of the fundraisers' status argument.[37] Do you want to be recognized and respected in your community as a "big man"?[38] Give a substantial sum to the Welfare Federation, and it will ensure that your generosity is known. The federation willingly participated in treating charitable giving as a matter of reputation. When the second campaign of 1931 appeared certain to fall well short of its goal, the *Vancouver Sun* quoted a campaign worker as having said that the federation had shown who were the "real citizens" of Vancouver and who were merely "living on their reputations."[39] Repeatedly, spokesmen for the federation referred to the moral failings of Vancouver's wealthiest men.[40] The 1933 campaign chairman, industrialist T.S. Dixon, was not above saying publicly that the federation people knew exactly who, among the wealthy, should be ashamed of their small donations.[41] In their reproaches, federation campaigners challenged Vancouver's well-to-do to make their names not by lavish personal spending but by generous giving. One editorial entitled "Pay Your Bills" made this argument in a particularly shaming way. It contrasted, on the one hand, the generous donations to the federation made by retailers who had a hard struggle to get by because their wealthy clientele failed to pay up their credit accounts with, on the other hand, the pocket change doled out at the door of palatial houses by men known for their splendiferous entertaining. "Pay your bills" not only to the merchants, the editorial suggested, but also by donating to charity, which is nothing less than the debt you owe to your community.[42] Just as consumer ads did, the federation publicists appealed to status aspirations. They sought to harness for philanthropy those energies so effective for other forms of marketing, even while their advertisements censured "greed" as a source of human suffering.[43]

While the federation campaign might seem logically to have been in competition with consumerist desires, it actually helped to legitimate spending on status goods. The campaigns entirely accepted status desires and pride of reputation as motives for charitable giving. Indeed, a 1932 federation ad suggested giving to charity the identical amount one spends on luxuries, thus integrally connecting expenditure for personal display to charitable giving. This connection was depicted in the ad by a crude figure of a weigh scale, representing the notion of "balance" that is often associated with justice (see Figure 9).[44] Implicitly stated was the comforting notion (for the wealthy) that the enjoyment of luxuries (one of the privileges of wealth) was culpable only when expenditures on enjoyment outweighed one's gifts to the needy. Giving to the federation was an efficient way to mitigate the guilt that the federation itself earnestly attempted to instill. Status could be pursued quite selfishly, through "unselfish" donations to the federation. Like consumer advertising, the federation campaign methods both sought to inflame a need and to supply the means of assuaging it.

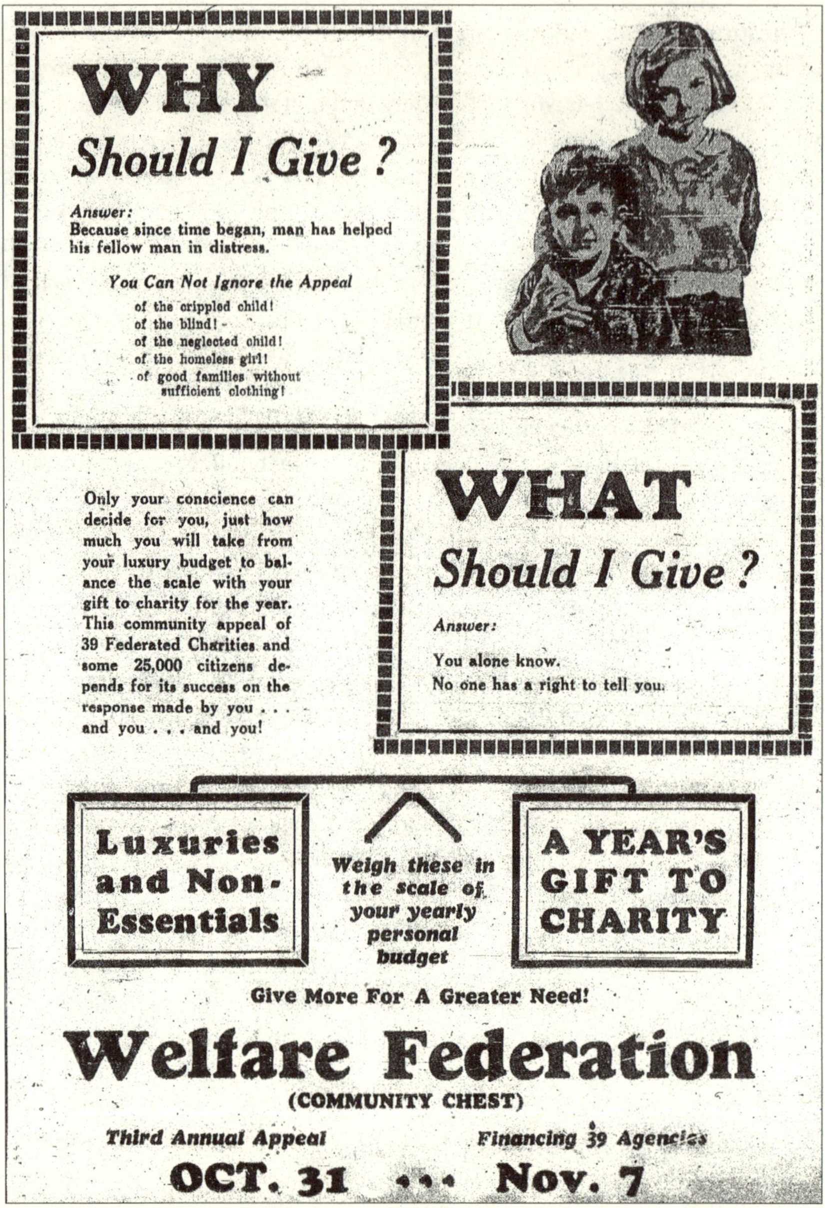

FIGURE 9 "Why Should I Give? What Should I Give?" ad, 1932. Evident here is the notion that one's charitable gifts should be at least as great as one's personal spending on luxury items, with a logic that both criticizes selfishness and offers a means of atoning for it. (*Vancouver Sun*, 25 October 1932, 13)

Even those Vancouverites whose "luxuries" consisted of a soft drink or a cigarette could be reached by these arguments, albeit in a class-specific way. A nickel a week would purchase a satisfying sense of superiority over the delinquent rich. Giving to charity could be a means of expressing contempt for *some* of the well-to-do, in terms that the federation officials' speeches (and their newspaper coverage) clearly authorized. In headlines such as "Great Corporation and City Newsboy Lead Chest Giving," the federation's promoters sought to fashion a common identity that joined the moral poor and the moral rich as the "unselfish" and distinguished them from the selfish others who do not "do their share."[45] So did cartoons like the 1935 front-page one titled "Indifference?" (see Figure 10).[46] In shaming the well-to-do who were just "living on their reputation," the federation rhetoric argued that the social status (and implicitly the legitimacy) associated with wealth had to be earned. The conservatism lay in the message that great wealth *could* be legitimized, made to seem fairly acquired and justly enjoyed for private purposes even during the hard times of the Depression. And, moreover, when

FIGURE 10 "Indifference?" cartoon, 1935. While fundraisers lambasted the morally inadequate rich, they invited working-class donors to identify in a fellow feeling of self-righteousness with those well-to-do citizens who did contribute according to their wealth. (*Vancouver Sun*, 5 November 1935, 1)

the federation lambasted the morally inadequate rich, it invited working-class readers to set aside what Carolyn Steedman calls their "proper envy" of the entire capital-owning class and to identify in a fellow feeling of self-righteousness with a morally sanitized subset of the well-to-do.[47]

The "Dear Jack" Ad: Making Charity Masculine

The class theme I address in the above discussion of reputation is touched on in another ad from the first 1931 campaign: the "Dear Jack" ad (see Figure 11).[48] In addition, this ad more explicitly addresses the gender theme mentioned above in the discussion of fundraising as a form of women's sociability.[49] The ad offers the text of a letter from an imaginary Vancouver business owner or manager (let's call him Bill) to his acquaintance, Jack, with the text set in a frame of images of those the federation proposes to help and a picture of one of the more attractive helpers. In the letter, Bill models the appropriate sort of guilt, expressing shame that he has been ignorant about "the Welfare Work of the City" and that he has given so little in the past. He also suggests the alleviation of guilt by an expiatory sacrifice of spending on "amusements and luxuries." Bill is offering Jack, for a relatively small price, a way to feel secure in his property. The cheerful youth playing baseball, shown as one image of need, is implicitly someone who might otherwise be idle, resentful, and undisciplined. Without the youth services the federation supports, it is implied, such a youth might turn to theft and vandalism or develop a propensity to question the rules of the economic game. In other sources, this implication was made specific, nowhere more so than a 1935 federation ad entitled "Youth at the Crossroads," in which the palliative effect of boys' clubs on the injuries of class is supposedly evidenced by the fact that "in five years of depression not one Vancouver Boy Scout has run foul of the law!"[50]

But this ad speaks to more than just the dynamic of middle-class guilt (and its associated fear of the envious). It also offers protection against a pejoratively coded surplus of moral sentiment. The federation writers moving Bill's fingers over the imaginary keyboard do not encourage Bill or Jack to dwell on fears or to agonize over their failings. "I didn't mean to preach a sermon, Jack," Bill says, repudiating charity's associations with religious moralism. It is Jack's "social conscience" that Bill seeks to awaken, quite a dispassionate state of mind compared with the infinite (and more morally demanding) empathy with pain evoked in sermons and symbolized for Christians by Christ on the cross. As a *Vancouver Sun* editorial writer would assert

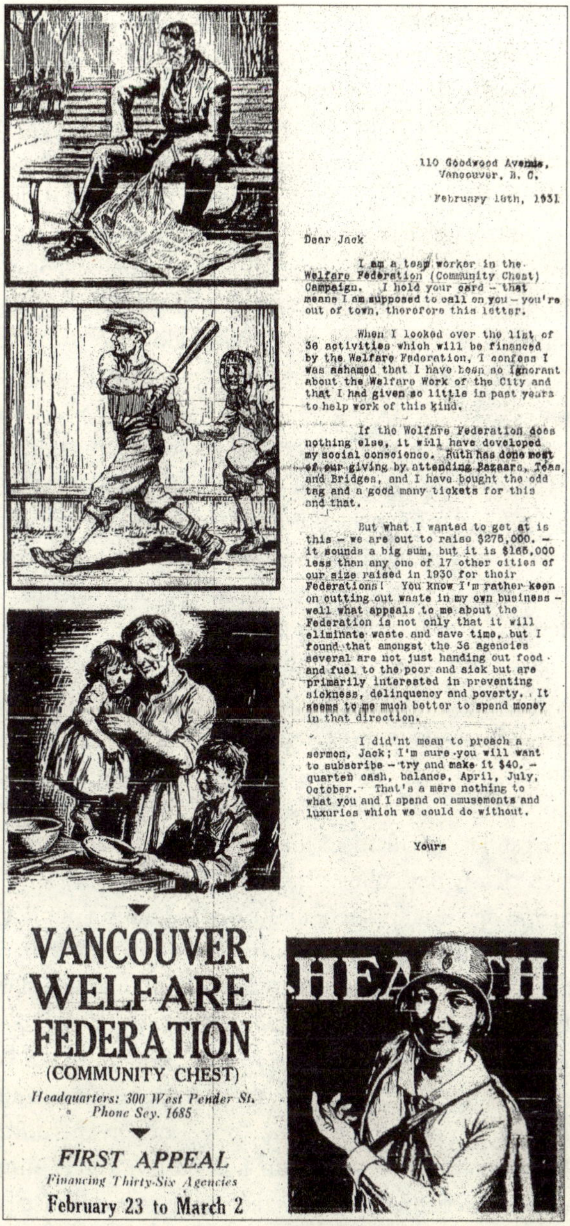

FIGURE 11 "Dear Jack" ad, 1931. This ad attempts to strip away some of the feminine associations of charity fundraising, in particular the perception that giving to the poor was an occasion for emotional self-indulgence by women and effeminate men. (*Vancouver Sun*, 21 February 1931, 14)

in 1935, "no one, we believe, hands out money for anything these days, in any ecstasy of Christian fervor."[51] Consistent with this dismissal of intense feeling, specified as Christian, the appeal of the text of the 1931 ad was clearly to Jack's mind, not to his heart. Federation will "eliminate waste and save time" by co-ordinating efforts. Several of its agencies work toward "preventing sickness, delinquency and poverty." That is a better way to spend money, Bill concludes, than just "handing out food and fuel to the poor and sick" (the sort of activities one's heart might find immediately compelling). Bill puts the federation case to Jack as a business proposition, one that is not primarily prompted by sentiment. It is by speaking to the reader's anticipated identification with the rational businessman that this particular ad seeks to have its effect.

This is, of course, an appeal to a class-specific identity. But it was also an appeal meant to strip away some of the feminine associations of charity fundraising, in particular the perception that giving to the poor was an occasion for emotional self-indulgence by women and effeminate men.[52] The fundraisers' notion of familiar gender roles in charity was presented early in the "Dear Jack" letter: "Ruth has done most of our giving by attending Bazaars, Teas, and Bridges, and I have bought the odd tag and a good many tickets for this and that." Both husband and wife participated passively, as consumers, but comparatively the wife is shown as being more actively involved in charity. To encourage an enlarged and more active role for men in this work involved two approaches. One was to represent charity women in ways that minimized the gender specificity of their charity work. The other was to promulgate various clearly masculine images of charity activity.

The first approach was apparent in the way federation publicity suggested that being "business-like" was a possibility for women in welfare work and was not simply a masculine identity. The "chief humanitarian of the women's division of the [John Howard] Society," Miss Ethelwyn Paterson, was featured during the second 1931 campaign week in the series "Business Romances of Successful B.C. Women," a front-page column that ran intermittently in the *Vancouver Sun*. Like its companion series, "Boyhood Dreams and Manhood's Realities," "Business Romances" told an individual's career story in such a way as to enable readers themselves to recognize and embrace business opportunities in their own lives.[53] In discussing Paterson, columnist Andrew Selwyn found himself perilously approaching a "sob story" and admonished himself to hold to the column's practical purpose: to offer career advice. In this business biography, sentiment threatened to undermine the narrative.

Ultimately, however, the columnist was able to forgo at least one kind of sentiment and to describe Paterson not as selfless and noble but as hard-working, intelligent, and successful, saving the community thousands of dollars, and seeking and finding "joy and pleasure" in her work.[54] Pursuing pleasure and success, not self-sacrifice, was the "business" value affirmed here. This affirmation contradicted one of the keystones of Victorian womanly ideals but suited the notion of a modern woman.

This was not simply a contrast between a self-seeking single business-woman and a self-sacrificing married one. Even married women who were not employed could be and were praised as "business-like" in federation publicity. In the coverage of the launch of the second 1931 campaign, women's chairwoman Mrs. A.Z. Delong and her vice chairwoman Mrs. C.E. Blee were said to "have been putting in longer office hours on the job than any business girl in the city." Another woman, Mrs. R.J. Sprott, had given "sales talks" to the women canvassers in each district so that all were "fully trained for their self-appointed jobs." In short, the report noted, "very business-like is the entire arrangement." Hard-working, aggressive, and well-organized seem to be the virtues implied by "business-like" in this context. The reporter underscored how remarkable he found this accomplishment in a women's organization: "And only one job of the innumerable ones involved is being held by a man."[55] Both the federation and the women who volunteered in its work were being served, after a fashion, by this angle of coverage: the federation appeared thoroughly modern in the possibilities it opened for a female citizenship of contribution, and the middle-class wives thus described were offered a type of praise more commonly afforded to their husbands.

By describing women as hard-driving, success-seeking, thinking people (an identity that may well have been welcomed by many women), modern charitable fundraising discourse thus reduced some of charity's feminine associations. Also clearly evident in the federation discourse were attempts to make specifically masculine subject positions available for men, particularly for those men who would not be the organization's top officials. Howard Falk adopted various means to accomplish this goal.[56] Addressing the Rotary Club, Falk managed to link enthusiasm for federated fundraising in Montreal to a key icon of masculinity in the interwar years: veterans. In Montreal, he asserted, the first federated appeal was "carried through largely by the young men just back from the trenches."[57] Throughout the five years of federation fund drives examined here, military (or sporting) vocabulary – "firing line," "team captains," "privates," "battle," and (most consistently) "campaign" itself

– revised charitable fundraising's feminine associations.[58] So, too, did information such as the biographical sketch of federation volunteer and (after 1934) campaign publicity writer Blair Clerk, whose stellar war record and sporting accomplishments took up two-thirds of the newspaper report of his having been hired by the federation.[59] Clerk's background clearly implied that this business of raising funds for charity was properly something a man's man could do.

The focus on men's involvement in the federation was particularly intense in the second 1931 campaign. At the opening rally, on October 24th, Falk called for an increase in numbers of and commitment from "rank and file" men workers. In the first 1931 campaign, eight months earlier, the canvassing by men of the city's workplaces had fallen far short of the campaign organizers' expectations. In his remarks at the launch of the second campaign, Falk explained this failure by suggesting that "most of the social service work of the city had been left to the women in past years." Implying that "the women" were therefore experienced canvassers, he affirmed that he expected the women's division would meet its quota. But among "our men," he continued, "we need a greater sense of citizenship and civic responsibility."[60] By the end of the fall 1931 campaign, in early November, the gender competition rhetoric had risen to the level of banner headlines on page 1 of the *Vancouver Sun:* "Are Men Going to Let Women Beat Them in the Welfare Campaign?" and "Men Have Just One More Day to Prove Their Supremity [sic] over Women."[61] These banners were no doubt intended to promote what the *Vancouver Sun,* a year later, reported as a spirit of "friendly rivalry" between the men's and women's divisions.[62] But it was not a symmetrical rivalry. The banners used the taken-for-granted inferiority of women as a means to shame men into more active participation in fundraising.[63]

Gender competition was only one dimension of the attempt embodied in the federation method to borrow from business, particularly from sales, a spirit of competition, to provide appropriately masculine emotional fuel for the engine of rational charity. In the "Dear Jack" ad, to incite Jack's support, "Bill" says other cities Vancouver's size have raised larger amounts than the one set as the Vancouver campaign's goal. Implied is a challenge: surely we won't let Vancouver "come in last." Throughout the second 1931 campaign, this spirit of intercity competition was explicit. Montreal's results were reported at the beginning of the front-page stories on the Vancouver campaign's progress. In remarks to campaign workers, chairman George B. Harrison twisted the emotional screw of civic pride: "Surely the citizens of Vancouver are not going to allow the third city in Canada to be put to shame."[64] Similarly, the campaign organizers mobilized competition among districts within both the women's and the men's divisions, offering prizes for the district that collected the greatest percentage of its quota and for the best team captain. In "Our Whole Town's Working," E.S. Roberts describes two fictional businessmen laying bets on whose "boys" will turn in a better performance as canvassers for the drive.[65] A sporting attitude complemented the military metaphors to make the federation method consonant with common-sense ideas of masculine pursuits. Again the cartoonists helped, using images of a fairground strength test or the rush for a touchdown as images of the canvassers' efforts (see Figure 12).[66]

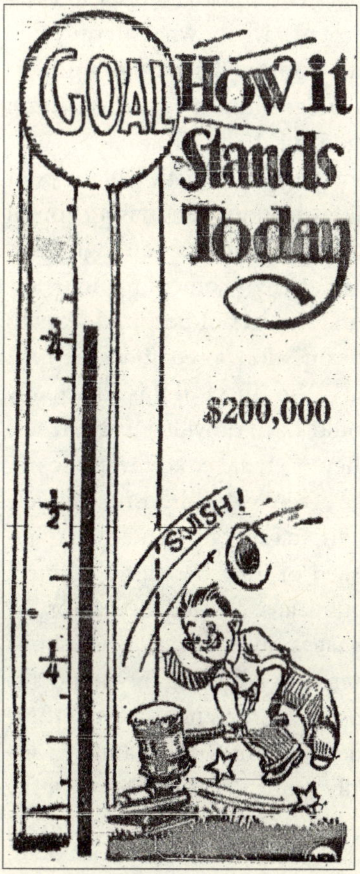

FIGURE 12 Illustrations of sporting men corresponded neatly with the spirit of competition that fundraisers borrowed from business to provide emotional fuel for the engine of rational charity. ("How It Stands Today" cartoon, 1931, *Vancouver Sun*, 2 March 1931, 1; "One 'Back' to Get Past" cartoon, 1932, *Vancouver Sun*, 5 November 1932, 1)

Finally, two of the images in the "Dear Jack" ad suggest an aspect of the federation appeal made not only to men as canvassers but also more generally to men as donors. One of them is the only source of a simple and direct emotional appeal in the ad, and that is the picture of the sad-looking fatherless family. The reader, if male, is implicitly invited to picture himself as the missing breadwinner. The invitation was made explicit in one of the 1934 ads, which asserted that this family was "Nobody's Business" unless "you" make it yours.[67] "You" might equally be a female or male reader, but for a man to make this family "his business" was inevitably to step into a kind of father position. The attraction of taking on this position was arguably enhanced in these ads when the artists rendered the single mother as young and pretty, like the ideal moms in ordinary consumer advertising (see Figure 13).[68] The "Dear Jack" ad does not do this: the mother is depicted with "lines of care" on her face. But in other federation ads or *Vancouver Sun* illustrations, the classic needy mother (who is almost always shown with only two children, a boy and a girl) is a pretty white woman, her hungry thinness indistinguishable, in some cases, from the slender silhouettes of the fashion illustrations in the paper's retail ads (see Figure 14).[69]

Was the urge to give supposed to be promoted by a depiction of the poor as not only deserving but also attractive? Did it help the fundraising appeal to show the Health League nurse as a sweet-faced twenty-something? These questions may be unanswerable, but certainly there is something here borrowed from consumer advertising, a sense that images of beautiful women attract attention. "Are they necessary?" was the question posed under the 1931 ad illustrated with a picture of a pretty nurse.[70] The "they" in this ad actually referred to jails and hospitals, but they would have provided a much less engaging image than the girl does. If the "they" were taken to mean the images of pretty girls and children under the age of ten[71] who almost exclusively represent both the needy and the helpers in these fundraising ads, the question "are they necessary?" might well be asked of the federation's ad men. And these advertising experts would no doubt have answered "yes, for the human appeal." A "human" appeal such images no doubt provided; however, given the campaign publicists' avid interest in attracting the support of men as volunteers and donors, it is perhaps not surprising that only these attractive images, and not ones of rugged male goodness, for example, were deployed to serve as the conventional, mildly erotic, "human" hook of the advertising image.

FIGURE 13 "Bran Is Good for You" ad, 1933. Whether in consumer product ads or in social advertising, a pretty girl was part of the regular toolkit that commercial artists used to produce an effective ad. (*Vancouver Sun*, 30 October 1933, 7)

The "How Big Is Your Heart?" Ad: The Class Counterpoint

In these various forms of appeal – shaming, enticing, affirming the possibility of manly charity – men seem to have been addressed as a homogeneous gender. But in the years from 1932 to 1935, increasingly vocal socialist or

FIGURE 14 "Help!" 1932. Attractive single mothers were featured prominently in the chest ads of the 1930s. Fatherless families offered what was then considered a sympathetic image of need. Appealing to women to identify with the pretty woman's woes, the ad also invited men to help out this woman. (*Vancouver Sun*, 3 November 1932, 1)

left-wing criticism resulted ultimately in campaign publicity that targeted men of the working class in particular. The criticism from the left deplored some of the federation's sentimental and non-rational appeals, with the result, it seems, of making the federation strategies more rather than less reliant on emotion.

One element of the socialist criticism appeared in the press in 1932, in a scornful paragraph by socialist *Vancouver Sun* columnist Bob Bouchette. Commenting at the end of the federation's third campaign on the campaign's repeated failure to collect the amount its experts had set as Vancouver's attainable quota, Bouchette offered both a practical explanation – in the present business conditions, people are too uncertain of their own income to give any money away – and a more politically pointed one: "Organized charity has put on the same show twice, has flopped twice. Apparently the public doesn't like the show. The only alternative is to take the production out of private hands and make it a government affair."[72]

Bouchette's mocking "show" metaphor underscores how recognizably the federation campaigns duplicated the entertainment aspects of "old-fashioned" charity events. Exuding hard-boiled rationalism, Bouchette also had a little fun with the federation fundraisers' claims to be business-like and unsentimental. He pointed out that, in his view, the whole "principle of voluntary charity" was grounded in feeling, not reason: "[Voluntary charity] leaves altogether too much to the personal whim of the giver. The size of a contribution to the Welfare Federation might conceivably be governed by the condition of the 'prospect's' liver at the time when the Community Chest canvasser paid a call on him. No business – and the Community Chest is supposed to put welfare on a business basis – could possibly operate efficiently in the face of such haphazard methods."[73]

In other words, federation, in spite of its claims to be otherwise, relied on the essentially unpredictable movements of feeling instead of the fixed policies recommended by reason and capable of being incorporated into statutory entitlements. Voluntary charity, by its nature, could not be rationalized. Rationalization inevitably led to making care for the needy a public responsibility. To make welfare "a government affair" offered some prospect of success in Bouchette's view. But all that the federation was accomplishing, Bouchette suggested, again borrowing one of its own rhetorical touchstones to use against it, was to create a series of failures that were "humiliating to the spirit of the city."[74]

Others on the left criticized the federation in more explicitly socialist terms. Most strikingly, according to the federation chairman in 1935, canvassers had repeatedly found over the years that, at some doors, residents refused to give a cent to a "capitalist racket."[75] It might be, of course, that federation executives made up this story and told it in the belief that it discredited socialists as ungenerous. However, a later source suggests that "capitalist racket" was genuinely a phrase with which socialists critiqued the Community Chest movement. In 1950, Canadian Congress of Labour official Pat Conroy used the term "racket" to describe Community Chests. Conroy argued that, like the charity sports rackets, the chests were too costly in relation to the funds they provided for meeting needs.[76] It also seems very likely that part of the "racket" charge in the 1930s was the criticism made in 1944 by some Toronto unionists. They charged that the same businessmen urging generous giving to the needy through charity were the ones whose low wages and callous use of labour made working-class wage earners unable to take care of their own needs, for example by purchasing the kinds of life and health insurance that would obviate the need for a whole range of social services.[77] Certainly, when mining magnate Austin C. Taylor spearheaded the first fundraising appeal, class-conscious Vancouver working people might have felt that his prestige was tainted by the reputation of his notoriously exploitive industry.[78]

The 1933 federation ad "How Big Is Your Heart?" shows the first real effect of a socialist or communist critique of the communications strategy of the fundraisers (see Figure 15).[79] The text of the ad asked, "shall we stop to argue about the rights and wrongs of why suffering should exist? Shall we quibble about other possible – or impossible – ways of meeting it? No! Let's act as our hearts dictate! It boils down to just one question: HOW BIG IS YOUR HEART?"

This ad clearly relies more heavily on sentiment than did either of the 1931 or the 1932 campaign materials. The federation had to move beyond its ostensibly rational appeal because, in fact, nothing in the federation's rational appeal clearly established that highly organized annual fundraising was better than a state-managed means of collecting money to meet welfare needs. Faced with socialist arguments, federation publicists resorted vigorously to the sentimental appeals they had earlier forsworn.

As well as tailoring their sales pitch to answer the criticisms of their ideological competitors, some of the federation's volunteer officers and newspaper supporters went on the offensive against socialist statism. The mild

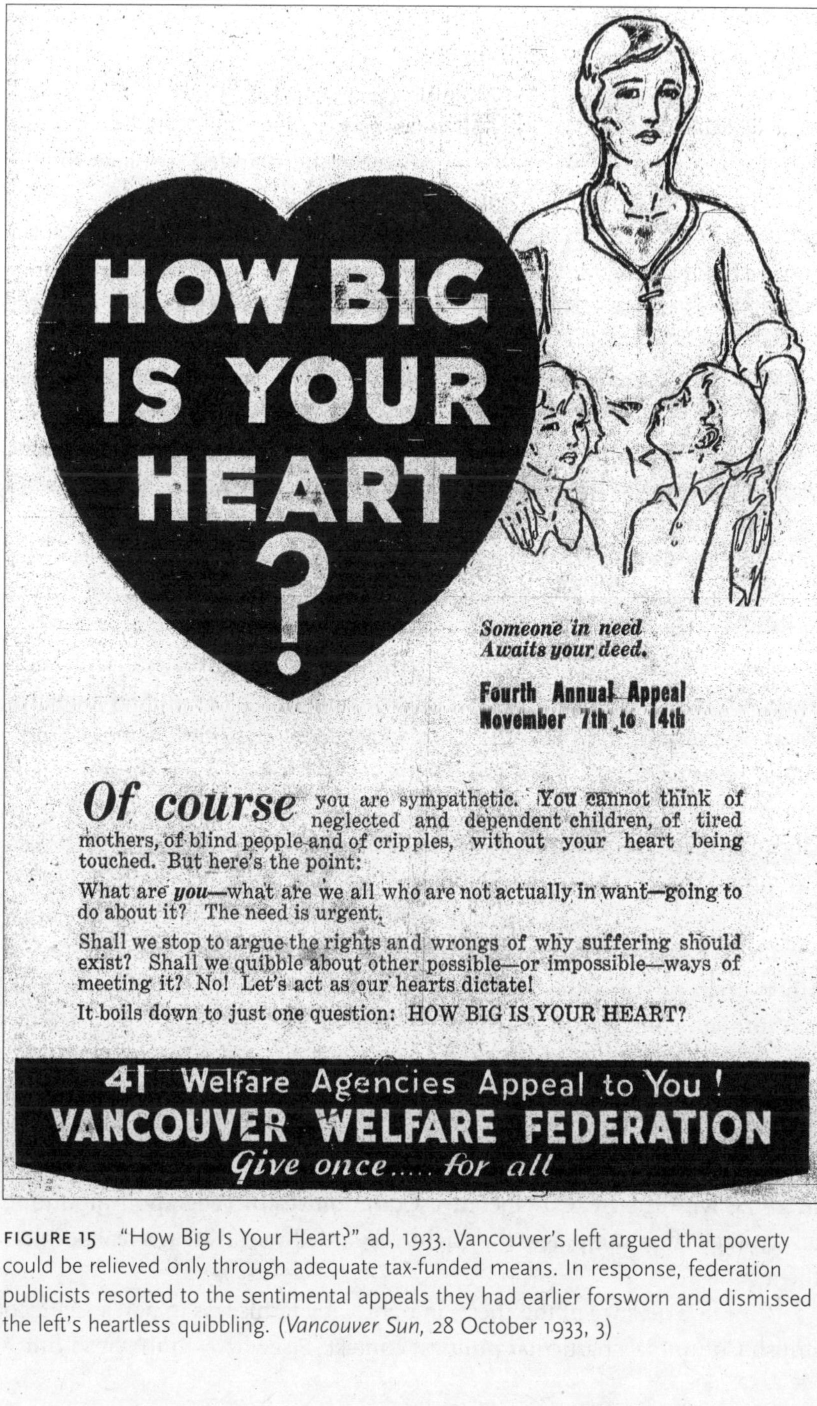

FIGURE 15 "How Big Is Your Heart?" ad, 1933. Vancouver's left argued that poverty could be relieved only through adequate tax-funded means. In response, federation publicists resorted to the sentimental appeals they had earlier forsworn and dismissed the left's heartless quibbling. (*Vancouver Sun*, 28 October 1933, 3)

protest against politicizing charity (or even reasoning about it) that the fundraisers expressed in the "How Big Is Your Heart?" campaign of 1933 was supplemented in 1934 by outright anti-statist polemic. In the *Vancouver Sun* of 13 October 1934, its owner and editor (and active Liberal) Robert Cromie published the text of the national broadcast he planned to make for the Canadian Welfare Council's appeal in support of all of the country's Community Chests: "Communism or Capitalism," he began, "is the only basis on which Vancouver and our Canadian cities can discuss their various Community Chests." He went on to say that, if Canadians wanted an economy that allowed "individual initiative, individual opportunity, and individual reward," then Canadians had to accept individual responsibility for charitable giving. Otherwise, the alternative was "Russia." Casual charity – a Christmas hamper or a handful of coal – was inadequate to stave off what Cromie clearly felt was the horrendous possibility of state expansion. The chest's "scientific" method of giving "according to one's worth, one's business volume, or earning power," he concluded, "is the only method for those who do not want to see themselves and their fellow citizens, turned into mere units of [a] communal socialistic group."[80]

Cromie was not merely an isolated extremist. Other federation leaders took a similarly ideological tone in more private forums when they sniped at their socialist critics.[81] They, like Cromie, made much of the theme of "individual responsibility" – not just for the needy but also for the fortunate, whose responsibility was inherent in their good fortune.[82] And provincial Liberal leader Duff Patullo, in a letter to Cromie in 1933, the year before Patullo became premier, used language very like that of Cromie's 1934 article: "If we are to continue to enjoy the individualism which is now ours, we must be prepared to carry not only our own burden, but the burden of others unable to carry the load."[83] Arguing for the preservation of individualism through collective responsibility, Patullo could make his case – for the expansion of tax-funded welfare programs – and Cromie could make his – for the benefits of rational charity. On the basis of this ideology, both of these men (and many of the federation leaders) regarded themselves as the opponents of socialism and defenders of a more compassionate capitalism. In 1933, with the BC Co-Operative Commonwealth Federation mounting an active election campaign, they rightly regarded socialism as a real political threat.[84]

Cromie's defence of the chests in right-wing terms was in part specific to British Columbia's particular political context. Elsewhere, in the head office of Canada's federated fundraisers, the Community Organization division of the Canadian Welfare Council, his proposed 1934 charities broadcast speech was not welcome. There division head Marjorie Bradford gently asked Howard Falk to find another leading Vancouver businessman to speak in the national broadcasts. Cromie's message, she wrote, "may be all right for Vancouver's present state of mind, but I don't think it would go down in Montreal or the eastern cities. We have been keeping quiet on the subject of riot insurance." She wanted someone capable of "putting the thing a little less baldly."[85] She would probably have accepted more comfortably Vancouver businessman H.R. MacMillan's 1933 observation that the well-do-do could not enjoy "peace of mind" and the "privileges" of wealth "without accepting the duties and obligations of good citizenship."[86] In Vancouver, though, active socialist organizing helped to push businessmen such as Cromie off MacMillan's moderate track.

The Women's New Era League Protest

Part of what gave Cromie's remarks their particular edge of animus in 1934 was a criticism of the federation published in the *Daily Province,* a newspaper that competed with Cromie's *Vancouver Sun*. The criticisms originated with a distinctive BC organization, the Women's New Era League (WNEL). Formerly a women's suffrage organization, the Political Equality League, the WNEL was still active in 1934.[87] In combination with labourite or socialist sympathizers in the City Council, in the months between the 1934 and 1935 federation campaigns, the WNEL mounted a sustained attack on the federation and its methods. In this attack, a socialist critique was combined with women's grievances and a regionalist protest. The result of this three-pronged attack would be new defensive strategies in the 1935 federation campaign.

On 20 June 1934, the *Daily Province* published a detailed statement from the WNEL headlined "New Era League Asks [for] Department of Public Welfare. Are Critical of City Organization under Mr. Falk." Its list of complaints about the federation was the result of at least six years of simmering irritations between some of the city's women's organizations and men's service clubs, such as the Rotary and the Gyros, which had joined with the Board of Trade to initiate the federation in 1929. Both camps seem to have felt a sense of ownership about charity work in Vancouver and how it should be conducted. Tensions in relations among these groups had developed during discussions of child welfare in the mid-1920s. The debate had pitted the advocates of foster care (including prominent WNEL member, juvenile court judge, and Liberal Helen Gregory MacGill) against the proponents of modern orphanages (including H.R. Glass, insurance executive, Children's Aid Society [CAS] president, Conservative, and later federation officer).[88] The results had been a defeat for MacGill and the construction of a new orphanage, the Children's Aid Society building, erected in 1928 and financed by men's service club fundraising. That year MacGill pointed out that the service clubs had effectively wasted money by conducting a child welfare survey to demonstrate need but had refused to offer or to explain possible sources of funding for services to meet the needs identified. Later the provincial government altered the regulations of the province's Mothers' Pensions program, in part because of Howard Falk's influence. The revised program exerted stricter control of beneficiaries, which violated the ideals WNEL members had successfully seen included in the program's original design.[89]

Tensions mounted between men's and women's service organizations when, in August 1933, the Vancouver Women's Building Inc. turned to the federation for financial help and was refused. The building had been constructed in 1926 through intensive fundraising by women's groups, but the building's directors were finding it difficult, by 1933, to continue paying its remaining debt. At the same time, as they knew, the federation was discussing its need for new office headquarters. The Women's Building representative, Helen MacGill, appealed to the federation Board of Directors to relocate the federation as a tenant in the Women's Building and thus save the latter's finances. Clearly indicating the strained state of relations between the federation and at least some of Vancouver's organized women, MacGill pointed out that not to take this step would worsen the "unwitting rivalry" between the federation and women's groups.[90] However, in October 1933, the federation board voted to refuse the Women's Building offer and chose instead to make their new offices elsewhere. The new location was the Children's Aid Building, a choice that irritated relations between the federation and MacGill's sympathizers. Having been convinced by Falk and his associates that foster care was generally preferable to congregate care, the CAS had belatedly followed "amateur" women social workers' earlier advice and had closed its substantial, modern orphanage. By renting it to the federation, the CAS then "stole" the tenant that would have saved the Women's Building.[91]

It was out of this context of real, and not especially friendly, gender competition that the WNEL, early in 1934, asked City Council to make some effort to control the federation. Council formally asked the federation to provide council with a list of employees and their salaries, an explanation of which powers the federation exercised over member agencies, and a justification of why some children housed in the new CAS building had been removed to make room for the federation offices and placed in the old Alexandra Orphanage. When the federation replied by inviting councillors and some of the WNEL members to a meeting, council refused to attend, some of its members regarding the invitation as evasive, in effect a means of telling "the council to go to hell." Council was the representative of "the public" and had a right to know how the federation was spending the money the public had contributed. Although one alderman, W.J. Twiss, was active in the federation and rose to its defence, others (H.J. De Graves, J.H. Shinnick, and "labour" representative Walter Deptford) showed a touchy sense of council's dignity having been affronted.[92] What followed over the next three months was an exercise in public relations management by the federation that resulted in two of its most senior and prominent volunteer leaders, Victor Odlum and W.E. Payne, being sent to Victoria to discuss the situation with "the government."[93] The fact that the federation's decision to send them to Victoria took place just two days after the *Daily Province* published the WNEL critique suggests that the WNEL had succeeded in casting politically telling aspersions on the federation.

As a response to the campaign methods of the federation, the WNEL's June 20th statement shows, as Bouchette's 1932 critique had, how readily the federation's means of appeal could be deployed against them and in favour of more state-centred means of organizing welfare. The WNEL's opening shot was both a sentimental one and one that showed a more critical awareness of class power than the federation publicity did. The federation's fundraising methods cruelly pressured lower-income people, they alleged. Moreover, in some cases, employers went beyond exerting federation-authorized pressure on employees and actually made payroll deductions for the federation without employees' consent. "Many workers who can't afford to give must," the WNEL charged, leading to sad situations such as that of a man who, having "donated" to the federation, was unable to save for Christmas presents for his children, while neighbours received Christmas packages as charity from a federation-funded agency. The federation's rational methods were thus disparaged as in fact repellently unfeeling.[94]

The WNEL also disputed the federation's accountability claim, represented in the "1931 Budgets" ad, while affirming public accountability as a democratic value. Pointing to the federation's initial resistance to supplying City Council with data, the WNEL alleged that the federation conducted its affairs in "secrecy." Rather than being the genuine community effort lauded in campaign speeches, federation seemed to be the project of a coterie of insiders. Accountability was essential, the WNEL argued, but "semi-public" agencies could not provide it. "We have a Legislature at Victoria and a council in Vancouver, elected by the people, paid by the people, responsible to the people." These elected bodies were the ones that should "co-ordinate and administer our public service." In effect, the WNEL's critique suggested that federation itself was guilty of the kind of wasteful duplication of services that the federation claimed to prevent. Federation was duplicating the administrative functions that properly belonged to governments. Furthermore, federation had not succeeded in incorporating all charities, so its claim to manage centrally the money Vancouverites gave to charity was inaccurate. Only government could genuinely (and accountably) co-ordinate "all public services" by "taking them entirely out of the hands of private or semi-public organizations."

On a whole series of particular administrative choices, the WNEL alleged, federation had failed to live up to its claims to expertise and probity. Here the criticisms were a flock of chickens coming home to roost: the CAS building story and the story of the Mothers' Pensions "reforms" were retold as evidence of incompetent planning and poor social work practice. And once again the federation's rhetoric of community pride was used against the federation. These mistakes had been made by outsiders who were not "familiar with our social history and ideals" and who therefore had undone the work done by BC women. Falk was described as "a man from a socially backward city like Montreal," under whose influence the government had reneged on a promise made by J.W.deB. Farris, a Liberal attorney general in the 1920s (and a federation participant in the 1930s).[95]

Most offensive were the high salaries paid to Falk and the other "outside workers" with whom, the WNEL alleged, he had staffed this supposedly Vancouver institution. Like the changes to the mother's pension, the payments to outsiders were characterized as disrespectful to BC people. Falk himself was allegedly paid more than the mayor, the city comptroller, the superintendent of education, and the head of the city relief department. The city's most senior male school principal, laden with credentials, learning, and administrative responsibilities, earned less than half of Falk's salary of $6,600.[96] Why should these local public servants be paid less than an "easterner?" The WNEL could play the western pride card as well as the federation did. The federation salaries were also derided as wasteful. In addition to Falk's salary, the WNEL averred, the federation paid nine more salaries to people administering its funds. All this was money that was diverted from the needy, they charged. They also argued that federation agencies were similarly squandering donations. For example, the Family Welfare Bureau's annual report showed that "some $26,000 of our money [had] been spent and [of] that $9160 had reached the needy." Salaries were the bureau's single largest expense.

The WNEL neglected to note here that the bureau was primarily a counselling agency and naturally spent most of its budget on salaries. But the animus against social work and administrative salaries was not surprising from a middle-class women's organization, for which unpaid social work had been an important part of the women's role in life. It must have chafed to see others, seemingly less competent, raising money to pay themselves to do work that these women had done for free. The Women's Building episode, not mentioned in the WNEL statement, can only have been a spark to an accumulating tinder pile of resentment between women's and men's service organizations. When, in 1943, Helen MacGill wrote *The Story of Vancouver Social Service,* giving capsule histories of thirty-six welfare societies, the men's service clubs were not included at all, and her coverage of the Vancouver Welfare Federation was noticeably cooler and less celebratory than that given to even small and tenuously struggling ladies' hospital auxiliaries. There were, in fact, two worlds of social service in Vancouver, even within the Anglo-Christian "world" about which MacGill wrote. In this milieu of mid-twentieth-century charity, the separate spheres still existed. But, as with the conflict over socialist ideology, Vancouver's particular political history may have heightened the atmosphere of gender conflict. In the origins of the Halifax Community Chest, suffrage campaigner Agnes Dennis led other organization women into successful collaboration with the men's business community without hearing dissenting voices.[97]

While the WNEL's criticism draws our attention to the rivalry that had grown up between men's and women's service groups in the 1920s, the WNEL and its sympathizers were not alone in casting Vancouver charity work in a separate spheres mould. Federation itself had always run the fundraising campaign out of two separate campaign headquarters: in 1935, the women's headquarters was in the year-round federation offices (on one of the main thoroughfares in middle-class residential Kitsilano), and the men's was downtown in the business district (at 734 West Hastings). This arrangement no doubt complemented the other efforts to allow men canvassers to avoid feeling they were part of feminine charity work. After the tensions of early 1934, however, a new approach to managing gender difference seems to have been required. It seems that retaining the support of women canvassers and women donors became newly salient for the federation's publicists. The earlier efforts to avoid feminine signifiers were balanced in 1934-35 by indirect responses to the WNEL charges and increased references to women in feminine terms as charity workers and donors.

The "Angels of Mercy" Ad: Victorian Femininity Reprised

In 1934, the most direct response to the WNEL was a story told by a former campaign chairman, T.S. Dixon, addressed to "those who have any doubt of the value of what is being done by the various social service agencies."[98] He spoke of having "heard" of two citizens – a mother and daughter from Kerrisdale, a prosperous suburb – who had decided to pay visits to some institutions supported by the federation. He gave their full names and addresses, as if to confirm that they were not a publicist's fiction. He reported that they were concerned that their visits might be "an annoyance" but instead found they were welcome and were assured that "too little interest was being shown by the public." They toured the Central Clothing Bureau (probably the Cordova Street clothing depot, whose unknown management and antecedents the WNEL had criticized in its June statement), YWCA, Crippled Children's Home, Institute for the Blind, Victorian Order of Nurses (VON), and CAS. In a supposed quotation from the daughter, the narrative concluded, "it is surprising just how little the general public knows of the many very necessary activities carried on under the one central financing organization which prevents over-lapping of interests and brings trained and yet most interested and understanding care to the many charities." No "secrecy" here was the scarcely subtextual message of the story as a whole. If a "citizen" does not know about federation agencies, said the voice between the lines, it is her own lack of interest that is to blame.

Other than this story, the 1934 campaign materials made little in the way of distinctive appeals to women. But a story told by the women's division chairwoman, Mrs. J.S. Eckman, foreshadowed a theme that reappeared in 1935, a theme that suggested that the organization was having to make a special effort to attract and motivate women canvassers. As the *Vancouver Sun* report read, "Mrs. Eckman told of one worker, a woman of quiet, retiring disposition, who had felt she was not the type to canvass successfully. She had, however, decided that she would do her best in view of the great need, and in the hope that every person she met could not but feel a personal responsibility to share the cost of maintaining the federation agencies. This woman, whose name she had been pledged not to give, was a member of a team which had raised $600 up to that morning. Of this total the woman of whom she spoke had turned in $565."[99] Here was a canvasser image suited to women who might have found the whole atmosphere of silver trophies and "friendly rivalry" entirely too extroverted and egotistical. She is an image of self-sacrifice. In the 1935 version of the story, "retiring women" are praised for "overcoming their natural diffidence for the good of a cause."[100] The especially feminine touch in the 1934 story is the woman's modest unwillingness to have her name mentioned.

In 1935, the women's rally to launch the campaign was, as mentioned earlier, the first truly "society" women's event for the federation. The report of preparations for it assured readers that "feminine Vancouver ... would not see the drive fail in its objective because of any lack of self-sacrifice on their part."[101] This comment inaugurated a new appeal to married women to "sacrifice" for the campaign as canvassers and donors. The ad that represented this new emphasis in the 1935 campaign was "Angels of Mercy" (see Figure 16). The first of the newspaper ads run that year, it began, "Angels of Mercy. Nurses, Doctors, Social Workers, and last, but by no means least many hundreds of kindly people – mostly women – mothers themselves, who find time out of their busy domestic lives to serve in a hundred ways those less fortunate." The illustration shows a motherly woman about to feed some hot soup to a bedridden young man. News stories emphasized the hardships women canvassers endured in their service to the community: "Rain or shine these one thousand [women] workers sacrifice the greater portion of the entire ten days," walking "many weary miles" to cover Vancouver's residential districts.[102]

The Monday after the women's rally, the *Vancouver Sun* editorial put the focus on the need for sacrifice from women as donors. The editorial deplored the housewife's tendency to refuse a donation on the ground that her husband gave at the office: "Thousands of wives can divert at least a small part of their household allowance or their spending money. The fact that husbands are giving is not always enough. The wives have also a stake in the community. They should be glad of an opportunity to help pay for it."[103]

And a few days later the newspaper offered apparent proof of the power of the press. It seems that one Vancouver housewife met with objections from her husband when she asked him to increase her household budget so

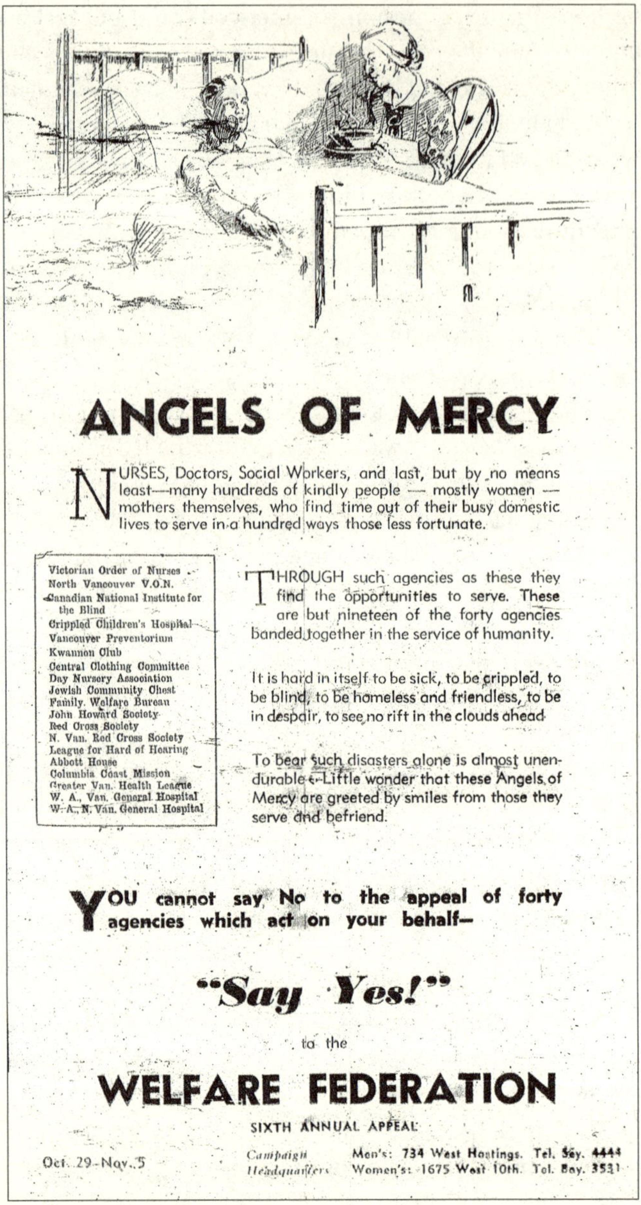

FIGURE 16 "Angels of Mercy" ad, 1935. Encountering challenges from some of Vancouver's social activist women, the federation appealed to women's pride in their volunteer social work. However, with its reference to Victorian separate spheres, the ad likely annoyed rather than mollified feminists such as Helen Gregory MacGill. (*Vancouver Sun*, 29 October 1935, 2)

that she could make a personal donation to the federation. When he refused, saying his donation should do for both of them, she tried to arrange with a business with whom she ran a monthly account to show an extra twenty-five cents per month on her invoice. She could then use that invoice as a means to get the increased household budget from her husband, which she would then give to the federation rather than pay to the merchant. "And at least," the newspaper story sweetly concluded, "she would feel that she had been able to play her part."[104] Clearly, in some families, the federation's notion of individual responsibility went against the more deeply ingrained idea of the family's "individuality" as being embodied solely in the husband. When, for example, the City Council decided to include women in the city poll tax, the city solicitor was instructed to draft the city charter revision in such a way as to avoid billing the tax to "housewives and other women not drawing wages in a direct manner."[105] In this step toward full citizenship as taxpayers, women found that their individuality still consisted of their labour outside the family collective.

While the Women's New Era League, with its suffrage antecedents, was undoubtedly interested in seeing women undertake citizenship responsibilities, the Welfare Federation's promotion of citizen obligation as individual self-sacrifice was a feeble form of citizenship compared with the broad-ranging social involvement of activists such as Helen MacGill. The federation's responses in 1934 and 1935 to the simmering anger of some of Vancouver's organized womanhood would hardly have mollified those for whom the federation's selfishness had cost them the Women's Building or the liberal provisions of the Mothers' Pensions Act. But the more frequent allusions to quasi-Victorian ideas of feminine charity in 1935 may have countered the robustly sporting, business-centred image the federation publicists had generated in the first four campaigns. The WNEL critique had had an effect, even if it was certainly not the one they would have wanted.

The "$350,000 – a Lot of Money!" Ad: The Communitarian Civic Imaginary

Similarly, the criticisms from the left, to which the WNEL had contributed, elicited an attempt from federation publicists to counter the impression that the campaigns were foisting an unwelcome culture of contribution on resistant Vancouver working men. The 1935 ad headlined "$350,000 – a Lot of Money!" (see Figure 17) came closest to conveying the federation's alternative vision. It promoted the giving of small amounts, in a context in which the responsibilities of the rich were spelled out: "Five hundred rich people and business firms will contribute at least $190,000 – another fifteen hundred well-to-do people will contribute $60,000. *That leaves $100,000 to come from 248,000 people; of whom 33,333 can certainly contribute. If they averaged $3.00 each, it would suffice. Some will give more – some will give less.*"[106]

This ad suggests that the federation was making a fair request of "the little guy" because the "big fellow" was doing his share too. Not surprisingly, federation leaders got "their big thrill of the day" when the Vancouver City Firefighters' Union came forward with donations that seemed to indicate working-class endorsement of this vision. The story began with a recitation of the pay cuts the firefighters had suffered, the shortness of their earning years, the city's unwillingness to pay the extra premiums required to include the firefighters in the municipal group insurance plan – in short, with evidence of the individual firefighter's need to save every penny. The narrator went on to celebrate the firefighters' record of "community spirit," especially their having given over some of their wages so that fellow municipal employees in the parks board could be retained. This "community spirit," he implied, explained why, in spite of their having little enough to spare, "every man signed up." The chairman of the Industrial-Commercial Division (formerly the Employees' Division) was quoted as saying, "there was no pressure on them. When they understood rightly what it was all about they got into the game gladly, and as a matter of community responsibility." Union president Ernie Young reportedly said, "I feel proud of my pals and our union."[107] Possibly, this is what he said. But it is a little more difficult to take at face value (although equally difficult to dispute with direct evidence) the assertion that no pressure was applied. In light of the WNEL criticisms about federation-authorized forcing of "donations," though, it is easy to see why this assertion was an essential figure in the story's tableau of universal citizenship.

Even more remarkable than the firefighter story was the success the federation reported in having both the Vancouver Longshoremen's Association and the Canadian Waterfront Workers' Association commit to canvassing their memberships for donations.[108] This was remarkable because these unions were the offspring of a complicated and violent labour dispute that had split the longshoremen's union into an ultra-left-wing union (the former of the two) and a right-wing employees' association. The dispute, which involved not only these unions but also a mean-minded employers' association and a police attack on a union march, tore through Vancouver's waterfront earlier

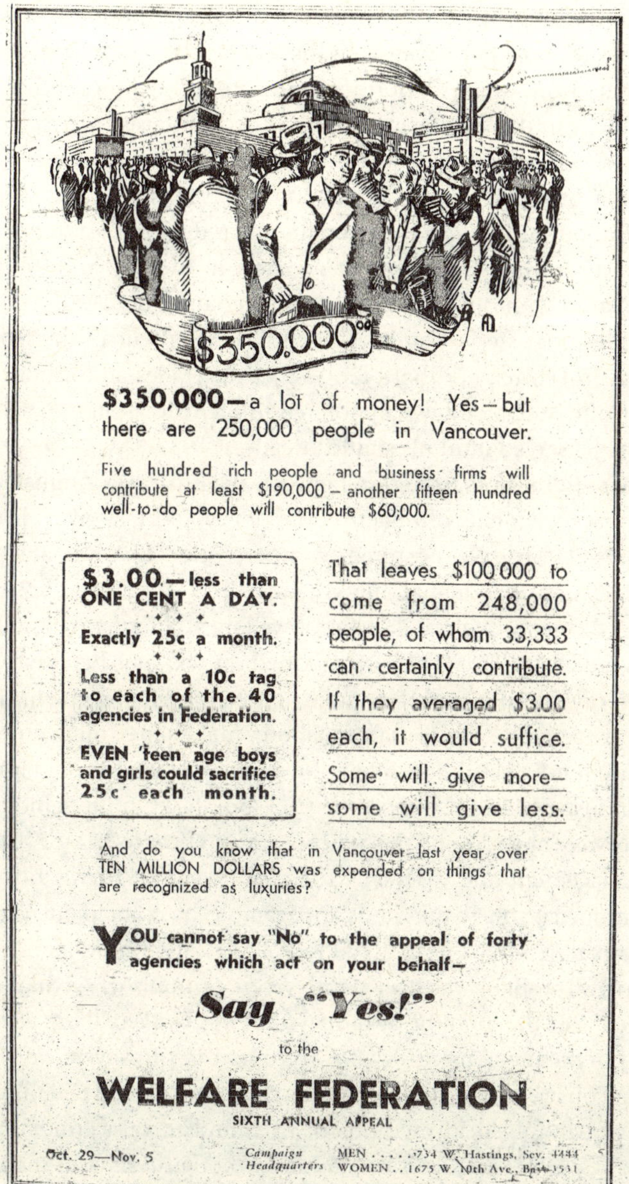

FIGURE 17 "$350,000" ad, 1935. At the heart of the chest idea was a remarkable blend of altruism and selfishness. As this ad suggests, the federation offered a way to fulfill obligations that would keep individuals' expenses to a minimum. Class suspicion and community spirit combine here in a mildly uncomfortable mix. (*Vancouver Sun*, 25 October 1935, 4)

in 1935 and was the object of a royal commission of inquiry.[109] It is unclear, to put it mildly, how participating in the federation's fundraising exercise fit into the waterfront unions' priorities in this troubling time. In fact, it seems only too likely in this case that the federation fundraisers were exaggerating their success with a bird that was still very much in the bush and perhaps never would be in the hand. The report, however exaggerated it may have been, is important because it represents the federation's attempt to show itself as transcending the forces of division in the city and uniting Vancouverites in a common goal for the city as a community. And, indeed, 1935 saw a modest first step toward real inclusion of labour in the federation's leadership. In February of that year, Vancouver Trades and Labour Council member Colin McDonald was appointed to the federation's board of directors, where he served until his sudden death in 1937.[110]

Further efforts at consultation between the business-dominated federation and some elements of organized labour would take place in the later 1930s. These efforts were inspired by a perception that labour's power in industrial relations was dramatically growing. In 1937, Falk's successor, George Davidson (former provincial director of welfare and future national director of the Canadian Welfare Council), reported on relations between American chests and organized labour. He spoke of the practice in some firms "across the line" of coercing donations from labour, making payroll deductions to a community fund a condition of employment. As a new, more radical Congress of Industrial Organizations, the CIO took hold in these industries, he said, firms were abandoning this practice, in an effort to reduce "friction between management and workers." The result was not necessarily that employees stopped giving to the chests; for example, he pointed out, the number of donors had increased from 5,700 to 6,300 at one Bethlehem, Pennsylvania, company (probably the steel plant), where compulsory "giving" had been abandoned. But the amount of money that the workers there gave was, in total, half of the previous year's take. So American firms were worried.

In Vancouver, he said, the moral was clear. "We should feel thankful that we have not indulged in methods of this kind to raise funds in our I-C [Industrial-Commercial] division and even though results in the past have not compared with results in other cities, the chances of labour unrest disturbing our relations with employee groups are distinctly less than in American cities." He called for the federation to continue to rely on "pressure from within the individual himself" – workers' own moral feelings – or "pressure from within employee groups themselves" – the same kind of mechanism the chests relied on when working with middle-class and elite groups. "Pressure from above," he acknowledged, could produce a "brief period of spectacular success," but for lasting support from wage earners and organized labour only peer pressure or personal conviction would work.[111]

By July 1939, the federation's interest in working with unionists bore some fruit. The labour council was far from happy with several of the federation's member agencies, but it agreed to seek representation on the federation's board. After the outbreak of war in September, the federation reorganized in a variety of ways. The Trades and Labour Council (the more conservative of the city's two labour councils) was invited to participate in that reorganization, and several labour men served on the war chests' board and committees during the war. In 1942, both of the city's labour councils were leading a canvass for funds among their member unions, and the president of the more left-wing council, the Canadian Congress of Labour affiliate, was a member of the federation's social-planning section. Among unionists, labour participation in the federation would remain controversial, as would particular federation policies.[112] But that the federation wanted such participation and was willing to include representatives from labour councils was no longer in doubt by 1942.[113] Business firms were complaining in 1943 that "labour in War Industries" was not "doing its share," and fundraisers worried that "Welfare Federation is far from being completely sold to labor." But they felt confident that the labour councils were "not hostile any more."[114] Without a sentimental era of trust having dawned, a negotiated basis of cross-class co-operation was beginning to emerge. A gesture that indicated this new regime was the name change from Welfare Federation to Community Chest in 1944. "Labour groups" had requested the change so that they could participate in community service without having to associate themselves with "charity."[115] These developments in the 1940s grew out of the relations between labour and the federation in the 1930s.

While this chapter has concentrated on the class and gender divisions that militated against the far-from-disinterested dream of community harmony that structured the federation appeals in the early 1930s, there were also religious and ethnic tensions troubling the Vancouver Welfare Federation's claim to be Canada's most inclusive united appeal.[116] Although a complete narrative of these conflicts would anticipate the contents of Chapter 4, it is worth noting here that Protestant-Catholic tensions and anti-Asian feeling also featured among the challenges to "unity" within the federation in 1934 and 1935. With one exception, all the Catholic charities withdrew from the federation just before the annual campaign in 1935.[117] The relationship between the Catholic Church in Vancovuer and the Welfare Federation was a complicated one in which the church disputed the degree of federation control over the social work practice and spending decisions of church agencies. The relationship was not helped by Protestant perceptions that Catholic donors contributed less than the Catholic agency budgets used.[118]

Within the same few months, relations to the Chinese community were no doubt frayed by the federation budget committee's insistence in 1935 that a hospital serving "Chinese incurables" was "the responsibility of the state," even though, in the 1934 campaign, a committee of federation canvassers directed by Howard Falk and the European-Canadian manager of a Chinatown bank had raised from the Chinese community donations of $1,280 in a single week.[119] Race anxieties were also apparent in the soothing story told of a Japanese storekeeper who gave a donation to the general fund as well as to the special Japanese division fund. Like the stories of "community spirited" unions, this narrative was undoubtedly designed to represent the ideal of peaceable community that the federation "sold" to satisfy the wishes of those Vancouverites anxious about social fears and hatreds.[120] It is really little wonder, with such social conflicts clustering around the federation like thunderheads, that Falk, whose personality and salary made him a lightning rod for criticism, began looking for a new job in 1935. He and the federation's publicists had aggressively promoted a common moral project for "everyone" in Vancouver. In doing so, they had probably fostered in some people warm sentiments of belonging, and, if the publicity was not simply a tissue of outright lies, they had elicited some remarkably generous donations from working-class people who had few nickels to spare. But they had also provoked hard-headed challenges to the social power the federation exercised and criticisms of their vision's controversial political implications.

Reason, Sentiment, and Citizenship

The early promoters of Community Chests in Canada were addressing a practical problem: how would existing charities be financed during the years when Canadians, and especially the well-to-do, were carrying the new tax burdens required to pay off the war debt and to finance the schools, highways, and urban sanitation systems that changing technologies, demographics, and public health standards demanded? Faced with this compelling competition for taxpayers' dollars, the task of charity fundraising undoubtedly called for vigorous and innovative measures. Simply to assume that rational citizens would understand their obligations would not ensure that charities' deficits were financed. What seemed to be needed was a forceful and effective way to persuade a mass public of their obligation to supply resources to meet welfare needs. In the early years of Canada's Community Chests, charity fundraisers made some rational promises and realistic claims for the federated appeal method. But they also engaged in representing needs, both material and political, that were beyond their power to satisfy. They promised deeply desired but unattainable reconciliations.

They offered community solidarity, that shop-worn yet endlessly desirable political good, attractively combined with the maximum of individual freedom. In appeals like the one made in the "$350,000 – a Lot of Money!" ad, they offered a vision of a way to fulfill obligations that would supposedly ensure that understandable human needs were met yet would keep to a minimum every individual's responsibility. This ad and similar devices promised to assuage guilt and to remove the fear and envy endemic to the relationship between the haves and the have-nots or among different strata of "the fortunate." To broaden its appeal, the federation sold its services as the voice of those "little fellows" carrying the burden of financing a caring society, against the irresponsible rich, whose indifference made the cost of social solidarity higher for everyone else.

In thus trying to craft a common moral position, the federation was simply performing what liberalism understands to be the essential role of civil society: forming a basis for co-operative citizenship.[121] In the name of fostering community solidarity, the federation campaigns both deployed and attempted to destroy social identifications that competed with universal citizenship. This chapter has shown several ways that class and gender identities were used to generate a supposedly motivational-friendly competition. But federation fundraisers were careful to contain the conflicts associated with these identities by linking them to overarching civic and moral subject positions. "Everyone" was clearly made to mean "citizens of Vancouver" or "you who are unselfish."[122] Within such representations of community, donors were constructed as individuals, not as members of potentially competing groups. As an individual, each was equally responsible to share in the burden of responding to need.

Hidden by this feature of the fundraisers' representational language, however, was the reality that citizen obligations varied not only in degree among individuals but also in kind among groups. Some of "Vancouver's citizens," after all, had extensive power to control public policy and the distribution of the economy's resources. Some citizens could make economic and political decisions that would determine not only how needs would be met but also who would find themselves among the needy. Others – the wage earner, the housewife, the voteless Chinese Canadian – could only help to supply the palliative services that the larger socioeconomic system made necessary. With a "semi-public" agency in charge of social services, the most active citizenship role available to most would be the charity canvasser, a kind of volunteer tax collector. The presence in Vancouver in the early 1930s of well-organized and politically viable labour and women's groups helped to draw attention to these political implications of federated fundraising rhetoric. In contrast, in Halifax and Ottawa, the fundraisers were able to carry on in the 1920s and 1930s without any serious engagement with left-wing labour.[123] The federation's superficial response to criticisms and, overall, the fundraisers' simplistic and sentimental incorporations of difference into representations of community revealed a deep ignorance of or disregard for the more fundamental disparities in power that genuinely divided the citizenry. Engaged in a liberal project, they displayed the characteristic weakness of liberal politics: the incapacity realistically to accommodate structural differences in power. Yet their apparent commitment to inclusion, part of their efforts to increase donations from working-class people, provided the basis on which more effective inclusion would slowly be built during the war and afterward.

In the social advertising of the interwar years, however, it is clear that it was the business equivalent of liberalism's political panacea – education. Education is supposed to create a common culture of reason and "civilized" emotions, which forms the basis for a community of both values and interests.[124] Advertising similarly works toward fashioning a common mind but more deliberately deploys non-rational means to that end. Like commercial advertisers, federation fundraisers worked with the guilts, anxieties, loyalties, and longings among their "market." They sought to heighten those feelings, to create a kind of demand for fulfillment or relief, and then to supply their "product" as a means of satisfying the demand. Far from simply proposing a rational solution to a practical problem, they exploited status hunger, class resentments, and gender rivalry. In Vancouver's distinctive political culture, this approach generated unintended political consequences. The federation constructed a social sentiment – a broadened sense of citizen obligation – that was consistent with the individualism of a predominantly liberal political culture. The steady increase in numbers of donors suggests that this sentiment had a wide appeal. Paradoxically, though, in arguing for modern charity – expert, efficient, convenient, accountable, trustworthy, and equitably required of all citizens – the federation opened up to criticism only the continuing role of irrationality in funding social services through donations. Inadvertently, the case it made for modern charity served just as well, indeed even better, as a case for the tax-based welfare state.

4 Race, Charity, and Democracy: Organizing Inclusion, 1927-52

The Community Chest movement's goal of reorganizing charity on an inclusive, universalist basis meant more than just engaging in public relations exercises. It meant coming up with means by which different social groups could participate in a shared, egalitarian, democratic decision-making process. As tensions between labour groups, women's groups, and a male-dominated business elite in Vancouver showed, this sort of joint effort was unprecedented and fraught with difficulty. But it was an undertaking that could not be avoided if indeed everyone was equally to be addressed and engaged as a donor to a mutually administered community fund. Viewed as an exercise in social advertising, the project looks thin, a nearly transparent facade behind which stood something selfish and coercive. But the effort to recruit cross-class support for social services had begun, by the 1940s in Vancouver, to move beyond social rhetoric to have concrete consequences. Not only were workers' nickels being harvested by the fundraisers, but also men from the mainstream of the labour movement were being incorporated into the leadership of the fundraising project. As I have argued in more detail elsewhere, prejudice against the intelligence and character of unionists presented a formidable barrier to their inclusion in the leadership of federated fundraising in the interwar years and even, residually, in the 1950s.[1] Thus, I would suggest that each step toward including working-class men among those who had both the right and the ability to manage donor dollars was a step toward a more democratic organization of community leadership and, consequently, of social citizenship.

The ideological work of social advertising was complemented in community organizing work by the mechanisms of representation that chest organizers devised. Of course, both advertising and representative structures might be trivial gestures that could leave social hierarchies undisturbed. But both also could be used for making real improvements in the democratic character of Canadian civil society. In this chapter, I will make two further arguments about the role of the chests in that democratizing tendency. First, I will show that, in race relations, there was a parallel to the inclusion mechanisms that chests, especially Vancouver's, had begun to develop across class lines. This parallel appeared in the origins of Ottawa's Community Chests. For that case, I will show that anglophone Protestant fundraisers included a racial other, French Canadians, for one purpose: to exact from them more substantial donations. In other words, fundraisers from a socially dominant group included representatives of a racialized group in their chest management to make sure that this "racial" group carried what the dominant group thought was "their share" of the so-called burden. Inclusion was meant to discipline French Canadians in the new culture of contribution. Like the inclusion of labour men in the chest leadership, this was a base-broadening exercise whose fundraising logic gave it a momentum that did not require, at first, any fundamental change in social prejudices. But, as I have already hinted in the previous chapter, the institutional mechanisms born out of classism or racism could also begin to produce the conditions in which such biases could be effectively challenged.

Second, the Ottawa case also raises the question of which was a more democratic method of administering relief – through private charitable agencies or tax-funded public agencies? Could a private welfare bureau be a democratic agency for relief distribution? In the 1920s and even as late as the middle of 1932, the answer in Ottawa seemed to be yes, at least in the minds of those who believed that aldermanic ward heeling was a perversion of representative democracy. Since 1925, in an attempt to remove any risk that relief giving could be used for vote buying, the city had delegated to a private agency, the Ottawa Welfare Bureau, the work of administering the payment of tax-financed municipal relief. The Board of Trade, the Council of Women, and the labour council had criticized the patronage practices that had corrupted the municipal offices. The solution implemented in 1925 had the support of the business groups and relief-giving agencies, and the others were involved in the organizational process that, by 1932, folded the Welfare Bureau into the Community Chest.[2] The bureau was a private agency in a specific sense: its office rent and staff salaries were paid for by donations from the community, and its directors were all volunteers, elected only by the Welfare Bureau's own subscribers. Some of the money it spent on helping out clients came from donors.

But after 1925 it occupied a distinctive place at the boundary of private charity and public finance: the bulk of its relief payouts came from the city treasury. By 1932, relief payments had become so controversial that this system was no longer sustainable, and a wholly public system of relief administration replaced the earlier hybrid.[3] The crisis in the relief system exploded in the same year that a proposal for federated fundraising was finally accepted. These two events were connected. And the connections show how competing conceptions of accountability and representative citizenship were in play in the 1930s. The federation's organizers heaped scorn on the corrupt form of democracy, shot through with ethnolinguistic log rolling, that they believed constituted civic politics. But they acquiesced at the end of 1932 to civic control of relief to protect for private charitable fundraising a realm of moral consensus and civic unity. This non-relief charity would be a sort of patrician association of self-described enlightened citizens, in which the city's two racial communities would each contribute to and benefit from charity on the basis of agreed-upon moral principle, not politics.

Race in Ottawa

To understand the story of the birth of the Ottawa federated appeal and its significance, we need to understand the sense in which racism figured in Ottawa of the 1920s and 1930s. Recent comparative histories and sociological studies have shown that racism is not only or necessarily confined to relations between people of different skin colours.[4] To allow us to compare racist intergroup relations through time and across cultures, historian George Frederickson proposes the following definition of racism: "an ethnic group's assertion or maintenance of a privileged and protected status vis à vis members of another group or groups who are thought, because of defective ancestry, to possess a set of socially relevant characteristics that disqualify them from full membership in a community or citizenship in a nation-state."[5] This definition has four features that make it useful for historical analysis. First, it emphasizes the protection of a dominant group's interests as a defining feature of racism. This feature allows us to see how changes in circumstances could alter the stakes in social negotiations and thus might heighten, diminish, or change the focus of racist ideology and practice. Second, it refers to "socially relevant characteristics" as the attributes on which racists focus: these characteristics, too, may clearly vary according to economic and other historically variable factors. Third, the linking of these features to "defective ancestry" is crucial in distinguishing racial from other politics of hierarchy – it is this move that cloaks the historically contingent in the garb of perdurability. But the calculation of ancestry is itself a culturally determined practice and so is part of the historical variability of racism. And fourth, and especially important for welfare history, in this definition the racial other is excluded "from full membership in a community or citizenship in a nation-state." The history of welfare in general (and of the federated charities in particular) is centrally concerned with changes in what count as the benefits and obligations that accompany citizenship, understood broadly as including both legal and customary entitlements and duties.

If the Community Chests' democratizing of charity entailed a diminution of racism, then we should expect to see changes in the degree of inclusiveness of two aspects of citizenship. One would be that the chests would make more inclusive the range of groups of people who enjoyed full membership in the community in terms of having their welfare needs met. In this sense of citizenship, the chests appear as service providers, either competent and fair ones or not. Charities, like states, could serve various racial constituencies well or poorly and participate in defining the "white" or racially dominant community by the charities' choices about whose needs are to be given priority. Judged on this criterion, a more democratic, less racist, mode of charity organization would not distinguish among the needy on the basis of "defective ancestry" or the imputed presence or absence of "socially relevant characteristics." The other change to assess would be the extent to which the racial other was included in the citizenship of contribution. It is easy to see how a racist exclusion of a particular category of people from citizenship could come from a characterization of those people as non-contributors. If the chests helped to democratize citizenship in this sense, then we should expect to see perceptions of contribution change so that race is no longer a significant category of assessment or so that contributions of all racial groups are appreciatively recognized.

The Ottawa story meets these criteria of democratization because of change over time in the francophone-anglophone relations in that city's federated fundraising organization. That these were race relations is perhaps difficult to recognize in twenty-first-century Canada. The racial other in the story is the French Canadian, and in Canada today no one speaks of French Canadians as a race. In fact, we scarcely use the ethnicized "French Canadian" terminology any longer. The only "French" Canadians are recent immigrants from France. The normal terms we now use fall into two categories. One is linguistic – "francophone" or sometimes "French-speaking." The other kind of term refers, in various ways, to sociopolitical identities: for example, francophone Québécois or Acadien or Franco-Manitoban. But as recently as the early 1960s, it was publicly acceptable to refer to "the French" and "the English" as Canada's two founding "races," just as the Victorians had.[6] In the early decades of the Community Chests, concerns about racial bigotry expressed in Canadian public discourse were more often concerns about French-English relations than about relations between whites and non-whites. These latter kinds of race hierarchy did, unquestionably, exist in Canada. And if the focus of this chapter were on Vancouver, then the change in the relationship between Asian Canadians and the chest could provide the basis for the same kind of argument about race and social inclusion.[7] But the history of race in Canada, and in particular its relation to charity, is importantly illuminated by the story of the reduction and near elimination in Ottawa of "the French" as a racial other. This aspect of race is important as a distinctively Canadian part of race history. And it is valuable as a hopeful story of how a racialized difference can change into a more readily integrated linguistic one.

In Ottawa in the 1910s and 1920s, anti-French racism was intense. In those years, when the federated charities movement was beginning in Canada, Ontario was painfully, sometimes violently, divided on the question of the language of instruction in one part of the publicly funded school system. In particular, the issue was whether instruction in all Catholic separate schools would be in English or whether, in some Catholic schools, in largely francophone communities, a combination of French and English instruction would be practised throughout elementary school.[8] This, the Ontario schools question, was at its most acute between 1912 and 1927, although it had roots in the 1880s and branches in the 1930s and beyond. It was fought out in and indeed centred on Ottawa because of that city's large francophone population and important educational institutions. Ottawa's Catholic population was nearly 60 percent francophone.[9] The Ordre de Jacques-Cartier, a nationalist secret society for the defence of French Canadian interests, was founded in 1927 in the Ottawa suburb of Eastview in response to the aggressions of militant Protestantism.[10] And the Fédération nationale des femmes canadiennes-françaises (1914) and *Le Droit* (1919) also came out of the Ottawa area in this period as part of Franco-Ontarian nationalism.[11]

The angriest years of the Ontario schools question were the years in which the federated charities movement in Ottawa began. In those years, Ontario politics were structured by racism in the four ways that Frederickson suggests. First, the goals of some anglophones in Ottawa were resistance against "French domination." In particular, English-speaking Catholics in Ottawa perceived anglophone power in Catholic institutions as threatened. Ottawa's French-speaking Catholics, they warned, had created around the city "a cordon of French institutions, foreign in sympathy, aims, and objectives[,] all aimed at destroying English Catholic life."[12] The fight over schools developed and consolidated a perception that English Catholics faced "a French Canadian menace."[13] Such views indicate anglophone Catholics' concern to defend their position and privileges. Second, anglophone Catholics in Ottawa drew on a discourse of defective ancestry to distinguish between themselves and francophones. A good source for this discourse is a popular polemic published in 1918, William Moore's *The Clash! A Study in Nationalities.* In his chapter on "race superiority," Moore points to the use in early-twentieth-century Canada of a nineteenth-century race schema in which Europeans were sorted into three races, different physically and psychologically: the Nordic, the Alpine, and the Mediterranean. English Canadians who were even vaguely familiar with these terms described themselves as Nordic and French Canadians as Mediterranean. The former were naturally "rulers, organizers, and aristocrats," while the Mediterranean race was their "inferior in bodily stamina, – and, sometimes– [the Nordic's] superior in the intellectual arts."[14]

That French Canadians' ancestry was deemed inferior and not just different was evident in other views Moore attributed to his fellow English Canadians. Quoting a "friend" whom he described as "an Ontario high functionary," Moore reported these items of anglophone common sense: "The French-Canadians are illiterate," and "the French-Canadians of Northern Ontario are stupid." Such views of Franco-Ontarians' "socially relevant characteristics" surfaced frequently in, and as a result of, the debate about schools. The premier historian of these debates, Robert Choquette, offers several vivid examples. To illustrate from one critic of the bilingual schools, "the system [of bilingual instruction] in vogue in the schools renders it quite impossible for the young generation to rise above the intellectual level of the average Lower Canadian habitant; and, if it be allowed to continue, the Eastern counties [of Ontario] are doomed before many years to be as dark a spot on the map of intelligence as any portion of Quebec."[15] In the 1930s, anglophones in the Ottawa area described "the French" as thieving, selfish layabouts, living on the charity of the hard-working and community-minded "English."[16]

In these reports of anglophone views, we see three of the elements of Frederickson's definition of racism: fearful self-protection, attribution of defective ancestry, and allegation of deficiency in socially relevant characteristics. For the fourth, exclusion from full membership in the community or full citizenship, I turn to francophone sources of the period. Ottawa's francophones were sensitive to their disparagement as a racial inferior and aware of racism as a factor in access to social services. *Le Droit* ("The Right"), a newspaper founded in 1919 to defend the interests of Ontario francophones, was a dedicated reporter of prejudice. During the unemployment crisis of 1921, for example, the paper revealed that a francophone man who sought work at a municipal employment office was told that only the "British-born" would be given jobs, even though he had identified himself as a citizen of Canada, born and raised in Ottawa.[17] And when a new system of relief distribution was instituted in 1925, francophone aldermen and the Société Saint-Jean-Baptiste protested a year later that it was disadvantaging French Canadians.[18] The Fédération des femmes canadiennes-françaises fought to have just one francophone case worker for the Children's Aid Society. Ottawa was so divided on racial lines that organizers of the city's centenary celebrations in 1925 "forgot" to include any francophones on the planning committee. "The fanaticism of race," *Le Droit* declared, was "so well developed" in the city's English press that "they regard as inferior and corrupt all that is different from themselves."[19]

Complicating the racial identity of francophones was the fact that they shared with English-speaking Catholics a stigmatized minority religious identity. Some anglophone Catholics thought that "racial antagonism itself is only a cover for anti-Catholicism."[20] But such a clear separation of the two kinds of prejudice was more or less irrelevant for francophones. Being Catholic was perceived as part of the francophone identity. In that context, being anti-Catholic necessarily implied being anti-French. The militantly anti-Catholic Orange Order was as vehemently opposed to French-language instruction in Ontario schools as the English-speaking Catholics were, although for the Orange Order anti-Frenchness was wrapped up in a more general opposition to separate confessional schools. In Ottawa, the Orange Order's politics (with anti-French and anti-Catholic strands intertwined) were entirely respectable.

Not simply a Victorian phenomenon, Orange Order parades attracted big crowds in Ottawa as late as 1960.[21]

This, then, was the context of race relations in which charitable modernization, with its goal of universal contribution, came to Ottawa. As I will show, in a condensed version of a complicated series of events that took place over roughly six years (1927-33), the effort to reorganize charitable giving in Ottawa entailed a struggle over how to deal with the intensely felt racial hostilities in the community.

Race and Representative Democracy

The racial fissure was clearly evident in the first step taken toward federating Ottawa's charities. That step was a conference of the city's child welfare agencies, held in January 1927, with the goal of co-ordinating their activities, including their fundraising methods. Only 17 percent of those attending (i.e., seven of the thirty-nine) were identifiable as "French." This was disproportionately low in a city whose population was, in 1931, 23.5 percent francophone. Three of the francophone delegates came from one agency, St. Joseph's Orphanage, which served the francophone community. Many francophone agencies interested in child welfare were absent and essentially hidden from view.[22] The representation of Catholic agencies was scarcely more proportionate: in a city whose population was 41 percent Catholic, this conference, whose speakers included both Catholic and Protestant experts, attracted only five Catholic agencies out of the total of sixteen present. The circular letter inviting agencies to send delegates had emphasized that the conference, to be effective, must be "representative." But Ottawa's francophone Catholics had, for the most part, chosen not to participate. At subsequent meetings about federating charities, the pattern repeated itself. The Council of Social Agencies, whose initial organizational meeting took place nine months later, was similarly anglophone. And the following meeting to discuss federated fundraising in particular had just one francophone representative, the wealthy lawyer and future provincial politician, C.A. Séguin.[23]

It was, then, very much an anglophone group that decided to proceed with reorganizing public appeals for charitable donations in Ottawa into one orderly whole. In the following two years, their plans for doing so followed the prescribed methods of modern social work. They employed an eminent social worker and federation expert, Howard Falk, assisted by a paid staff researcher, to inventory Ottawa's social agencies and social needs and to produce a report outlining plans for future progress. Falk's most important professional contact in Ottawa was Charlotte Whitton. When Whitton appeared in the story of federated fundraising in Ottawa, in 1929, she was thirty-three years old. Since she had come to be the first paid executive of the Canadian Council of Child Welfare (CCCW) three years earlier, she had established a reputation for herself and her organization as the leading source of social welfare expertise in the dominion. The events of 1929-33 in Ottawa show her at the height of her powers. A native daughter of eastern Ontario, she was both deeply knowledgeable at an intuitive level and deeply invested in the standing she had as an expert on social welfare and community relations on her home turf. Her views on the race question in charity, though those of a single individual, can and should be taken as both well informed and strategically influential. Both Whitton and Falk, but especially Whitton, would bring to the exercise of organizing Ottawa's charities and charitable fundraising a concern with racial inclusion that would push Ottawa's anglophone elite well beyond what they had anticipated, even though not to a point beyond racism.

In 1929, in a letter meant to determine the conclusions of Falk's survey, Whitton recommended that a federated welfare fund in Ottawa should be divided along "racial" lines into an English and a French division. She asserted that "the racial distinctions and considerations separating English-speaking and French-speaking Catholics in Eastern Ontario are much stronger than the religious ones separating the former from the Protestant group." Were this fact to be ignored, and the federation divided along confessional lines into Catholics and non-Catholics, she (and her sources close to the Ottawa archdiocese) believed that the English Catholics would suffer an injustice. They would be a minority, forming "only about 20 percent" of the Catholic federation, but, on the strength of their past record as donors, they would provide "perhaps as much as 75 percent of the funds." Yet, as a minority in the organization, they would find their will dominated by the French-speaking contingent, and matters of "budgets, etc. would be drafted to favour [the French Catholic welfare agencies]." In the shareholder view of citizenship, which Whitton held, this was clearly an undemocratic state of affairs. The voice of contributors was overwhelmed by that of non-contributors. An additional problem in a French-dominated Catholic chest, she feared, would be that the English Catholics would be unable to impose the constraints of modern fundraising practices on the members of the religious orders, generally nuns, who staffed the agencies. The sisters took their orders from their Quebec houses, not from the archdiocese, so, Whitton thought, there was little hope that the nuns would consent to raise funds only as canvassers for the annual appeal of the federated charities. She concluded, therefore, that "it would be best to isolate [the French Catholic] agencies into their own federation, and allow them to handle their own financing in such ways as they saw fit."[24]

In these 1929 recommendations from Whitton, we see reflected the anglophone Catholics' concern to protect from francophone control the anglophone agencies and the money raised from the anglophone community. The anglophone group had more money, and linguistically they were a majority in the community. Their position was generally more powerful, then, than that of the francophones, except if engaged in a competition over Catholic resources. In such fights within the Catholic community, anglophones lacked the power of numbers and needed to rely on other resources to get their way. The occasional alliance with the Protestant community was a means to this protection of their vulnerable, even if also privileged, position in Ottawa's race relations.[25]

The strategy to protect privilege was combined with a full awareness that, by thus "isolating" francophones, the English-speaking community would save for their own agencies and clients the greater part of Ottawa's philanthropic dollars. Detailed research in 1932, using property assessment records and the income tax reports of Ottawa's population, would prove conclusively what Whitton and others already knew intuitively in 1929 – that the city's wealth was asymmetrically distributed along racial lines. Dividing the total personal wealth of Ottawa residents into the quantity owned by anglophones and the quantity owned by francophones, and then distributing those amounts on a per capita basis across those two populations, resulted in figures of $2,412 per capita owned by anglophones and $373 by francophones.[26] This is not to say there were no wealthy francophones, only that they were relatively few in a large population of mainly working-class francophones. To organize charitable fundraising by separating two such differently equipped communities would have made it impossible to meet the needs of francophones. This proposal, then, indicates Whitton's and the anglophone Catholics' willingness to disqualify francophones from the benefits of service and security that they believed the federated charities could provide to anglophones.

While consideration of service to francophones would re-emerge in later years, the central race question in 1931-32 was whether or how francophones would be included as citizens in another way – as contributors. The first proposal for federation, contrary to Whitton's 1929 suggestion of a "racially divided one," came in 1931, from a Council of Social Agencies that was entirely anglophone in its makeup and closely tied to City Council, the Rotary Club, the Board of Trade, and the Local Council of Women. In the organizational framework they proposed, neither religious identity nor linguistic identity was meant to be meaningful. Membership in the federation was to belong to anyone who contributed five dollars or more in the campaign. No provision was made for dividing responsibilities in fundraising along linguistic lines. When this proposal was brought up for public discussion, there was pressure from leading philanthropists to break it up into four funds, Protestant, Catholic, Jewish, and non-sectarian. In the end, the proposal for a single fund stood but with an important modification: donors would be allowed to earmark their gifts for particular agencies.[27]

Was this an egalitarian proposal in which francophone Catholics were being treated inclusively and fairly as fellow citizens, with a view to ensuring that the wealthier Protestant Ottawa would continue to help support the budgets of Catholic agencies? Perhaps it was among some of its framers. Not long after the single fund proposal survived its critics, some of these voices were heard in another planning meeting: "A general chest ought to be the aim, without too much stress upon our differences religiously, and ... the ideal in community service should be, as Mrs. Thorburn pithily put it, 'a hungry child is a hungry child.'"[28]

But a more negative view of the prevailing attitudes is sustained by the responses to these sentiments at this meeting. The head of the Council of Social Agencies (CSA), Social Services Commissioner G.S. MacFarlane, pointed out that "both newspapers and several large subscribers absolutely refused to accept such an arrangement." And Whitton, present at this meeting, as she was at so many others, said that the "strong personal prejudices of very large and influential givers" posed "practical difficulties" for any undivided chest.[29] In this context, then, we should see the insistence on the option to earmark funds as betraying the influence of Orange anti-Catholicism. In charity as in taxation, money talks.

Elsewhere in the Canadian politics of federated charities, this influence of Orangeism had led to ugly sectarian conflicts. In 1927, the Catholic charities had been driven out of the Toronto federation in response to Protestant objections that Catholics contributed much less and claimed, by way of clients calling on the agencies' services, much more than did Protestants. The latter also objected to the practice in some Catholic institutions of running "sweatshop" laundries that competed with "legitimate" laundry businesses. And Protestants in Toronto, as in Vancouver, disliked the degree of autonomous control that the Catholic Church authorities wanted to exercise over agencies whose mandates federation authorities wanted to determine.[30] In Halifax, too, the "ultra-Protestantism" of the chest's executive director, Gwladys Kennedy, had led to the compiling of separate lists of Catholic and Protestant donations to show that Catholic donations were inadequate in comparison. And she had given a sympathetic ear to a commercial laundry that had threatened to withdraw its chest donation because a Catholic agency in the chest advertised its own laundry business.[31] "Ultra-Protestants" objected to having their dollars going to the support of Catholic agencies, and this was a key reason for the insistence on earmarking donations.[32] In this context, the "undivided" chest must be seen not as non-discriminatory inclusion but as an imitation of the Toronto model, in which a Protestant-dominated board decided whether Catholics were contributing their share. In the event that they were not, their agencies could be expelled.

At the end of November 1931, then, a proposal that came from Ottawa's anglophone community was apparently accepted by the city's social agencies. But Whitton had been following events in Ottawa between her travels across Canada. When she discovered the proposed constitution, she determined to stop it. And she did. She went to the publishers of Ottawa's English-language newspapers and begged, urged, and even insisted that the papers refuse to support the proposed chest. The plan of organization was wholly inadequate, she claimed, rushed through by a small group and lacking the support of some of "the most representative agencies."[33] Within a few weeks, the CSA was complaining that the opposition of both English papers was making further progress impossible.[34] But, in fact, further progress in federation would have been possible had Whitton been put in charge, because she had the support of those essential fundraising tools, the daily papers. She agreed to take charge on one condition: that the CSA would co-operate with "other authoritative and influential groups of the giving public" and that it would cease to "ignore other strong elements of community life and activity, not [so far] represented within the council."[35] She was certainly right about one important exclusion: the francophone community had not been in any real way involved.[36]

Was it Whitton's goal to include francophones on a fairer basis? Probably not, if we consider her willingness in 1929 to isolate French Catholics in their own federation, regardless of the harm to the donor base of their charities. Yet inclusiveness was her goal by May 1932. In the first five months of that year, she consulted extensively, supervised research on the donor base of dozens of Ottawa agencies, assessed the patterns of wealth and religion in the community, and by May had devised a system of rationalized fundraising that, she believed, would survive in Ottawa. It needed to be a system that would meet the objections of certain wealthy Protestant donors who held Orange views about Catholic charities. It also needed to be acceptable to anglophone Catholics, afraid of French domination in Catholic agencies. And perhaps it also needed to reassure francophones that their needs would be met even if their collective donor capacity was small. To do this, she proposed three separate funds: Protestant (of which the Jewish fund would be a subsection), English Catholic, and French Catholic. Each would collect money for two different kinds of agencies: one kind would be those specific to their sectarian and linguistic community, while the other would be the non-sectarian agencies that served all comers. This proposal was unique in that Whitton frankly acknowledged the different donor capacities of the different communities, spelled them out in per capita terms, and said that each community's share of the non-sectarian budget would be in proportion to this research-based ratio of donor capacity. This was quite brilliant if the main goal was to produce a stable federation: on the basis of this agreed-upon scale of obligation, the Protestants would be less likely to drive out the Catholics, and the English Catholics would be deprived of a key grievance against the French Catholics. It accepted the realities of the unequal distribution of wealth in Ottawa but insisted that, within the framework of those realities, each community would contribute to the best of its ability. And each would have a decision-making body in which its community's views and values would predominate. This sounds fair, and, like the model of federation that Canada was built on, the plan of "unity in diversity" with co-operation where possible had a pleasantly pragmatic ring to it. As we shall see, however, when concrete steps were taken in 1933 to put Whitton's plan into effect, it was, for the anglophone element, too generous in the autonomy it gave francophones and, for the Catholic Charities director, too deferential to the prejudices of the Orange Order.

Race, Representation, and the Public-Private Division of Welfare

Before this problem in race relations came to a boil in 1933, however, a crisis in the city's welfare scene temporarily derailed progress toward a federation. The crisis began when, in the fall of 1932, some of the most notable social work, civil service, and business leaders of Ottawa mounted an emergency appeal to help fund the agencies that were delivering relief to the unemployed. Both in collecting the funds and in distributing them, the committee in charge of this appeal had to deal with Ottawa's race problem and with the class conflict attached to relief matters. At the centre of the conflict was the Ottawa Welfare Bureau (OWB), an agency that would be one of the highest-profile members of the Ottawa Community Chest. The attacks on the OWB, therefore, help us to understand the conditions in which federated fundraising in Ottawa originated. Moreover, the solution to the OWB problem and to the related issues around the emergency relief fund reveals the vision of democracy that underpinned the concept of this welfare federation and the movement more generally. It was a vision in which citizenship and, indeed, authority flowed from contribution.

Both the relief fund and the OWB were sharply criticized, as relief efforts in the Depression usually were. One of the relief fund's distinctive problems had to do with the relationship between unemployment relief and other kinds of services to the needy. If families needed VON's nursing services but could no longer afford them because of unemployment, would the fund give money to VON to compensate for lost fee income? If not, would VON have to lay off nurses or cut their already low salaries? Were the blind unemployed supposed to be provided for by the usual charities for the blind, or could they claim assistance from the general unemployment relief fund? Were the Christmas hampers that the city usually distributed to its relief clients a legitimate charge on the fund? If those relief recipients were disabled or elderly, rather than unemployed, then perhaps not. And in any case, those hampers usually were paid for by tax dollars, not donations, so why should donors take up the taxpayers' burden?[37]

These problems were a result of the fact that the relief fund money included not only donations raised in the October drive but also matching grants supplied under dominion and provincial unemployment relief legislation. The managing committee for the fund included a volunteer who could hardly countenance spending these tax dollars for a purpose not intended by law – the dominion comptroller, Watson Sellar. The plan initially proposed in October by the committee was to disburse three-quarters of the funds to the OWB, the Union Mission, and the Red Cross for their relief work and to keep a quarter ($25,000) to cover requests for fuel, food, and shelter made to the fund's own committee. But by early December, the absurdity of separating out relief from the whole matrix of family welfare led the fund's leader,

F.E. Bronson, on Whitton's advice, to promise that the fund would go to "all those services which private charity ordinarily provides." He cautioned, however, that the "expenditures would be arranged" so that the fund would not lose its eligibility for the matching grants.[38]

While this sort of legal problem was being sorted out, people in need were, of course, feeling very frustrated with the relief suppliers. Laura Chartrand of Le Foyer, a residence and employment bureau for women, said her agency could not get donations because everyone had given to the relief fund, but it was not helping her agency. Moreover, she had sent francophone clients to the relief fund committee, and they had found no one there who could speak French.[39] An organization of the unemployed called the Labour Reserve (whose name bespoke a Marxist analysis of the relief crisis) was worrying Thelma Williams, the director of the OWB, by conducting its own investigations of relief cases. From various quarters came accusations that politicians were interfering in OWB investigators' decisions about who got relief and how much. Allegations multiplied: the offices of the bureau were overcrowded, the staff rude, and decisions about disbursements unfair, mechanical, or both. The bureau, inexplicably it seems, had refused an offer from the Société St-Vincent-de-Paul of free space for a second office in Lower Town, the district where its francophone clients lived.[40]

Faced with these many criticisms, the bureau sought help from Whitton's CCCW. Whitton appointed a trio of Toronto and Montreal social workers to do a study, and on December 6th they delivered their report. When the OWB balked at some of their recommendations, Trades and Labour Congress president Tom Moore angrily pointed out that there would be nothing left to reform if the bureau did not "waken up to the discontent and bitterness" that its agency inspired.[41] Even Whitton, hard to imagine as a defender of the rights of relief seekers, recognized that incompetent social workers might inspire legitimate grievances; she supported the report's recommendation that the bureau build into its structure some means of appealing bad decisions.[42]

At stake in the problems presented by the relief crisis, and in the OWB as a focus of those problems, was, for the social welfare and political elites, the legitimacy of their city's distinctive combination of public and private welfare provision. That combination had to do with the fact that, in the public side of community leadership, the city government had had to accommodate in its structure the two politically important linguistic groups in the city. Indicating the continued emphasis in the 1930s on political representation by language groups was the appeal to voters made by Fulgence Charpentier, elected in the 1931 election for the 1932 Board of Control. In his election advertising, Charpentier pointed out that "it is of national importance that francophone taxpayers have an interpreter among the membership of the senior municipal administration."[43] A few years earlier the issue of a cancer hospital had shown why such representation was important. When a group of anglophone Protestant philanthropists proposed putting a cancer hospital in Catholic (and largely francophone) Lower Town, francophone Alderman Eric Quéry protested. Quéry pointed out his community's displeasure at having yet another such stigmatized hospital and mobilized voters successfully to block its creation. For Quéry or Charpentier, that success was no doubt a sign that democracy in Ottawa could be made to work for working-class francophones as long as they had a voice in the city government.[44]

For Whitton, however, the cancer hospital situation (and several others) meant that progress toward a needed welfare service (for Protestants, especially, in the cancer case) could be blocked by "municipal politics."[45] And in her view, moreover, Ottawa's "population make-up" (and the need or ability to claim benefits on the basis of "race") were what had made the civic relief system before 1925 susceptible to abuse for political purposes by aldermen.[46] As the historical literature on urban reform has shown, ties between disadvantaged ethnic communities and municipal officials were often deemed suspicious by middle-class guardians of the treasury such as Whitton.[47] Her views were probably shared among the anglophone elite. Admittedly, in the documents I have consulted, others were rarely so frank about the race dimension. But the business leaders who wanted to keep relief out of civic politics were very clear in their view that "aldermanic ward heeling" made for a bigger relief bill than was necessary.[48] In the name of keeping relief distribution out of the reach of elected officials, they did their best to protect the OWB system of administering relief.

One of the most cloak-and-dagger interventions came from a very influential public health physician, Dr. Robert E. Wodehouse. Wodehouse became the first chairman of Ottawa's welfare federation until October 1933, at which time he went from that volunteer position to become the dominion's deputy minister of pensions and national health. In his public health career with the Canadian Tuberculosis Association, since 1919, he had established financial support for its work from the life insurance industry. In 1932, he used his insurance industry connections to apply pressure to the chair of the OWB board, E.S. Miller. Miller was an insurance agent, and Wodehouse successfully asked the national head of Miller's firm to explain to Miller that he should accept a new slate of board members that Wodehouse and others had arranged for the OWB. In his letter to Miller's boss, Wodehouse explained that, to keep charity out of municipal politics, Bronson and others of Ottawa's philanthropic circles had decided that there needed to be "interlocking boards" that would co-ordinate relief and other welfare matters.[49]

In spite of using such insider connections and considerable political influence, however, those who wanted to reform the OWB to preserve it lost the battle. In the morning of 29 December 1932, a group of eleven "responsible citizens" (all anglophones) met in Chateau Laurier to discuss the relationship between the city and the OWB. The group included Bronson, Whitton, Wodehouse, Tom Moore, Canada's first woman senator, the *Citizen*'s editor-in-chief, and several of the men and women who would organize in the following year the new fundraising system. After "considerable discussion" – always a sign of distress and disagreement in the minutes of social work meetings – they agreed that, while it was essential to keep civic politics "within bounds," it could be accomplished in a new way, even if relief administration was returned to municipal administration, by ensuring that relief matters were supervised by a Welfare Commission that would be associated with City Council but not dominated by elected men.[50] Afterward the group adjourned for lunch, where they were joined by the mayor and Controller Charpentier, who were reportedly "favourably impressed" with the group's recommendation. The next day the mayor presented the plan for a Welfare Commission to the Board of Control. On December 31st, the *Ottawa Journal* reported that the commission plan had become the city's new policy.[51]

Although the anglophone welfare leaders had resisted the return of municipally managed relief, they made an important gain in letting go of this goal. Starting in 1933, the Ottawa Welfare Bureau would be free of the burden of unemployment relief. This meant that the agency had escaped from the storms of controversy over how taxpayers' dollars should properly be spent and had sailed into the more protected harbour of community service – from politics to morality. Relief administration would remain controversial in Ottawa for years to come.[52] But the Welfare Bureau, like the other agencies in the federation, would be able to avoid these debates and to present itself as simply doing the work of love and mercy. On this uncontroversial basis, the fundraisers no doubt hoped, the OWB would be able to appeal for funds without bringing into the new federation the "badly shaken prestige" and the outright risk of failure that it seemed stuck with because of its inept handling of relief work in mid-December 1932.[53] It had become necessary in Ottawa to sharpen the division between public and private welfare and to make the municipal government take on the responsibility of administering relief to make the new scheme of charitable fundraising viable. In effect, the local state had to do more in order that private welfare work could survive and prosper.

Race and Coercive Inclusion

Only one more challenge remained if the federated fundraising scheme was to unite, rather than divide, the forces of private social work in Ottawa. Or, to describe the project less sympathetically, only one more problem confronted the self-described responsible and representative citizens in their efforts to gain control over fundraising in the city. That problem, or set of problems, was how to overcome resistance in some quarters of Catholic Ottawa to Whitton's confederal plan. That plan's resemblance to the British North America Act did not much help to alleviate concerns among agencies whose donor support came only from francophone Catholics. Given the lower per capita income in that community, these agencies were not likely to do very well out of the proposed Whitton plan. Nor could they have felt much en couraged by the early stages of planning.

As practical steps began to be taken, in December 1932, to put the plan into effect, francophone community leaders were notably absent from the steering committee.[54] Over the next six months, it became increasingly clear that their proposed inclusion was in fact coerced. The Whitton plan had given the francophone charities their own "province," as it were, an arrangement that had its disadvantages but at least promised autonomy. By June, however, the anglophone Catholics had managed to force their francophone fellows into a single Catholic chest. According to Whitton, the Catholics were planning to "iron out their quarrels within their own Board." In this move, certain of the anglophone Catholics planned to argue, when they wanted to pursue particular agendas that conflicted with the francophone-dominated archdiocesan headquarters, that the Protestant chest was insisting on these measures as conditions for their support.[55] This tactic was an anglophone racial alliance across sectarian lines.

It was not enough, however, to form the basis for a single anglophone chest. The Irish Canadian director of the Catholic Charities, Father Armstrong, told the Catholic chest board in June 1933 that he preferred a single chest fund. But when Catholics protested the apparent doubling of effort in having two separate but simultaneous campaigns, with separate committees and canvassers and boards, the leading English Protestant volunteer, lawyer Kenneth Greene, said the two funds were necessary "so that responsibility could be squarely placed."[56] Here, again, was the Protestant paranoia about the inadequacy of Catholic contributions and unaudited spending. In private correspondence, Whitton was even sharper: if Ottawa's Catholics thought that a sum raised from the general public would be handed over to a Catholic organization to administer, then they could think again. Before that would happen, the whole federation plan would be abandoned, or a Protestant and non-sectarian fund would finance agencies only on the condition that no Catholic clients were served.[57] As late as July 1933, with a campaign planned for October 1933, these drastic options were still being considered as the Catholic community struggled to work out its own internal differences. Fears that they could not raise the expected amount led to concerns that Catholic agencies would end up without adequate funding.[58]

At the outset, those fears appeared to be groundless. In the first campaign of the Ottawa Financial Federation, both of the sectarian fundraising objectives were met and exceeded. But the threat to francophone Catholic agencies was a real one, and soon its practical consequences appeared. In 1934, after the second campaign, a shortfall appeared in the budget of a key agency for the francophone Catholic community, St. Joseph's Orphanage.[59] The St. Joseph's board of directors made it clear, in the newspapers, that federated fundraising was to blame. The centrepiece of the federated charities method – only one annual appeal – meant that many of the fundraising methods used in Catholic parishes were prohibited to member agencies. Protestants had coerced Catholic charities into joining the chest with the threat that to stay out would cost them the support of Protestant donors. But, in the knife-edge budgeting of the main francophone orphanage, it had turned out that keeping Protestant support had not been sufficient to balance the loss (about $4,600) of revenue from francophone Catholic parishes. An organization that had been devised in English Ottawa, and largely by Protestant Ottawa, was failing to support the needs of francophone Catholics. Over the following ten years, Ottawa's federated charities repeatedly fell short of meeting their annual fundraising goal, most often in the Catholic and non-sectarian fund.[60] This meant that Protestant agencies' budgets were met, but Catholic ones took cuts of as much as 18 percent. This was the enforced accountability that certain large Protestant donors and the English-language newspapers had called for as a condition of their support.[61] Its ugly side was the shortage of funding to Catholic agencies.

In spite of these conflicts, the activists and staff of the Ottawa chest (or chests, as they carefully called themselves until 1952) had some right to congratulate themselves for having devised a mechanism of bringing together in joint action three communities among whom considerable tensions existed. I have called these racial tensions, both in keeping with the language of the time and to signal their significance for the politics of inclusion and social citizenship in the period. The federation fundraisers were emphatically not the most racist of Ottawa's residents. They may disappoint us morally because their elevated invocation of civic unity coexisted with organizational practices designed to accommodate ultra-Protestant and anti-francophone prejudices. But it is possible to see, beginning in the fundraising efforts of the chests in the late 1930s and accelerating in their organizational practices in the 1940s and 1950s, that modernist fundraising could transcend the social prejudices ingrained in its origins.

For example, the separation of the appeal into two sectarian funds made visible the charitable contributions of Catholics, both French speaking and English speaking. And, after several years of chest operations, this visibility began to have an effect. By 1939, efforts were being made to alter the chest's image as a project of the anglophone and Protestant community. One suggestion was that second in command in the campaign committee be not one individual but four vice chairs to represent "the religious and racial groups of the community." Making sure that there were francophone canvassers for the francophone commercial district was another proposal.[62] Separate funds and thorough canvassing strategies had made different communities' patterns of giving more visible, but this structure also inspired conscious attempts to minimize those differences by constructive effort. The modernist impulse of the Community Chests was to deny that donor capacity was a racial given; the federated fundraising enterprise defined itself as a skilled exercise in increasing the number of donors and the size of gifts.

But the universalist conception of citizenship worked in another way deliberately to understate racial differences. Whitton had seen federation as possible in Ottawa only if its organizers accepted as reality the racial and religious bigotry endemic to the city. But once the chest was established, its second executive director, Joy Maines, recast the story of race relations in charity. When Maines, in 1942, reviewed a pamphlet being written by a national social work organization to celebrate the Ottawa chests' successful accommodation of diversity, she insisted that the title "Three Chests in One: It Can Be Done!" should say "two" instead of "three" (and in so doing erase the French/English division within the Catholic chest). She wanted to minimize, not emphasize, racial differences, she said. And she insisted that the pamphlet's editors cut entirely the passages that treated religious prejudice as an inescapable fact of life.[63] Most significantly, she asked that they edit out, as "dangerous to the Chest," the dollar figures Whitton had published in 1932 as the various per capita shares each group owed to the non-sectarian funds. She was counselling a deliberate forgetting of the chests' origins. And that should make us uncomfortable. But what she was asking to be suppressed from memory was a moment when francophobia and anti-Catholic sectarianism won the day. Her instincts in this, on the terrain of practical fundraising, were surely not wrong. In drafting a model for future action in other communities, it made sense to redescribe as co-operation what had begun, in Ottawa's particular circumstances, as coercion.

The Beginnings of Genuine Inclusion

In annual meetings, the chest speakers continued to assert their engagement in "the co-operation of all racial and religious groups in one united effort to maintain social services for the benefit of everyone in the community."[64] But in 1951, after eighteen years of supposed co-operation, the chests were still having less success than they wanted in soliciting donations and volunteer participation from francophones. The director newly hired in 1951, a young American named John Yerger, diagnosed this as a weakness in the Ottawa situation. If Ottawa were to fund its social services adequately, the federated charities would have to do a better job at reaching French Canadians. Another new figure, Joseph Laycock, recently appointed to head the Ottawa Welfare Council, was also keen to increase francophone participation. Laycock and Yerger undertook a simple but significant new measure to achieve that goal. With the encouragement of the Canadian Welfare Council (CWC), they hired the chests' first francophone organizer, Marie Hamel (seconded from the CWC), for a year in 1952. She secured the volunteer services of Éveline Leblanc (a civil servant) to serve as a French-language liaison officer for the chests' public relations work. By Leblanc's efforts, French-speaking volunteers were appointed to all the public relations committees. The work of these volunteers was supported by a part-time, paid francophone staffer. A further measure of integration was the appointment in 1955-56 of the Community Chest's first francophone president, a funeral director named Horace

Racine. Racine had a distinguished record of service to the francophone community, having held leadership roles in its main nationalist service organizations, such as the Société Saint-Jean-Baptiste and the Club Richelieu. He had also been an activist of the Ordre de Jacques Cartier.[65] In 1951, Racine had been the second francophone speaker ever to speak in French at the annual meeting of the Community Chests.[66]

These small steps indicated that the federated charities were beginning, in the 1950s, to think more seriously about what might be the conditions for a more genuine manner of including francophones in the Ottawa chests. The background to these innovations was a larger step that had been taken without fanfare in 1947. After that year, the annual report of allocations to agencies no longer was broken down to show how much came from the Protestant fund and how much from the Catholic one.[67] Although the separate funds continued to exist until 1961, and fundraisers tracked the federation's success in reaching the different linguistic and faith communities, the reduction in public reporting of contributions by religion signalled that the initial rationale for the separate funds had lost some of its social meaning. Had anti-Catholicism still been vigorous in Ottawa's philanthropic circles, this change in the reporting of how dollars were distributed would not have gone unnoticed. The amalgamation of the Protestant and Catholic boards in 1952 and the elimination of the dual chests entirely in 1961 would symbolize in turn the declining force of sectarian feeling in Ottawa.

The origins of this change lay in the materially motivated beginnings of the chests. Surrounded by religious bigotry and racial prejudice, the chest organizers had tried to make it appear that the Ottawa Community Chests were the agent of a united moral community, engaged in uncontroversial works of love and mercy. Whitton called the men and women who undertook this organizing "very representative" and "responsible" citizens. In reading widely in her writings and in the political debates of the day, I have come to the conclusion that these terms come from a particular discourse of political democracy, one that hearkens back to the philosopher-rulers and the guardian class of Plato's *Republic*.[68] The representativeness of people such as Bronson and Moore, Séguin and Racine, Wodehouse and Cairine Wilson did not consist in their being mouthpieces for interest groups engaged in power struggles. Rather, qualifiers such as "very" or "most" for the term "representative" point to another meaning – representation as exemplification. The most representative people were not embodiments of a type in all its strengths and weaknesses; rather, they were Platonic exemplars. In this discourse, their right to decide how to manage the common business of a community came from their moral worth and intelligence. They could represent without being elected because their contributions to their community were self-evident. That they came from various and separate spheres of life enabled them, collectively, to oversee the integration of those spheres in common action. And their deliberations were underwritten by an assumption that the different aspects of the social world were not fundamentally in conflict. They, as exemplary citizens, could share a common viewpoint on the public questions of their day.

These political assumptions seem to be quaintly undemocratic today, although, to be sure, some of us still hope there are admirable people among our community and political leaders. But the assumptions I outline above are part of the democratic tradition, however suspect a part. They are the tissue of elite democracy, explained in Plato's *Republic.* Given its origins, this conception of democracy might most accurately be called classical. It was clearly part of the stock of political ideas used by individuals such as Whitton, university educated in the liberal arts, including the classics, in the 1910s. Its influence was explicitly attested in 1938, when a representative of the United Church of Canada, Reverend James Mutchmor, defended policy making by elite volunteers. He asserted that this kind of policy making followed the model of patrician rule in "the old Greek city" and was thus the "very essence of a democracy" because in it "citizens, as citizens, *without going through the routine of an election,* offer themselves for voluntary service."[69] The American journalist Walter Lippman endorsed this sort of reform leadership in the 1920s, and in the 1950s philosopher Karl Popper excoriated it as the seedbed of totalitarianism.[70] Exercises such as the Kidd Commission in British Columbia in 1932 and, in Ottawa, the deliberations of Whitton and her allies in a Chateau Laurier meeting room represent this strain in Canadian political culture. So does the federation movement.

As a mechanism of decision making, this classical democracy had not been adequate to the challenges of the Depression. On the assumptions of these self-described representative people, the problems presented by the unemployment crisis were insoluble. And this made for political heat, when those who suffered from the lack of solutions refused to have their sufferings ignored. The more literally representative forms of the elected municipal government offered a more open channel for the reception of grievances as well as the mechanisms with which to punish ineffective leadership. When the federation sought to distance charities from the control of municipal officials, they were hoping to protect decision making from what they perceived as the irrational and selfishly short-sighted dynamics of electoral politics. And it is easy to see that, in doing so, they were also protecting their own power from a more broadly democratic form of accountability.

However, if we fail to understand that they believed in the legitimacy of authority based on contribution, we will overlook the moral world in which this protection of welfare from politics might have seemed to be in the interests of both humanity and accountability. Whitton was right to complain when a city official unilaterally raised relief rates only a few days before the municipal elections, even if her objections might not have been the same as those of a relief recipient infuriated by the arbitrariness of relief rates.[71] Whitton was joined in her dislike of politically motivated relief distribution not just by the penny-pinching rich but also by men in the city's labour council and perhaps by the self-appointed investigators of the Labour Reserve. The effort to keep the financing of welfare work within a non-partisan moral world also helps to explain the potential of the federated appeal organizations to help build a more socially diverse community leadership. Across "race" lines in Ottawa, as across class lines in Vancouver, the attempt in the 1930s to integrate a critical other into the deliberative councils of this philanthropic leadership was motivated by fundraising logic. But it also came from the logic of representation in which contributors showed their moral merit by their contributions and so earned a part in the leadership of the community.[72] When the so-called war for democracy increased the capacity of the working class to contribute, and raised the political costs of social exclusion, the fundraising experiment begun in the 1920s and 1930s would begin to help broaden the country's social leadership.

Before leaving behind the chests' formative decades and moving on to discuss the fate of charity in the world of the emerging national welfare state, we should pause to look back. On the eve of the Second World War, the chests' history could be seen to support two apparently competing interpretations of the federated fundraising project. On the one hand, the fundraisers had created, in the mechanisms of the chests, organizations that affirmed an egalitarian citizenship of contribution. Similarly, much of their advertising and publicity had relied on universalistic images of citizenship in which no group or kind of person was seen automatically as a dependent, unable to help in meeting community goals. In my analysis so far, by comparing taxation and charities discourses, I have pointed out that the legitimacy of a voice in public affairs was seen by the fundraisers, and by business and professional people more generally, as being based on giving money, whether through taxation or through donation. Consequently, it was significant that fundraisers sought to include in their community organization project, however superficially, housewives, working-class men, and groups that had been subject to racist social exclusion. This inclusion had some of its roots in religious tradition, and attempts to transcend religious prejudice, even if less than fully successful, should be recognized as a movement toward a society in which common citizenship mattered more than particular differences. Seen in this way, the base-broadening strategies of the chests provided a foundation for a future democratization of social leadership in the cities where chests operated. The attempts at inclusion also helped to disseminate a new understanding of citizenship as implying not only a stockholder perspective but also a consumer one.

In contrast to this positive interpretation of the chest, I have also pointed out that the fundraisers' explicitly acknowledged reason for their inclusive practices was to increase donations, in particular to get more money for social services from groups that the fundraisers thought had not given their fair share. Some of those alleged delinquents were the very wealthy, and it is easy to see the legitimacy of the fundraisers' shaming tactics. But when the objects of fundraisers' complaints were low-income wage earners or socially disadvantaged ethnic groups, the strategies devised to extract small sums from their overstretched family budgets were less clearly about fairness of contribution. In the Ottawa case, different ideas about fairness clashed, and when, in spite of concerted efforts at accommodation, these perspectives proved to be irreconcilable, coercive tactics were used to force the Catholic community into co-operating with the chest project. And even though the Vancouver chest directors Falk and Davidson claimed to have rejected coercive methods of payroll deduction, it is hard to discount as wholly impossible the allegations of enforced giving that the federation's critics made in 1934. Employees who felt or who were, indeed, forced to give part of their wages to a project chosen by the employer might reasonably have failed to see any distinction between bad, coercive taxation and good, voluntary charitable giving.

In each of these interpretations of federated fundraising, there is an idea of the chests' relationship to citizenship that can be applied equally to charitable giving and to taxation. In the first, the chests look like a democratic gesture by the urban business elites to extend to others a chance to participate in social leadership on the terms in which those elites believed citizenship was earned. Whether donors or taxpayers, if you contribute, you have a voice. In the second, the inclusive gesture appears coercive and self-interested, an attempt to enlist others forcibly in a project of social governance to which they have not consented. Whether taxpayers or donors, you will be forced to contribute so that the social burdens on capital will be lightened. Are these truly alternative perspectives on the fundraisers' contribution to developing citizenship? Or are they reconcilable?

We might question the plausibility of the second interpretation when we realize how small a proportion of the funds collected actually came from the expanded base of small donors. Is it likely that anyone really cared, for financial reasons, about the minor effect of small donations on fundraising totals? In Vancouver in 1936, an analysis of giving showed that those who gave small amounts, in spite of their large numbers (62 percent of all donors), provided only about 9 percent of the funds collected. Complaints in Ottawa in 1939 about low per capita donations suggest a similar phenomenon, and a 1950 analysis of Halifax giving showed that, even if all donors of up to ninety-nine dollars were counted, their contribution was only 27 percent of the total collected.[73] Small donations of the sort that housekeeping budgets and working-class incomes could provide were not going to do much to ease the financial burden on capital or higher-income earners. If these donations mattered, then surely it makes more sense to see their importance as resting on symbolic and political effects. Enlisting many people as small donors was indeed most important as a means of including them in the community of contributors.

But rather than returning immediately to a confident appraisal of this modernized charity as a progressive political project, let us recall a theme from the 1920s taxation debates. In the 1920s, fiscal conservatives proposed that more people be included in the ranks of taxpayers, in the hope that more people would thus feel themselves to be stockholders and would therefore resist the politicians' tendencies to spend extravagantly. Could enlisting people as donors to charity have been meant to have a similar effect? Was increasing the number of people who felt obliged to subscribe to the chest campaign supposed to help extend to a wider community of small donors a passion for the control of agencies' spending? Would the defenders of private charity find themselves fighting against the meeting of needs, with large donors finding allies in small donors against the demands of the social work agencies? Or would engaging more people as donors increase their awareness of welfare need and, when they appreciated the scope of the necessary spending, convince them that taxation was the only effective method of funding social services? Would the professionally organized appeals for funds serve, in effect, as a public relations campaign for the value of social work and the worthiness of those social workers served? In assessing the impact in the 1940s and after of the federated fundraising system, I have looked for both of these configurations of opinion. And I have found both. Whether or not the federators of fundraising meant, by monopolizing charity, to set limits on public spending, the outcome of their efforts would be, in the 1940s and 1950s, something quite other than forestalling the welfare state.

5
How Charity Survived the Birth of the Welfare State

Before the Community Chests achieved their success in recruiting large numbers of donors, people could only speculate about the possible effects of mass charitable giving on attitudes toward need and obligation. But by the late 1940s, evidence on this question began to emerge. The chests had succeeded in recruiting a large percentage of the adult population as donors to the federated appeals. By 1944 in Vancouver, the city for which I have the most complete donor data, almost a quarter of the population donated to the Community Chest (see Appendix 1). This rate of participation had risen to approximately 27 percent in 1950, very close (within a percentage point) to typical North American participation rates in Community Chest giving. To appreciate how significant this rate was as an indicator of the involvement of people in contributing to social welfare, we may compare donor numbers to income tax payers. Only 19 percent of the Canadian population paid income tax in the census year 1951. If we focus the comparison on urban adults, then we find that about 25 percent of this group were income tax payers, compared with nearly a third (approximately 30 percent) of adult Vancouverites who were giving to the chest.[1] The growing number of cities in which there were federated appeals also indicated the increasing number of donors to modern charity in the 1940s. In 1939, eleven Canadian cities had federated appeals; by 1948, this number had more than quadrupled. The first doubling took place during the war, but the growth was not merely a temporary response to crisis. Between 1945 and 1948, the number of chest communities in Canada rose again, from twenty-four to forty-seven (see Appendix 2). In the chest communities, giving to the federated appeal was probably a more common way of contributing to social welfare than was paying income tax. Both practices were widespread in the late 1940s, however, and growing.

In the circumstances of these levels of charitable giving and taxpaying, it is not surprising that, during the 1940s, the question of how to finance and administer welfare services was an important part of political debate. Some Canadians thought private charity's day was past. Should all welfare needs be met by tax-funded government programs? Or was there a necessary role for social agencies funded entirely or significantly by donations? How should the cost of welfare services in taxation or donation be distributed? These were the themes of the debate about the public/private division of welfare. In its largest reach, the debate encompassed the long-standing competition between socialist and capitalist ideologies. In the 1930s, it had very often been conducted in highly polarized ways. But in the 1940s, this controversy began to take shape in immediately practical terms, because of fundraisers' efforts in the 1930s, because of the new challenges that fundraisers faced during the war, and because of the uncertainties around what returning to peace would mean. More than simply a commitment to the idea of private charity, it was threats to their institutions' survival that forced Community Chest fundraisers into new strategies to defend the role of private agencies in the emerging welfare state.

The well-known shift of Canada's political parties during wartime toward support for a much expanded array of tax-financed social programs should be seen in light of this fundraising problem. The Co-Operative Commonwealth Federation's (CCF) support from voters and poll results in 1942 and 1943 brought home to party organizers of all stripes the reality of the shift in public opinion.[2] The Conservative Party renamed itself the Progressive Conservatives, and the Liberal government famously flip-flopped on family allowances, enacting in 1944 this measure that Prime Minister King had earlier described as unthinkable.[3] By the end of the war, Canada had an unemployment insurance system, the wage-supplementing family allowances, and old age pensions. And Parliament was seriously discussing health insurance. International examples and the language of the Atlantic Charter suggested that the way forward was toward tax-funded health and welfare services. In the infancy of Canada's welfare state, it seemed that charities might reasonably be left behind as part of the failed system of the 1930s.

But that did not happen. Not only did the federated fundraising movement surge forward in the 1940s (see Appendix 2), but public opinion polling in 1948 also showed that a majority of Canadians (59 percent of the representative sample) supported a continued role in social service for local voluntary groups supported by charitable donations.[4] Of course, "a majority" was not all. When the pollsters sorted the responses by the federal political vote of their subjects, they found that CCF voters were only 49 percent in favour, while the proportion of others supporting the voluntary sector was correspondingly greater. Canadians certainly wished for a reformed country after the war, but they apparently thought that a better world was one in which charitable giving and non-governmental agencies had a role to play.[5] Even with public opinion support for both an expanded role for government in welfare, and a continued role for private agencies, there were, however, considerable challenges for governments and fundraisers. Governments needed to decide legislative priorities and taxation levels, and the fundraisers, correspondingly, had to choose which services to support and where to set campaign goals. These challenges were related. Would governments be able to rely on successful private charities to help minimize public demand for programs and so keep taxes down? Would fundraisers encounter donor resistance if taxation levels rose too rapidly or too high or if public agencies were seen as providing all the necessary services? In the conditions of wartime, these questions became acute. Both in the similarity, on an abstract level, of the challenges faced by fundraisers and policy makers and in the interconnectedness, on a practical level, of the two mechanisms of financing social projects, taxation and fundraising came close together during the Second World War. In this crucial period, the making of the welfare state and the development of charitable giving were in fact both parts of a common exercise in defining needs, determining appropriate recourses, and organizing the financing and administration of the response to needs. They were related elements in an evolving culture of contribution.

Although taxation is enforced by law and charitable giving is not, an examination of developments in each in the 1940s reveals that both faced legitimation problems during the war. On the taxation side, the dominion government had to design a plan for financing the war that would be perceived as effective and fair. If it failed, then it would face certain risks. If it increased the money supply too sharply and thus produced severe inflation (described as a "hidden form of regressive taxation"), then it would encounter the kind of worker revolt that had brewed after 1917 and boiled over in 1919. If the government relied too heavily on income taxation, then the possibility arose of tax evasion and onerous enforcement measures, costly in both policing efforts and electoral prospects. If it misjudged the willingness and capacity of Canadians to defer personal spending in favour of saving, then the sale of government bonds – the Victory Loan campaigns – would fail.[6] By 1943, the finance minister was clearly aware that frustration among the electorate threatened the government's financial strategy. His budget speech in March that year was, in effect, an exercise in fundraising rhetoric, following the well-worn strategy of asserting (regardless of reality) that the campaign for funds, as it were, had been successful and enjoyed the unanimous support of the community:

> Taxes and loans are not exactions from the people by a government. They are weapons which the people through their elected representatives and the free methods of democracy have fashioned for their own use and their common purpose. We cannot all man guns and planes and ships; we cannot all build guns and planes and ships, but the Canadian people have shown by the reception which has been given to each succeeding wartime budget that they are ready to wield these weapons, each according to his strength and all against the people's enemies. They are ready to accept their share in each increase in the effective organization for war of which the budget is but the financial counterpart.[7]

Whether seeking support for warfare or welfare, an active state faced a predictable array of complaints, each addressed in this passage. The state's measures had been criticized as coercive, impersonal, corrupt, alienating, and unfair. To these anti-statist grievances, the finance minister's rhetoric provided a condensed reply. The elements of war finance are not corrupt measures worked out through partisan machinations and then imposed coercively on the people, he claimed. They are not the impersonal exercises of a government that acts merely in its own interests: they are an expression of a community's united spirit, expressed through democratic processes.

Both accusation and reply were no doubt partly true, and a history of taxation would explore to what extent the politics of taxation succeeded in legitimating the methods of war finance. I wish here simply to make the point that the legitimation problems that taxation faced during the war and immediately afterward had their counterparts in the problems that charitable fundraising encountered in these years. While taxation represented the public solution to the problems of financing collective provision for need, and faced anti-statist attacks, the critics of charitable fundraising, the private method, held that tax-financed services would be better than donation-fuelled ones. The typical complaints against charity were that it was wasteful, inadequate to meeting need, and, in multiple ways, unfair. These criticisms had been expressed throughout the 1930s. They had been treated as threats to the legitimacy (and therefore the money-raising capability) of modern fundraising, and in both Vancouver and Ottawa (and to a lesser degree in Halifax) steps had been taken to respond to these threats. But when fundraisers faced the new challenges of wartime, pressure mounted on the chests to respond more effectively. In what follows, I will trace these threats and fundraisers' responses as they developed in the late 1930s and the war years. The result of this practical struggle over who would give what and how was that charity survived the war to prosper afterward. It lost some of its old tools in the process, but it gained new ones that made it part of the welfare state rather than its alternative.

Charity as Inadequate

By 1939, there was a clear record of success in Canada's Community Chest cities. But it was also a record of failure. To be sure, the total number of dollars raised and donors enlisted had typically increased every year since 1935. But in Vancouver, Ottawa, and Halifax, the fall campaigns rarely reached their goals.[8] During campaigns, the rhythm of the newspaper coverage went from early excitement about promising returns, to worry that more donors and donations were needed, to impassioned statements about what dire consequences would ensue if the goal was not met. Then, in the final campaign dinner, when the outcome was reported and prizes distributed for good work done, speakers emphasized the satisfaction of progress made, even if the goal was not quite met. The fundraising incentives underpinning this rhythm of reporting are obvious. But even the more systematic stocktakings that were presented several months later at the annual meetings were also crafted with an eye to fundraising effectiveness. While the reports of the executive directors were more balanced than those of campaign captains, and were suitably bolstered by financial statements, they were still fundraising documents. Predictable motivational purposes informed the remarks addressed to volunteers at the annual meetings and to reporters who covered those events: celebrating their common project and identifying achievable goals for improvement. In this spirit, naturally, the sober reporting of steady progress was balanced by an acknowledgment of "constant failure" to meet the budgetary needs of the agencies whose funding the chests supposedly guaranteed. And beyond even that obvious failure was a further one. There remained conceivable social service goals that the community might seek to achieve: for some agencies and some chest fundraisers, the status quo seemed not to be good enough.[9]

In spite of the acknowledgments of their shortfalls, the chests' trumpeting of their mounting success was difficult for some of the public and some of the member agencies to accept quietly. Irritations that had developed in the 1930s would produce in the 1940s some bitter criticisms of the processes of chest budget control, goal setting, and canvassing. In Ottawa, as we have seen, the impact of campaign shortfalls was distributed along sectarian lines: failures in Catholic fundraising translated into cutbacks only in Catholic agencies. But even on the Protestant side of that chest, the budget committee chair reported in 1938 that "continued failures to reach the objective" made it "doubtful if loyalty to the Chest principle will continue" among the agencies. Campaign committees, he pointed out, were protected from the agencies' anger and frustration in a way that the budget committee was not.[10] In Vancouver, that anger had been mitigated somewhat because the Welfare Federation was able to draw on other sources to make up the campaign shortfalls. The first successful campaign had created a reserve fund to be used for unexpected needs. It had been supplemented from time to time from a variety of sources when particular agencies failed to spend some part of their budgeted funds for the specified purposes and had to return some money as surplus.[11] In addition, the funds collected during campaigns earned some interest revenue because they were held in a common account and disbursed in quarterly payments to the agencies. The interest revenue earned on that account was added to the reserve fund. Thus, in Vancouver, relations between the agencies and the federation were eased by the use of this fund. But situations in Ottawa and Halifax were different. Ottawa lacked this contingency fund. Halifax kept one but did not spend from it as often as Vancouver did.

In general, the charge that federated fundraising was inadequate was most clearly justified in Halifax. In particular, the case of the Halifax Children's Aid Society (CAS) points most dramatically to the way the chest budgeting process could produce failure even in the case of campaign "success." CAS in Halifax had struggled badly under the pressures of the Depression. In 1930, there were only thirteen new wards, while in 1934 there were forty-two. With no increase in staff, the number of continuing wards for which casework supervision was required rose from 125 in 1930 to 279 in 1939.[12] In 1938, CAS asked for a nearly doubled allocation from the chest in order to hire new caseworkers. It was refused, with the observation that there was a limit to how much money could be raised in Halifax. The chest advised CAS to live within its means. CAS president S.R. Balcom, a rising young businessman who would go on to represent Halifax as a Liberal MP, lambasted the chest's directors for not increasing the campaign goals, but to no avail.[13]

During the war, the staff shortage caused by underfunding at CAS became even more troubling. Overcrowded housing and the strains of transiency and family separation increased the number of children needing protection and parents needing help.[14] Nonetheless, even in 1942, after a campaign that had exceeded its goal and raised twice the money that chest fundraisers had thought was Halifax's limit, CAS found it impossible to get money for more staff. In a particularly infuriating gesture, the chest's rather conservative executive secretary met its 1942 request for a further $5,952 with a tiny increase of $200. Imagine, then, the incendiary effect when CAS board member Lillian Farquhar discovered in 1943 that the chest had a reserve fund of $40,000. When the 1944 campaign raised $14,500 in excess of its goal, and disbursed none of the surplus to the agencies, relations between the chest and the agencies were seriously embittered.[15] At the annual meeting a few months after the end of the campaign, the chest president referred to critics in odiously self-righteous terms, calling them "thoughtless and improvident" and "irresponsible extremists."[16] He was defending a budgeting process supposed to bring business scrutiny to the operations of agencies to ensure that all possible economies were practised. But when the Halifax chest budget committee simply ignored uncontroversial claims of need made by the agencies, it was perverting its intended role. Its tight-fistedness gave credibility to the criticism that the chests could not adequately finance essential services.

In the short term, the result of this failure of the chest process was the beginning, in 1942, of provincial grants for the operating budgets of CAS branches in Nova Scotia.[17] This was not a purely welcome event. With government money, some feared, would come government control. For the antistatist element in the Community Chest movement, one of the most important fundraising arguments was that, if charity proved inadequate to its task, then government would take over.[18]

From this argument proceeded an aversion to unemployment relief work by chest agencies. In the case of the Ottawa Welfare Bureau, the relief crisis in the early 1930s sent some of the chests' family service agencies fleeing from their earlier semi-public role in distributing municipally funded grocery orders and home heating fuel to unemployed heads of families. Unemployment relief was too big and too politically charged to be navigated safely using the fundraisers' unsubtle moral compass. In Ottawa's 1934 campaign, future Liberal minister of national health and welfare and Montreal chest board member Brooke Claxton stated the commonly used distinction between donation-based services and tax-funded ones: "While [government relief programs] make life possible, it is the job of the federated charities to make life worth living and to recreate the spirit of self-respect. Moreover, the task of handling child and family welfare and providing recreation welfare for the young necessarily falls within the scope of the federated charities. We do not conflict with, but supplement the work of government boards."[19] This was the public/private distinction that fundraisers and social workers used in the 1930s, and it was supposed to shield their agencies from the criticisms that pummelled relief distributors.

In Vancouver, as in Ottawa, the Welfare Federation had supposedly worked within this model and had tried to present itself as outside the business of unemployment relief. In its 1937 canvasser guide, it argued that the need for charity was as great as ever, even though unemployment was not so bad. A saving on relief expenditure, it further asserted, was "a saving to the government, not to the private agencies, which have never given unemployment relief." Strangely enough, this apparently false statement was true, after a fashion. For example, even though the Central City Mission, which provided shelter and food to homeless men, was a federation member, its 1935 allocation from the chest was only $2,000. This money paid the salary of a minister, Reverend J. Colwell, who worked there as a religious social worker. Strictly speaking, then, no federation money directly bought food or paid for other expenses relating to daily expenditures on the men's material needs. Most of the mission's budget for literal relief expenses came from the room rental fees paid by residents ($16,507 in 1930), supplemented by modest municipal and provincial grants ($2,500 and $2,000 respectively in 1930). Donors had given only about $1,000 in 1930 to the mission. When the federation's first director, Howard Falk, assessed the mission as a prospective member agency in 1931, he concluded that it was "anything but charitable" in its practices and, indeed, "anti-social in its result." By the latter, he meant that the mission made homeless men more angry and more alienated rather than less so, in part by giving them lice. He made numerous recommendations about improvements needed to make the mission an acceptable recipient of charitable dollars, including compliance with municipal public health bylaws.[20]

It seems, however, that these recommendations were not followed. Yet the mission became a member of the federation. Thus, when unemployed men seeking food and shelter were fed unwholesome slop and given verminous beds, the federation seemed to be in part responsible. And, in part, it was. In 1936, the federation found a way to separate itself from the stigma of the mission's dreadful service while still helping to finance the social work aspect of the mission's operation. It created an entity called the Abbott House Association, whose sole purpose was to provide counselling services for the men who used the mission. After 1936, on the federation's roster of agencies, the (by then) infamous Central City Mission was replaced by this mysterious new entity. Possibly, no one was deceived. To add to the grounds for confusion, in 1940 the federation reinforced its apparent connection to relief by adding to the Abbott House Association a Men's Service Bureau that helped men new to Vancouver and looking for war industry work to find jobs and, if necessary, to establish their eligibility for municipal relief. But in confining its support to these counselling and referral roles, the federation had found a way to stick to its apparent principle, that private charity financed social work and left relief work to the government.[21]

The legacy in the 1940s of this and other similar episodes from the 1930s was that it was understandably difficult for the public to see the difference between the social work services funded by the federation and the provision of material relief. Would anyone who had not taken advanced training in social work have readily understood the complex message that Ottawa's campaign planners thought needed to be emphasized in their fall 1938 campaign? "The following points should be stressed in campaign publicity: 1. The distinction between public relief and private agencies' services; 2. The increased burden on Community Chests' agencies due to reduction in relief and the stringency of present relief regulations; 3. The limitations of government aid to those in need; 4. The purpose and need of character-building services; 5. The advantages of the Community Chests. It was also agreed that the appeal should be based on the spirit of charity rather than on the fact that helping those in need is good business."[22]

As this passage shows, fundraisers were asking the public to accept that charitable giving was meant solely to provide services other than relief but also to believe that reductions in public relief meant that charities needed more money. The latter claim was certainly true. People went to family service agencies for reasons such as desertion by a husband, inability to care for their children, mental illness, or difficulties in making ends meet or finding a job. In periods of relief crisis and cuts, some of those people inevitably needed not just information but also money or food or things such as eye glasses. Thus, family agencies frequently found themselves giving out short-term, emergency relief.[23] Each of the chests studied here, consistent with its view of the public/private division of welfare, deplored the failure of public relief agencies to meet the needs that government was supposed to address. In Ottawa, it was also true that the leading businessmen and other prominent citizens who served on the chest boards told the city to live up to its responsibilities. In Vancouver, the director reported to the federation's annual meeting that private agencies were at the limit of what they could do as a "cushion or safety valve" to prevent the collapse of the public relief system.[24]

The blend of social work and business prestige that the chests had at their disposal was thus put to work in service of making tax-funded relief more effective at its supposed purpose, which in turn was supposed to leave funds and energies available to the private agencies to do their job of personal service. But paradoxically, by emphasizing the impact of relief cutbacks on the private agencies, fundraisers only ended up reinforcing in public opinion the perception that charity was something to do with the dole rather than the provision of services such as first aid training, child protection, home nursing, or libraries for the blind. Needs such as those that the Halifax CAS addressed were hidden from view so long as "charity" commonsensically meant grocery orders and fuel supplies. The inadequacy of public relief, even when bolstered by private agencies, thus helped to create the impression that "charity" had failed and should be replaced by social insurance and more intensive government management of the economy.

The popular association of private charity with relief giving had led to mixed benefits for fundraisers in the 1930s. While it attracted critics, it also made available to fundraising enterprises the sympathy that many Canadians felt toward the unemployed and their families. By the late 1930s, however, the fundraisers were starting to think that the costs of the popular confusion were greater than its advantages. And once the war worked its transformative effect on labour markets, the chests would discover that some of the willingness to give had come from the perception that their agencies primarily took care of jobless breadwinners and the homeless unemployed. In the booming economy of the early 1940s, fundraisers would encounter with new force the charge that charity was not only inadequate but also a pointless waste of money.

Charity as Wasteful

The Community Chest leaders argued that one of the advantages of their method was that it rationalized social service and campaigning for funds and thus made sure that the money people gave through them to charity was used in the most efficient way and without wasteful duplication of effort. The problem with that rationale for modern charity was that, as I pointed out in Chapter 3, it was immediately appropriated by those who wanted to see government take responsibility for meeting welfare needs. They argued that there were two kinds of charities: ones that were necessary, and that therefore should be government funded, and others that were more-or-less-ineffective pet projects of people who persisted in running small operations of dubious value. The tone of urgency that the Community Chest campaigns adopted was, in this view, either an argument for tax-based financing that would render the essential services secure or an unwarranted inflation of the importance of the services that the campaign represented.

In the late 1930s, the chests tended to respond to such critics in two ways. One was to regard them, rather dismissively, as people who grasped at any excuse not to give. In one such analysis, it was suggested that these people were never going to give much anyway, so the cost of their disaffection was negligible.[25] The other was to concede, whether sincerely or not, that government funding and management might be preferable but that any decent person would see that, in the meantime, charitable donations were necessary and the chest method the least inefficient. Developments in the early war years made the chests increasingly sensitive to allegations that the services for which they campaigned were unnecessary.

The most startling example of such a development came during the fall 1942 campaign in Vancouver. The Vancouver *News/Herald* reported the story "City Hall Employees Turn Down Appeal from Welfare Federation":

> Arguing that unemployment in the city "is a thing of the past" and that "the need for a Community Chest no longer exists," the City Hall Employees' Association as an organization has turned down the annual appeal of the Welfare Federation this year.

> Walter Scribbins, business agent for the association, said that the majority of their members felt that necessity for the community chest no longer exists. "We feel," he added, "that the present is a good time to close down public charity appeals."
>
> He referred to rosy prophesies by politicians for after the war, and said the association would like some indication of good faith.
>
> "Would you rather go back to tag days?" asked Mayor J.W. Cornett.
>
> "No," Scribbins replied, "but the funds should be raised by government taxation. Unless someone presses for a showdown it will never be done," he added.[26]

The *Daily Province* also covered the story, quoting Scribbins more fully:

> We would like some evidence of good faith in the rosy future that is promised. When it is said it is impossible for the government to find another half million [the 1943 chest campaign target] for welfare work when it is spending that every minute for the war, we just don't believe it. Let us [not?] go back to those trying days. Let the government pay this cost with money from taxation. Let the government give some indication of its intention to do things differently in the future. We have the same right as any other citizen [to decide] where to put our money. We merely say that in the opinion of the majority the need for a Community Chest no longer exists.

And in the familiar mode of this debate, Alderman John Bennett retorted, in the chest's defence, "that until the government assumed responsibility for welfare institutions they must be kept open by public subscription."[27]

Clippings describing this episode found their way to the de facto head office of the Canadian chests, the Canadian Welfare Council (CWC) in Ottawa. They were sent by one of the staff members of the social planning section of the Vancouver federation, Edgar Brown, to George Davidson, that federation's former executive director (also former BC director of welfare) and now head of the CWC. In a chatty, gossipy letter, Brown told Davidson, his former boss, that the point of view in the clipping was one that the chest met "continually, not only among labor groups but in 'A.'" (The "A" section was the name given to the list of the biggest donors to the chest. And apparently they were as restive about the pressure to give to charities as the civic workers were.) As Brown put it, "the financing of [welfare services] by annual appeals accompanied by ballyhoo seems to be more and more difficult, not because money is lacking but because many people, thinking of social security and economic changes, are impatient of 'charity.'" He pointed out that he had heard two retorts to the familiar defence that Alderman Bennett had offered. One was that stopgaps just postpone a "proper solution," and the other was that "welfare services are promoted by the 'ruling class' to keep people partly satisfied and quiet." The latter, the more left-wing point, was heard even beyond the predictable "militant labour men," he noted. It was the "penetration" of Vancouver's political life by "the CCF ideology" – which Brown told Davidson he personally welcomed – that was going to have "repercussions on privately-financed welfare services."[28]

More than just a concern about wastefulness was involved in this critique, and I will return to its other elements below. But importantly it was about inefficiency and wastefulness, the waste of time and effort involved in the "ballyhoo" of fundraising. Taxation was quiet and routine, and the amount of money that could be raised by income taxation, at least in good economic times, was so large that the relatively trivial number of dollars sought by fundraising campaigns could, it seemed, easily be supplied from the public purse. Everyone would thus be saved considerable effort. And, in 1942, that effort was intensified because the competition for dollars was so fierce: Victory Loans, Red Cross, taxation, and war services all targeted Canadians' suddenly larger incomes and wartime altruism, and many people still had to deal with debt and deferred needs from the 1930s.[29] Aware, since 1939, that war needs made the most compelling claim on Canadians' feelings of generosity, the chests did not want to be seen to be asking for anything other than the most undeniably necessary services.[30] They wondered if their agencies were "welfare luxuries."[31] And at the same time, the point of view indicated by the civic workers meant that the presence in the chests of necessary agencies, ones that might seem more appropriately funded by taxation, could be the ground for donor protest and even withdrawal.

There were three kinds of response to this awkward situation in which the needs represented by the chests had to be made to appear worthy but not suitable for tax-based funding. One was rhetorical, another social scientific, and a third institutional and political. The rhetorical move was easy and obvious: faced with competition from war charities, fundraisers used both "home front" metaphors and sympathy and admiration for the soldiers to leverage dollars for domestic welfare services. The guide for Halifax canvassers is typical: "Children, wife, and home are the chief concern of the man overseas. He is fighting for them and they cannot be overlooked in an all-out war effort ... The enlistment of men tends to disrupt families, leading to family discord, to broken homes, leaving children homeless, and increasing the number of illegitimate births. These difficulties add to the work of many of our Agencies."[32]

And, in a similar vein, the CWC's national journal told the anonymized case story of "A Soldier with Worries." A soldier wrote to the family welfare bureau to ask it to send a social worker to see his son. He and the boy's mother had divorced in the 1930s, and the father had given the boy to friends as a foster child. But he lost his job and stopped sending money to the family, which his son took as a sign that his father no longer cared about him. Communication ceased between father and son. In response to the father's request, the welfare bureau social workers visited the son, helped him to get a job that he liked, and encouraged his "sporting interests." They also reported to the father, the soldier, about his boy's "progress." The point of the story, for fundraising purposes, was that the father wrote to the welfare bureau to say "I cannot express in words or writing how much I appreciate your interest in my boy. Knowing this, helps me to keep my chin up and at times it does need a shove."[33] A soldier's morale was being supported by the services of a family welfare bureau's social work staff.[34] Most generic was the fighting front/home front analogy: "The man in uniform offers his life – we can offer only our money and time to fight this war at home ... To keep the home front safe and to keep that sacred obligation to our fighting force away from home, is our job."[35] It would have been easy to respond cynically to such appeals, and my point here is not to claim that everyone was persuaded by them. Rather, it is to point to fundraisers' ability to adapt their depiction of need to suit changing circumstances. When, at the end of the war, the chests lost the leveraged power of sympathy for soldiers, they would find yet other ways to channel the currents of public sentiment.[36]

For people who were not easily moved by advertisements evoking soldiers and broken families, social science offered other wartime arguments for the value of charities. In Ottawa, the Ottawa Council of Social Agencies (CSA) supplied fundraisers with research to back up their claims about the need for their services. Complaints about youth crime in Ottawa in 1943 prompted the CSA to do a study to provide evidence of the need for delinquency prevention services. This was precisely the sort of service, it argued, that was still important, indeed more seriously required, in the superheated economy of wartime. Wage-earning youth and shortages of housing spelled trouble. The CSA meant that there would be kids on the streets with money in their pockets and not enough gymnasiums or supervised skating rinks and social clubs to keep them constructively busy. Gambling, drunkenness, and sexual recklessness among the young might well be expected if the community did not provide wholesome alternative activities.

The CSA researchers found that, although there had been in 1941 and 1942 a "marked increase in *serious* offenses committed by juveniles," in general there had not been an "alarming" increase in youth crime. In fact, there had been no increase: rates in both 1930 and 1937 had been higher. This happy state of affairs did not stop them from finding a need, however. The research showed that most of the offenders came from areas that lacked "amenities for the young." That the listed areas were also ones that had suffered poverty and social stigma for decades before the war was not noted. A simpler message, and one more useful for fundraising, was that recreational agencies deserved donor dollars because the absence of such agencies produced juvenile delinquency.[37] It was in the interest of those raising funds for social work agencies that the donor public be worried about juvenile delinquency. "Wartime jitters over juveniles" were not simply the result of generalized anxiety but a predictable consequence of the emphasis in the wartime chest campaigns on a kind of service that fundraisers thought would attract donations to the chest as a whole. In other words, this was, at its origins, specifically a fundraising panic, not a moral panic.[38]

A more rational conclusion about increased need was drawn from a study of the social work labour market. In 1942, Vancouver's Marjorie Bradford produced a 5,000-word report for a national conference showing in detail for British Columbia what everyone in social work intuitively knew by then – that there were not enough staff for the work that needed to be done. According to Bradford's study, there were 375 social work jobs in British Columbia and 250 people in place. Of those 250, 75 had no general social work training, much less the specialized preparation that their particular jobs really required.[39] This meant, for example, that there might be social workers in courts who did not know how the courts worked, social workers in tuberculosis control who could be too overworked to prevent further infections, and social workers in family counselling whose youth and inexperience could make their usefulness somewhat questionable for middle-aged couples in crisis.

Not only did the social worker shortage cause these problems for the agencies' effectiveness, but it also raised their costs. To keep staff, chests and their agencies had to pay people more. The labour shortage meant wage competition. The Vancouver chest lost a director to a war-related job in Ontario that paid twice his Vancouver salary. Even in tight-fisted Halifax, the chest's leading executive, Gwladys Kennedy, got a pay raise in 1943 (possibly her first since 1928). The increased budgets of member agencies, which fund-raisers presented to the public as increasing need, were in part the result of the wartime labour market's upward pressure on social work salaries.[40] This reason for budget increases had less curb appeal than did abandoned children or brave soldiers, but it was part of what maintaining a system of private social work meant during wartime. The inflation and social work labour shortages of the late 1940s would only prolong this phenomenon into the postwar years. They also added to the challenge of defending increasingly expensive private agencies, which, like the chests themselves, were chronically suspected of wasting money, whether on extravagant salaries or on unnecessary services.[41]

As wartime pressures to avoid waste brought the cost of private social work under special scrutiny, the institutional and political efforts of the chests began to shift in favour of saving donor money not only by rationalizing within the private sector but also by shifting new responsibilities to governments. In Halifax, the shift was merely rhetorical, although it was remarkable to see in 1940 the new president of that conservative chest express enthusiasm for the day coming when the chest agencies' services would be financed by taxation.[42] In Vancouver, however, the concern about "welfare luxuries" led to more substantial developments.

Within the Vancouver Community Chest, there were multiple agencies dealing with veterans, with tuberculosis, with summer camps for children, and with home nursing. Most of these separate organizations maintained their own administrative staffs. Were all of these independent organizations truly necessary? There were also special-purpose hospitals in the chest, and some thought that these expensive and complex organizations were really essential public services. In 1942, in response to such criticisms, the Welfare Federation created an eight-member "committee on coordination of agency work." Chaired by unionist and aspiring Liberal politician E.A. Jamieson, the committee studied agencies and met with government officials.[43] This humble, banal work of co-ordination was full of menace for some and promise for others. Even into the 1950s, tempers flared when co-ordination and its related subjects were raised. Some of the agencies' representatives, who sensed that their place in the chest was vulnerable, protested the chest's attempt to shift more responsibility to government or to force amalgamations. And even within the chest, there were strong differences of opinion on how these issues should be handled for the best fundraising effect. From the fights about co-ordination came hard-won and fragile compromises about how private and public responsibilities should be divided.

In the course of its work, Jamieson's committee laid down a general principle to describe the role of private charity: it should support new kinds of social services. If a service became valuable and necessary, then the private agencies should ask governments to take on the funding of the service. If not, then the money should go elsewhere. No service should continue to be supported by donors just because it had managed to survive: an agency's existence was not "conclusive proof" that its work was "either necessary, or in all cases desirable."[44] The following year the chest board endorsed by formal vote an amended version of this statement. Considerable debate and politicking must have gone into the one phrase that was changed. In the final version, a service's success was to trigger a request from the chest to "municipal and provincial governments ... to contribute financially to the fullest possible extent." In the Jamieson committee's version, there had been less enthusiasm about continuing private management. To the committee, a service's success meant "the government should be approached with a request to take it over."[45] The committee's version treated tax-funding as necessarily and properly entailing government management, whereas the compromise version allowed for the persistence of various "semi-public" combinations of public funding and private direction. Here was a crucial division on what constituted democratic accountability, the appropriate mechanism to prevent the waste of public money. But in both versions of the new principle, it was clear that fundraisers themselves wanted to avoid making a pitch to the public for agencies whose usefulness might be questionable or whose eligibility for public funding might be successfully argued at city hall or in Victoria.

Beyond this level of consensus, however, conflict existed among and between fundraisers and agency representatives on exactly which agencies, or more precisely whose agencies, should be pushed into the possibly unwilling arms of the city or the province. To the Jamieson committee's roughly

2,500-word report, the chest budget committee replied with close to 9,000 words of comment. In each of twelve areas, the two groups grappled with the complex mixtures of public and private funding that sustained the various agencies. The issues around the Crippled Children's Hospital were typical. Was the 1941 change in the Hospitals Act, which gave the Crippled Children's Hospital per diem subsidies for patients for the first time, enough to make this very expensive agency a bearable burden for private charity? Or was this kind of hospital analogous to the chronic care hospitals already fully financed and operated by the province? Was the chest, as a major funder of the hospital, entitled to ask the government to take over this hospital? Or was the hospital's own volunteer board, who felt most strongly that they were the owners of the agency, the only body that could appropriately address the minister of health on these questions? The budget committee urged that the chest be restrained in its approaches to the government on the question of the Crippled Children's Hospital.

In spite of this urging, however, representatives of the chest continued over the next four years to discuss the future of the hospital with the provincial health department. The hospital board, unhappy with the chest's intervention, threatened to quit the chest and go to the public for donations on their own, presenting the chest as a miserly villain in the process. This threat saved the hospital's spot on the chest's roster of member agencies. So, too, did the fundraisers' awareness that children's health charities helped to bring in donor dollars. Suffering but smiling children were an important image for a charity campaign. Nevertheless, as the hospital example indicates, tensions persisted in the relationships between the chest and its agencies as the latter struggled for some decision-making autonomy within their complex net of funding sources. In 1954, yet another committee on public-private relations would be struck. Already, in the 1940s, however, it had become clear that, in the context of mixed funding, there would be struggles over authority.[46]

Fundraisers' claims to be asking the public for the minimum necessary to meet the real welfare needs of the people enabled fundraisers to say "none of your money is being wasted." To say that credibly, they needed to have control, but increasingly it seemed to be impossible. The only agency that Jamieson's committee actually killed, though not immediately, was a small women's group, composed entirely of unpaid volunteers, who visited TB patients. This was hardly a stunning victory for efficiency.[47] It hints, however, at a skepticism among the rationalizers about the value of feminine volunteer social work. Social work that seemed to be mere womanly wailing and weeping, or at best quiet caretaking without rehabilitative effect, would be harder for the embattled chests to defend against the critics of wasteful spending, no matter how useful pity was for opening wallets.

During the war, the expanding public welfare bureaucracy increased the market value of social work labour. It was the fundraisers' task to enable private agencies to compete in that market. In the 1940s, that meant working with the resources of sympathy most readily available and throwing off to governments any services they would agree to fund. At the same time, however, it entailed insisting that private agencies had a distinct value and purpose and that money given to them was therefore not money wasted. Out of the imbroglios of the 1940s thus came a rationale for private agencies that would shape the fundraisers' contribution to social programs in the 1950s: the commitment to innovation, known later as the demonstration role. On this rationale would depend the later success of the chests in claiming that the private charities were an essential part of the new welfare state system.

Charity as Unfair

In the 1940s, the socialist criticism of charity as a poor substitute for economic justice continued to be expressed as part of a general argument for rights-based income redistribution. From this perspective, charity was just one part of a larger problem of unfairness in which wage earners' labour produced luxuty for employers and anxious insecurity for workers and their families. This view of the whole capitalist system as unfair would continue to appear in left-wing and labour politics, albeit increasingly under attack or politically marginalized, through the 1940s and 1950s. In addition, however, there were new notions of fairness or unfairness in charity that emerged as a response to the chest movement's expansion and success. From this perspective, charitable giving was a normal part of citizenship, but the particular methods of fundraising or of spending charitable dollars could be more or less fair. Critics pointed out that, although they were willing to give or to do their fair share, something was wrong either in the distribution of the burden of giving or in the methods fundraisers used to extract and distribute donor dollars. In these complaints, it is easy to hear echoes of taxation grievances, and therefore it should not be surprising that the responses and remedies the chests devised were drawn from the toolkit of tax fairness.

From their beginning and into the 1940s, the federated charities discourse, like tax talk, used the term "burden" to describe the responsibility they asked contributors to undertake.[48] In 1945, in response to complaints that taxation and charity combined made that burden too heavy, Halifax's fundraisers defended the chests: "He who withdraws support from the needy in order to apply this amount against his tax bill, is simply shifting to very thin shoulders his fair share of a universal burden of sacrifice."[49]

Here, as in the 1930s Vancouver advertising, the emotional force of the appeal comes from the feeling of compassion for fellow citizens, forced to carry a burden that others have shirked. In the 1940s, as in the 1930s, campaign committees meeting to assess results were told by canvass captains that some donors thought too much was being asked of them and not enough of some other groups. Regular givers of substantial amounts disliked being asked to give more every year or being recanvassed in the weeks after the campaign to increase their donations so that the target could be met. Accompanying this complaint sometimes came the assertion that the chest had to find more new donors. Meanwhile, fundraising executives analyzed donation patterns and demographic data on income cohorts and repeatedly found, in all three cities, that per capita giving was lower in their city than elsewhere and that their wealthy citizens were poor givers. Their points of comparison (not always identified) were the donor demographics provided by the Community Chests and Councils of America. The more accommodating tax law of the United States may have boosted the numbers of large donations by making charitable giving more remunerative for the enormously rich. Whatever its basis, the complaint that the rich people of Canada did not give enough was, like the image of the beleaguered regular donor, a claim of unfairness – that those who enjoyed wealth gave less than they could. And this class critique from below was matched by one from above. From Vancouver's business community in wartime came the complaint that workers in the war industries were not contributing their fair share to welfare work. New Canadians in particular, they suggested, needed to be taught their duty as citizens to be donors.[50]

In pursuit of their campaign goals, fundraisers continued their efforts to reach ever-wider circles of potential donors. None of the techniques tried was fundamentally different from those used in the 1920s and 1930s. But when canvassers met the objections that a prospect had given at the office or had given at home, it was perhaps a sign that people felt the coverage of their market had become entirely too thorough.[51] These objections may also have indicated that some people thought it unfair to be asked to make two donations from one breadwinner's wage packet. Labour spokesmen gave more formal expression to war workers' feelings of being unfairly beleaguered by fundraising campaigns. In 1941, Trades and Labour Congress president Tom Moore wrote:

> That Labour is anxious and willing to do its part is again demonstrated by the generous appeals that have been made for the Red Cross, auxiliary war services, and other worthwhile community efforts. Workers have accepted, without protest, the heavy impositions of the National Defense Tax and the inclusion of many previously exempt among the income tax groups. In fact, they have supplemented these financial demands of the Government by voluntarily agreeing to wage roll deductions for the purchasing of War Savings Stamps, Certificates and Bonds. Added to these is [sic] the contributions now being made to the unemployment insurance funds. In view of acceptance of all these added financial burdens, it is foolish to denounce wage earners as profiteers.[52]

While no chest campaign captain would have been so tactless as to sling such a stinging accusation as "war profiteers" in public, shaming the non-giver was nevertheless part of the fundraiser's stock in trade. The chest method of consolidating appeals was designed precisely to keep shaming language valuable and effective by preventing its overuse. In Toronto and Hamilton, workers in war industries found refuge in special Employee Chests, designed by fundraisers to minimize the delicately described "adverse reaction" that beleaguered war workers might reasonably have had to the numerous calls on their larger but not infinite pay packets.[53] Nationally, the CWC negotiated with the minister of war services and the minister of national revenue to ensure that a few weeks early in the fall fundraising season would be kept free for the chest campaigns to avoid competing directly with other claims on the people's pockets.[54] But even though spacing out and consolidating appeals was meant to prevent constant irritation of guilt-ridden consciences, the annual appeal was itself undeniably full of implications that people had not given enough and should open their hearts and wallets more fully and again.

That the shaming tactics of the chests had a coercive effect is strongly suggested by the existence of defaulting donors, who apparently succumbed to the power of the appeal and gave what they could not afford to give. About 3 percent of donors in any given campaign fell into this category. In a large place like Vancouver in the middle of the war years, there were over 1,800 people who did not or could not fulfill their pledges. Some of them perhaps had said yes cynically to the canvasser, simply for the sake of appearance; others no doubt had had a turn of bad luck and unexpected expenses; yet others were probably the victims of a too-generous impulse and an insufficient income. Most would no doubt have said that they had been pressured to give. Their delinquency, then, was a perverse result of the chests' attempts to distribute more widely and thus supposedly more fairly the burden of contribution. The chests' reputation for coercive pressure may have mounted over the years as office staff hunted down the donors who were delinquent in paying up on their pledges. Notices, phone calls, and, in Halifax, personal visits from the chest director must have made some people feel as though they had bought furniture on an installment plan they could not afford and had fallen into the hands of a collection agency.[55]

Those who celebrated charitable giving as voluntary in contrast to compulsory taxpaying might have been puzzled by accusations that unfair pressure was applied to extract donations. If social pressure were the only tool at the fundraiser's disposal, then those accusations would indeed have been dubious. But an Ottawa insurance company president in 1938 wondered if, as an employer, he might be crossing the line between persuasion and coercion when he lectured his staff about the importance of giving to the chest. His talks resulted in more donations to the chest, to be sure. But was this a result of his convincing eloquence, or did staff suspect that he watched the published names lists to check for compliance?[56] And when a firm used payroll deductions as a means of channelling staff donations to the chests, employees might fear retaliation, petty or otherwise, by employers if they did not join in the boss's project. Tax-like in its ease and efficiency, payroll deduction deprived employees of the privacy in which they could make free choices about charity. For people who felt vulnerable in their jobs, whether salaried workers in an insurance company or waged workers in a shipyard, there could have been a fear of pressure to give that was more than just social pressure. These concerns had been heard in the 1930s; the increasing use of payroll deduction in the war years (with income tax coming off for the first time in September 1942) upped the tension around this technique of getting donations.[57]

While applying pressure to potential donors was the whole purpose of their campaigns, fundraisers walked a fine line between fair and unfair techniques. Both had an element of force, but social pressure counted as fair, whereas threats to employment were unfair. To avoid the appearance (and perhaps the reality) of unfairness, chest fundraisers turned to mechanisms of representation. Fundraisers knew that donors' feelings of fear and hostility might be lowered if the prospective donor felt that the canvasser was not one of "them" but one of "us." When charitable giving was organized through religious associations, such reassuring identifications were obvious. A more universal, less particular basis of unity, like the citizen identity evoked by the Community Chest, required that the fundraising process obscure or actually alter its limited social base. If the federated appeal looked like something that Boards of Trade and social workers had cooked up for their own purposes, then donors who saw those groups as alien or hostile would likely experience the appeal as coercive, as though "those people" were trying to get something from "us."

From their beginnings, the chests used various persuasive techniques and organizational methods to prevent or overcome such reactions. Wartime pressures brought on a new round of efforts, not only of the rhetorical sort but also of the sort to increase, in particular, worker representation in the management of community fund appeals. In Ottawa, in 1943, the chest began work on an employee chest plan like those used in Toronto and Hamilton. Although it failed to implement this plan, the idea had taken hold that labour representation on committees and boards, or even more substantial measures of worker control, was crucial to increasing employee contributions.[58] Vancouver's wartime chest co-operated with the labour councils in several projects and also with appointed Liberal labour man Edward Jamieson, head of the controversial co-ordinating committee, to the chest's most important body: the budget committee.[59] Only in Halifax did worker representation fail to appear on the wartime chest agenda; there labour and in particular organized labour were courted only after the war, from 1949 onward.[60]

These efforts at increasing labour representation had a material purpose: they were deliberately designed to increase wage earners' contributions to charity. But they also had a larger political meaning. American practices during the war were held up as models for Canada, both by social workers and by union men in the 1940s and later. It is not surprising, then, that the Revolutionary War expression "no taxation without representation" summed up the viewpoint that, if workers' money were demanded, then workers' representatives must be on the deliberative councils of the chests.[61] The logic of classical democracy that connected voluntary contribution and legislative authority made a business-dominated chest seem increasingly unfair as wage earners' dollars flowed into its coffers. The choice that the chest faced seemed to be this: include representatives of the smaller donors, who en masse were beginning to make a real difference in the amounts collected, or risk having the whole project of charitable giving rejected in favour of that other representative organization, elected government. Those who advocated an end to private charity might reasonably have thought that their views had a better chance of affecting social services if decisions about those services were made by people whom they had elected. Because labour's bargaining power rose during the war, both because of mass organizing and market conditions and because of workers' increasing potential as donors, the pressures of wartime fundraising made the chest movement's leaders think, again, and harder, about labour participation in the management of the people's donations.

To some figures in the chest leadership, the political reasons for increasing labour participation seemed even more important than the immediately material ones. Musing in response to the civic workers' protest, George Davidson of the CWC expressed this view in a letter to his friend and fellow social work administrator, Edgar Brown:

> For my own part I feel that the real approach to the problem [of legitimating charity] must be made on the basis that private welfare agencies occupy the same place in the welfare field that private trade unions, private educational institutions such as universities, and non-state churches occupy in their respective fields. I think that chests must make clear that there are certain democratic values in citizen participation through private agencies and welfare effort, but I also think, of course, that before chests can talk very much about democratic values, they will have to make the Chest movement and the private movement really democratic for a change. You and I both know what a big change is involved in that.

Davidson went on to point out that, in depersonalizing the connection between particular services and donors, the chests had made less immediate the participatory element in charitable giving. From this undermining of the direct connection between agencies and their donors came the chests' potential obsolescence. If that was the problem, Davidson suggested, then there were two solutions: "The Chest, in the years that follow the war, will survive, if it does survive, not so much on its own merits [as a convenience to donors] as on the real worth of the private agency programme, and the extent to which these programmes make possible democratic citizen participation ... If the American Chests can bridge the gap with labour, the answer may be found somewhere in that experience."[62]

It was the middle of a late-November night in 1942 when Davidson wrote this, full of passionate conviction about the importance of his theme. He had been more cautious a month earlier in a message to CWC staffer Eurith Goold. In response to her suggestion that the CWC should push chests more aggressively into a program of labour participation, Davidson cautioned that the CWC could not go "out on a limb."[63] He knew from Vancouver experience that, among the volunteer leadership of the chests, real opposition existed to having labour involved, even though there was also real support in the social work community as a whole. In the 1940s, class prejudices made labour participation neither a trivial gesture nor a natural, taken-for-granted development. But efforts to make genuine labour participation a reality would continue through the 1950s, culminating in new forms of labour-social work co-operation.[64] In fundraising circles, the origins of those developments lay in the debates about the value of private charity during the Second World War and the threats to its legitimacy from those who doubted the fairness of elite, classical democracy.

In with the New, on with the Old: The Second World War as a Turning Point

The war turned out not to be as bad for the Community Chests as the fundraisers had feared in the war's early months. Canadians shelled out more dollars for the chest campaigns in the war years than ever before, and donor numbers continued to rise, even though Canadians were also meeting mounting calls on their pocketbooks for war-related donations and income tax contributions. Chest fundraisers continued their established practice of listening to the criticisms of charity that were funnelled to campaign planners through the system of canvasser reports. They heard fresh objections in the war years because of the perceived end of unemployment, the beginning of adequate income assistance, disputes about saving for postwar reconstruction, the salary expectations of social workers, the distribution of the donation burden, and the prospects of converting private services to public auspices. In response, various chests tried new approaches or new versions of old ones.

Wartime needs, real or imaginary, gave them a chance to define clearly the difference between their agencies' services and unemployment relief. They acknowledged that philanthropy was inadequate to mass income security and argued, apparently convincingly, that, in spite of that fact, charity had other valuable purposes and should continue to exist. By adopting war-related symbols of worthy need, they again made themselves vulnerable, at war's end, to appearing irrelevant. But images are adaptable, and in the post-war campaigns they would find other ways to appealingly depict need. More fundamentally, to defend themselves from the charge of wastefulness, they refashioned the old public/private distinction to position charitably funded agencies as part of a new welfare regime in which public provision could expand without eliminating the reason for most private agencies' existence. A key feature of this distinction was the demonstration function of private agencies. Commitment to this function, and the concomitant insistence on adequate publicly funded income security, meant that these largely business-driven fundraising organizations could be made palatable to social democratic and liberal unionists. The class tensions about who was carrying the burden of charitable responsibility began to be eased when labour councils became more closely involved in chest management. Relations between fundraisers and member agencies were tense, in some places more than others, as setting fundraising goals at a level appropriate to agency needs remained controversial. But the outline of the postwar broadening of social work services and the raising of standards was beginning to emerge in some of the wartime research on needs and salaries.

The war was, indeed, a turning point in tax-funded income assistance. Rather than militating only in favour of expanded state services, however, the circumstances of war and the legacy of the Depression also helped to build the groundwork for private charity's growth in wartime and beyond. Fund-raising campaigns responded to changes in legislated provision, but in years to come the fundraisers' adaptations would themselves have consequences for public welfare. To justify their existence, the chests undertook, in effect, to become public relations agencies for social work, making the case for needs other than income assistance and for new levels and kinds of provision beyond even the existing social services. In response to the notion that "there can't be much hardship" in times of full employment, they argued, in the words of a 1948 radio ad, "Brother, there's always hardship. Misfortune's choppin' away at somebody, good times or bad, winter, summer. There's illness, accident, death. There's waywardness, crime, villainy, cruelty ... Somebody's always being hurt."[65] Their ability to make this sort of case convincingly, and indeed their general reputation as welfare authorities, would rest on the effectiveness of their money-raising methods. The successes of the wartime appeals positioned them to make the value of many social services part of the general knowledge and common sense of the Canadian urban public and the decision makers from whose desks future social programs would come. The first six or seven years after the war would present new difficulties. But the foundations laid in the fundraisers' successful wartime adaptations helped to make sense of the Community Chests as part and parcel of the new Canadian welfare state in the 1950s.

6
Reconstructing Charity: The Postwar Politics of Public and Private, 1945-66

The Community Chests had survived the war far more successfully than they had expected. But the transition from wartime to a new welfare order in the first decade after the war was painful and uncertain. The logic of a revised public/private division of welfare had been sketched out during the war years, but its implementation during reconstruction was difficult. No one knew for sure how to organize the communications that would be necessary to co-ordinate the work of private and public agencies. Indeed, it was not always clear what work each type of agency would do. These uncertainties provoked a spate of nasty spats among the compassionate and community minded. Different elements within the welfare community vigorously fought for their vision of what the "right" mix of public programs and private services should be. Lurking behind this debate was the old contest between socialism and capitalism, newly elevated into geopolitical drama as the Cold War took shape.

Difficult as the issues of the day were in these large terms, they were made even more so by the politics and personalities of their local settings. Deeply committed people, aware of the stakes in reorganizing social provision for a new future, worked desperately and fought hard to defend or advance their (sometimes bloody-minded) positions. In the federated fundraising organizations in each of the three cities in this study, the reconstruction years saw controversial hirings and firings, resignations and reorganizations, conflicts with both agencies and donors, and bleak predictions that the chest method might be abandoned. The tensions inherent from the beginning of the federation sharpened in the uncertain years of reconstruction. In contrast to the 1930s, however, the federations in 1945 had become established institutions, and their adherents (staff, long-time board members, dependent agencies) wanted continuity in their world. They wanted the chests to survive.

It was also clear by 1945 that expansion of public provision was part of the future. Survival of the chests depended, then, on finding for their fundraising program and their member agencies a method of coexistence and co-operation with state agencies. It seemed certain that public agencies would grow and change, so the chests and their supporters sought not simply to preserve all existing private programs but also to develop general principles that would enable private agencies to shift and expand in complementary ways. Their place in the future was to be secured not by perpetuating antistatist antagonism but by joining the new and growing regime of social security.[1] Some of the chest agencies might be abandoned, others might leave to become tax funded, new ones might be created, and existing ones might expand and grow. All of these prospective developments would need to be chosen, explained, and promoted by budget committees and canvassers, public relations committees and campaign chairs. Many felt that, if they succeeded in getting the principles of the new division of welfare right, then the chests would survive. If they did not, then the chests would cease to exist. This sense that they teetered between survival and extinction explains the emotional intensity of the postwar reorganization of the chests.

To survive, they needed, as always, to succeed. It quickly became apparent that the question of what counted as success was still debatable. On the one hand, many new chests were created in the immediate postwar period, which seemed a clear sign of the movement's success. On the other hand, in the existing chest cities, campaign results showed the same mix of increased giving, but failure to meet targets, that had troubled fundraisers in the 1930s.[2] Was this success or failure? Increasingly, the definition of success appeared to be a matter of politics. This was a change from the optimistic consensus of the 1920s, when it was possible for both chest organizers and agencies innocently to hope that existing social services merely needed help with financing and perhaps some elimination of duplicate services, and agencies' budgets could be covered. Since then, the critiques of the 1930s and 1940s had raised the possibility that, even when campaign goals were met, social services might fall short of meeting real needs.

Moreover, it was possible that the proper function of private charities was to innovate in social work and to redefine common-sense notions of "real needs." But who could properly define the needs or the dollar amounts minimally required to meet them? The efficiency claim that underpinned the federations' annual campaigns was that the campaign target represented "the absolute minimum necessary." If campaign targets were not met, what really were the consequences? Did a failed campaign mean real failure to provide for crucial welfare needs? Or was failure only the result (as some thought) of social workers' overblown, self-serving representation of what was necessary to maintain social peace and reasonable well-being for all?[3] Did campaign shortfalls mean that private charity simply could never be adequate and that governments should finance social services in addition to income support? Or were failed campaigns only a temporary feature of post-war economic uncertainty, to be replaced by success once things settled out and reorganization and improved campaign techniques proved their worth? On these questions, various constituencies disagreed.

The working out of answers to these questions would result in a reorganized federated fundraising movement, with a permanent role in a new public/private division of welfare, even though that role continued, and still continues, to change. In the process of the chests' development during the long 1950s (1945-60), fundraising continued to contribute to the expansion of the welfare state. Rather than collapsing in the face of a crisis or being reduced to insignificance by an aggressive state, the federated appeals made the need for state expansion evident by themselves being expansive, important, and successful on some measures (and thus demonstrating "need" and their own social salience) yet also by frequently failing to attain fundraising targets. The solutions that people in the chests and councils devised to the problems of the reconstruction years themselves became the grounds for renewed and profound criticism of the fundraising federations in the 1950s and 1960s. The state of affairs in welfare in 1960, both public and private, can be explained in part by the solutions fundraisers found to the threats that they encountered during the reconstruction decade.

In general terms, the threats to success fell within five categories: increased costs, a perception of lessening needs, dissatisfaction among member agencies, donor skepticism and frustration, and ideological opposition. The responses can be similarly summarized: reduce costs and increase revenues, persuade donors of the legitimacy of higher targets, change organizational structures to ease relations with agencies and donors, expand coverage while controlling costs, and pre-empt or counter ideological critiques. In this chapter and the next, I will present stories from the period that indicate how these general phenomena, apparent nation-wide, manifested themselves in each of the three cities. Each narrative shows how a large transformation in political culture took shape in local struggles and engaged participants in power relations fractally, at multiple levels, from the interpersonal to the institutional to the ideological. Through associational networks, partisan politics, and individuals' career paths, social politics and high politics connected in many ways, even while the people involved were trying to clarify and more sharply distinguish the public/private division of welfare. In this chapter, the focus is on the sharing of responsibilities in child welfare and unemployment assistance, both areas in which the chests felt deeply threatened. These are stories of the political manoeuvring within and between institutions and governments. The next chapter looks outward from the institutional politics of the chests. By analyzing in that chapter the chests' responses to donor fatigue, I show how the chests put on welfare state camouflage, presenting their organization and the needs they served in the cultural language of the new welfare regime. In these two chapters taken together, I show how the culture of contribution promoted by the chests led to particular new public programs, developed associational forms for an inclusive deliberative democracy, and promoted the standards of justice and care by which the Canadian welfare state was legitimated (at least for a time) at its zenith.

The Firing of Gwendolen Lantz: Gender, Generation, and the Growth of the Welfare State

In 1945, fifty-six-year-old Gwendolen Lantz had been the executive director of the Halifax Children's Aid Society (CAS) for twenty years. For those years, Gwladys Kennedy, Lantz's contemporary, had been the chief executive officer of the city's Community Chest. In 1945, both were about to encounter the future of social welfare, manifested in the province's newly appointed director of child welfare, Fred MacKinnon, and in a principled young clubwoman, Lillian Farquhar of the Junior League. Farquhar's attempt to reform the chest and MacKinnon's to repair the Halifax CAS combined to shape a climate of conflict in the city's social work circles that lasted until 1952. Personalities mixed with party politics, and gender conflicts meshed with generational ones. In the end, both Kennedy and Lantz would be replaced by young male social workers. In the process, hostilities between private charities and the provincial Department of Public Welfare would be replaced by a closer partnership. And both the chest and the CAS would expand and adopt new methods. In this story, we see the early stages of a process that would produce across Canada, by the early 1960s, the effective demand for the Canada Assistance Plan of 1966.[4]

The career paths of the CAS's Lantz and the chest's Kennedy were parallel. Both came from rural Nova Scotia and had earned a university degree in the 1910s. Both could claim to have been new women of the 1920s, having been pathbreakers in their working lives. Lantz was the first professionally trained social worker to be employed in the city, and Kennedy, in 1925, was a businesswoman taking on, in the Community Chest, the management of a wholly novel enterprise. While Kennedy was married and Lantz remained single, neither had children, and both therefore were free to devote themselves single-mindedly to their professions.[5] And, by all accounts, each did. Through the challenges of the Depression and the unrelenting demands of wartime Halifax, a city swamped with struggling families and sojourners of all sorts, these two women put in long hours of social service on modest salaries.[6] Both were infamously poor delegators, with Kennedy doing clerical work and Lantz casework, even though they were both nominally supervisors and executives. Each developed a reputation for imperious certainty, having purchased considerable authority with the hard coin of self-sacrifice and the more dubious currency of a secretive management style.[7] Their tendency to do nearly everything themselves was warranted, apparently, by their organizations' small budgets. Neither the CAS nor the chest was able, it seemed, to hire enough junior staff.

On the question of the CAS's staffing, the courses of Kennedy's and Lantz's otherwise parallel lives collided. This happened because the Children's Aid Society was both a public and a private agency – sometimes called semi-public. It was public in the sense that its work was partially governed by the Child Protection Act, and its services to children were financed partially by disbursements from the provincial government, on a per capita basis for each ward. After 1943, there were also annual grants from the province, made to assist with operating costs. But it was also a private association in that its policies were set by a volunteer board, albeit within some statutory constraints. And even after 1943, charitable donations from the Community Chest paid for over 80 percent of the Halifax CAS's operating budget, the largest part of which was staff salaries (see Table 1). In this sense, too, then, CAS was a private agency: the donations that enabled it to function came from the chest's annual campaign. Thus, when Lantz and her staff were swamped by the high caseloads of wartime Halifax, and begged for help, it was the chest's budgeting that they were challenging. And, as an American observer from the Junior League noted, it was Kennedy, and not the chest's somewhat sclerotic volunteer board, who truly made the Community Chest's

TABLE 1

Distribution of major revenue sources, Halifax CAS

	1949		1960-61		1966-67	
	$	%	$	%	$	%
Chest	10,733	78	31,999	49	31,376	23
City	1,000	7	7,165	11	24,198	18
Province	2,000	15	25,645	40	80,750	59

budget decisions in Halifax: "The board is so grateful to her for relieving them of any work that they are a rubber stamp for what she dictates."[8]

Kennedy's domination of the chest's decision making was extremely annoying to Farquhar. And, as Kennedy would learn, an annoyed Farquhar would take on even a well-entrenched opponent. Farquhar was a double threat. She was an agency activist, having served since 1940 on the board of CAS, and she was a significant donor to the chest, well connected among other wealthy donors. She thus represented two of the chest's most important constituencies. Her personal authority was also considerable: she was equipped with skills that made her credible to national and international supporters. As a member of the Junior League, Farquhar had received specialized training in social work and was connected to an international community of similarly qualified women volunteer leaders.[9] In 1944, she was also appointed as the maritime regional representative of the Canadian Welfare Council (CWC) advisory committee. This was a clear endorsement by that national organization of her viewpoint on chest reform and chest-agency relations.[10]

Since early 1942, taking up where other CAS board members had left off, Farquhar had struggled to have the chest grant to CAS increased to pay for more staff. The board's response, no doubt dictated by Kennedy, expressed her perspective as a fundraiser: that Halifax had limited resources for charity and that CAS was being given its fair share of the funds the chest was able to raise. In 1943, however, Farquhar discovered that the chest had a substantial surplus carried over from year to year as a kind of "rainy day" reserve fund and a source of interest income. She was outraged, telling the CWC's George Davidson that "the Community Chest has no right to withhold public funds which are given for the purpose of helping the agencies and alleviating suffering." Farquhar threatened to withdraw her own donation and suggested menacingly that other donors might also do so. She felt, as her New York advisor reported, that "the sense of trusteeship of the public money is apparently unthought of by this board."[11]

To remedy this central problem, Farquhar took aim at the organizational culture of the Halifax Community Chest. There were two problems with that culture. As one of her allies, Gwendolyn Shand of the Halifax Council of Social Agencies (CSA), would note, it set up a bitter conflict between agencies and the chest, keeping agency workers well outside any decisions about fundraising targets or agency allocations. It was as if Kennedy did not even see the council as relevant to the chest. There was no actual representation of the CSA on the chest's board, and between Shand, the council's director, and Kennedy there was no love lost.[12] The other problem was that the same people had been serving on the board pretty much since the chest's origins: it was, in Farquhar's view, virtually a "closed corporation" even though Farquhar herself had gained membership. Her most strenuous and persistent campaign was to see the chest's constitution rewritten so that board members would serve only three-year terms, on a staggered rotation, and so that the social agencies, through the council, could appoint their own representatives. Although, by 1945, she had begun to feel that it was useless to struggle any longer, she gained enough support from her various networks to persist through to success in 1950.[13] While the rewriting of the constitution in this period depended on her doggedness, the question that troubled her – the accountability of the chest to its member agencies – was a more general one, to which I will return below.

Following the renewal of the Halifax chest's board membership in January 1950, a wave of change swept through the organization. In the spring of 1950, the new board, with Rotarian and Northern Electric manager Marshall Wilson at the helm, commissioned a major survey of the chest by the CWC.[14] Perhaps its key recommendation was that an assistant be employed to help the overburdened Gwladys Kennedy. In 1951, thirty-six-year-old George Hart was hired as the chest's "manager." A schoolteacher from Prince Edward Island with a 1942 MA in English literature from Acadia University, Hart had been an education officer in the navy during the war and had attended the Maritime School of Social Work. He had directed the Cumberland County, Nova Scotia, CAS for two years. His most recent position had been as second-in-command to Fred MacKinnon at the provincial Department of Public Welfare.[15] In the conflicts between chest, council, and Children's Aid, Hart had stood with MacKinnon and the council as a critic of Lantz.[16] And he no doubt agreed with MacKinnon that the chest should have raised its grant to CAS.

Soon after Hart was hired, the chest's community organization and campaign techniques began to change, moving into the mainstream of modern federated fundraising. By 1953, for example, payroll deductions at workplaces had been so successfully implemented that the need to continue the house-to-house canvass was being questioned.[17] In the fall campaign of 1953, "employee donations" were 67 percent higher than in the previous year.[18] Kennedy must have begun to feel the loss of her accustomed control because she resigned in June 1953, amid apparent protest by the board.[19] Not long after her departure, Hart held up the case of the Ottawa chest, captained by a young American fundraiser, John Yerger, as an example of effective PR methods for a chest that was successful because it was "young in spirit."[20] In the fall of 1954, after Hart had put in his first full year as chest director, the campaign target of $177,000 (7.2 percent larger than 1953's target) represented the biggest year-to-year increase in the dollars sought since Hart had joined the chest.[21] The results of the campaign that fall were impressive: the target was not only met but also exceeded. Hart's adventuresome view of what was possible was vindicated. Halifax gave exactly double in 1954 what it had given in 1947, a 37 percent increase over seven years in the per capita rate of donations.[22]

Also indicating a change in norms, if not in substance, was the 1955 appointment of Aaron Zive to the board as a representative of the city's Jewish community. The Zive family had been involved with the chest for years, but formal acknowledgment that they were representing Haligonian Jews marks the chest's adoption of a standard of diversity in its concept of representation. Hart also spearheaded the chest's energetic attempt to enlist more agencies as members, culminating in the important addition in 1957 of a major national agency, the Red Cross. He was a key figure in the transformation of the chest into the united appeals, the chief innovation in federated fundraising in the 1950s. Hart would leave Halifax's chest greatly changed when, in 1958, he moved to Ottawa to become the director of the CWC's chests and councils division. His success in solving Halifax's persistent problems no doubt recommended him for the national job, as perhaps did the presence in 1957 on the CWC's national executive of Wilson, who had been both chest president and council president during Hart's years in Halifax.[23]

Another of the emerging solutions to the CAS problem was the removal of Gwendolen Lantz as the agency's director. Lillian Farquhar's efforts to improve CAS had always been tempered by her concern not to hurt feelings. When Fred MacKinnon took on this project, a less tender regard for the city's volunteer elite emerged. Battle lines were drawn and sides chosen. It took him five years to wrest control of CAS from Lantz. In the process, MacKinnon deployed his personal persuasive abilities within the Council of Social Agencies as a member of that council as well as the regulatory power of the provincial department, enforced by control of provincial grants. This was not just a power struggle driven by ego. The evidence MacKinnon assembled about the failings of the Halifax CAS included heartbreaking stories about how Lantz's rigidity had kept children from their parents and had driven single mothers to despair. He wanted Lantz to go so that the agency could be improved. In his view, the public authority had the right and the responsibility to set standards of service. In contrast, Lantz thought he completely misunderstood the role of the provincial department. And at least some of the public, catching wind of the question, began to think "the government" was failing in its duty to vulnerable children. The political currents that the CAS controversy generated drew in the minister of welfare and other heavyweights as the threats to the reputation of this quasi-public agency began to look like potential election campaign material. With a leading government minister unhappy about the state of the Halifax CAS, rumours about a potential government takeover of the agency began to circulate. They worried some members of the council and became another reason to push harder for changes at CAS.[24]

Tracing events between 1948 and 1952, as I have done in a more detailed narrative elsewhere,[25] we can see that the decisions made by social workers, whether public or private, depended for their implementation on the agreement of the chest. In Halifax, real financial clout remained in the chest's hands. And the chest on its own would not have forced the firing of Lantz. As Kennedy admitted in April 1952, the chest's budget committee had been concerned about "the whole matter" of CAS for "several years" but had not protested, "hoping things would correct themselves." By 1952, however, the Welfare Council was determined to force the issue, even while aware of the consequences for fundraising of doing so. At one of the crisis points in the 1951-52 events, the council president accused the chest of being "afraid of" an October 1951 report that recommended Lantz's removal. The council president knew that chest fundraising depended on presenting the agencies as faultless providers of essential services. Exposure of Lantz's record would have highlighted the falsity of those images. When, finally, the chest accepted that it would have to threaten to cut off its support of CAS to force Lantz's resignation, it tried to do so before the fall fundraising campaign.[26] The timing of the chest's intervention suggests the chest thought that newspaper coverage of the Lantz-CAS story risked damaging the images of those who did the firing as well as bringing to light questions of the adequacy of CAS's work over the previous twenty-five years. These matters fundraisers were loath to expose.

Aware of the chest's reluctance to take on the CAS problem, the Welfare Council delayed officially transmitting its report to the chest until May 1952. In fact, it only did so when it had concrete evidence that its support for the firing of Lantz could be presented as *preventing* bad publicity. In April 1952, Welfare Council president Fred Fraser got a call from Frank Doyle, associate managing editor of the city's leading daily, the *Chronicle-Herald.* Doyle told Fraser that the newspaper had been receiving increasing numbers of complaints about CAS but had not published them. If something was not done soon to remedy the problem, he said, the newspaper would have to speak out. He knew that CAS had had the recommendation to fire Lantz since the preceding October. Indeed, it had probably been Doyle who had told the council a year earlier that the newspapers did not want to "hurt the whole welfare structure," but they thought there was something wrong when $14,000 of donors' gifts was being paid by the chest to an inadequate agency.[27] With Doyle's phone call in April 1952, handling "the situation" in secret, as Kennedy would have preferred, was no longer possible. By October 1952, Lantz had been forced to resign.

She was replaced at the beginning of 1953 by a young social worker and war veteran, Thomas Blue, who had graduated in social work from the University of Toronto in 1948 and had since worked both in the federal family allowance division in Newfoundland and as a CAS director elsewhere in Nova Scotia. That year the provincial subsidy to the Halifax CAS rose approximately 350 percent, to almost $9,000. This seems to be a clear extension of the grading grant principle, introduced in Nova Scotia in 1950, by which the provincial department's assessment of the quality of CAS's management determined the extent to which it was willing to subsidize a society's operations.[28] The pressure for more spending on social work labour in CAS had so long been a point of conflict that this additional funding from the province can hardly have been unwelcome in the chest. With MacKinnon's former staffer, George Hart, at the helm of the chest and MacKinnon himself an active member of council, it is not surprising that neither Community Chest nor Welfare Council resisted the increase of public funding as an unwarranted expansion of the state.

Throughout the 1950s and into the early 1960s, the Halifax CAS sought increased funding for staff salaries, both from the chest and from the provincial and municipal governments. Under way was a near-constant negotiation of the burdens of financing and caseload, with mandated responsibilities moving back and forth across the public/private line. At the time of Lantz's departure, Kennedy investigated the potentially money-saving possibility that CAS might be closed down and its work folded into the responsibilities of the chest's main family services agency. Her queries in that direction were discouraged by the CWC, and she was advised that this sort of planning might best be done by the Welfare Council, where both public and private, chest and non-chest, agencies were represented. In 1955, with an increased allocation from the chest, CAS was supposed to take back the responsibilities for adoptions and family allowance supervision that, because of its staff shortages, it had earlier passed off to the provincial department.[29] In 1960, when CAS had to take on the caseload of the defunct Halifax Infants' Home, it managed to get expanded funding from both the government and the chest. But, contrary to the flow of mandates in Halifax, the CWC nationally took the view that programs that were "very costly" and that "involve[d] the use of police power" – both features of child protection work – were increasingly coming to be seen as public responsibilities.[30]

The ongoing perplexity about the public/private boundary was again reflected in a 1962 Halifax Welfare Council study that proposed something very like what Kennedy had suggested in 1952: the amalgamation of CAS and the Family Services Bureau, with the combined agency taking on the child welfare casework that the provincial department was still doing. By 1964, CAS was incurring significant deficits ($4,700 in 1964, with a $10,000 shortfall anticipated in 1965). In this context, the chest no longer defended CAS's private status as depending on its operating budget being privately funded. Rather, the chest insisted that financing most of the work of CAS was a public responsibility, regardless of the role of the volunteer board.[31] A 1964 study of the Halifax CAS by an Ontario expert concluded that the province should supply CAS's operating budget. That year the city refused to increase the CAS grant, and in March 1965 the united appeals president told his board that the member agencies' needs were greater than the amount that fundraising could collect in the city.[32] A month later MacKinnon summoned chest officials to discuss the prospect of increased assistance from the province for CAS.[33] By CAS's 1966-67 budget year, the balance in CAS funding had decisively changed.

The reason for MacKinnon's new approach to the chest was that, in the spring of 1965, MacKinnon was preparing to bring to CAS's perpetual problems of funding and staffing the new money that would flow into the province via the Canada Assistance Plan (CAP). CAP is best known for increasing the federal contribution to social assistance programs (i.e., "relief" or "welfare"). But one of CAP's other components was a new commitment to federal cost sharing in the funding of non-governmental social services, such as the Children's Aid Societies. Planning for CAP had been under way among federal and provincial welfare bureaucrats since 1960. In 1965, politicians in central Canada brought to the fore proposals to include child welfare in the charmed circle of cost-shared programs. CAS and Community Chest leaders must immediately have noticed the striking resemblance between their own fundraising arguments and the logic of these policy proposals. Spending money on preventive work with children, all agreed, was a means of reducing dependency (and therefore unemployment relief claims) among adults. Inadequate funding had meant excessive caseloads and poor performance in preventive work. Even the administrative arguments that bureaucrats made were similar. Just as there was no good reason to have different funding sources for the Family Services Bureau and CAS when they both handled cases of child neglect and abuse, so too there was no real difference between the children who were helped through mother's allowances and those supported through CAS wardship arrangements. In the design of legislation, as in the allocation of the functions among private agencies, amalgamation was the best path to cost savings and rational service delivery.[34] The debates in the chest and council circles during the 1940s and 1950s about how to organize and finance child welfare thus stocked the policy shelves with arguments based on private agencies' and fundraisers' history of planning and financing child welfare. The carriers of these arguments to the CAP planning table included Fred MacKinnon and nationally R.E.G. (Dick) Davis of the CWC, both of whom participated actively in the CAP discussions. They brought to national policy making the arguments that had been honed in the CWC and in local settings such as Halifax.[35]

While the chests supplied ideas to the policy developers, CAP would make a more material contribution to the chests. CAP was welcomed in 1966 as promising to solve the chests' chronic problem of campaign shortfalls. Halifax's chest director since 1958, Arch Jackson, told the 1966 annual general meeting that he had an eight-point plan for solving that problem. Four of his eight points had to do with making sure that privately raised "volunteer dollars" were not spent on agencies whose work was "fully the responsibility of government." A month later chest president Gordon H. Thompson told board members that the record of "near-misses" in chest campaigns could be changed if private charity was careful to stay out of areas of public responsibility. He acknowledged that donor support had never risen to the extent required by private charities, but he thought that now the "gap between funds raised and funds required for expansion of services" could be closed. Here, in speaking of expansion, he was asserting the demonstration role of private charity. The implementation of this view of private charity was launched two months later, when the chest's budget committee, in agreement with the Welfare Council, decided to phase out the budget for CAS, except insofar as CAS developed new services.[36]

In 1952, Gwladys Kennedy had suggested to the CWC that the chest budget committee might make the City Council's granting decisions for social agencies.[37] In making this proposal, she had shown her allegiance to the classical elite democracy, of the sort Whitton had espoused, in which chest boards were "more representative" than city aldermen. She had not understood, it seems, the emerging logic of the new public-private relationship. By 1958, when her successor, George Hart, left the Halifax Community Chest to go on to national prominence in the Canadian Welfare Council, the province was experiencing its New Deal under Stanfield's Conservatives, and increased provincial responsibility for the Children's Aid Societies was a sign of the emerging shift in the balance of welfare responsibility. The reconstruction of relations among social work planning, the state, and fundraisers had ended the careers of two women who had been pioneers of modern welfare work.[38] But even though these individuals lost their power, both CAS and the chest emerged from these events enlarged and still influential in the world of social policy.

Reconstructing Chest-Council Relations

As well as illustrating the continuing power of the private side of welfare work, even in the changed postwar child welfare regime, the interconnected stories of Lantz and Kennedy also show how relations with the emerging welfare state were changing the relations between the Community Chests and the Welfare Councils. The chests were losing some of their weight as sole funders, and the councils were adding or expanding their public welfare sections. The agencies represented on the councils were often restive at the budgetary restrictions imposed by the chests, but they also knew that their own viability depended on the effectiveness of the chests. Criticism of the chest, then, was a dangerously double-edged sword for the agencies to brandish. Yet it was a tempting tool because the fundraisers were extremely alert to public criticism. The Halifax chest may have had a reputation for conservatism in national social work networks, but its secretiveness was only an extreme example of a bias that was present to some extent in all chest fundraising. Criticism of any part of the private welfare apparatus was to be avoided, especially around campaign time. For example, when the Children's Hospital left the Vancouver chest in 1947, canvassers were warned to speak very diplomatically on this subject to avoid offending this popular charity's many supporters.[39] The move to a new head office in Vancouver in 1948 was publicized but with care not to "adversely affect the campaign."[40] In Ottawa, later in the 1950s, worry about the operations of the Big Brothers organization (possibly about sexual issues) was framed as a failure to meet professional standards that, in affecting the image of the chest, risked harming the fundraising campaign.[41]

Public relations considerations thus tied agencies and fundraisers together like partners in a three-legged race. While the agencies ultimately needed the fundraisers more than the fundraisers needed them, a successful fundraising campaign did depend on the co-operation of the member agencies. Some canvassers came from agency boards; agency staff served as speakers and sources of promotional information; some agencies would host tours for the public.[42] "Popular" agencies, which usually meant child-serving ones, could seriously embarrass the chest by leaving it.[43] Agencies were apparently shifting from the supplicant mode of the chests' early years to a more assertive posture. Halifax's council director, Gwendolyn Shand (not to be confused with the other Gwendolen), wrote that the council disliked having to disagree with the chest, but "it is the responsibility of a Council to protect and to fight for its agencies, when necessary ... We would even be justified ... in exerting more pressure."[44] Chests began to hear demands from more agencies for funding that was adequate to hire qualified, professional staff and provide a high standard of service.[45] The three new, university-level schools of social work (bringing Canada's total to five by 1946) equipped their students with a body of expertise and a self-perception as autonomous professionals that heated up the simmering conflict with volunteers, especially board members.[46] And the continuing shortage of social work labour made it possible for younger social workers, especially the even scarcer men, to back their views by threatening to leave.[47] The ferment that Fred MacKinnon, himself a formally trained social worker, fostered in the Halifax Welfare Council was thus simply one example of this larger process in which social workers sought better funding for their agencies or related goals and used the threat of bad publicity or other forms of pressure to try to extract concessions from the chests.[48]

Elsewhere in the country, other conflicts between chests and welfare councils also centred on who would define social work standards, who would plan services, and who would allocate funds.[49] In general, this was the problem of social planning, linked in one direction to business rationalization and in the other to economic planning, the hallmark (to some eyes) of communism. In Canada, as elsewhere in the North Atlantic world, planning for postwar reconstruction was framed in terms of freedom versus tyranny, efficiency versus waste and injustice.[50] Prime Minister Mackenzie King's mantra in the postwar years was that "the planning and direction of government must be exercised in such a way as to increase, and not to decrease, the opportunities for individual freedom and initiative."[51] In 1943, Ottawa's chest and council director, Joy Maines, also signalled an awareness, from a social worker's standpoint, of the ideological landmines that studded the route toward a systematic approach to meeting needs: "'Social planning' is a phrase that is sometimes avoided because it has been seized upon for political purposes." The implicit solution she offered, in a sentence, prophesied a political strategy that only began truly to be implemented in social services by "client" involvement following the welfare rights movement of the 1970s: "Planning becomes offensive only when there is lack of participation on the part of those for whom planning is done."[52] In the postwar period, this ideological tension mapped onto the contrast between coercive totalitarianism versus capitalist freedom, a pattern of association that would provide both fresh material for fundraising and fresh ammunition for the united appeals' critics.[53] But within the federated fundraising movement in the late 1940s and early 1950s, this war of ideologies also had immediate practical implications for the relations of chests and councils.

With vocabulary such as the "open society" versus "serfdom" available for their use, chests and councils sought in their internal structures to represent constitutionally the integration of voluntary citizen leadership with authoritative planning by unelected experts. Donors were figured as expressing their free, and likely sentimental, choice in the marketplace of charity, persuaded by the sales efforts of the campaign team, while social work planners sought to set campaign targets that met objectively defined needs for which a rational case could readily be made. In the following chapter, I will address the rhetorical strategies by which participants in the chest system sought to integrate these different projects. Here the point is that this problem also existed and had to be addressed at the mere and messy level of local interests, both institutional and individual.

Ottawa, like Vancouver, had managed the problem of reconciling campaigners and welfare experts by maintaining one person as the director of both the fundraising chest and the planning council. This joint position had been senior social worker Joy Maines' role since 1936.[54] When she departed to head up the Canadian Association of Social Workers in 1945, her replacement, Sidney T. Smith, survived five years under the relentless workload it entailed. (He left social work entirely after his ordeal in the Ottawa chests.) In 1951, American fundraiser John Yerger took on the job Smith had vacated but quickly parlayed his success as a fundraiser into a separation of the two roles. In 1953, Joseph Laycock was hired to head up Ottawa's Welfare Council. That year a long-time volunteer leader in both planning and fundraising, Beverley Thorburn, exacted a promise from Yerger that the council's planning would continue to influence the allocation decisions of the chests' budget committees.[55]

In Vancouver, simmering conflicts between big donors and social worker Marjorie Bradford, the wartime director of both chest and council, heated up to a fully boiling power struggle after she headed off to do refugee relief work for the United Nations. The donors won, at first, with the appointment of businessman Hugh Allan as the new director. But the council remained part of the chest as a division parallel on the organizational chart to the campaign section. Directed initially by a young woman, Dorothy Klingler, to whom Allan failed to accord adequate professional respect, the planning division of the chest had a bumpy start. After Klingler's departure, one CWC official, Nora Lea, was actually warning professionally trained women not to apply for Klingler's old job because of the difficulty of working with Allan. By August 1946, Klingler had been replaced by the very diplomatic Ivor Jackson, who was no professional but a veteran of the federation's early years. As I will show below, this led to effective co-operation between chest and council in at least one policy area. In 1953, Allan left to run for political office, to be replaced by a young social worker, Howard Naphtali, whose relations with the council in the 1950s were largely congenial.[56] In each of these cities, reconstructing charity entailed conflict between chests and councils. The solution in each was to appoint new personnel, usually younger men.

Typified in the Halifax story by Fred MacKinnon, George Hart, and Thomas Blue, these were a new generation of social workers, a cohort that included an increased proportion of men, usually relatively young and usually war veterans, who displaced more senior women in social work's higher administrative ranks.[57] As Halifax's Gwendolyn Shand would write in 1955, "many positions which had been traditionally filled by women, are now being invaded by the men."[58] It was a gender transition that was also a generational one as the social workers of the pioneering 1920s, nearing the end of their working lives, faced the daunting challenge of negotiating a new relationship between government and private charity. As James Struthers argues, the association of masculinity with managerial roles had always militated against the upward occupational mobility of women social workers. But in these cities, the replacement of women directors by men also shows that the postwar context had made masculinity more compellingly a requirement of management in private charity. Working with and, as necessary, challenging the mainly male heads of provincial and federal departments were likely additional reasons for boards who associated maleness with public leadership to prefer male applicants. While this pattern was bad news for women's equality in the social work profession, it marked the persisting and even increasing prestige and importance in the 1950s of privately funded charities. If the fundraising game had been reduced to insignificance by the incursions of the welfare state, then ambitious, smart, young men such as John Yerger, Howard Naphtali, and George Hart would not have sought these jobs. Rather than being reactionary conservers of an old welfare regime, they were active participants in the creation of a new public-private relationship.[59]

Shifting the Burden: Fundraising and the Unemployment Relief Question

In Halifax, child protection services had been the central issue in the restructuring of public-private relations. The chest's attempts before 1952 to keep costs down in this area clearly subordinated the quality of service to the limits on what donors appeared to be willing to give. After 1952, with two young men from the new generation of social workers directing both CAS and the chest, an alliance between public and private officials emerged. A lesson that boards of private agencies and the chest everywhere might well have learned from this process was that expansion of public provision, government "takeover" if you like, had the benefit of relieving private charities' fundraisers from the constant pressure to increase campaign targets and risk failure in meeting their objectives. In this inference, which appears paradoxical only from a doctrinaire standpoint, government expansion was not inimical to the charitable sector but could in fact make charities more successful.[60] In Nova Scotia's child welfare story, this logic merely resigned the chest to a project that had begun within the state. In Vancouver, however, the same fundraiser's logic, combined with other calculations of what was good for the chest's survival, spurred the chest to initiate a campaign for greater public spending on unemployment assistance.

In 1956, with the Unemployment Assistance Act, the federal government finally accepted, after decades of resistance, that it had to take more responsibility in providing income support to employable people who were unemployed and in need. As Struthers has shown, this development was the result of three main considerations by the federal government. It wanted to avoid unduly expanding UI entitlements, it needed to give the provinces something in return for federal control over income tax, and it felt a political threat from the pressure applied by private charities.[61] In his discussion of the last element, Struthers refers interchangeably to "Canadian social work" and "private charities" as the source of pressure. In his account, there seems to be no need to distinguish, within those general categories, between fundraisers and social workers. But Gale Wills, in a book focused on the tensions between business-based fundraisers and service-oriented social workers, argues that, in Toronto, the fight for unemployment assistance (UA) was carried on by the social workers in the Welfare Council, not by the fundraisers in the chest. Her apparent implication is that, in this crucial phase of the expansion of the welfare state, fundraisers were at best indifferent and at worst hostile to the expansion of statutory entitlements to unemployment relief. But in Halifax, Ottawa, and Vancouver, fundraisers' commitment to the survival and expansion of social services, financed by donations, dictated a commitment to the expansion of the welfare state with respect to income assistance. For example, Halifax's chest director George Hart, in a 1957 debate about adjustments to the province's poor law, insisted that private welfare agencies could not cope with the effects of inadequate public assistance. "There are dozens of families in Nova Scotia now near to starvation," he said dramatically, and according to journalist Mary Casey he drew the inference that the impossible demands on private welfare agencies were caused by the inadequate public relief provisions for such struggling families. And in Ottawa, the chest director was an essential member of delegations to the provincial government when the city sought improved funding for municipal relief.[62] By exploring the Vancouver story in some detail, we can see how and why both the fundraising and service-delivering elements of private charities were important advocates for better public relief. In the postwar period, neither was any longer willing to act as the safety valve for an inadequate public system.[63]

That said, redefining roles in relief was very difficult. Already in the late 1930s, the chests had already begun in the late 1930s to pressure municipalities to improve their relief programs, on the argument that the subsistence level of support was a government responsibility. And weathering the wartime critique of charity had prompted fundraisers publicly to promote the notion that chest agencies met needs other than subsistence ones. In the postwar period, however, the challenge was to make this division of responsibilities work.

In Vancouver, the chest and council's activity in this work was shaped significantly by four people: Hugh Allan, Ivor Jackson, Dorothy Klingler, and Ann Angus. The gender competition that Wills has described for Toronto in this period was also evident in Vancouver's chest-council relations in the 1940s. Allan and Klingler got off to a bad start. Klingler, a young, American, professionally trained social worker, came to the council staff job without realizing that Allan was the director of both the chest and the council, newly combined under Allan's directorship in 1946. This meant that he was her boss. Allan epitomized the sort of chest leader whom social workers generally disliked: he had been involved in hospital fundraising and management but had otherwise no social work experience. He was, moreover, fresh from a high administrative position in the military, and, although reportedly a charming man, he was strongly committed to managing through chain of command. He was hired in a job search in which being a man was specified as a requirement, and he reportedly tended not to take women seriously as equals. In a psychoanalytic moment, Nora Lea of the CWC described Allan's efforts to monitor communications in the organization as "symptomatic of a deep-seated feeling of insecurity on the part of this man who is trying to resolve his fears by resisting any activity on the part of his member agencies without his knowledge." Before Allan's appointment, the volunteer members of the council had relied on Marjorie Bradford's effectiveness as a joint director in negotiating relations with the chest, and the bad match between Klingler and Allan left the volunteer agency representatives struggling to have their voices heard. Lea deplored Klingler's attempts to incite revolt among the agencies and urged them instead to "manipulate" Allan more carefully. Klingler quit, no doubt in frustration, leaving behind an unquiet chest-council relationship.[64]

On the volunteers' side, in 1949, a new leader named Ann Angus emerged in the council. University educated, a poet and an essayist, Angus was familiar with the highest levels of Canadian policy discussion through her warmly companionate marriage to Henry Forbes Angus, UBC political scientist and member of the Rowell-Sirois Commission. Ann had lived in Ottawa during her husband's wartime secondment to the federal public service and came back to Vancouver with the prestige and perspective of experience in another chest and council. An activist in the Vancouver Children's Aid Society (non-Catholic), she was part of the successful campaign to secure more municipal and provincial financing for the needs of Children's Aid wards and for the preventive work of the society. Between 1945 and 1947, these innovations in the public-private division of funding for child protection work in effect supplemented the resources available to all agencies through the chest. Effective in increasing her own agency's funding, Angus expressed some frustration in late 1947 with what she perceived as a reluctance to engage in "planning" by the chest and council's board of directors. Her frustration led her to take a more active role in the management of the chest and council: she served on the board between 1949 and 1952 and was chair of the social planning committee during 1951. While she was chair, she arranged for a study of the need for a referral centre to help people in crisis and to "interpret to the citizens the services of both public and private agencies."[65]

Finally, Ivor Jackson, who replaced Klingler in the head staff position of the council, worked successfully with both the chest and the council. Not himself a trained social worker, he was genuinely committed to innovation in social work. During his time as council director (1946-52), he supported research into new approaches to sexual psychopathy, alcoholism, drug addiction, disability services, and delinquency issues. As well as engaging in these efforts to expand the scope of private welfare work, Jackson succeeded during his tenure in having the city relief office (officially the Social Service Department) made a member of the chest's social planning committee. As he pointed out to the chest's board in 1947, if the private agencies were to become a small minority of health and welfare services, then a planning body that included only private agencies would cease to be of use. He was aware that unemployment would shape the charities' work, and he knew that the private and public agencies needed to make plans together for their respective roles. A veteran of the Welfare Federation's homeless men committee in the 1930s, he was, however, strongly opposed to any engagement of private charities in unemployment relief work.[66]

Nonetheless, contingencies seemed repeatedly to return to the chests' agencies the responsibility of giving people money for subsistence. These contingencies may be sorted into two types. One was government aversion to taking responsibility for relief. Between 1945 and 1955, every level of government was trying hard to escape having to support unemployed workers whose needs were not met by social insurance. This avoidance was part of the larger process in which the fiscal relations of the Canadian federation were being renegotiated. By 1947, every province except Ontario and Quebec had agreed to withdraw from certain tax fields so that the federal government could expand its revenue base and thus deliver new or expanded welfare programs, including unemployment relief. But when the provinces did not get the promised return, in the form of federal grants, they found their budgets inadequate for their health and welfare responsibilities. So they disputed the proposition that they were responsible for the care of employable people who were unemployed. The federal government's assumption through UI of responsibility for some of these people, they argued, meant that it was responsible for all.[67] At the same time, in each province in this study, there was in the mid-1940s an expert assessment of municipal-provincial relations in the matter of social assistance. In British Columbia, the Goldenberg report recommended that the province assume complete responsibility for unemployment relief, as did George Davidson's study of Nova Scotia. In practice, none of the three provinces did so.[68] Overall, governments at every level, from the local to the national, faced the anxiety of not knowing how much or whether unemployment levels would rise, and each wanted therefore not to acquire a fixed responsibility for an expense of uncertain dimensions. Government budgets at all levels were being strained by other kinds of welfare spending too. Expenditures for hospitals, veterans' services, and child welfare, in particular, were increasing.[69] In this context, representatives of each level of government took hard positions, limiting or denying their responsibility for unemployment relief.[70] As a result, unemployed workers inevitably turned to charities.

The other obstacle to change was that the definition of "employable" was not a matter of plain fact. It was a matter of judgment. The regulations for social assistance in British Columbia required a medical certificate to attest to unemployability, but when a relief applicant had no organic malfunction municipal administrators were empowered to judge his or her degree of fitness to work. Moreover, social workers argued, there were psychological impairments to employability that, though not medically certifiable, were real. For instance, in the course of the 1947-48 campaign to get new UA legislation, some Vancouver social workers described cases of breadwinners whose "inadequate personalities" made it difficult for them to get or keep a job and whose dependents therefore had suffered "acute hardship." They questioned whether the threat of such hardship would be enough to make these "inadequate" breadwinners truly employable. They further queried whether it was "wise" in terms of "eventual cost to the community" to withhold food and shelter assistance at the risk of harming children. The new head of the city's Social Service Department may himself have been sympathetic to such concerns, describing his office as having moved on from "giving assistance in kind to giving kindness in assistance."[71] Another determinant of employability, as the provincial department of welfare acknowledged in 1947, was the state of the labour market. People who might have found work or a place in the forces during the war could now be rejected by less desperate employers. "It is impossible," a chest committee concluded, "to determine, except on purely arbitrary lines, as to whether or not a person is employable or unemployable, unless one relates the degree of employability to the opportunities for suitable employment, and the ability of the unemployed person to not only obtain but continue in employment."[72]

In the context of legislation based on "employability," these ambiguities in the term became maddeningly pertinent to people in need as government agencies, and the chest itself, all sought to avoid expanded responsibilities for relief. In 1946, "GJ," a member of the Greater Vancouver Unemployed Organization (GVUO), wrote about what happened when determinations of employability conflicted. The National Employment Service (NES) turned him away, claiming he was unable to work, but the city's Relief Office thought he was employable so denied him relief. For a worker to insist he was employable thus meant he had to turn to his neighbours for something to eat. Many workers, he argued, were thus trapped between the federal employment agency and the city relief authority. He concluded on a political note based on a class analysis: "The S.S. [NES] is working under control of police, the employers and government. The workers must to controll S.S. and the Relief Office throughout."[73] As far as the responsible provincial minister was concerned, however, a different sort of politics was required. In response to a letter from the GVUO's president, Provincial Secretary George Pearson wrote, also in 1946, that social assistance is "provided for persons who through sickness or other disabilities, are unable to provide for themselves. It is our view that Unemployed workers who exhaust their Unemployment Insurance and cannot obtain employment are the responsibility of the Federal Government and representations should be made to the Federal Government for an extension of Unemployment Benefits to such persons."[74]

For social workers in the Family Welfare Bureau, the problem was the heartbreaking inadequacy of what they could do for desperate people seeking help. As the bureau's director, Mary McPhedran, wrote, with dry understatement,

> We do not consider that a voluntary agency should assume responsibility for basic services such as food and shelter. Yet when families with small children come to us utterly destitute, and the public authorities tell us that they are unable to assist them if they are employable, we have been forced to do something about it. Our Relief account for the whole year could be easily used up in a few weeks for these families if we provided adequate maintenance. Consequently, anything we do for them is likely to be unsatisfactory from their point of view as well as from ours.

For the social workers of the Welfare Bureau, politics meant collecting data on relief cases and stories of people harmed by the UI regulations and collaboration with the chest's social planning committee in mounting a persuasive lobbying effort. Together with the chest and council, they sought to abolish "the distinct categories of 'employable' and 'unemployable'" so that "eligibility for public social assistance [would] be determined on the basis of actual need."[75] (In this goal, they foreshadowed a standard of eligibility that would not be embodied in legislation until the CAP of 1966.)

Although the Vancouver chest and council had begun a national lobbying effort on this question as early as April 1947, three years before the Canadian Welfare Council's national campaign, the Vancouver struggle over relief intensified in January 1948.[76] On January 13th, the *Vancouver Sun* published an editorial whose last sentence, apparently a mild suggestion, was experienced by the chest and council as a public relations disaster. The editorial described "six youths in their late teens," no more than "footloose youngsters," who found themselves in police court on vagrancy charges and at risk of jail time because they were unable to find work. The editorial praised the service that the Salvation Army provided to men who appeared in court on vagrancy charges but concluded that it "ought to have more assistance than it does, and other social agencies might well bestir themselves to lend a helping hand."[77] The Salvation Army had only recently joined the chest and council as a member agency: the chest campaign that had just finished (and failed) in the fall of 1947 had been only the second for the Salvation Army as a chest agency. If the salvationists had insufficient "assistance" and other social agencies were failing to "bestir" themselves, it might well have looked bad for the fundraisers. After all, they had been rather vocal, for years, about the success of their agencies in keeping youth out of the courts. Thus, the *Vancouver Sun*'s apparently subtle criticism, though softened by a velvety subjunctive, was nonetheless a stinging rebuke.

Not surprisingly, then, the chest and council responded. Director Hugh Allan wrote to the premier and to the deputy minister of welfare about the unemployed issue. Although his letters no longer exist, the fundraisers' earlier and later stands on this question suggest that the letters must have contained a request for the government to contribute funds to help in unemployment relief. The result of the letters was a subsidy from the province for an emergency referral centre at the Salvation Army hostel, where, between February 12th and March 5th, meals and beds were supplied to men who otherwise would have been rejected by the city's relief office. On February 24th, during the weeks when the referral centre existed, the annual meeting of the chest and council took place. In his speech at that meeting, Allan called for the dominion government to take financial responsibility for unemployment relief. His speech launched a two-month campaign directed at Prime Minister King, Minister of Labour Milton Gregg, Vancouver MPs, and BC senator Ian MacKenzie. The Family Welfare Bureau supplied ammunition to the chest in the form of information about the scope of the problem and the kinds of homeless and hungry men, women, and children who were casualties in the wars of definition and jurisdiction. Ivor Jackson orchestrated the campaign. Hugh Allan signed the letters and so asserted the interest of fundraisers in the question. In the letters to politicians, according to Jackson, it was emphasized that "the Chest and Council are not only concerned with the immediate situation but with the general policy of excluding employable persons from eligibility for assistance. When proposals have been made regarding the extension of eligibility for Unemployment Insurance benefits or an increase in the amount of benefits[,] we have tried to point out that the underlying weakness of the whole social security programme remains the same so long as there are no comprehensive social assistance provisions."[78]

One of the documents that Jackson prepared for this campaign concluded with a two-pronged jab, emphasizing the danger to the state and the insufficiency of private charity: "The whole matter is one of considerable urgency as private funds are not available to relieve the distress which is increasingly reported by our member agencies and as a result a serious volume of criticism and antagonism is being built up against the Department [of Welfare] and the Government."[79] Indeed, the MP for Vancouver-Burrard, opposition member and war hero Colonel Cecil Merritt, took full political advantage of the opportunity to link the chest's failure and government relief administration.[80]

Although the campaign in the winter of 1948 was especially intense, Vancouver's chest and council persisted in lobbying for unemployment assistance over the following ten years and for improved social assistance, generally, throughout the 1950s. From the city and the province, they repeatedly sought funding for a referral centre that would both help the unemployed and provide credible data on which the case for federal participation in unemployment relief might be based. In turn, the city sought their support in pressuring the federal government. George C. Miller, at various times a Conservative Coalition MLA and the mayor of Vancouver, led the attack on the King government, an attack that briefly succeeded when, in a 1948 federal by-election, a CCFer defeated the Liberal incumbent in Vancouver Centre. In the run-up to both the 1949 federal election and the 1953 provincial and federal elections, the chest and council board convened meetings of the mayor, MPs, the city social services officer, and leading relief agencies to take the message to Victoria and Ottawa that the promise of federal responsibility proposed in the 1945 Green Book had to be fulfilled.[81]

Important though lobbying was as a form of political action, it had limits. In 1950, Hugh Allan's frustration was growing as Premier Byron Johnson denied that there was a "serious problem," even while federal Minister of Labour Milton Gregg and Mayor Charles Thompson acknowledged that there was.[82] Allan noted that, because of government inaction, the Legion and the unions were no longer (if they ever had been) content to accept the chest as the leader in this cause. Instead, they had organized their own lobby group:

the Veterans Labour Action Committee.[83] Because of the chest's history of seeking to foster labour participation in fundraising, this was a worrisome development, and in Cold War Vancouver it must also have seemed a potential home for the class-conscious politics of the GVUO. Allan's own solution to the frustrations of the chest-led lobbying campaign was to resign as chest and council director and to run for provincial office himself, in Vancouver-Burrard. A riding that had been home to one provincial welfare minister (George Weir) and, after 1953, would elect another (Eric Martin), Vancouver-Burrard had shifted loyalties across the political spectrum, returning between 1934 and 1952 CCF members, Liberals, and both Liberal and Conservative coalitionists. Like his allies Merritt and Miller, Allan ran as a Conservative, only to be crushed along with the rest of that party in the Social Credit landslide of June 1953.[84] However unlucky his choice of party, Allan's running for office indicates that electoral politics had become important in the chest's effort to escape the burden of unemployment relief. It must have been clear to Allan that private charities' fundraisers needed more vigorous allies in the provincial government. Given how thoroughly the chest was involved in the intergovernmental politics of unemployment assistance in this period, it is hardly surprising that a chest activist crossed the line from social to electoral politics.

The chest's reasons for engaging in UA issues were complex. Both principle and institutional interest played a part. Indeed, the two sorts of motivations were thoroughly blended when the chest formulated and defended the public-private division of welfare responsibilities. On the institutional side, unemployment relief posed a distinct threat to the chests' interests because of the unpredictability of unemployment crises. In the chest method, budget allocations to agencies were supposed to be set for the coming year based on the previous year's expenditures and anticipated needs. The policy of keeping funding to an absolute minimum made the chest's budget committee unsympathetic to proposals for open-ended allocations for emergency relief. Yet agency directors could not predict for any given year how many families or individuals would appear, destitute, in their offices.[85] So it was entirely possible that, in a given year, an agency's emergency relief fund, meant to tide people over until some other, regular source of income could be found, might suddenly be exhausted. It was not that the agencies were faced with supporting all of the employable unemployed. But even the small numbers who appeared at their doors might quickly use up their budgeted funds. In

January of 1948, for example, the Family Welfare Bureau's report on relief applicants listed only twenty-one relief cases, all men and all but three with children to feed. To the bureau, this counted as a crisis because it had so little to give these families, and it knew that at least fifteen of them could anticipate absolutely no money other than what the bureau could give them. Forty-four children under sixteen thus had for their prospect of regular meals only this private charity's inadequate relief fund to rely on.[86] In the winter of 1950, the chest office itself hired a social worker for two months to field requests for assistance. The worker responded to 160 applications, directing the 110 of them judged to be completely destitute to the Salvation Army, the Catholic Charities, and the Returned Soldiers' Club. Of the total 160, only a few were eligible for public assistance. Allan pleaded with the city to relax its eligibility regulations, but he was refused.[87]

While it may seem that these small numbers were hardly an insupportable burden for private charities – surely only a few thousand dollars would have covered the need – the results of the 1948 and 1949 campaigns put this amount in a different light. The 1948 campaign had been the first to meet its goal since 1945. Even the campaign chairman for 1948 had acknowledged, however, that the objective ($775,000) was at least $125,000 less than the agencies needed.[88] Moreover, chest president E.V. Chown pointed out that the success had been the result of a high-pressure, post-campaign canvass of prominent business firms. The "success" had been achieved by suggesting to the owners of these businesses that, "if the Chest failed to reach its objective it would have to go out of existence."[89] The lesson for goal setting was not lost. In the summer of 1949, even before the agencies' budgets were in, Lyman Trumbull, the chairman of the fall campaign (and a prominent member of the Conservative Party), urged the board to get started on deciding the amount to be sought. From his point of view, that amount had to be "a realistic one, in order to ensure the carrying forward of our success of last year."[90] The goal set for the fall of 1949 was $850,000, an increase of $75,000 from the previous year but $50,000 less than what the agencies had requested. The results were a disappointing $751,539, which may well have suggested to Trumbull that his view of "realistic" had been discounted.[91] Allan speculated that uncertain business conditions had worked against them and noted toward the end of the campaign that prospects were giving as "a defensive argument" the 3 percent sales tax and an increase in "hospital dues payable on the 1st of October."[92] The campaign shortfall left chest president Chown with the demoralizing task of convening a special meeting of the agencies' representatives to discuss how the chest would deal with the consequences.[93]

The solution settled on at that meeting represented, on the one hand, the application of normal business administration principles and, on the other, the kernel of an ongoing public relations problem. After several options were discussed, the president proposed, and those attending apparently accepted, a sort of compromise. Instead of imposing a standard reduction to all budgets of 12 percent (to match the percentage shortfall), the chest would use money from its surplus fund to augment what was available from the campaign. But this did not mean that a full \$850,000 would be provided. That would have drained entirely the surplus fund, which was, at the end of 1949, \$58,360. It had been as large as \$112,604 in 1944.

How was it that, even though the Vancouver Community Chest had met its campaign goal only three times since 1930, and even though agencies repeatedly cried out for larger budgets, there was a surplus fund? The answer lies in the fact that such funds were and are part of the normal business budgeting process: they are meant to ensure that funds will be available to cover spending commitments even if unexpected costs arise or anticipated income does not materialize. Additions to the chests' surplus account in any given year usually came from three sources. One was revenue from unexpected payment of pledges. Every year, in the chests' accounts, an amount of approximately 1 percent was deducted from the campaign "results," under the heading of unfulfilled pledges. Minus that amount, the pledge total was the amount of money that realistically would be available for agency spending. If more pledges were honoured than expected, then this revenue, which usually was about a quarter of 1 percent, or approximately \$3,000, would be credited to the surplus account. Another source of money was funds allotted to particular agencies' budgeted purposes in the previous year but not actually spent for those purposes. These funds had to be returned to the chest and were credited to the surplus account. Also, interest earned on the chests' considerable bank balances went into their surplus accounts.

Even though these accounts were augmented in these ways every year, the chests' books could also show that the chest and council spent more money in a particular year than had come in during that year. When that was so, the shortage was made up (and the books balanced) by a transfer from the surplus account. Even in years when the public gave insufficient funds for the agencies' purposes, then, the result was not unpaid rent and unpaid staff. For example, during 1950, when the campaign for 1950 funds in the fall of 1949 had fallen short by nearly $99,000, precisely $2,892.59 from the surplus fund ended up being paid out to cover agency expenditures approved by the finance committee.[94] The campaign shortfall had indeed meant that less was spent by the agencies than they had anticipated in the estimates on which the goal had been partly based. But on the other hand, when there were unavoidable expenses beyond what the campaign revenue could cover, the surplus account provided a cushion.

For members of the public to whom balance sheets and accounting were unfamiliar, the mysteries of the surplus account may have seemed impossibly remote from the question of whether the chest method was succeeding or failing and whether there was really enough money to increase agencies' emergency relief budgets in times of sudden spikes in unemployment. The chest's budgeting methods were, however, the source of both the real moral question and the public relations problem that unemployment relief presented. At issue was the question of what kind of emergency might warrant spending of funds held in reserve. If a children's hospital or shelter suddenly lost part of its roof in a windstorm, there needed to be funds to pay for its repair, and the surplus account would be adequate. But meeting the income needs of the unemployed and their dependents if there was a sudden sharp increase in unemployment would quickly drain the chest's surplus account, which would immediately make all of its other services more vulnerable.[95] The chest's budgeting principles were adequate to meet the contingencies at work in social services agencies, but it might well have seemed wrong to set aside a large enough reserve to compensate for the limits of the nascent UI system when such a large reserve would be maintained at the cost of services such as child protection and home nursing care. This blend of practicality and principle, then, explains why the chest would not permit agencies to take on, without any constraint, the provision of relief to the unemployed. But the hidden workings of the surplus account must have raised suspicions about the reality of "the absolute minimum" when, in its absence, agencies survived.

If refusing to act as relief agencies was necessary to protect other chest services, then it was also essential in public relations terms. This might not seem so obvious. After all, when the chest held to its principles and refused to increase the resources for emergency relief, it was vulnerable to accusations that it was not acting as a good representative of the community's neighbourly impulse. The general public still tended to think that the chest was a relief agency, and, if the needs of the unemployed were not met, then the chest's power of fundraising risked being harmed.[96] But the chest fought this perception. When chest representatives spoke to the public in this period about what would happen if a campaign did not make its target, they were careful not to say that the unemployed would be without food and shelter.[97] And, more importantly, the chest fought with governments. To be seen to be acting as the community's conscience, the chest had to badger governments about their obligation to meet the relief responsibility.

Also at stake for the fundraisers in maintaining a clear separation from relief giving was the risk of a certain kind of donor resistance. In British Columbia, taxation resources had been turned over to the federal government so that a national unemployment relief program would be implemented. So far it had not been. Given the importance of that grievance in BC politics, some donors would have been reluctant to give charity dollars to a purpose that their taxes had been intended to meet.[98] It is hard to imagine that the kind of pressure tactics used in 1948 would have succeeded again if the large donors who were also large taxpayers thought that the chest was asking them, in effect, to pay a second time for unemployment relief. When, on the national scale, chests and councils protested that the burden of relief was beyond their power to carry, it was not that they had tried but were unable to carry that burden. It was that the responsibilities they understood to be theirs alone – for social services – became more difficult to fulfill when governments failed to carry out their responsibility for the income needs of unemployed workers. The chests protested not the size of the relief burden but the mere fact that they were forced into relief giving at all.

Public-Private Politics: Neither Competition nor Rescue

Both the Halifax and the Vancouver stories I have told in this chapter show the complexity of the work entailed in developing a relationship between private agencies, the chest, and the state. The politics involved included social ones of several different types, from ego-fuelled conflicts between strong-minded individuals, to class antagonisms, to gendered and generational ascriptions of incompetence. Fundraisers and service providers tangled on the question of what constituted a reasonable accounting of social needs, condensed into the single controversial figure of the annual campaign goal. "Dirty work at the crossroads"[99] was not unknown between chests and councils as various constituencies (volunteer board members, donors, and social workers) manoeuvred for position. Newspaper editors weighed in as a voice of "the public," seeking from politicians or fundraisers, or both, a better job of spending donor and taxpayer dollars.

Immersed on one level in these complex social politics, the fundraisers did their best at another level to use whatever power they could muster, together with social workers, to engage in the high politics of public policy. The chests and councils waded into the bureaucratic battle of fiscal federalism, trying to make governments fulfill what seemed to them to be obviously a public responsibility: providing subsistence income for all in need. In their individual cities and nationally through the Canadian Welfare Council, the fundraisers backed the campaign for a federal unemployment assistance act with the prestige and public influence of their well-to-do board members and their public relations machinery. When BC premier Bennett wanted to persuade Prime Minister St. Laurent to take action, he told him that Vancouver's agencies "had exhausted their funds."[100] Ottawa's mayor (and earlier chest movement leader), Charlotte Whitton, took the same message to Premier Frost in 1954 when, accompanied by the Ottawa chests' director, she sought provincial help for the city's relief budget.[101] In 1955, a leading volunteer in the Ottawa Community Chests, Lawrence Freiman, was at the helm of the Canadian Welfare Council when it won what James Struthers calls "its most significant policy victory ... in federal politics." That victory consisted of forcing Prime Minister St. Laurent into dealing with the provinces on UA, an undertaking that would inevitably mean federal participation in a cost-sharing scheme.[102]

This was a victory for social work, as Struthers says, to be sure. But social work here should be understood clearly to include the financial planning and campaigning parts of social work, not only the social work staff of the agencies and councils. Freiman was a department store owner, not a social worker, and the expertise he brought to the table was sales and promotion, the power to make people buy a fundraiser's message. The power to sell was a force for change as much as were policy principles in the history of the UA act of 1956. Freiman's credibility when he deplored the effect of government irresponsibility came in part from his reputation as an effective retailer, not to mention his family's long-standing support of the Liberal Party.[103] Freiman's constituency within the social work community was the fundraisers who wanted to set reachable goals and to achieve campaign successes. Freiman was able to give voice to their unhappiness about having their campaign targets pushed up and the image of the agencies tarnished when governments expected the agencies to deal with the problem of unemployment relief or soaring child welfare caseloads. Chest fundraising in those circumstances was like trying to sell overpriced merchandise or an unreliable model of car. Insofar as they looked to government to "rescue" private charity, it was not the relief program that they wanted rescued but the viability of their campaigns and the smaller, low-cost, non-relief agencies for which they believed they could raise sufficient funds. In short, the chests' insistence on federal participation in UA and (later) in child welfare was in the interests of effective fundraising as much as (if not more than) it was in aid of adequate funding for social work.

The expansion of the public side of the public/private division of welfare responsibilities was important to the fundraisers because it would protect the chests against most of the threats to campaign success. When federal money was made available to UA and (with CAP) to Children's Aid Societies, expansion of the state took two of the most expensive elements of social work out of the chest agencies' ambit. The increased public funding reduced the costs to the chests of private agency work and helped to keep campaign targets low and attainable. The problem of low social worker wages or inadequate staffing would be solved, or at least transferred to government hands, which would remove a long-standing irritant in the relations between the chests and the agencies. With these relationships soothed, the threat of damage that angry social workers posed to the chests' image and appeal would be reduced. To the extent that donor frustration came from constantly mounting targets combined with rising taxes, a clearer division of responsibilities would make it clear that charitable giving was not just double taxation. In that way, one excuse for not giving would be removed. And with unemployment relief shown to be clearly the responsibility of public, not private, agencies, the chests would be able nimbly to sidestep the left-wing critique of charity as an unnecessary exercise in whitewashing the exploitive labour market that produced needy families. Together these arguments trumped, for practical policy-making purposes, the anti-statist opposition that persisted in chest circles among the Board of Trade men who continued to serve as canvassers, campaign chairs, and board members. No doubt more than once some of these men, such as Vancouver's Ralph Baker, shocked the CWC's representatives with their "not very progressive" views.[104] But those views were irrelevant when it came to deciding how an ideologically diverse organization such as the chest and council of Greater Vancouver would wield its policy weight. What determined the support that that chest and others gave to UA or to public funding for child protection services was ultimately their interest in the success and therefore the survival of the federated fundraising method.

While militating for expanded public provision, the chests were thus at the same time vigorously defending the usefulness and viability both of private charities and of the chest method of raising funds for those services. Expansion of the welfare state presented a complex mix of opportunities and problems for the private side of welfare, so the choreographing of sophisticated new steps in the public-private dance was necessary for the chests' survival in the 1950s. But in addition to the expansion of public programs, there were other sources of danger and promise for social work in the postwar world. The culture of contribution in Canadian society was also being reshaped by actors and circumstances other than the federated fundraising movement. I now turn to the chests' engagement with these other forces in a cultural politics of citizenship.

7
Justice, Inclusion, and the Emotions of Obligation in 1950s Charity

In addition to finding a place in the policy processes of the welfare state, the Community Chest fundraisers shifted their appeals in the 1950s to adjust to the cultural logic of the new regime. Like their predecessors in the 1930s, these social advertisers looked around them at the methods of consumer advertising and within the general culture for materials that could be used for their purposes. Their fundamental purpose – to raise money – was unchanged from the 1930s. But since the 1930s, their accumulated record of success and failure, the expansion of the welfare state, and the development of the social work profession subtly altered their campaigns' purposes and changed the emphasis on particular themes. Specifically, the chests confirmed and sought to complement rather than to criticize the underpinning values of the universalist and socially inclusive postwar welfare regime. For the chests, a notion of inclusion had been part of their appeal from the beginning. It had been elite centred, rooted in classical notions of democracy, but it was less exclusive than particular religious or ethnic models of charity had been. In the 1950s, building on this practice, they would continue to welcome, and sometimes to arrange, the inclusion of people from diverse social backgrounds in their organizations. Universalist values underpinned rights-based, statutory forms of help, to which all were equally entitled. The chests, though not lawmakers, creatively presented equality of entitlement and the commonality of vulnerability as part of their fundraising toolkits. When they chimed in with the politicians who celebrated public programs' service to "all the people," the fundraisers were again building on their past – namely, the base-broadening strategies of the 1930s. In their postwar use of universalist and inclusive discourse, the chests bolstered their fundraising work with cultural materials that they had helped to create.

More challenging than incorporating universalist and inclusive values was the problem of how to make charitable emotions part of a fundraising discourse that could fit comfortably with the welfare state. For the chest fundraisers, there remained an inclination to present the objects of welfare work as different: weak, pitiable, and faultlessly vulnerable, like the images of fatherless families that had been routinely used in the interwar years. Such representations were emotional incitements to provide care – an essential element in the fundraiser's toolkit. But they were not obviously compatible with a liberal, state-centred vision of welfare as the egalitarian provision of security for all. An egalitarian vision implied that both citizens' obligations as taxpayers and citizens' rights as potential beneficiaries emerged from a single conception of individuals as generalizably alike in both responsibilities and need. In this context, could fundraisers continue to use the formerly effective images of the pitiable needy without seeming retrograde? Would Dickensian images of the poor as dangerous, horrifying, and utterly pathetic seem irrelevant and perhaps offensively sentimental to citizens who now assumed that economic growth, expanding private insurance services, and new social programs prevented or provided for real need? If the Angel of Mercy had retired to her Victorian roost, and the professional social worker had taken her place, then were appeals to modern science now inevitably more effective than emotional ones? After so many campaign failures, would a sense of futility finally harden the public to any and all appeals for the pitiable needy?

These questions point to a dilemma that may be described as the contradiction between universalist values and care values. In their struggle with this dilemma, fundraisers in the 1950s anticipated questions that, in recent years, have become politically and intellectually important. Political philosophers and ethicists since the 1980s have been working out how to integrate these two sets of values in a revitalized account of what social policy can and should do. Universalist values invoke the use of abstract principle as essential to the making of policy and make fairness the central virtue of social justice. In this view, the diversity of citizens' needs and social positions is acknowledged, but policy makers are enjoined to imagine the objects of policy as notionally identical in order to apply principles fairly. In daily language, this model is expressed in the idea that there is no real difference, except for luck, between the poor and the comfortable. This way of working toward justice in social policy is both supplemented and challenged by care values. As a supplement, care values add an awareness of the contextual specifics of need and respond to the views and values of those affected by policy. In addition, however, the care ethic casts doubt on whether blind justice is justice at all. It requires that good policy making be done with a clear eye to uneven consequences and an alert ear to a wide range of different voices. It takes as its foundational assumption that citizens are not all alike, that some groups are more vulnerable than others, and that all of us will need individualized forms of care in the course of our lives. In its articulation by feminist philosophers, the ethic of care has brought aspects of women's social experience and feminism's struggles with equality and difference into the conceptualizing of social need and citizen obligation. Backed by the community work of social justice movements, the proponents of a care ethic have developed concrete improvements, such as social impact assessment tools, to help policy makers hear the voices of those whose lives their decisions affect.[1]

In the 1950s, the political context was quite different. Universalist values were in the ascendant, full of fresh promise and largely untainted by a record of perverse outcomes. The labour movement, a social force organized around the masculine role of family provider, was a key actor in the politics of social justice. Social work, though still a mainly female profession that was linked to social services, was developing ties to labour and was attracting and promoting young male leaders. Universalist values and masculine social experience were the indicators of progressive standpoints in social policy circles.[2] The "big ticket" income programs and the government departments that administered them stood at the centre stage of policy discussions. In this context, the charities and their fundraisers could not usefully persist in presenting themselves as the agents of care against an inadequate, ploddingly rule-bound state, as they had effectively done in the 1930s. Yet they were not confident that the state would take up funding the social services, nor were they prepared to let go of those agencies' work in dealing with the peculiarities and particularities of individual need. In providing supervised play for children and social support for the isolated elderly, or counselling for families in crisis and good homes for deserted children, their agencies were doing the work of care, as yet largely unfunded by the state and practically invisible to a universalist perspective focused on the breadwinner wage.[3]

To promote charitable giving in this context required the fundraisers to describe their project and to present a notion of need in terms that could blend with welfare state discourse. By the 1950s, the agencies supported by charitable fundraising had already developed an explanation of their services as a necessary complement to subsistence maintenance of public programs: the state provides the minimum, and charity discovers and addresses other unmet needs. In the 1950s, however, this rationale for their existence encountered fresh challenges. Both at the beginning of the decade, between 1950 and 1953, and again at the end, in 1957-58, debate flared about whether or not citizens should support the chests. At each of these moments, a very thoughtful individual, well positioned in the country's social leadership, attacked the chests. In these attacks, something new was held up as the threat to private welfare: donor fatigue. At its worst, donor fatigue might become donor revolt. In these critiques, the state appeared as potentially a welcome relief rather than a threat. In this phase of the debate about the merits of public and private welfare, modern fundraising was vulnerable as much for its similarity to taxation as for its difference from it. The problem was that charity, supposedly about care and choice, was beginning to seem coercive.

Raising the Alarm about Donor Fatigue

By 1950, urban Canadians were becoming accustomed to both the income tax and the Community Chest campaigns. But it would be too much to say that these systems of contribution were accepted unquestioningly. The newness of the tax system was sometimes the subject of bitter humour, as in this tidbit that was occasionally published in labour papers: "Officials of the Income Tax Division received the following acknowledgement of a blank [i.e., an income tax form] received by a citizen: 'Dear Treasury – I received your application blank, but I already belong to several good orders and do not care to join your income tax at this time.'"[4]

Ruefully, this wee joke points to the shift from a voluntary means of collective care (the fraternal order) to the compulsory one (the tax-based welfare state). Perhaps, reading this, we think, "the poor rube! He doesn't understand that he's in a new, less free world now." But other tax commentary of the period suggests that this joke's threat – that working-class taxpayers might not choose to "join the income tax" – touched on a real issue of the period. What was legitimate tax avoidance, and what was criminal tax evasion? As these features of the income tax system were discovered and debated in the late 1940s, it seems clear that the new taxpayers of the new welfare state were feeling the pressures of the system, weighing its costs and benefits, and giving or withholding their consent, not just at election time but also when they were completing their tax returns.[5] In the same way, prospective donors to the Community Chests were questioning the fairness and efficiency merits of modern charity and wondering out loud whether they should continue to give.

This questioning appeared in a concentrated way between 1950 and 1953. A flashpoint came in May 1950, when a Commons-Senate committee was hearing interventions on the subject of Old Age Security as Parliament moved toward a new federal Old Age Pensions Act. Speaking in favour of radical improvements to this act and a more systematic effort of the federal government to end poverty was the secretary-treasurer of the Canadian Congress of Labour, Pat Conroy. In the course of his remarks, Conroy contrasted a proper tax-funded social security system with the non-system of agencies funded by charitable donations. He called the Community Chests "a symbol" of what was wrong with charity, which he labelled an "organized racket." This term was a familiar element in the left's critique of charity, by which respectable charitable fundraising was derisively associated with the more dubious sort that did nothing more than line the pockets of con artists. But the increased participation by wage earners and the union movement in chest fundraising during the war made this old critique much more consequential now than it had been in the 1930s, when it was dismissed as the inevitable communist grumbling. Conroy was an executive of an organization whose members formed a large and influential segment of Canadian employees. And they provided as much as 30 percent of all donations made to the chests. So his critique was alarming, especially when, over the next month, it was echoed by unionists' voices in Toronto, Winnipeg, and Vancouver and reported in the national wire services.[6] In the face of the possible withdrawal of labour endorsement from the Toronto chest, a Canadian Welfare Council (CWC) staffer wrote to one of her colleagues, "it would mean a loss of hundreds of thousands of dollars to the Toronto Chest if they [Toronto's major industrial union labour council] did what they threaten to do."[7]

The presidents of Ottawa's chests led the local defence against Conroy's attack. According to the *Ottawa Journal*'s reporter, the Protestant chest's president fulminated about how wrong it was for a "responsible official of a responsible organization" to express such views. In a different vein, B.G. McIntyre of the Roman Catholic chest cried, "what does he want? Does he want every charity cut to a pattern, a prescribed pattern, regardless of individual needs? The Community Chests are the last remaining evidence of human kindness, of Christian charity in our communities. It's worth a lot. It's the voluntary effort that enables us to get along without the state assuming the whole burden. Human consideration for the needs of the next-door neighbour is what pioneered this country. That's the spirit of the Community

Chests."[8] In this framing, the chests stood for care and personal relations against mere rights and bureaucratic rigidity, with religion on their side of the binary and the rights-based, tax-funded welfare state on the other.

With the teams lined up this way, Conroy had no compunction in avidly defending his side. In a long, metaphor-rich letter to the *Ottawa Journal*'s editor the following day, he teasingly took credit for having incited, in the hostile reaction to his remarks, an unusual display of Catholic-Protestant unanimity.[9] And he pointed out that, in his remarks to the House committee's questions about the public/private division of welfare, he had made "a rather nice compliment to the volunteers engaged in the business of charity-giving." For most of the letter, however, he stingingly defended his view that the "horde of agencies" financed by donations was part of a "chaotic, inefficient and unsatisfactory" system that cost the Canadian people more than would a state-supervised welfare system designed to remove the causes of poverty rather than just tinker with its effects. Most charity workers know, he wrote, that "they are inadequately trying to deal with a social and economic disease, and that this social cancer can only be cured by major social analysis and treatment. This disease cannot be cured by temporary applications of hot and cold poultices of voluntary charity giving." In this turn of a figurative phrase, social science-based public welfare is modern medicine (entailing diagnosis, treatment, cure), and sentimental charity ("hot and cold") is old-fashioned nursing (applying poultices).

In spite of his claim to respect the idealism of fundraisers, the sting in Conroy's letter came from his contemptuous description of their campaign methods, which he argued had nothing to do with religion or real caring. The "racket," he alleged, lay in the link between charitable giving and status. Charity no longer "had the true light of Heaven in its Eyes." The first step in a campaign was not prayer; it was finding a campaign chair who was "a socially recognized success." The next step was to set up a military-style hierarchy in which "the buck privates, ... as usual, have to do all the slogging and dirty work." Conroy was outraged not only by this status machine's deployment of exactly the class hierarchies a good unionist should fight, but also by its exploitation of the ordinary guy's desire for respect: "The first unhappy individual to receive the impact of this well-organized campaign is the guy who has probably the equivalent of the price of a couple of plugs of chewing tobacco in the bank. He is hoisted on a level which he undoubtedly never dreamed he would be able to reach. He is placed on the 'Special Names' list, with the laurel wreath that accompanies the designation. And he is going to receive the necessary publicity of the amount of money that has been smiled out of him."

This is not about the "shedding of tears for the poor," wrote Conroy. "This is organization with a vengeance, with a precision that would make the Rockettes appear to be wearing Dutch clogs. It is the vested continuing interest that can only be dealt with on a basis of precise and ruthless organization." Conroy was characterizing charity as no more spontaneous, and no less coercive, than the state. Charity's coercions were social ones. He called these methods "Operation Pressure." This coercion, he claimed, was as effective as the taxman's: "The average household is paying more money per year to charitable undertakings than it paid a few years ago in income tax." And the joys of the community feeling that McIntyre claimed the chest agencies represented? Conroy nodded to the value of a "good heart," but then he savagely slashed those who help the "unfortunate ones," describing these volunteers or paid social workers as "professional keeners [i.e., moaners] who will not only be unhappy if they are not allowed to attend funerals or wakes, but also if they are not allowed to burst into people's homes and to smile and cry about the misery they hope to find there. Some people are just built that way."

Conroy's political rhetoric used a thumping blend of gender ridicule, class outrage, and self-congratulatory modernism and materialism to puncture the chests' balloon of equally self-congratulatory idealism. The gender element in this rhetoric flowed from a distinction between the supposedly real welfare issues, having to do with the paternal work of breadwinning, and allegedly secondary ones, related to the maternal work of care.[10] In this scheme of things, nursing and sympathy are necessary only when the real problem, poverty, remains unaddressed. Even the chests' military style of organization was made absurd in a feminized way by Conroy's comparison to the Rockettes. Defending working-class men against the pressures and coercions of the chests, Conroy called for them and others to exercise choice as citizens and to make rational choices rather than sentimental ones. Of course, his discomfort with charitable emotions such as sadness and pity betrays the other emotions, such as anger and resentment, that, in a comfortably masculine way, fuelled his passion for a rationally organized system of social security.[11] Turning around the dichotomy that makes charity about choice and tax about imposition, he appealed to the "best value for money" discourse of efficiency. Charity is a bad choice because it costs too much. The state's role is to use taxpayers' dollars sparingly and well. "Social analysis," not self-indulgent moaning, will produce intelligent care and genuine well-being. The well-organized, rights-based provision of services by the state constitutes true caring in this view, and emotion appears as pernicious sentiment. Small wonder that those who defended the chests as embodying the spirit of charity had a hard time accepting Conroy's compliments when they came packaged with this critique.

As Conroy's critique was echoed and extended in the *Financial Post* and CCF-affiliated unionists in Toronto amplified his points, the pressure on chests to improve their efficiency mounted.[12] It must have seemed that a massive donor revolt was looming on the horizon. In fact, it had already begun in Detroit, as journalist Sidney Katz explained. In an article published in *Maclean's* on 15 November 1953, Katz assembled in one place the rallying cries of the donor revolt. The article was called "The Unholy Mess of Our Charity Appeals." It became essential reading for chest leaders.[13]

Although Katz defended the chests rather than calling for their abolition, he was just as much inclined as Conroy to see inefficiency as an impediment to effective service and to see a kind of emotional deficiency as lying at the root of charitable inefficiency. In his description of the problems facing charities in the postwar period, he deployed a familiar contrast. On the one (deplorable) hand was the threat of irrationality, sentimentality, and waste; on the other (hopeful) hand lay the prospect that charities might still rise to a level of efficiency, order, and fairness that would earn the respect of both business and labour and thus ensure their survival. He thought that the chests, with improved discipline, might still be the heroes of the story. In Katz's view, rational charity had as much claim to represent true caring as public provision did. But, like Conroy, Katz also called for charity's emotional content to be reformed.

His analysis began with a description of the problems in the charitable sector. The article's lead put it in a nutshell: "The fierce and often selfish competition by hundreds of organizations for the Canadian charity dollar – with the apparent results of unrealized goals and exorbitant expenses – leads many confused and harried givers to echo Henry Ford's ultimatum [Henry Ford II, that is] that the fund raisers 'federate or perish' ... Business executives, labour unions, welfare officials, and individual citizens are becoming more and more outspoken in criticism of charitable appeals."[14]

To illustrate "exorbitant expenses," Katz referred to "the ill-fated Canadian 'March of Dimes'" campaign, from which *58 percent* of the $360,000 raised went to campaign costs. With respect to unmet goals, he claimed that almost half (twenty-nine out of sixty) of Canada's chest campaigns failed to meet their 1952 goals. He hastened to point out that this was not a sign that federated fundraising was more vulnerable than were individual charities to failure. To support this point, he gave the example of a campaign by the new Canadian Arthritis and Rheumatism Society, whose success at raising $400,000 paled in comparison with its goal of $800,000. And he noted that the chests retained their record of superior performance in keeping collection costs low: no individual agency did as well.[15]

Further to his concern about efficiency, Katz addressed the question of whether or not unmet goals really meant unmet needs and concluded that they did. His support for this claim was tangential but evoked more generally the gap between fundraising success and satisfying needs. For example, he pointed out that the campaign to raise money for polio research and victim support did exceptionally well because of the donation-drawing power of crippled children, but polio ranked forty-ninth in the causes of death. Heart disease, by contrast a common killer whose treatment arguably represented a more urgent health need, raised not a penny of charitable giving because no heart disease charity existed in Canada. Katz also contrasted the continuing success of the single-agency Red Cross campaigns, which raised $7.3 million in one year, while the chests, which represented "almost 900" agencies that "directly assist an estimated two out of every five Canadian families," raised only $12 million. While disavowing the implication that the Red Cross had more money than it needed, he insisted that the receipt by the chest of fewer dollars per agency meant that the chest's member agencies could not effectively meet the needs of "Canadian families."[16] The rational setting of priorities, rather than the potent but unreasonable appeal of certain kinds of need, would better ensure that adequate care was provided.

Another of the problems facing charity was the risk that the emotional wellsprings of giving might unnecessarily be drained. Both donor fatigue and volunteer fatigue loomed as threats when fundraising was inefficient. The "confused and harried givers" were warning that, if charities did not federate, donors would limit their giving. Referring to a 1952 study by Albert Shea, called *Corporate Giving in Canada,* Katz noted that 70 percent of charitable donations came from the combined giving of corporations and employees at work. But the frequency of appeals had become so burdensome to employers that their long-standing preference for charity over taxation was being strained.[17] Of course, this was not merely a question of emotion. Material interest was also involved. Echoing the taxation discourse's familiar theme of the "administrative burden" to business entailed by collecting taxes, Katz reported the complaints of firms that had to assign "highly paid executives, full time, to consider anywhere from fifty to fourteen hundred appeals every year." But tied into the complaints from business donors was a perception that economic pressures were bypassing altruism. Advertising firms, in particular, felt explicitly coerced into donating executive labour to fundraising: "You can't refuse when the request comes from an important customer."[18] Not only this specialized kind of volunteer labour but also the 112,000 canvassers needed every year by the chests alone were getting harder to find because of "low morale." Giving a curious example of the fundraisers' passion for psychological expertise, Katz reported that, "recently, a Montreal fundraiser became so worried about his volunteers that he enlisted the services of a psychologist to draw up a program that would banish their fatigue and low morale."[19] In the short term, the risks of volunteer fatigue and donor revolt were troubling. In the longer term, Katz hinted, they threatened the very survival of the charitable sector.[20]

To Katz and the people he quoted, the problems of the charitable sector stemmed from a failure of emotional morality. Since 1945, the growth of the Canadian economy had helped to sustain more and more charitable fundraising, especially in support of health services and research: the period had seen the creation of Canadian societies for cancer, arthritis, polio, deafness, multiple sclerosis, and paraplegia. There were at least thirty national appeals of various kinds. At the same time, universities, welfare organizations, churches and temples, and hospitals were conducting capital campaigns to repair and replace buildings that had suffered decades of neglect since the 1920s. No one disputed that all, or most, of these good works were necessary. But the phenomenon of proliferating appeals raised questions about morally sound or unsound emotion. Katz pointed to a paradox: all of this altruism had a selfish side. He quoted approvingly the national Community Chest president, Montreal manufacturer Carl Reinke, castigating the leaders of non-chest charities: "[They] are guilty of rivalry, jealousy, plain selfishness, suicidal shortsightedness and a lack of team work ... In the interest of the general welfare, it is time we stopped pussy footing about this problem for fear of offending somebody."[21] The main targets of the Katz article were the Red Cross and the Salvation Army, which were "deadlocked" in negotiations with the chests. These two national agencies were effective fundraisers that had, more often than not, refused membership in the chests. They believed that they did not need the support of the chest apparatus, and indeed it seemed that they could raise more money on their own.[22] While their assessments of their own interests might seem rational, Reinke's series of adjectives put these supposedly altruistic agencies on the side of irrational emotions ("rivalry" and "jealousy") and unhelpful "competition" against the desirable emotions that underpinned regard for "the general welfare" and the practice of "team work."

Katz's recommended solutions expressed what, to the chests and their supporters, was the general wisdom. One was to replace the chests with a new organization: the united fund. The exemplar of this solution was Detroit, where in 1948 business and labour had combined to limit their contributions to a single appeal and thus to force all charities to "federate or perish." Columbus, Ohio, had successfully followed suit in 1952. These were the foundational donor revolts. The other solution was also an American one: the National Information Bureau assessed the merits (including revenue and expense records) of national and international charities and made endorsements that were crucial to the credibility of these campaigns. Local versions of this sort of board were also necessary, and Winnipeg was celebrated as a Canadian city that had adopted this method. The problem of defining appropriate needs and attainable goals – that is, the problem of defining fair contribution – was also being addressed in the United States by a national budget committee, formed by the US chests and other national philanthropies. Nothing in this solution called for Canadians to care more or to be more generous. These solutions simply promised that good organization would allay painful emotions – frustration, guilt, rivalrous envy – and control disproportionate emotions – "sentiment" – that seemed to produce wasted effort. And the chests, remade during the 1950s as the united appeals, were still the best mechanism for doing this work of reforming contribution. Apparently a response to rational concerns about efficiency, this was nonetheless a call for a reformed emotional morality. Selfish competition would be replaced by co-ordinated and well-policed means of caring, charitable emotion disciplined by rational planning.

The problem posed for fundraising in the early 1950s, then, was that tax-funded social programs presented a model of efficient services, and a fairly distributed burden of financing those services, while charities seemed to be wasteful and to impose an intolerable burden on some contributors and volunteers. Rationalization of many appeals into one was being proposed, once again, as a solution, with new criteria for inclusion being its necessary means. In this view, both the defenders of the chests and the promoters of an expanded welfare state presented efficiency as a means to superior care. The efficiency value linked taxation discourse and charities discourse. In the latter, it was distinctively combined with a critique of sentiment and selfishness as morally unsound emotions that interfered with charities' ability to raise funds and use them efficiently.

The Power Politics of Inclusion

The exercises in rationalization that followed these critiques were conducted in the name of altruism. But the tools used and the social power deployed had little to do with love and much to do with fear. In the years after Conroy's complaint, organized labour sought involvement in the federated charities movement but expressed their involvement in fiercely unsentimental terms. As William Black of Vancouver's Hospital Employees' Union frankly pointed out, his membership was "fed up with the dunning and bumming that has been going on. From now on our union will make one collection each year and a committee will decide how to proportion the donations." Meanwhile, Toronto Labour Council president and CCFer Murray Cotterill warned that "charitable organizations are growing like weeds" and worried that this uncontrolled growth "might result in a refusal to contribute to any charity." His horticultural expression of donor fatigue was picked up by the Canadian Press news services and carried on the CBC national news, making the spring of 1950 a particularly anxious time for the chests. Seven months later the Toronto Labour Council issued a report of the Special Committee on Welfare outlining its position on the role of private charity and labour's part in the planning of welfare spending. The themes of that report would be repeated throughout the 1950s as "labour participation" continued to be a much-sought-after and sometimes achieved goal of the chests.[23]

For the chests, what was at stake in the rationalizing of charity appeals was more than just preventing donor fatigue or organized donor revolts. The chests believed that their oversight function was a source of informed control over the allocation of charitable donations among charities. If business or labour chose to set up its own internal allocation process, then the broadly representative deliberative bodies that the chests had been trying to fashion would be sidestepped. Funds might be given to single agencies outside the chest or to member agencies within the chest. Either way the threat was not simply to the amount of the bottom line; the chests also thought that independent action by business or labour threatened the sound setting of spending priorities. This threat existed if there was no co-ordination of appeals, but it was also present when co-ordination was inadequate.[24] Bodies that did not represent a variety of social constituencies (including the social workers who represented agencies) did not seem, to the chest fundraisers, to be competent at planning social spending.

In 1960, defending his Community Chest against the departure of a major disease charity, Vancouver's chest president Ross Wilson expressed this value in terms both of efficiency and of democratic rights: "Citizens have the right and responsibility to determine what health and welfare services are needed, thereby participating in their planned and orderly development."[25] While this might sound like a defence of government against charity, it was, in this context, a defence of the federated appeal organizations against fundraising by independent agencies. In this view, federated charities, by their inclusiveness, helped to improve the quality of choices made about how to meet needs. Modern charity was organized to channel altruism into efficient action, and chests were political institutions designed to make this organization democratic. In the process, however, they too were defending a group interest, that of social workers. The defence of planning was also a defence of consistent, reliable funding for the chests' member agencies and their staffs' salaries. If more agencies were to be added, then the social workers wanted planned additions so that the budgets of agencies already in the chests would not be jeopardized.[26]

In spite of worries about uncontrolled expansion, the chests, under pressure, began to invite more independent agencies to join. This effort was an international one, apparently initiated in the United States, and associated with the united fund method imposed by business and labour in Detroit in 1948. It was called the "open door" policy. Chests that pursued this policy offered non-member agencies flexible terms for joining. In the old system, member agencies had to account strictly to the chests for all of their spending, return surpluses of any sort, forswear all manner of independent fundraising, and confine their activities to the city in which the fund was based. These conditions had all but ruled out chest membership for national organizations such as the Red Cross. Successful and well-established charities observed that they did not need the help of the chest in fundraising; indeed, they expected that they might collect less through a chest campaign than on their own. So, for them, the incentive to give up autonomy and to add a layer of budget reporting and control was not obvious. For the disease charities, the prohibition against independent campaigns was especially unappealing because fundraising was one of their main methods of educating the public about the cause and prevention of the disease. With the open door policy, all of the restrictive terms under which agencies had previously joined were open for negotiation.[27] And herding charities through the open door were the big contributors with their "federate or perish" club.

All three of the cities studied here adopted some variation of the open door policy, with Ottawa taking it up with the greatest enthusiasm and effectiveness. Between 1952 and 1954, a newly hired, energetic, fresh-from-the-US director, John Yerger, carried on negotiations with the St. John's Ambulance, Multiple Sclerosis Society, Cancer Society, Salvation Army, Red Cross, and others. The Salvation Army stayed out, convinced that it did better on its own. But others joined, realizing that they faced objections from "powerful contributor interests" if they remained independent. Ottawa's most important employer, the federal government, tightly restricted permission to canvass the civil service. The chest had that permission, and getting access to it was part of what drew the Cancer Society and St. John's Ambulance into the federation. In addition, the Ottawa records provide an explicit example of a kind of donor pressure that must also have been used elsewhere. The minutes refer to a Mr. Southam (one of the newspaper-owning Southams) having refused requests from the Cerebral Palsy and March of Dimes organizations on the ground that these agencies were not members of the Community Chest. One of these two agencies immediately applied for chest membership.[28] By 1954, this sort of pressure had aroused objections in Halifax, where several board members and "some of the public" said that the chest was becoming "too aggressive" and was "departing from its early principles." Indeed, in 1954 in the midst of the Salvation Army's annual drive, the Halifax *Chronicle-Herald* had refused to use a CWC press release about the problem of multiple appeals. Only after the salvationists were finished was the newspaper willing to froth with appropriate rabidity about the scourge of proliferating charity campaigns.[29] By 1956, in spite of considerable effort by chest director George Hart, the Halifax chest still suffered the ignominy of being one appeal among many, with the Boy Scouts, the YMCA, and the Salvation Army still not member agencies. The only major success of the open door exercise in Halifax had been the addition of the Red Cross, the result of a policy change at that agency's national level.[30]

Vancouver held out more vigorously than the others for preserving the chests' budgeting and planning functions. Director Howard Naphtali told a visiting CWC advisor, Ralph Albrant, that the Vancouver chest and council had succeeded in broadening the federation without having recourse to the dubious methods of the united fund. In Albrant's summary, Naphtali "seemed quite disturbed by the high pressure methods that were being used in some places to get the nationals to participate and the discrimination against the old line Chest agencies which came about with more liberal treatment for new national agencies. He saw planning going out the window. He felt that the relative need of a service was not the main consideration but the whole emphasis was on getting everybody in at any price."[31]

The older agencies' "disgruntled" mood that Naphtali went on to describe was not only about different levels of autonomy. The older agencies also feared that including more new agencies might mean a smaller share of the total chest budget for each of them. This fear meant that directors such as Naphtali had not only to attract new agencies but also to assuage concerns and allay envies so as not to lose old ones. And as he found, alarmingly, in 1959, the new agencies might be hard won and easily lost. When the BC Heart Foundation departed after only a few years in the chest, chest president Ross Wilson predicted a fundraising crisis. The loss of other major member agencies was anticipated. A community committee was struck to investigate the state of fundraising for health and welfare agencies.[32] By August, the PR injuries had been assessed and bandaged. The crisis had passed. But the tone of panic in this episode confirmed what news reports from the United States suggested – that there was open conflict between the united fund and the major disease charities. And the fight was not always in any obvious way about providing better social services. By now, the chests had an institutional interest that, deny it though they understandably did, necessarily played a part in keeping their doors open to agencies whose campaigns competed with theirs.[33] Agencies disparaged the pressures applied by the chests. But the chests themselves feared the consequences of donor revolt. Donor interests, represented by big business and big unions, were the power behind these associational politics.

Care and Inclusion: Cross-Cultural Communication in 1950s Fundraising

In addition to the open door policy, with its mixture of reason and pressure, the chests in the 1950s moved toward two other kinds of inclusion: racial/linguistic and class. Both involved institutional integration and a measure of cross-cultural communication. Each also affected campaign advertising. To the limited extent that this cross-cultural work was successful, it entailed an attentive response both to the particulars of intergroup emotions and to the practical needs of subaltern groups. This kind of responsiveness was invisible in the universalist efficiency argument, even though the inclusions that made caring responsiveness necessary were prompted by the call for rationalization.

One of the racial/linguistic inclusions had to do with Ottawa's relationship to the francophone community located in Eastview (present-day Vanier, Ontario). This was a particular example of a more general problem of inclusion that the chests faced in all urban areas. Surrounding the old cities were suburbs or other smaller towns. Services such as the VON, the CAS, and the CNIB, whose agents dealt with people in their homes, found themselves called on to serve the suburbs. But the contributors lived in the city. Some suburban clients worked in the city and contributed to the city's chest. Others, however, were able to call on agencies that they did not help to support. The chests, anxious to prevent competition from suburban fundraising, began to organize the fringe communities.[34]

In Ottawa, this exercise entailed a particular difficulty. Between Ottawa, lying to the west of the Rideau River, and Eastview, on the other bank, there was a broad cultural gulf. Eastview was a low-income, largely working-class community whose residents were, in the defining majority, francophone and Catholic. As I pointed out in Chapter 4, there was a long and unhappy tradition of anglophone racism toward the francophone community of Ottawa, a racism compounded by class biases by middle-class anglophones toward residents of a largely working-class area such as Eastview. Reciprocally, Eastview residents regarded Ottawa as a separate and slightly hostile place.[35] Complicating relationships between Ottawa and Eastview was that Eastview was in fact not a suburb but a separate, independent municipality, with its own cash-strapped local government. When the Ottawa chests began to take on the amalgamation of the suburbs, Eastview nearly proved to be an indigestible morsel.

The chests' attempt to incorporate Eastview was triggered by Eastview's attempt in September 1952 to organize its own chest. The initiative came from Eastview's mayor, Gordon Lavergne, whose City Council owed $9,000 to the VON for services that it had given to Eastview households. The CNIB was also threatening to stop helping out blind residents of Eastview if that community did not contribute to the CNIB. With a poor and overstretched tax base, Mayor Lavergne looked to the federated appeal plan as an alternative source of funds for financing these sorts of services. He sought advice not from the Ottawa chest but from Henry Stubbins, then the director of the

CWC's chests and councils division. The new director of the Ottawa chests, John Yerger, read about Eastview's plans in the paper and sought out Stubbins to express a worry. If Eastview organized a chest, then the many residents of Eastview who worked in Ottawa businesses and the civil service might choose to donate to their own community rather than to the Ottawa chests. Stubbins advised Yerger to suggest to Lavergne a joint venture: a "metropolitan" chest.[36]

At a meeting with representatives of Eastview, both this option and another were raised. The other was a "branch" chest for Eastview, suggested by Yerger. In that plan, Eastview would get administrative support from the Ottawa office but would have its own board, budget committee, and campaign committee. And only funds earmarked by donors for Eastview would go to the budgets of agencies based in or serving Eastview. As Stubbins pointed out, that plan would do little to solve Eastview's problems. What was really needed was an arrangement that would truly share the wealth, an arrangement in which Eastview was treated as part of greater Ottawa. After the meeting, Yerger told Stubbins that there were two problems with that arrangement: "His leading people [were] indifferent and even hostile to Eastview, and ... his agencies in particular would resent the taking on of an additional load of this kind without specific financial guarantees." In Stubbins' summary of this conversation, he urged Yerger to try to "establish his reputation as a statesman" and convince the Ottawa leadership to change this "short-sighted, selfish attitude" and to recognize that Ottawa's "central economic position" entailed an obligation to offer a "fair share" to this neighbouring community. He suggested that a successful campaign in the fall of 1952 might incite a more generous mood.[37]

The hostility to Eastview that Yerger noted bears a clear resemblance to the hostility to francophone Ottawa that had been apparent in the organizing phase of the chests. Marie Hamel, in her May 1952 survey of the relations between the chests and francophone Ottawa, noted the view among chest leaders that donations from "the French-speaking group" were smaller than they could be. The francophone "leadership" was criticized for being ineffective. But Hamel offered other explanations: the chests had not been willing to use the parish organizational pattern, "which is so close to the heart of the French Canadians," nor had they taken seriously French Canadians' feelings about "running their own show."[38] Moreover, the bishop's appointee as head of the Catholic Charities, Father John Macdonald, had not proven acceptable to the francophone community. In these observations, she made known the emotional content of this institutional problem. As I argued in Chapter 4, Hamel's involvement in the Ottawa chests was an important step toward presenting a dominant culture with information about a subordinate one. Yerger's endorsement of her contribution would help to make that information significant.

Even before Stubbins' call for him to be a "statesman," Yerger had begun to work on cultural bridges between Ottawa and Eastview. At the suggestion of the bishop's appointee to the chest board, Father Vézina (whose parish was on the east bank of the Rideau), Yerger convoked a meeting of leading francophone citizens, several of them from Eastview. Yerger was still finding out about the sensitivities around francophone autonomy and the language of business. He and his anglophone publicity secretary, Freda Fripp, attended the francophones' meeting. Afterward Vézina pointed out that there was still a need for "a meeting of French-speaking Canadians only."[39] Rather than defensively asserting his right to be involved, Yerger agreed with Vézina's point. Yerger also agreed to supply French posters and publicity material in spite of their expense and his concerns that the publicity material was "not slanted the way it should be." Indeed, he agreed to produce a special leaflet for "the French-speaking group" and to allow it to be distributed at churches. Yerger was listening and learning. Had he been alert to the nuance of Hamel's language, he would have picked up the habit of using the term "French-speaking" or "French Canadians" rather than the anglophone Ottawans' historically idiotic and typically disparaging term "the French." As it was, he was still using "the French" later in 1952, during the Eastview negotiations, even while praising Hamel's help in opening up to him the "correct slant" on campaigning in francophone Ottawa.[40] In spite of this mixed record, however, Yerger was discernibly working toward making the Ottawa chests more inclusive of Ottawa francophones.

Over the next two years, his star rose in the Ottawa chests as he led them to their first successful campaigns in many years. Vigorous pursuit of the open door policy, the creation of a new executive director position for the Welfare Council, and the greater support for French-language public relations work all helped to make the chests flourish. Yerger's period also saw the end of the legal existence of two separate chests combined in one as well as the addition of Eastview and Nepean to the emerging metropolitan chest.[41] It seems likely that Stubbins was right, that success in fundraising and Yerger's resulting prestige helped Yerger to arrange the inclusion of Eastview in a metropolitan chest. The conditions of that admission were stringent, requiring specific commitments from Eastview about donor prospect lists and tax grants. But nothing in the final agreement specified that Eastview would only get earmarked funds. This might seem like a small victory. In fact, it was a big one. Earmarking would have signalled Ottawa's definitive rejection of Eastview as part of the community, entitled to its full benefits. And given that excluding a group from community belonging and benefit was so important a marker of racism, this small difference must be seen as a mitigation of Ottawa's racialized conception of Eastview.

Progress continued to be made toward cross-cultural inclusion, albeit still slowly, after Stubbins became the Ottawa chest's executive director in 1954. Eastview did not immediately rush to support the chest, nor did Ottawa leaders' suspicions of Eastview as a burden immediately disappear. But there were signs of efforts being made on both sides. One of the first shows on Ottawa's new French-language TV station, Channel 9, was a 1955 *Plume Rouge* variety show (hosted by Horace Racine). By 1957, the chests' need for a paid "French services" staff member had become solidly established. In 1959, the board observed with satisfaction that services to Eastview had been fully integrated into all of the member agencies.[42] If this was indeed the case, then what was implied was some bilingual staff in all the agencies.

At the level of campaign organization (as distinct from office and social work staff), the worries about and efforts toward integration continued.[43] In February 1961, Eastview lawyer Jean Paul Filion spoke of deficiencies in the "French-English balance in Eastview and throughout the campaign organization" and called for "adequate French representation in all divisions and committees." Later that summer the campaign committee lamented that the chest did not have "an effective image" in Eastview. Gearing up to the fall campaign, Filion's publicity committee contacted the Fédération des femmes canadiennes-françaises, influential priests, the Chamber of Commerce, and other Eastview organizations. A poster was prepared for display in the stores of Eastview, proclaiming that 6,000 local residents had benefited from "their Community Chest." By 1963, continuing dissatisfaction both with collections in Eastview and with francophone representation in the campaign organization led to the creation of an Eastview division. By this means, the chest board hoped "to provide more incentive and challenge to the Eastview canvassing organization."[44] As an echo of the accountability mechanisms provided by the original separation of Protestant and Catholic chests, this move probably indicated some continuing anglophone suspicion that "the French" were not carrying their share.

But the earmarking formula of the 1930s was not revived. And at the same time, the Ottawa Community Chests had been renamed the Ottawa and District Community Chest, a name change that eliminated the last trace of the original "federal" constitution and marked the addition of several suburbs to the organization. Another sign of integration across cultural lines was that, from 1962, annual meetings were addressed in both French and English rather than having honorific snippets of French appear at the edges of English speeches. Print copies of translations of speeches (both English and French) were circulated at the meetings. Finally, in 1964, the Ottawa chest eliminated the separation of French and English, Catholic and Protestant, in the core work of budget review.[45]

In all of this, in both the cultural tensions and the attempts at social integration, we should see at the community level themes that would also play out during the 1960s in national politics. How could the minority francophone communities in Canada be, in their own terms, fully a part of the public life of predominantly English-speaking political entities? The experience of the Ottawa Community Chests seems to have been part of a continued and perhaps broadened struggle by Franco-Ontarians in the early 1960s to assert their right to representation in community organizations and to have social services and public institutions available in French. The steps taken in that direction by the Ottawa chests in the early 1950s show the chests' role as a symbolic site of social inclusion across cultural divides. Operating from the premise that inclusion would incite contribution, the chests attempted to recognize and accommodate the facts of real difference. This work entailed a mix of emotional appeals combined with practical aids to communication.

The work going on in building relationships between Eastview and Ottawa not only expressed the practical necessities of municipal integration and the political aspirations of Franco-Ontarians. Its rhetoric also drew on the human rights and civil rights culture of the period, while its practices contributed concretely to extending social rights. In postwar Halifax, as in Ottawa, rhetorical gestures of racial inclusiveness began to appear in fundraising discourse. For example, in 1949, just a year after Chinese Canadians got the right to vote, Halifax's Chinese community was congratulated in heavily stereotyped terms for its support of the chest campaign.[46] In an editorial entitled "Well Done, Friends!" the community was praised for having paid up on all of its pledges to the chest:

> By thus aiding a useful community effort, the Chinese people have done well – and have set an example to the rest of us. Their example is the more striking because the Chinese, generally, have a way of looking after their own people and make relatively few requests to community agencies. But in this and in many ways they display a sense of citizenship. They make as little trouble as possible. They work diligently. And they go quietly about their affairs ... Above all, the Chinese have a great gift for minding their own business, which is not a bad practice for any of us.[47]

By representing the social marginalization of Chinese Canadians as a virtue rather than a threat (presenting Chinese Canadians not as denizens of hidden, shadowy slums but as successful, privacy-respecting Canadians), this text reflected the rights talk of its moment. Unfortunately, one word, "generally," carried the stereotyping taint. In the late 1950s, the Halifax campaign slogan, "Need Knows No Creed," showed the chest (now the united appeal) playing its role as part of the civil rights culture.[48] And perhaps the depiction of several African Nova Scotian women as team captains in the 1957 drive was part of a deliberate attempt to make the annual campaign seem less exclusively a white organization.[49] These efforts hint at the influence on fundraisers of the civil rights atmosphere of the period.

In Vancouver in the 1950s, ethnic inclusion became more than just a campaign technique. In 1954, a civil rights organization became a member agency of the chest, which began to advertise "Action against Discrimination" as one of the services that donations would help to fund. The agency that did this work was the Civic Unity Association (CUA). It had been formed in 1950 by CCF activists such as Knute Buttedahl and Arni Arnason, following an initiative in Seattle. Nineteen fifty-eight seems to have been a particularly active year, or at least the news coverage that the CUA got that year was carefully harvested by the chest's record keepers.[50] The CUA helped a young man, Douglas Wong, to prove that there was housing discrimination against Chinese Canadians in the city's west end and made his experience part of the basis for a petition for provincial human rights legislation. The CUA also supported a Sikh family who found their house purchase challenged by racist neighbours. As it happened, so did the head of the Labour Council, Lloyd Whalen, who was that year also the president of the chest. Saying that "we don't want any Little Rock ugliness in Vancouver," Whalen pointed out that the men of the family were members of his union (the IWA) and that they were "fine boys, good workers and an asset to the community."[51] In this incident, featuring the collaboration of a charity-funded social service agency and community unionism, we can see one of the positive consequences of earlier attempts in Vancouver to make labour a real part of the social leadership.

The inclusion of labour was both institutional and in an important way cross-cultural. In seeking to include organized labour, fundraisers tried to speak to the issues of working-class culture. Some of these issues were represented in the union movement's taken-for-granted notion of what counted as real need. Unionists' objections to charity had long been marked by a conception of need that was entirely based on a critique of market relations of exchange. Exploitation of labour by capital produced workers unable to secure their own or their dependents' subsistence needs. In the socialist version of this view, the very distribution of the means of life through jobs was unjust. But even in a left-liberal critique of class relations that accepted labour markets as a reality, the justice issue was the inadequacy of the wage – poverty. Either way the call was for economic reform that would make adequate means of subsistence a citizen's right. Union leaders, whether socialists or liberals, were necessarily engaged in seeking both more adequate incomes for their members and other workers and reliable backups for income in the form of legislated income support programs. Charity, with its careful scrutiny of the character and circumstances of the needy, was abhorrent because of its dispensers' assignment of responsibility not to the failures of the market but to individual shortcomings.

Social workers and the chest's fundraisers attempted to describe need in ways that would both appeal to this view of the male breadwinner as central and make a case for the value of care services to supplement the wage and support the breadwinner, on an analogy to the work of wives and mothers. An ad from Halifax's 1956 campaign represents the essence of this effort.[52] The ad's visual focus was a drawing of a giant, ruggedly handsome, smiling man in overalls carrying a lunch can. He looks down in satisfaction at a collage of buildings, trains, mine shafts, and planes – his manly sphere of work. The headline called out, "Construction and Building Workers – How MANY Will You Help?" In smaller type were listed those who, according to the ad's second level of headline, "need your help":

- Homeless children
- Sick children

- Youth
- The aged
- The crippled
- The blind
- People hurt in accidents
- Other fellow workers and members of their families who suffer misfortune.

While everyone in this list potentially lacked an adequate income to meet needs, most were commonsensically dependents, non-workers. It is also worth noting that "men out of a job" or "men unable to support their families" were not on the list (even if they may have been hidden in the last category). Instead of problems with employment, this interpretation of welfare emphasized the needs of people unable to solve their problems through working for a living or through bargaining for a better deal from an employer. This interpretation thus carefully avoided offending the view that income security is a right and that providing it is the responsibility of the state or a state-regulated market. In so doing, it is recognizable as part of an overall strategy to engage labour in fundraising. In Halifax in 1956, the chest had been pursuing this strategy for seven years, since 1949. The results of the chest drive in 1956, when this ad appeared, were impressive – more than double the 1949 collection. And the campaign report in December noted that giving by "employees" had risen by 54 percent over their 1955 contributions.[53] The Halifax fundraisers must have thought that their appeal to labour was working.

The view that the 1956 Halifax ad represents was being presented in labour-social work workshops, press releases to union publications, and talks by social workers to union organizations in the 1950s. And social workers were being careful to respect labour views, at least in public. An American publication in the CWC files pointed out that labour's participation in chest fundraising depended on the chests' ceasing to present charity as "the answer to the threat of the 'welfare state.'"[54] Absences are notoriously hard for historians to prove, but my survey of the fall campaigns through the 1950s shows that this particular line of appeal had indeed been removed from the chests' repertoire. It seems that the chests had accepted that silence on this point had become, by the mid-1950s, a "cost of doing business" with the labour movement.[55]

Calculated though that change probably was, social workers active in the chests in the 1950s were also increasingly likely to share views of need that labour had traditionally endorsed. Unlike influential figures such as Howard Falk in the 1930s, social workers in the 1950s were less likely to be contemptuous of "merely supplying money" as a means of helping troubled families. In an analysis of British Columbia's social assistance allowances that Pat Conroy might well have endorsed, the Vancouver chest's social planning section told the province's deputy minister of welfare that "the present situations which brought the families to the attention of the [family service] agencies were caused or aggravated mostly by deprivations during the childhood of the parents."[56] In other words, these social workers (both volunteer and professional) were advocating for adequate income assistance in the present to prevent family breakdowns in the future. With this view emerging in some social work circles, the scope of disagreement between organized labour and social workers about welfare need was shrinking.

In the community services committees in unions and in the labour participation committees on chests that were established in Vancouver, Toronto, and eventually Ottawa and Halifax, we can see the growing area of shared cultural ground between labour and social work. There were more unionists promoting welfare services, and they themselves were likely to be active on a Labour Council community services commmittee or in a union counselling setup. Vancouver's chest had Labour Council member Charles Lamarche on its paid staff as a labour participation liaison, and there were Labour Council volunteers such as Fred Ibsen in Halifax and Kathleen Marsden (both social worker and unionist) in Ottawa.[57] Whether volunteer or paid, these activists defended the labour movement's involvement in welfare services from other unionists' familiar criticism that charity substituted for proper public income support. For example, Toronto's united appeal labour liaison staffer, auto worker unionist Moses McKay, called the work of caring "social service" and reserved the contemptuous label "charity" for the private distribution of material relief. He and his associates opposed the use of charity in any circumstances other than brief emergencies.[58]

By the end of the 1950s, an enlarged and less gender-bound view of welfare need was being actively promoted by national labour leaders. The welfare needs that they endorsed were no longer only the rights-based ones related to the breadwinner's wages but also included the social services akin to the housewife's work of care. This view of welfare need helped to reduce class tensions on welfare issues. By redescribing charity, chest fundraisers and national labour leaders helped to play down class differences and to define a place for unionists in the community of the charitable. The image of a manual worker as a provider of caring services was in its time as important an image of cross-cultural inclusion as, for example, the African American women actors who began to appear frequently as women judges in TV crime dramas in the 1980s, well ahead of Black women's significant representation in the American judiciary. Similarly, the introduction of francophone staff and French-language campaign literature was, for 1950s Ottawa, a more important cross-cultural gesture than, for example, today's graduates of Canada's French-immersion programs might recognize. In the same vein, the efforts at including people of colour in the 1950s fundraising organizations, while paltry, were also significant. They too were signs that the terms of inclusion in Canada's social leadership were beginning to change in the 1950s.

The Revision and Preservation of "True Charity"

The inclusion of more agencies and more social groups was one strategy for defending against donor revolt. Practical exercises in negotiated belonging, these inclusions were arranged through deals, pressures, and emotional gestures. In the fundraising campaigns themselves, the work of inclusion concentrated more specifically on appeals to emotion. In this aspect of the defence against donor fatigue, the fundraisers creatively adapted their ads and events to the discursive figures of welfare state discourse. This entailed both developing alternatives to pity and perpetuating its use by way of preserving the emotions of true charity.

Fundamental to nineteenth-century charity, and present still in the early days of the chests, was the view of the objects of charity as belonging to an entirely different element of society than the givers of charity. However, it was possible to see emerging in the late 1930s and flourishing in the 1950s an alternative view of charity. In this new conception of the nature of contribution, the giver is also a consumer. Charity, like tax-based social insurance, is a collective means of guarding against risk.[59] In this view, the citizenship of contribution entails not the stockholder's stance of ensuring that the poor do not waste donors' dollars but the consumer's stance of ensuring that services one might use are adequately funded and of decent quality. This is a fundamental change in the political subjectivities or the citizen identities associated with welfare need. While derived in part from efforts to include working-class donors, the shift to citizen as consumer became an important part of the chests' fight against donor fatigue.[60] It marks the emergence of the egalitarian welfare state as a cultural form in which need is a universal condition and citizenship entails a general entitlement to help in times of need.

In the federated fundraising movement, this conception of citizenship was encapsulated in the phrase "everybody gives, everybody benefits," or its reverse "everybody benefits, everybody gives." In the campaigns for 1947, 1948, 1949, and 1950, this new and distinctively universalist slogan was central. In 1948, the president of the Canadian Congress of Labour (CCL), Aaron Mosher, concluded his endorsement of the chest campaigns by saying, "knowing that 'everybody gives, everybody benefits,' I am confident [CCL members] will respond generously." Furthermore, this slogan (in its "benefits/gives" order) was incorporated into the Red Feather logo in both Canada and the United States. In a 1953 campaign postmortem, one Vancouver fundraiser, Doris Mellish, regretted that it had not been used more intensively in the campaign. But it continued to feature nationally in publicity materials. A united appeal television commercial used it in 1957, and by 1959 a social worker reviewing the fundraising strategies for recreation agencies referred to it (in its "gives/benefits" order) as one of nine "commonplaces of the business."[61]

Themes of mutual aid and the use of social services as a normal part of everyone's life also appeared in various other ways during the 1950s campaigns. In a 1957 meeting to discuss methods of attracting contributions from wage earners, Ottawa's campaign committee set about acquiring a basis in research for the claim that "everybody benefits." It had member agencies count the services they had supplied in a three-month period to employees of firms of 100 or more, including the civil service. These data were to be used as pre-campaign "cultivation material" – in other words to educate prospective donors on the reasons they should give. In a host of other ways, the chests propagated the message that welfare services were for everyone. The idea was to communicate to "Mr. Average Citizen" that "he, a close friend or relative, is receiving, or has recently received, help from one or more of the Red Feather Services." A 1954 Vancouver pamphlet for a referral service used Victorian graphics to depict the "old-fashioned" notion of need as entailing only services for the poor, contrasted with modern images and typography to support the pamphlet's message that "new-fashioned" social services had something to offer everyone. And the National Council of Women attempted to quantify "everyone" with the usefully vague statistic that agencies funded by the chests served about "40 per cent of the Canadian population" – not quite everyone but still an impressively large proportion of the nation. The author of a news story about Toronto labour men visiting chest-financed social services cleverly combined sentiment and self-interest by reporting the reactions of these men to the clients of an occupational therapy agency: "One toughened trade unionist watched in silence. 'It kind of tears at the heart,' he finally said. Another nodded agreement and added, 'It makes you grateful for your health.'"[62]

Mutual aid was more than just the pursuit of a shared self-interest as individual consumers of services. Part of the chests' publicity work was to present an emotionally appealing notion of co-operation and sharing. A striking photograph in a Halifax ad illustrated the concept of "everybody": hands marked by various signifiers of youth and age, wealth and poverty, joined together in one strong circle, with a little child's hand on top, supported by the others.[63] Another Halifax ad asked donors whether they "could be happy" in a city "which neglected its children, gave no helping hand to the blind, denied medical and nursing aid to those who couldn't pay, or shirk[ed] its obligation to the aged?"[64] In this view, individual happiness also had to be collective. This was a consumer role derived from the communitarian logic of private insurance marketing, in which the provident purchaser of life insurance served not only himself but also his community by joining with other policy holders to distribute risk by co-operating in investment and to carry his share of responsibility by providing for his dependent family.[65]

The Red Feather radio show in 1951 made an especially dramatic case for the notion of charity as mutual aid, deploying metaphorically the intensity of marital love and interdependency. In an emotionally charged exchange between a husband and wife, the wife pleads with her skeptical husband to understand why she does volunteer social work, visiting the recently bereaved, administering insulin to a blind diabetic. He thinks she's subjecting herself to unnecessary suffering. Her reply is that he feels this way only because he's young and strong now but that one day he'll understand "we can't exist independent and alone. We all depend on one another, and we can't leave them alone just because this day is their turn at misfortune." She implores him to help her in her work by understanding the value of what she does. "Don't make it hard for me! Help me to go on." And then a chorus sings "You'll Never Walk Alone." Here it is the fundraiser and the social worker, as much as the people she helps, whose needs are foregrounded. But the conception of need she represents is a communitarian one: we are all subject to a common condition of vulnerability. This value, and the connection between individual and community well-being, were explicitly affirmed at the end of the program: "Community is a fraternity of families. These broken families become your responsibility. Their influence affects the happiness of your home."[66]

In this example, it is easy to see the continuing use of pity even in a mutual aid type of appeal. Pat Conroy might well have found in that ad a prime example of "professional keening" – a contemptible display of self-indulgent sentimentality. Each of us has, for various reasons and at different times, a personal sense of the frontier between sentiment and genuine emotion. And this individual sense is not only biographically formed but also determined by social position and historical conjuncture.[67] In labour's long fight for welfare rights, sentimental views of poverty (along with moralistic ones) were tools wielded by the historical enemy. A unionist such as Conroy had every reason to be alert to such sentimentalizing and to seek to disable it by mockery. From another standpoint, the CWC sought to battle corporate donor fatigue by circulating an American business leader's speech that urged corporations to eliminate "altruism or paternalism" from their support of community services. They should consider their contribution to be motivated simply by "enlightened self-interest."[68] But the disparaging of emotionally inspired giving is only one of several standpoints that we need to distinguish in order to understand what was particular to the role of emotional appeals, and pity in particular, in the chest fundraising of the 1950s. Another position, one that I would like to recapture for an integrated view of justice and charity, was also present in the 1950s.

This was the view that there was in the motive of giving an important moral and social good.[69] In this view, one part of the benefit of charitable fundraising was that it taught the comfortable not to be complacent. Appealing for donations was important because it showed prospective donors that others in their world suffered afflictions that everyone should care about and take action to mitigate. In short, it spoke to its audience's capacity for love. This conception of fundraising's purpose is separate from any measure of the adequacy to need of the dollars it raises. Fundraising simply and usefully serves to affirm the value of certain kinds of moral emotions. In the 1950s, the emergence and extension of rights-based methods of relieving need seemed to threaten to outmode certain desirable emotional motivations of care. This concern was not unique to the 1950s. For decades in Canada, and for at least a century in more urban and industrial places, a feared loss of "neighbourliness" had been part of the cluster of anxieties that surrounded the formation of mass society. But it is easy to see that there were particular triggers in the 1950s, with the supposed complacency of affluence and the increased security afforded by the expanding welfare state. Among those historically specific triggers were the united fund movements' own methods and successes.

The success of the chest and the danger it posed to charitable feeling became the target of the controversy-loving pastor of Toronto's First Unitarian congregation, Reverend William P. Jenkins. In 1957, *Maclean's* published a piece by Jenkins called "Why I'm against the United Fund." In it, he set out the pleasantly maverick view that the more charitable the appeals the better. Unusual though that position was, his arguments in support of it were not idiosyncratically his alone. Others in the social work and fundraising community were raising and would continue to raise several of the points that he made in 1957.[70] One was that giving to omnibus "charity" stopped people from really thinking about which needs mattered most and so inhibited their development as responsible, caring citizens. Making giving "painless" through payroll deductions meant that the chests encouraged the sidestepping of an important moral act: deciding to sacrifice one's own immediate satisfaction in order to care for another. And the use of pressure (whether from an employer, a union official, or one's business peers) to extract donations removed choice entirely from the charitable act. "This is, in short, not giving but taxation," Jenkins concluded.

He disputed the chests' claim that their mechanisms of representation and inclusion really gave citizens a voice in the admission of agencies or the allocation of budgets. So the chests' fundraising was not only taxation but also taxation without representation. Jenkins was opposed, he said, to "taxation by social, business, or economic pressure." Pressures to conform he disliked, in particular, because they made a lie of the celebratory Cold War contrast between the constraints of Soviet society and the freedoms of the West. "We are made social outcasts if we do not support the United Fund." He called for the return of charity to individual agency appeals so that citizens could be "free to make our own choices in at least one small area of life." He praised the Salvation Army's independence and thought it justified by its belief that "the gift without the giver was bare." In a nicely modern twist at the end of his jeremiad, he pointed out that most of the united fund agencies should be tax funded because they are "community necessities." Only when such agencies became public institutions, supported by real taxation, would citizens truly have a "voice and a vote" in spending priorities. In Jenkins' view, impersonality and pressure had helped the chest to collect donations but had also helped to undermine real feelings of care and responsibility – true charity.

The debate sparked by Jenkins' remarks and by subsequent nationally publicized critiques on the same themes seems to have been particularly vigorous in Ottawa.[71] For four years, between 1959 and 1962, that chest's campaign committees discussed and disagreed about the role of emotional appeals in their campaigns. In March 1959, a campaign committee brought in a consultant from the United Community Funds and Councils of America, Bert Williams, to offer his advice on contemporary campaign methods and issues. He told them that it was important to play down the "necessary machine type of organization" and instead to inject "more emotion in the Chest appeal." Although Ottawa's fundraisers followed this advice, the campaign in the fall of 1959 also included a strongly stated appeal to self-interest. This feature of the campaign prompted several citizens to write letters of protest to the chest, calling for an emphasis on truly charitable motivation. These letter writers complained that the chest appeal seemed to be "losing its charitable nature." They explicitly expressed opposition to the appeal to self-interest. For another constituency, the alternative to self-interest was not heightened emotionalism but an appreciation of and commitment to the work of the agencies. A meeting of the member agencies in early 1960 concluded that, "although emotional publicity has its place, it must not become the major item and that the public must have a constructive picture of the aims and ideals of member agencies of the Chest."[72]

Following these two criticisms of the 1959 campaign, the campaign committee decided to ask the public relations group to modify its materials to "give somewhat more emphasis to helping others and the need for sacrificial giving." But the question was not yet settled. The criticism of the chest as a big, impersonal machine continued to circulate and to rankle. For some, the solution was charitable emotion – pity for the needy – but others defended "duty," "community," and "enlightened self-interest" as being "as important as the concept of charity." The Christian concept of "sacrificial giving," which made the motive of charity an intrinsic part of charity's merit, was invoked both in 1960 and in 1961. Early in 1962, a further campaign committee meeting concluded that both efficiency and charity themes had to be included in the chest's public relations. So thoroughly had this question been discussed that it was able to conclude as a matter of policy that "needs were [to be] given greater publicity than the campaign organization in about a three to one proportion roughly."[73] The addition of both "about" and "roughly" belies the mathematical precision of the 3:1 ratio and suggests how controversial this question remained. But the formula indicates a hard-won consensus and makes clear that, consciously at least, these fundraisers thought that they should make pitiable need the primary focus of their appeal for contributions.

Not yet settled by a neat formula, however, was the question of whether the emotional type of appeal was an adequate representation of the actual work done by the member agencies. Here we come to the nub of the problem with the representation of need in these campaigns: as its emotional freight grew, its range of references to real social work and real clients narrowed. The images of the needy in chest advertising in the 1950s used a small number of pictures to stand for many diverse agencies. Unlike the smaller federations of the 1930s, which had been able to show photographs of each agency in their ads, the larger the federation the more abstracted from concrete particulars the images deployed in the annual campaign to show how donations would be used. Compounding this practical pressure in the 1950s was a shift in the design norms of newspaper advertising. The latest thing in ad design was a single big photo or illustration that had a particular kind of aesthetic: not just squarely centred, still-life images but asymmetrical, active shots. Less text, more image. This notion of effective advertising necessarily entailed picking fewer images to stand for "need."

In addition to these effects of immediate circumstances, the abstractions of need in the 1950s chest ads may also be explained by fundraisers' view of how charitable feeling and the real work of social services were linked. From the social work staff of agencies came the message that realistic explanations of their services and of clients' needs should provide the appropriate incentive for giving. They wanted to see that narratives based on the stories of actual people were used in the year-round educational efforts of the chests. Central to the agencies' view on this question was their feeling that campaign goals could be set higher, and successfully met, if truly meeting needs was the deciding factor in setting goals. By contrast, campaign chairs tended to take the view that true accounts of the dimensions of need were irrelevant to campaign success because they had no direct relation to the donors' motivations in giving. For campaign purposes, an emphasis on unmet needs seemed to fundraisers even to be potentially harmful in its impact on giving. It "created some concern about the apparent 'bottomless pit' of voluntary health and welfare."[74] In this view, the specifics of what clients needed and what agencies provided risked scaring off donors.

Some thought that even the more abstract representations of need also risked inciting donor fatigue. The latest advertising and public relations wisdom suggested that an emphasis on the "crippled children and needy families" was actually counterproductive. As international motivational psychology expert Ernest Dichter explained, such images created an aversive subconscious reaction. In a report circulating among fundraisers in 1958, Dichter argued that the prospective donor, faced with such images, feels that, "the moment I give to these people, I am somehow assuming responsibility for their difficulties in an irretrievable fashion." Perceiving this responsibility as overwhelming, the donor would become less willing to give. In Dichter's view of the psychology of donation, the most effective strategies were based on the "brutal" manipulation of the self-centred, infantile, unconscious mind. Journalist Peter C. Newman noted that Dichter's analysis seemed to be confirmed by a 1957 Toronto ad that heavily pressed the shame button. Even though it sparked letters of protest, donations made in the forty-eight hours after the ad appeared totalled $1.5 million – the most ever raised by the city's annual appeal in a single two-day period. Not surprisingly, then, some fundraisers regarded critics such as Jenkins as merely naive about the relations of means to ends. Toronto's 1957 campaign chair said, "I don't know Mr. Jenkins, but has he ever tried to raise nine million dollars?" And to accusations of unfair pressure tactics more generally, Ottawa chest member Norman Smith retorted in 1962 that "a million dollar campaign is not a tea party."[75]

To counter the associations of their campaigns with pressure and futility, the chests tried to connect their appeals to power and pleasure. One of their ways of doing so was to make the chest campaign fun and cheerful. Campaign launches had always had an element of razzmatazz. But the 1950s campaigns became a festival of fashion shows, charity sporting events, variety programs, celebrity appearances, competitions, comedians, and fireworks.[76] These events symbolized affluent optimism and community togetherness. In one football example, a campaign chair kicked off the campaign and the game with a helium-filled ball whose easy, inevitable, and infinite rise conveyed an obvious message.[77] Niche marketing began to appear in the form of exclusive dinners for big givers and low-cost nights out that were accessible to families on tighter budgets. Bingos and lotteries were proposed by some communities, but, as Suzanne Morton has shown, some charity fundraisers continued to find the use of gambling distasteful.[78] Some of the late Victorians' suspicion of charitable bacchanals apparently remained.[79] But not much.

In connecting giving and playing, fundraisers reinforced the notion of the contributing citizen as a consumer.

Another method of making charity pleasurable was to present the needy in a purified form, the better to incite in donors an enticing fantasy of benevolent potency. As Jackson Lears has shown in relation to consumer advertising, twentieth-century advertising techniques were not about the material qualities of the goods displayed but about their fetishized meanings.[80] In the 1930s, the imaginary of a peaceable community assumed a particular importance among these meanings because of Depression-era anxieties about social conflict. And another image, the fatherless family, seemed, in the face of a highly politicized unemployment crisis, to be less dangerous and complex a figure of need than the jobless worker. By the 1950s, the meanings of dependency were in the process of changing. Consequently, so too was the array of emotionally charged materials most likely to be used in representing need. As Nancy Fraser and Linda Gordon have argued, psychological explanations of dependency had begun to displace economic ones.[81] Changes in the chests' preferred images of the needy confirm this shift. No longer able, in a period of affluence, to rely on hunger as the image of need most likely to be perceived as "real," fundraisers had to illustrate symbolically the other kinds of need that member agencies served. As one campaign chair told his canvassers, they were campaigning "not only for funds but for love."[82] In this enterprise, they used images drawn from family life, the "natural" home of love. Natural though familial love may be, however, the images that chest fundraisers thought would effectively deploy it for charity had changed over time.

In the 1930s, the chests' canvassers for love had been able freely to use the image of a pretty woman with two (or sometimes three) young children as an appealing icon of need. Those who planned the campaigns in fact favoured this image above others. As Ralph Blanchard, the administrative director of the Community Chests and Councils of America, wrote to his counterpart, Marjorie Bradford, in the CWC in 1936, "the so-called mother interest will predominate in the poster design and it will again have three figures, two children and the mother."[83] But by the late 1950s, the mother had all but disappeared. In the 1957 campaigns of Vancouver, Ottawa, and Halifax, only one mother image was used.[84] Most striking is the fact that, in the Vancouver campaign's series of twenty-two agency ads that year, mothers as such did not appear at all. In the two ads explaining foster daycare and a home for unmarried mothers, only the children, being cared for by others, were presented. It seems that, for fundraisers, the needy mother, like the unemployed worker, had become so tainted by moral complexity that she could no longer be sentimentalized into an imaginary object of safe benevolence. By the 1950s, the mothers' allowance system supposedly filled in for the absent breadwinner. What apparently remained, then, was a psychological kind of dependence in which the needy mother lacked not merely a breadwinner but also mental health or some other, less clearly boundaried, necessity. It is easy to imagine that the needy mother might thus have seemed to demand the sort of ill-defined and potentially endless form of care that Dichter warned against evoking.

Two other family figures, whose needs for care were less morally ambiguous and conceivably easier to satisfy, were the lonely elder and the sad little girl.[85] One of a series of celebrity ads from the end of the 1950s, featuring fiddler Don Messer, exemplifies this frequent sort of appeal.[86] Messer tells a folksy story about an old woman in his childhood neighbourhood who gave the kids cookies and told them stories. But she was a sad figure because "no friends or relatives ever seemed to bother with her ... Then one day I saw her striding down the sidewalk to the bus stop, her whole face bright as a new penny. She'd found new friends and a new purpose in life at a club for senior citizens sponsored by the money we give each year, the United Way." Now, Messer grew up in New Brunswick between 1909 and the late 1920s in a small town called Tweedsmuir where there was certainly no United Way or Community Chest, no bus system, and probably no seniors' club. So this was an especially flamboyant farago of fictional images. Factual truth was patently not what the fundraiser who designed this ad thought would prompt contributions. The point of the ad was to incite affectionate pity and to present one type of member agency as a simple solution to a simple problem.

The even more central figure of need was the sad little girl. In images such as Figure 18 of the sad girl crouched in a gravelled corner, shadowed by bars, it is certainly possible to see problems of poverty.[87] But the image is "open" enough to suggest a broader need for care. In a single pure and abstract form, the little girls that became emblematic in the 1950s chest campaigns represented needs for counselling or companionship or comfort as distinct from needs for income. That is, they appealed specifically on behalf of the particular kinds of services that belonged to the chests. In the 1957 campaign, the Halifax ads carefully listed the kinds of care the agencies offered and nowhere mentioned unemployment or poverty. Admittedly, the

FIGURE 18 "Somebody Thought that *One* Gift Didn't Matter" ad, 1957. This rich image of need was taken by an American social worker, United Way volunteer, and skilled amateur photographer, Daniel J. Ransohoff. The girls who became emblematic in the 1950s chest campaigns represented needs for counselling or companionship or comfort as distinct from needs for income. ("Daniel J. Ransohoff, 71, Booster for Cincinnati," *New York Times*, 16 June 1993, 24; Halifax *Chronicle-Herald*, 29 October 1957, 13)

1957 Ottawa campaign did list "the destitute" among those whom the chest helped, but it also itemized five other categories of need. And of Vancouver's twenty-two agency ads in 1957, only four described even part of an agency's purpose as enabling its clients to work and earn their own support.[88] The remaining eighteen ads emphasized efforts to end discrimination, to build community relationships, and to support families (and especially children) suffering from a variety of health and personal problems. The sad little girl, like the lonely old man and woman, usefully represented these kinds of social work agencies.

The agencies' services were not as widely understood or perhaps as widely accepted as those of the public programs supposedly now meeting income needs. To present the needs served by these agencies, fundraisers used abstract symbols of care whose effectiveness rested on images of people assumed to be naturally dependent on help. These images allowed fundraisers to sidestep questions about the actual scope of needs less obvious than hunger or homelessness. The ads asked donors to imagine themselves not as breadwinners but as caring mothers and companionate fathers. As consumers of community caring, they were buying the services of social workers, recreation directors, nurses, credit counsellors, addiction researchers, and others to stand in place of these family figures in doing the work of care.

The quantity of need that existed for this sort of care was an imponderable. What was certain was that, in the 1950s, the market for the labour of the professionals who supplied it was highly competitive, so the abstract symbols that incited pity and donations had as their most immediate purpose making it possible for agencies to meet the reasonable wage and pension demands of staff.[89] This practical sort of need was hardly a trigger that would make the dollars shoot out of donors' wallets. Thus, the salary and pension needs had to be hidden while the case was being made for the services of care. And at the same time, the case for care had its own value: reminding a broad public that charitable emotion was part of a democratic citizen's character and that the discursively feminine work of social service belonged in a modern welfare regime alongside income programs.

The Impersonal Personal

In the interwar years, the struggle of the chests had been to establish their legitimacy and attract mass participation. In the war years, they felt threatened by competition from war charities and by suggestions that charity's day was over. Establishing themselves during the 1940s as part of the new welfare regime meant asserting that they served an important social function as demonstrators of need, as developers of new standards for an adequately caring society. It also meant, in reality, doing the work of promoting better income assistance policies. By the 1950s, fundraisers began to fear that their success was threatened by donor fatigue and donor revolt. And, indeed, powerful donors in business and labour were calling for the chests to live up to their promise of making private welfare efficient. "End multiple appeals!" was the cry that condensed that demand and prompted the chests to embark on a fresh and aggressive organizational campaign. They opened their membership admission door to competing agencies and tried to redecorate their appeals with signs and symbols that would attract critical or social subaltern groups and to engage them as donors, canvassers, and participants in planning. Among themselves, they struggled over the question of which targets could be met and how different sorts of appeals might figure in the success or failure of campaigns. From outside their committee rooms came the criticism that the chests were more like a parallel (and morally dubious) system of taxation than like true charity. The chests feared this criticism because of its potential to foment donor resistance.

The struggle around donor resistance was a new stage in the relation of charity to the welfare state. Some of the voices of donor resistance were entirely accepting of the importance of charity but thought that high-pressure fundraising was a contradiction in terms. Giving could not be giving if it was coerced. From this perspective, charity was valuable as a complement to the state, a necessary site for the expression of morally important emotion. This criticism posed no fundamental challenge to the continuation of private welfare. And the outrage about coercive fundraising was entirely compatible, as Reverend Jenkins showed, with a call for the creation of new, tax-funded social services. From another perspective, however, other critics of the chests' impersonality and pressure tactics meant to point to the futility of private welfare in general. This perspective, which had its roots in the traditions of labour's left, lost much ground in the 1950s as the newly expanded union movement accepted that involvement in community services offered respectability to labour and possibly political influence. In 1964, a vigorous attack on the chest by Pat O'Neal from the left wing of the BC Federation of Labour was merely a call for the reform of some chest practices and the piecemeal conversion of some agencies to management under government auspices. He publicly disavowed ever having told anyone not to donate to the united appeal or any other "legitimate charitable campaign."[90] Charity was no longer vulnerable to the criticism that it was a weapon against the welfare state: its demonstration function committed it wholly to encouraging the shift to public responsibility of generally accepted services. The anti-statist hammer was no longer part of the fundraisers' toolkit, and its critics could not turn it against fundraisers.

In other ways, too, the responses made to the threat of donor revolt in the 1950s worked, like the demonstration function argument, to make the chest organization and campaigns wholly compatible with an expanded and expanding state. The organizational innovations and the inclusion practices prompted by the panic about multiple appeals expressed values that blended smoothly with public welfare discourse. Efficiency, fairness, representativeness of the community (electorate), and representation of the donor (taxpayer) were all common terms in liberal democratic welfare state talk. The chests had worked hard to blend into the political scenery. Judging from the terms in which they were criticized, they had succeeded too well for some people's taste in making the charities resemble the welfare state. Supposedly the expressions of a caring society, both the chests and the social programs of the welfare state seemed rather to be coercive and inadequate to the job of meeting needs. At the end of the 1950s, the slogan "everyone gives, everyone benefits," might have been cynically rephrased as "everyone is pressured, and no one is satisfied."

In this context, fundraisers' use in annual campaigns of social events and sentiment was merely another kind of pressure tactic. Neither the mass rally launching a campaign nor the United Way movie night entailed participation in a community project in the way that, for example, actual volunteer social service did. Such fundraising events were just methods of creating a sense that "everyone" is involved and thereby creating a norm of contribution as part of community belonging. This is a subtle coercion that had little to do with care, even though it bespoke universality and a superficial social inclusion. In addition, the abstract icons of need that the campaign ads laid out in their sweetly appealing monotony, while meant to incite feeling, were themselves quite impersonal. If the personal is about particularity, then these images were no more invitations to a personal charitable relationship than pornography is to a personal sexual one. Idealized images of need are meant to trigger emotional automatism: impulse, not moral reflection. Again it is easy to see such methods as being designed to bypass conscious choice and charity.

In their appeal to a generalized, almost biological, response to universal human vulnerabilities, these ads worked within the universalism of a liberal welfare state culture. If small children and the elderly are the needy, then we are all sometimes the needy during the span of our lives. But need actually comes in many human forms. Most make more complex demands on our emotions and moral reasoning than do innocent children. Both in fundraising and in social policy work, people ask what is a "sellable" representation of need. The answer is rarely, for example, multi-problem adult men convicted of sex crimes. One solution to the risk that such predictable biases pose is the liberal universalist one: to wear a mental blindfold when setting up systems to meet human needs. This is a good and important solution. By that means, the goods available as human and citizen rights are distributed to the sweet and the sour alike. But the blindfold solution has a political weakness. That weakness lies in the feature that it shares with the sentimental charity ad: its abstraction of the needy. Being represented without particular traits and getting help without particular emotions, the holders of universal rights (and the programs that confer those rights) are vulnerable to attack by opponents who effectively use images of particular unattractive, supposedly undeserving, recipients to rouse emotions of disgust, envy, anger, and fear. These aversive emotions are deployed to discredit programs whose recipients' entitlements rest on the recipients being imagined as abstract citizens without traits. In the welfare state regime, it could be that fundraising for private charity might help to close off this line of attack on rights-based programs. It could be the job of fundraising to make compelling, emotionally charged representations about needs for community and caring in ways that would underscore the value both of charities and of tax-funded programs. And today's United Way advertising often does just that. But at the end of the 1950s, the fear of donor fatigue drove fundraisers to use threadbare, sentimental images of need. Designed to counter allegations of impersonality, this emotional appeal itself was impersonal.

Conclusion: Similarities, Differences, and Historical Change

Between local and national networks, private and public agencies, necessity and principle, new ways of defining and (always inadequately) meeting social obligations emerged. My account of this process began in 1920s Halifax. There, in a shattered city, the problem of financing social services was both a taxation problem and a fundraising one. Handfield Whitman and his Board of Trade friends persuaded the men and especially the women running charities that a financial federation would solve both the chronic and the acute problems of balancing their agencies' budgets. A certain measure of his persuasiveness came from the tools Whitman and his cohort proposed to use. Innovations such as systematic accounting, a disciplined sales force, and arithmetical formulas to set campaign targets were like tested methods in business and public administration, and they appealed both to an audience of businessmen and to newly enfranchised middle-class women seeking acceptance in their new status as citizens. Still, fundraisers faced the challenge of convincing everyone else that their show was worth applauding. To meet this challenge, they drew on advertising and public relations techniques. In Vancouver, fundraisers put on their show in front of an exceptionally tough audience. There was audible heckling from the left and from a well-connected women's organization. Nevertheless, the show went on, and the paying audience grew. Donor numbers increased, suggesting strongly that people were attracted by the Welfare Federation's message of individuality and community, probity and pity.

But the federation movement was more than just the display entailed in the annual campaign. The chests were also decision-making, deliberative institutions whose representativeness was meant to provide a deep and solid foundation of inclusive participation, one that would legitimate the planning function of the chest and incite contributions to the work of its member agencies. In this work, the interwar years were not especially encouraging. In

Vancouver, the integration of the Catholic charities proved unmanageable, and in Ottawa Protestant organizers collaborated with anglophone Catholics to force a confederal merger on the francophone community of Ottawa. Halifax made only minor efforts to reach out to wage earners and Catholics and apparently did not even think to include the Nova Scotia Home for Coloured Children as a member agency. In all three cities, attempts to include labour always had an element of coercion. Nothing in the chest idea at its origins indicated an impulse to transform inequalities among social groups.

The closest that the chest project came to confronting the structural social differences in the Canadian cities studied here was Charlotte Whitton's solution to the cross-cultural impasse in Ottawa. Elsewhere, the idea that "everyone" should and could participate in this project reduced social complexities and variations in giving power to a moral binary – the selfish and the unselfish. On the one hand, this kind of thinking was profoundly conservative, tending to reinforce social hierarchies. A poor showing from the industrial neighbourhoods of Halifax made it possible for business-based fundraisers to disparage wage earners and their families as ungenerous. If the Vancouver firemen could stump up a decent collective donation, then other workers could be made to seem morally substandard. On the other hand, the idea of universal participation was rich in democratic potential. Combined with the view that contribution entitled the donor to a voice, this idea led to unionists being on the committees that designed a new and smaller place for charity in the welfare state. Edward Jamieson's committee work in studying duplication among Vancouver chest agencies, Fred Ibsen's call for the Halifax chest to address labour in labour terms, Moses McKay's work as a paid labour liaison officer for the chest – these were all part of a changed landscape in the social politics of Canadian cities during and after the Second World War. The substantial inclusion of organized labour in the chests in the 1950s was a move toward more democratic communities. The organizational techniques designed for the practical purpose of inciting donations from the broadest possible population led fundraisers, in the context of the 1940s, to see a much larger project – "to make the Chest movement and the private movement really democratic."[1] In this way, the chests' innovations in organizational technique – the tools of power – helped to change the definition of the problem their work was meant to address.

The federation movement also had complex effects in the world of middle-class gender relations. On the one hand, the modernization of charity was also a masculinization. Women leaders such as Vancouver's Helen

Gregory MacGill, Halifax's Gwendolen Lantz, or Ottawa's Thelma Williams were all sidelined, some of them rather roughly, in the postwar years. They had been accustomed to a welfare regime fuelled in large measure by the low-paid or volunteer labour of women. But as Canadians became more and more persuaded of the value of social services, the demand for social work labour began to force wages up, and they began to be breadwinner wages. The increasing prestige of enterprises such as the chests and the expanding Children's Aid Societies also made staff positions men's jobs. At the same time, however, women volunteers such as Ann Angus and Lillian Farquhar continued to occupy leadership roles in the planning and publicity work of the chests. Indeed, the continuing involvement of middle-class women with this kind of large-scale charity enterprise probably gave them a wider scope for their abilities. Their role in the 1950s was not hived off in a separate women's campaign headquarters. Conflicts between the agencies, represented by social workers, and the chests, dominated by businessmen, could and sometimes did have a bitter edge of gender conflict in the 1950s, as Gale Wills has argued. But these conflicts nonetheless were also contests between political programs and institutional interests rather than being directly about whether or not women should have a voice in public affairs. The addition of ambitious young men to the ranks of leadership in private charity was hard on the careers of women social workers, but in a still-sexist public sphere this gender shift in social work leadership was not a bad thing for the weight of influence that the chests could bring to bear in public policy processes.

By the mid-1950s, the chests were a well-established institution in urban Canada. Their leaders and many volunteers had succeeded in making a new structure for the financing of social services. Alas, while fighting with every means at their disposal to meet the needs of social agencies, they frequently failed to do so. When the cities' brightest business and professional talent could claim they had done their best, the very competence, creativity, and energy of chest staff and volunteers helped to make the case that voluntary means were inadequate to meet social needs. First, in the 1950s, this argument was used by fundraisers such as Hugh Allan to improve or create income assistance programs. Then, in the 1960s, the same logic led to the federal-provincial financing of services such as the Children's Aid Societies, with the Halifax CAS saga forming part of the material that decision makers considered. It was true, then, that the inadequacy of private charity led to the creation of the welfare state in these specific ways. But that inadequacy was not as clear in the struggling 1930s as it was in the affluent 1950s. And it was always the *combination* of effectively deployed expertise with insufficient revenue results that made the chests influential in state formation. What made the case for more public funding convincing were the several decades of hard-fought charity campaigns. The chests' enormous success in increasing participation and multiplying many times over the amounts collected was the evidence needed to show that even the most determined fundraisers could not meet the needs that Canadians were coming to believe had to be met. The problem of meeting need, it turned out, was not irrationally organized charity but voluntarism itself. Even charity, in its modern 1950s form, had to turn to methods that bordered on coercion. A fundraising toolkit designed to keep voluntarism alive had the effect of making visible the limits of voluntarism and produced fresh reasons for preferring "public charities."

By the late 1950s, the chests had become an established institution. The Red Feather appeal, as their annual campaigns were generally known, was part of North American urban culture. These campaigns allowed people to participate in a ritual of caring, inclusive community. But the very established nature of the united appeals made them a target for critics of complacency and conformity. Along with the now-forgotten Reverend Jenkins, a now-better-known controversialist of the period, journalist Pierre Berton, took on coercive charity in 1961 before he took on spiritually empty Christianity in his 1965 book *The Comfortable Pew.*[2] The united appeals were an attractive target because of the contradictions that had emerged over the thirty or more years of their existence. Supposedly about care, they had been repeatedly and convincingly criticized for their inability to set attainable campaign targets that actually reflected what the social agencies said was needed.

The united appeal leadership had become thoroughly practised in meeting such criticisms. Addressing critics in the 1960s, leaders would point to the record of increased government spending on welfare and claim credit for having goaded the government into doing better and spending more. They acknowledged that agencies' needs were not always met but argued that fundraisers could only generate a consistent source of charitable donations if goals were meetable and campaigns therefore successful. It had become the settled common sense within united appeal campaign circles that campaign goals were the result of exercises in compromise.[3] Implied in this response was an allegation that critics simply lacked the ability to find the reasonable middle point and were not sufficiently mature to be competent actors in public life. This view of critics was made explicit in 1969 when Victoria's campaign chairman replied to criticisms from an NDP MLA, social worker

Dave Barrett. He had said of the UA campaign, "what a sham, what a mockery, what a sixteenth century attitude toward community social welfare services." The fundraiser retorted, "I've known [Barrett] since he was a little wet-nosed kid – I hope one day he grows up."[4]

The celebration of the campaigns as expressions of compromise was bound to inflame opposition in the political climate of the mid- to late 1960s. Maturity and compromise were not especially valued among some important actors new on the political scene. One of those new actors was the Student Union for Peace Action (SUPA). A 1965 CBC current affairs show, directed by Ted Koch, used SUPA and the youthful, uncompromising style of its activists as a point of contrast to the united appeal's place as part of the establishment. The opening shots highlighted the proximity of the appeal's Toronto headquarters to Queen's Park, and the script's neutral description of the organization took on a disparaging tone because it was accompanied by footage of a mechanized mailing list being cranked out by the latest office automation technology. The contrast to SUPA was succinctly expressed by a SUPA volunteer saying that her work was not about "replacing a system with another system."[5] Giving directly of one's own time and energy to help solve community problems was, for SUPA and other new social movements, more likely to produce socially just solutions than was giving money to the chests.

Faced with this sort of criticism, one response by the chests was to try to include representatives of the new social movements in the chests' planning process, just as labour had been engaged in the 1940s and 1950s. But this strategy could and did backfire, sometimes loudly. For example, Vancouver chest board member Alex Bandy, representing a welfare rights agency called the Unemployed Citizens Welfare Improvement Council, described the annual appeal on campaign kick-off day as "a charade that provides big business with a tax dodge and cheap public relations." Even though some of the goals of the welfare rights movement – to make the welfare state more democratic and to extract adequate income assistance from government – were compatible with the chest tradition, others were not. It would not be possible to integrate into the federated fundraising movement goals that entailed explicitly challenging "the system" – capitalist market relations, electoral democracy, and mediating voluntary associations. Its founders had hoped the Community Chests would become, in effect, part of the power structure of Canadian cities, and they had succeeded in making them so. As a result, the chests were in no position to entertain seriously goals that were not compatible within the assumptions of the chief beneficiaries of the system. But it is worth noting that the defenders of charity, faced with attacks from the left, did not retort with calls to retrench the welfare state or with assertions that the chests helped to keep taxes low. Instead, their defence lay in their continuing contribution to expansion of the democratic welfare state.[6]

In the four decades that this book covers, comparisons between charity and the state formed the common-sense substrate of debates about social policy. In these contests, the point being made by comparing public and private was typically that one or the other of these systems for providing food, shelter, and help was entirely better than the other. The assumption was that they were fundamentally different systems. I have argued, however, that there were deep similarities in the categories and assumptions of private and public systems. Whether it was the data collection methods, the universalist conception of the contributors, the evolution of a consumer standpoint in place of a stockholder one, or the abstraction of the "less privileged" into rights holders or sentimentalized tokens, the organizing conceptions of obligation, voice, and need were shared across the public/private divide. Both modern charity and the welfare state rested on a common culture of contribution, even though within that culture fierce ideological divisions were possible.

In showing the existence of this culture of contribution, I mean to suggest something about how skilled public actors organize support for their projects. The Community Chest fundraisers exploited the cultural similarities between taxation and modern fundraising to navigate the turbulent ideological waters of their day. In the ideologies they encountered, three points of supposed contrast were particularly important: reason versus feeling, compulsion versus freedom, and democratic accountability versus self-interested or arbitrary elite governance. But at a cultural level, none of these was a simple description of historical fact about public or private provision. Consider, first, reason versus feeling. The chests used charitable emotion in their fundraising campaigns, to be sure, but their participation in modern rational administrative culture was clearly apparent in their commitment to planning, their careful assessments of donor capacity, their "discovery" of needs on the basis of research, and their orchestration of combined action by thousands of volunteers. Some of their early activists, such as Ivor Jackson, defined the federation project explicitly against older models of charity in which wealthy individuals luxuriated in the pleasures of personal benevolence.[7] And not only were the chests deeply committed to rationality, but it is also easy to point to ways in which the state was not. For instance, in comparison to the chests' budget allocation processes, the setting of social services budgets based on electoral calculations only substitutes a calculation coloured by ambition or other aggressive emotions for one based at least partly on a feeling of helpful interest and concern. The desire to get one's party re-elected is no more purely rational than the wish to see VON better staffed. And the fear or dislike of social assistance recipients evident in the rhetoric and practices of some public actors – civil servants or politicians – hardly suggests that a clear-headed rationality was always guiding the agents of the state. Even benefits conferred by right come from policy processes in which both fear and compassion play their parts, and few if any of our income assistance programs have been administered without some measure of discretion. Even in the most "rational" programs of the welfare state, emotions, charitable and otherwise, have played a part. In this way, public and private were not dichotomously different.

Next, consider compulsion versus freedom. Apparently, compulsion has clearly distinguished taxation from charity, public from private funding. One can choose one's charities but not one's tax contributions (at least not without the help of a clever tax accountant). As critics of the chest method pointed out, however, fundraisers had some effective means of coercion at their disposal. Some, such as social pressure among peers, were considered fair. Others, particularly between employers and workers or between businesses and their bigger customers, were the subject of protest. A nurse recently arrived in Canada from Great Britain in the late 1950s described the routine of getting paid at the Royal Victoria Hospital. Lining up with the other nurses to get their pay envelopes, she was surprised to find, standing next to the payroll clerk, the hospital's head nurse asking her what her donation to the Red Feather appeal would be.[8] The compulsion she experienced at that moment was no more easy to evade (and conceivably less so) than the impersonal pressures that the Department of National Revenue could bring to bear by the threat of auditing a business's books. Still, the taxman had the police and the courts at his disposal, and the punishments for evading tax could be severe. Further research into tax evasion and enforcement is necessary before I can offer a definitive picture of just how far and how effectively paying taxes was compelled and how far a willingness to pay – genuine voluntarism – featured in the history of twentieth-century taxation. In the early decades of the century, some tax authorities thought income tax was so easily evadable that it "is almost [regarded] as voluntary, and is considered pretty much in the same light as donations to the neighbourhood church or Sunday school."[9]

Were we to have an empirical rather than a mythic version of Canadian tax history, we would be able to say how great a difference in voluntariness lay between direct taxation and charity during the debates about the financing of welfare at mid-century.[10] Here, by showing the element of coercion in mid-century fundraising methods, I have argued that in at least one way this dichotomy was not always perfectly clear.

Finally, and most compellingly, another certain objection to claims about the similarity of public and private is that, however well researched and rationally planned the spending of charitable dollars may have been in the hands of the chests, and however coercive their methods, the people who made the spending decisions were self-appointed and therefore less accountable to the popular will than were government decision makers. This objection is right on the point of fact. The question raised by this point, however, is whether the processes that legitimated decisions of public policy makers, and their enforcement, were more democratic than the decisions made by the volunteer leadership of the Community Chests. The democratic character of elected government in mid-twentieth-century North America has been the subject of a large literature and considerable debate. The removal of decision making from lawmakers to bureaucrats, the vitiating of election campaigns by public relations gamesmanship, and the role of party finance in compromising politicians' responsiveness to the full range of interests among the electorate have all been sources of concern about the health of twentieth-century democracy. Set against these concerns about electoral democracy, the chests' deliberative bodies, by the mid-1950s, do not seem to have been so much less representative of and responsive to the public than was Parliament. In proximity to their publics, an important mechanism of accountability, they were arguably more democratic, not less.

If the cultural underpinnings of public and private financing of provision were not so thoroughly and necessarily separate and not so different in mid-twentieth-century Canada, then what should we make of the ferocious ideological debates about the merits of the two? Were the participants in these debates merely hiding material interests behind a facade of political debate, engaging either in mystification or in self-delusion? If they were, then we might think the explanation of events is best served by ignoring the ideological clamour and exploring material interests. The story of the chests certainly supports the view that there were economic interests such as tax reduction or income redistribution at play. But the story of the manifold interactions between the charities and the government and their use of common cultural tools also suggests that the ideological debates about similarity and difference were not merely surface noise, distortions of reality to be cleaned away to understand what happened. Rather, the fundraisers used these ideologies in ways that affected state formation.

Consider a summary list of the main qualities attributed to public and private during the twentieth-century welfare debates, from the statist and the anti-statist viewpoints (see Table 2). The fundraisers' use of this discourse was innovative. Fundraisers claimed for private charity both the positive attributions from the anti-statist binaries and those made for the public in the statist pairs. In different strategic contexts, before and after the creation of the major national income assistance programs and the broad-based income tax, the purposes that this mixed discourse served for fundraisers changed. In the earlier period, the prevention of state expansion predominated, and in the latter period the preservation of private charitable organizations was central. Both purposes were effectively served by the fundraisers' use of ideological language.

Rather than dismiss this fundraising discourse as merely misrepresentation and mystification, however, we should see it as having valuably contributed to the cultural context of state formation. The effect of charities defending their existence in terms that they shared with the proponents of state expansion was to help organize the coexistence of and collaborative action between

TABLE 2

Binary descriptors of public and private welfare

	Public	Private
Statist	Rational	Sentimental
	Universalist	Particularist
	Inclusive	Exclusive
	Democratically governed	Elite governed
	Modern	Traditional
	Professional	Amateur
Anti-statist	Impersonal	Caring
	Arbitrary	Sensitive
	Corrupt	Responsible
	Spiritually empty	Religious
	Dangerously experimental	Time tested
	Self-interested	Altruistic
	Compulsory	Voluntary

the agencies of the state and the organizations of civil society. Both the eliciting of donations and the winning of votes depended on presenting a welfare enterprise in culturally endorsed terms. In the rhetorical work of both the chest fundraisers and their critics, we see being made and tested the terms in which a democratic welfare state could be established and consent to its imposition of taxation be secured. This process is not finished. Both politicians and fundraisers will continue to talk about obligation and care, efficiency and accountability, inclusion and responsiveness. Neither private charity nor public rights naturally embody all of these or other imaginable democratic virtues. And, while binaries may be necessary both as a tool of thinking and as a tool of politics, reality is not so neatly arranged in pairs. With their ideologically messy and multi-faceted methods, the chests blurred political binaries and creatively contributed to historical change.

Appendices

APPENDIX 1

Number of donors to annual campaign for funds, from first campaign to 1961

Year	Halifax	Vancouver	Ottawa
1925	1,700 or 2,400		
1926	3,500		
1927			
1928	4,400		
1929	5,700		
1930	5,700[a]	4,200[b]	
1931	5,479	20,520	
1932	6,031	23,028	2,993 or 2,944[c]
1933		23,774	2,800
1934	10,680 (est.)	24,790	
1935	10,700	24,925 or 26,400[d]	
1936		28,223 or 27,300[e]	
1937	10,669[f]	33,481 or 29,200[g]	23,000 (approx.)[h]
1938		33,449 or 33,100[i]	
1939	almost 12,000	35,588	
1940		50,178	25,391
1941		53,000	
1942		58,500 (est.)	
1943		63,000	
1944	17,300	76,356	
1945		73,731	43,000+[j]
1946			
1947			
1948			

▶

APPENDIX 1

Year	Halifax	Vancouver	Ottawa
1949		85,475	
1950		93,032	
1952		99,000+	
1954			76,000
1956			84,600
1960			84,000
1961			95,000

NOTES: Unless otherwise indicated, these numbers are drawn from the 1926 campaign clippings and, for subsequent years, the minutes of the annual meetings in UWHD; the annual reports or the executive director's reports in UWLM; and the minutes of the annual meetings or goal-setting reports in UWOC.

a Minutes, meeting of chest council, 20 February 1931, NSARM, UWHD, MG 20.

b "Welfare Rally," *Vancouver Sun*, 23 October 1935, 2.

c "A Report on the Social Services and on a Possible Basis of Financial Federation for the City and Area of Greater Ottawa," May 1932, LAC, CCSD, MG 28 I 10, vol. 43, file 213, 109. The smaller figure comes from a shorter, printed version of this report, which may be found in LAC, Charlotte Whitton Papers, MG 30 E 256, vol. 21.

d The lower figure is from the annual meeting report in 1936; the higher figure is from the 1938 annual report.

e The lower figure is from the annual meeting report in 1936; the higher figure is from the 1938 annual report.

f Gwladys Kennedy, Executive Secretary, report, 28 February 1938, LAC, CCSD, MG 28 I 10, vol. 228, file 228-16.

g The lower figure is from the 1938 annual report; the higher figure is from the executive director's report to the meeting of the board of directors, 10 February 1938.

h Minutes, meeting of division chairmen and campaign committee, 9 December 1937, UWOC.

i The lower figure is from the 1938 annual report; the higher figure is from the 1941 annual report.

j "Report of the Campaign and Publicity Committees," re 17 September-13 October 1945, UWOC.

APPENDIX 2

Total number of cities with one or more Community Chests

1917	1	1941	14	1948	47
1918	2	1942	13	1950	49
1922	3	1943	18	1951	50
1925	4	1944	21	1952	52
1933	7	1945	24	1954	57
1937	9	1946	25	1956	66
1940	16	1947	40	1958	74

NOTE: Some cities, usually larger ones, had two or more chests, organized by religion. Cities that organized "United Home Services" campaigns during the war were not counted as chest cities until and unless they converted after the Second World War to peacetime chests.

SOURCES: The data are drawn from the annual Community Chest campaign results reported in *Child and Family Welfare*, its successor, *Canadian Welfare*, and J. Irving Oelbaum, "Community Chest," *Canadian Welfare* 24, 7 (1949): 67-68.

Notes

INTRODUCTION: PUBLIC AND PRIVATE IN WELFARE HISTORY

1 The major centres were Toronto, Montreal, and Vancouver. The smaller ones were Ottawa, Halifax, Winnipeg, Hamilton, and Regina. General studies of the Community Chests or studies of particular chests may be found in Eleanor L. Brilliant, *The United Way: Dilemmas of Organized Charity* (New York: Columbia University Press, 1990); John R. Seeley et al., *Community Chest: A Case Study in Philanthropy* (Toronto: University of Toronto Press, 1970); Aileen D. Ross, "Organized Philanthropy in an Urban Community," *Canadian Journal of Economics and Political Science* 18, 4 (1952): 474-86; Roy Lubove, *The Professional Altruist: The Emergence of Social Work as a Career, 1880-1930* (Cambridge, MA: Harvard University Press, 1965), 183-219; Gale Wills, *A Marriage of Convenience: Business and Social Work in Toronto, 1918-1957* (Toronto: University of Toronto Press, 1995); Anne MacLennan, *Red Feather in Montreal: A History* (Montreal: Red Feather Foundation, 1996); and Stephen Speisman, *The Jews of Toronto* (Toronto: McClelland and Stewart, 1979), Chapter 16. The Montreal and Toronto Federations of Jewish Philanthropies were commonly credited with being Canada's firsts; see, for example, J. Irving Oelbaum, "Community Chest," *Canadian Welfare* 24, 7 (1949); and "Who Is My Neighbour?" 1946, Library and Archives Canada (LAC), National Film Board (NFB) Fonds, item 150637. However, in the Montreal case at least, the Federation of Jewish Philanthropies in 1917 was an associated charities organization whose fundraising methods were wholly traditional. The modern fundraising element was added in 1923 when a businessmen's committee was created to improve this aspect of the work. Seventh Annual Report of the Federation of Jewish Philanthropies of Montreal and Constituent Societies, 1923, Canadian Jewish Congress National Archives, MB1/B/11, 4, 7.

2 "Results of United Community Campaigns in Canada for 1958," *Canadian Welfare* 34, 2 (1958): 75.

3 The discussion of the "chest idea" in the next two paragraphs draws on the records relating to the initial organizational efforts in the 1920s of the Halifax and Vancouver federated appeals. These records are mainly to be found in two collections:

Nova Scotia Archives and Records Management (NSARM), Records of the United Way of Halifax-Dartmouth (UWHD), MG 20, and City of Vancouver Archives (CVA), Vancouver Board of Trade (VBT), Add. Mss. 300. In the first of these two collections, the key documents are in vol. 1717, a scrapbook; see, especially, the clippings for May 1925. For the second of these two collections, the key documents are in vol. 5, 319, report by W.C. Woodward, chairman of the Retail Merchants' Bureau of the Vancouver Board of Trade, 4 May 1922; vol. 146, insert at 44, "Minutes of Meeting of Organizations Called to Receive a Report Prepared by the Special Committee re Community Chest," 26 June 1923; vol. 8, insert at 487, "Minutes of a Special Meeting of the Council of the Vancouver Board of Trade," 8 November 1928; and "Expert Urges Chest System of Charities," *Vancouver Star,* 13 August 1929, 7. Some of the same themes appear in the origins of Toronto's Federation for Community Service, described in Jacquelyn Gale Wills, "Efficiency, Feminism, and Co-Operative Democracy: Origins of the Toronto Social Planning Council, 1918-1957" (PhD diss., Department of Social Work, University of Toronto, 1989).

4 I do not mean here the war income tax launched in 1917 – it applied to a very small percentage of the Canadian population. See Chapter 1 for a further discussion.

5 Dennis Guest, *The Emergence of Social Security in Canada,* 3rd ed. (Vancouver: UBC Press, 1997), 84-87; John H. Taylor, "Sources of Political Conflict in the Thirties: Welfare Policy and a Geography of Need," in *The "Benevolent" State: The Growth of Welfare in Canada,* ed. Allan Moscovitch and Jim Albert (Toronto: Garamond, 1987), 148-49; Mary MacKinnon, "Relief Not Insurance: Canadian Unemployment Relief in the 1930s," *Explorations in Economic History* 27 (1990): 51-52; Allan Irving and Patricia Daenzer, "Unemployment and Social Work Practice: An Historical Overview – 1929-1987," in *Unemployment and Welfare: Social Policy and the Work of Social Work,* ed. Graham Riches and Gordon W. Ternowetsky (Toronto: Garamond Press, 1990), 272; Pierre Berton, *The Great Depression, 1929-1939* (Toronto: McClelland and Stewart, 1990), 49-50. Berton's rather imprecise account of the 1929 debate about the responsibility of the federal government to spend on unemployment relief quotes parliamentarians listing the strains on missions and soup kitchens along with the strains on municipal governments as signs that existing resources were unable to cope in the face of an enormous unemployment crisis. For an example of the normal use of "public charity" as distinguished from "private charity," see Vancouver Welfare Federation, Chairmen of Budget Committee and Board of Directors, to Archbishop Duke, 29 June 1933, LAC, Records of the Canadian Council on Social Development (CCSD), MG 28 I 10, vol. 253, file 253-10.

6 Colin Jones, "Some Recent Trends in the History of Charity," in *Charity, Self-Interest, and Welfare in the English Past,* ed. Martin Daunton (New York: St. Martin's Press, 1996), 52.

7 James Struthers, *No Fault of Their Own: Unemployment and the Canadian Welfare State, 1914-1941* (Toronto: University of Toronto Press, 1983); James Struthers, *The Limits of Affluence: Welfare in Ontario: 1920-1970* (Toronto: University of Toronto Press, 1994).

8 Pat Armstrong, "The Welfare State as History," in *The Welfare State in Canada: Past, Present, and Future,* ed. Raymond B. Blake, Penny E. Bryden, and J. Frank Strain (Toronto: Irwin Publishing, 1997), 52-73; Neil Brooks, "The Role of the Voluntary Sector in a Modern Welfare State," in *Between State and Market: Essays on Charities Law and Policy in Canada,* ed. Jim Phillips, Bruce Chapman, and David Stevens (Montreal: McGill-Queen's University Press, 2001), 166-216; Samuel A. Martin, *An Essential Grace: Funding Canada's Health Care, Education, Welfare, Religion, and Culture* (Toronto: McClelland and Stewart, 1985); Lester M. Salamon, *Partners in Public Service: Government-Nonprofit Relations in the Modern Welfare State* (Baltimore: Johns Hopkins University Press, 1995); Alan Wolfe, *Whose Keeper? Social Science and Moral Obligation* (Berkeley: University of California Press, 1989).

9 Ellis W. Hawley, for example, notes the parallels between the prescriptions of contemporary American conservatives and the partnership strategies of President Herbert Hoover and goes on to argue that the failure of the Hoover strategy in the 1930s has relevant lessons for today's politics. Ellis W. Hawley, "Herbert Hoover, Associationalism, and the Great Depression Relief Crisis of 1930-1933," in *With Us Always: A History of Private Charity and Public Welfare,* ed. Donald T. Critchlow and Charles H. Parker (New York: Rowman and Littlefield, 1998), 161-90.

10 In a distinctive variation of this option, David C. Hammack argues, to continue the metaphor, that philanthropy bounced. That is, various forms of donor-funded social services found new fundraising strategies that helped them to continue to be useful, if not to meet all the needs of the unemployed in the 1930s, and indeed to expand in the 1940s. David C. Hammack, "Failure and Resilience: Pushing the Limits in Depression and Wartime," in *Charity, Philanthropy, and Civility in American History,* ed. Lawrence J. Friedman and Mark D. McGarvie (New York: Cambridge University Press, 2003), 263-80.

11 Lizabeth Cohen, *Making a New Deal: Industrial Workers in Chicago, 1919-1939* (New York: Cambridge University Press, 1990), Chapters 2 and 5, especially 218-38.

12 David Beito, *From Mutual Aid to the Welfare State: Fraternal Societies and Social Services, 1890-1967* (Chapel Hill: University of North Carolina Press, 2000), 228-29, 231, 234. British historian Stephen Davies argues similarly for the British case that nineteenth-century fraternalism offers a valuable model for twentieth-century welfare reform. Stephen Davies, "Two Conceptions of Welfare: Voluntarism and Incorporationism," in *The Welfare State,* ed. Ellen Frankel Paul, Fred D. Miller, Jr., and Jeffrey Paul (New York: Cambridge University Press, 1997), 39-68. The philosophical view of obligation that underpins these interpretations is spelled

out (and Beito's research is deployed) by David Schmidtz, "Guarantees," in *The Welfare State,* ed. Ellen Frankel Paul, Fred D. Miller, Jr., and Jeffrey Paul (New York: Cambridge University Press, 1997), 1-19.

13 David Beito, "A Conversation with David Beito," 21 July 2000, http://www.fcpp.org/publication_detail.php?PubID=210.

14 Nancy Christie, *Engendering the State: Family, Work, and Welfare in Canada* (Toronto: University of Toronto Press, 2000), Chapter 6.

15 Mariana Valverde, "The Mixed Social Economy as a Canadian Tradition," *Studies in Political Economy* 47 (1995): 33-60.

16 Lynne Marks, "Personal Ties and Poor Relief in Small Town Ontario," *Studies in Political Economy* 47 (1995): 61-87; Margaret Little, "Charity and the Moral Regulation of Motherhood," *Studies in Political Economy* 47 (1995): 89-109; Paula Maurutto, *Governing Charities: Church and State in Toronto's Catholic Archdiocese, 1850-1950* (Montreal: McGill-Queen's University Press, 2003); Shirley Tillotson, *The Public at Play: Gender and the Politics of Recreation on Postwar Ontario* (Toronto: University of Toronto Press, 2000); Renée Lafferty, "Child Welfare in Halifax, 1900-1960: Institutional Transformation, Denominationalism, and the Creation of a 'Public' Welfare System (PhD diss., Department of History, Dalhousie University, 2003); Magda Fahrni, *Household Politics: Montreal Families and Postwar Reconstruction* (Toronto: University of Toronto Press, 2006).

17 Several collections, both historical and interdisciplinary, make this their unifying question, and others touch on it extensively: Donald T. Critchlow and Charles H. Parker, eds., *With Us Always: A History of Private Charity and Public Welfare* (New York: Rowman and Littlefield, 1998); Martin J. Daunton, ed., *Charity, Self-Interest, and Welfare in the English Past* (New York: St. Martin's Press, 1996); Ellen Frankel Paul, Fred D. Miller, Jr., and Jeffrey Paul, eds., *The Welfare State* (New York: Cambridge University Press, 1997). See also Jane Lewis, *The Voluntary Sector, the State, and Social Work in Britain: The Charity Organisation Society/Family Welfare Association since 1869* (Aldershot: Elgar, 1995).

18 Geoffrey Finlayson, *Citizen, State, and Social Welfare in Britain, 1830-1990* (Oxford: Clarendon Press, 1994).

19 Richard S. Tompson, *The Charity Commission and the Age of Reform* (London: Routledge and Kegan Paul, 1979), Chapter 9.

20 Judith Fingard, *The Dark Side of Life in Victorian Halifax* (Porter's Lake, NS: Pottersfield Press, 1989), 171-72; Andrew Jones and Leonard Rutman, *In the Children's Aid: J.J. Kelso and Child Welfare in Ontario* (Toronto: University of Toronto Press, 1981), Chapter 3; Jane Ursel, *Private Lives, Public Policy: 100 Years of State Intervention in the Family* (Toronto: Women's Press, 1992), 333-35; Harry M. Cassidy, *Public Health and Welfare Reorganization: The Postwar Problem in the Canadian Provinces* (Toronto: Ryerson Press, 1945), 41-52; Heather MacDougall,

Activists and Advocates: Toronto's Health Department, 1883-1983 (Toronto: Dundurn Press, 1990).

21 Bernard Vigod, "Ideology and Institutions in Quebec: The Public Charities Controversy, 1921-1926," *Histoire sociale* 11, 21 (1978): 167-82; Valverde, "Mixed Social Economy," 44-48; Robert Bremner, *American Philanthropy* (Chicago: University of Chicago Press, 1960), 95-96.

22 Mark D. McGarvie, "The *Dartmouth College* Case and the Legal Design of Civil Society," in *Charity, Philanthropy, and Civility in American History,* ed. Lawrence J. Friedman and Mark D. McGarvie (New York: Cambridge University Press, 2003), 91-106.

23 Oelbaum, "Community Chest," 68-69. Oelbaum's account begins in 1939, but the community organization division that Oelbaum describes existed before the war. See LAC, CCSD, MG 28 I 10, vols. 157-62.

24 Bremner, *American Philanthropy,* 133; David G. Duff, "Charitable Contributions and the Personal Income Tax: Evaluating the Canadian Credit," in *Between State and Market: Essays on Charities Law and Policy in Canada,* ed. Jim Phillips, Bruce Chapman, and David Stevens (Montreal: McGill-Queen's University Press, 2001), 408-9; for the role of the welfare federations in campaigning for that exemption, see minutes, meeting of the executive committee, 18 June 1930, NSARM, UWHD, MG 20.

25 Christie, *Engendering the State;* Margaret Jane Hillyard Little, *"No Car, No Radio, No Liquor Permit": The Moral Regulation of Single Mothers in Ontario, 1920-1997* (Toronto: Oxford University Press, 1998); Struthers, *Limits of Affluence,* Chapter 1; Ruth Roach Pierson, "Gender and the Unemployment Insurance Debates in Canada, 1934-1940," *Labour/Le travail* 25 (1990): 77-103; Dorothy Chunn, *From Punishment to Doing Good: Family Courts and Socialized Justice in Ontario, 1880-1940* (Toronto: University of Toronto Press, 1992).

26 James Struthers, "'Lord Give Us Men': Women and Social Work in English Canada, 1918-1953," in *The Benevolent State?* ed. A. Moscovitch and J. Albert (Toronto: Garamond Press, 1986), 126-43; Judith Ann Trolander, *Professionalism and Social Change: From the Settlement House Movement to Neighborhood Centers, 1886 to the Present* (New York: Columbia University Press, 1987); Linda Gordon, "Social Insurance and Public Assistance: The Influence of Gender in Welfare Thought in the United States, 1890-1935," *American Historical* Review 97, 1 (1992): 19-54; Tillotson, *Public at* Play; Sara Z. Burke, *Seeking the Highest Good: Social Service and Gender at the University of Toronto, 1888-1937* (Toronto: University of Toronto Press, 1996).

27 Frank Prochaska, *The Voluntary Impulse: Philanthropy in Modern Britain* (London: Faber and Faber, 1988), Chapter 4.

28 Carmen Nielsen Varty, "The City and the Ladies: Politics, Religion, and Female Benevolence in Mid-Nineteenth Century Hamilton, Canada West," *Journal of*

Canadian Studies 38, 2 (2004): 151-71; Lucia Ferretti, *Entre voisins: La société paroissiale en milieu urbain: Saint-Pierre-Apôtre de Montréal, 1848-1930* (Montreal: Boréal, 1992), Chapter 4; Brian Clarke, *Piety and Nationalism: Lay Voluntary Associations and the Creation of an Irish-Catholic Community in Toronto, 1850-1895* (Montreal: McGill-Queen's University Press, 1993), 84-85; Lynne Marks, *Revival and Roller Rinks: Religion, Leisure, and Identity in Late-Nineteenth-Century Small-Town Ontario* (Toronto: University of Toronto Press, 1996), 75-79; Wendy Mitchinson, "Canadian Women and Church Missionary Societies in the 19th Century: A Step towards Independence," *Atlantis* 2, 2, Part 2 (1977): 60-63.

29 Kathleen D. McCarthy, "Women and Political Culture," in *Charity, Philanthropy, and Civility in American History*, ed. Lawrence J. Friedman and Mark D. McGarvie (New York: Cambridge University Press, 2003), 179-98; Ruth Crocker, "From Gift to Foundation: The Philanthropic Lives of Mrs. Russell Sage," in *Charity, Philanthropy, and Civility in American History*, ed. Lawrence J. Friedman and Mark D. McGarvie (New York: Cambridge University Press, 2003), 199-216.

30 Laura Tuennerman-Kaplan, *Helping Ourselves: Power, Giving, and Community Identity in Cleveland, Ohio, 1880-1930* (Kent, OH: Kent State University Press, 2001), Chapter 4.

31 See, e.g., Wills, *Marriage of Convenience*, 133.

32 Bremner, *American Philanthropy*, 140.

33 Lubove, *Professional Altruist*, 172-73, 180, Chapter 7.

34 Walter Trattner, *From Poor Law to Welfare State: A History of Social Welfare in America* (New York: Free Press, 1974), 222.

35 Daniel J. Walkowitz, *Working with Class: Social Workers and the Politics of Middle-Class Identity* (Chapel Hill: University of North Carolina Press, 1999).

36 For Guest's descriptions of charity, see *Emergence*, 16, 32-24, 38-39; and Irving and Daenzer, "Unemployment," 283.

37 Wills, *Marriage of Convenience*.

38 MacLennan, *Red Feather*; Struthers, *Limits of Affluence*, 21, 101-4; Speisman, *Jews of Toronto*, Chapter 16.

39 Desmond Morton, *Fight or Pay: Soldiers' Families in the Great War* (Vancouver: UBC Press, 2004).

40 Seeley et al., *Community Chest*; Ross, "Organized Philanthropy." The article by Ross gives a particularly good overview of the major changes in fundraising just after the Second World War. She has relatively little to say about the role of labour in the chests except to acknowledge that relations between capital and labour in her city were atypical (480n16). Her study was based on various agency and chest records, interviews, and participant observations in the annual appeals of "Wellsville," especially the YMCA and the "Community Chest" (Montreal's Protestant Financial Federation).

41 Ross, "Organized Philanthropy," 485-86.

42 Lubove, *Professional Altruist.*

43 Daniel T. Rodgers, *Atlantic Crossings: Social Politics in a Progressive Age* (Cambridge, MA: Belknap Press, 1998).

44 For such a broad interpretive trend, the number of examples is vast. A particularly expert and telling example that shows the merits of the approach is Margaret McCallum, "Corporate Welfarism in Canada, 1919-1939," *Canadian Historical Review* 31, 1 (1990): 46-79.

45 See Chapter 4 and Conclusion.

46 In Canada, this influence is apparent in William Gairdner, *The Attack on the Family* (Toronto: Stoddart, 1992), in which he approvingly quotes (80-81) a leading Reaganite commentator, Charles Murray. For an American critique of this notional separation of public and private, see Salamon, *Partners,* 1-5, Chapter 2.

47 Books and essays from these various literatures that particularly influenced me while writing this book include Andrew Barry, Thomas Osborne, and Nikolas Rose, eds., *Foucault and Political Reason: Liberalism, Neo-Liberalism, and Rationalities of Government* (Chicago: University of Chicago Press, 1996), especially Nikolas Rose, "Governing 'Advanced' Liberal Democracies," 37-64, and Pat O'Malley, "Risk and Responsibility," 189-208; Stuart Hall, "Gramsci's Relevance for the Study of Race and Ethnicity," in *Stuart Hall: Critical Dialogues in Cultural Studies,* ed. David Morley and Kuan-Hsing Chen (New York: Routledge, 1996), 411-40; Iris Marion Young, *Justice and the Politics of Difference* (Princeton: Princeton University Press, 1990); Nancy Fraser, *Justice Interruptus: Critical Reflections on the "Post-Socialist" Condition* (New York: Routledge, 1997). For a synthesis of the debates between Young and Fraser, and a call to add a political element to their relatively more economist and culturalist analyses, see Lawrence C. Feldman, "Redistribution, Recognition, and the State: The Irreducibly Political Dimension of Injustice," *Political Theory* 30, 3 (2002): 410-40.

48 The conception of the role of language in social action that underpins this paragraph comes from my integration of material from an interdisciplinary array of theorists. The emphasis on the interactive determination of context and actor comes from Bruno Latour, *Pandora's Hope: Essays on the Reality of Science Studies* (Cambridge, MA: Harvard University Press, 1999), Chapter 2; Diana T. Meyers, *Self, Society, and Personal Choice* (New York: Columbia University Press, 1989); and Diana T. Meyers, "Decentralizing Autonomy: Five Faces of Selfhood," paper presented at the Department of Philosophy, Dalhousie University, 20 August 1999. On the role of language in making social change and its use as a tool for tracking social change, see Quentin Skinner, "Language and Social Change," in *Meaning and Context: Quentin Skinner and His Critics,* ed. James Tully (Cambridge, UK: Polity Press, 1988), 119-32; Richard Rorty, *Contingency, Irony, and Solidarity* (Cambridge, UK: Cambridge University Press, 1989), 12-20; and Mariana Valverde, *The Age of Light, Soap, and Water: Moral Reform in English Canada, 1885-1925* (Toronto:

McClelland and Stewart, 1991), Chapter 2. My understanding of the cultural processes by which a conceptual binary such as state/society (or charity/taxation) works to organize social relations and to affect events has been shaped by Jonathan Dollimore, *Sexual Dissidence: Augustine to Wilde, Freud to Foucault* (Oxford: Clarendon Press, 1991), Chapters 14 and 19; Joan W. Scott, "Gender: A Useful Category of Historical Analysis," *American Historical Review* 91, 5 (1986): 1053-75; and Jeffrey C. Alexander, "The Binary Discourse of Civil Society," in *The New Social Theory Reader: Contemporary Debates*, ed. Jeffrey C. Alexander and Steven Seidman (New York: Routledge, 2001), 193-202.

49 In the introduction to *The Limits of Affluence*, Struthers delineates six different analytical perspectives from which welfare history has been written. Like him, I find myself having drawn on them in this work. Centrally, this book is an example of the new institutionalist approach. But the social context within which the world of leaders and politicians operated is best described in terms developed by neo-Marxist and feminist scholars, and my emphasis on democratization owes something to the social democratic perspective. I hope also that the Foucauldians' view of modes of government offers some of the same strengths as the older political culture literature, even if its limitations are also similar.

50 A good summary of social theory and research traditions concerning this question of how micro- and macrolevels of social organization interact is Jeffrey C. Alexander et al., *The Micro-Macro Link* (Berkeley: University of California Press, 1987).

51 I owe particular debts (for Vancouver) to Robert A.J. MacDonald, Robert Campbell, Mark Leier, Todd McCallum, and Andrew Parnaby; (for Ottawa) to John H. Taylor, Jeff Keshen and Nicole St. Onge, and Robert Choquette; and (for Halifax) to Judith Fingard, David Sutherland, Janet Guildford, and Suzanne Morton.

52 My understanding of this methodology is based on reading the work of its practitioners, including, for example, Anne McClintock, *Imperial Leather: Race, Gender, and Sexuality in the Colonial Contest* (New York: Routledge, 1995). However, descriptions of the methodology's conceptual underpinnings may be found in Mary Poovey, *Uneven Developments: The Ideological Work of Gender in Victorian England* (Chicago: University of Chicago Press, 1988), 15-23; and Stanley Fish, "Interpreting the *Variorum*," in *Is There a Text in This Class? The Authority of Interpretive Communities* (Cambridge, MA: Harvard University Press, 1980), 147-73.

53 My thanks to Jessica Squires, whose interest in the ideological work of consensus building on taxation questions in the Rowell-Sirois Commission helped me to develop my earlier thinking on this point. Her argument on the commission's work of fabricating apparent consensus is presented in "Ideological Formation and Liberal 'Consensus': Reading the Rowell-Sirois Commission" (MA thesis, Department of History, Dalhousie University, 2003).

54 "Citizenship of contribution" is Finlayson's phrase in *Citizen*.

55 As Jane Lewis has observed of Victorian voluntary organizations, they should be seen not as alternatives to the state but "as part of the way in which political leaders conceptualised the state." Lewis, *Voluntary Sector,* 8; see also Jean-Marie Fecteau, "État et associationnisme au XIXe siècle québécois: Éléments pour une problématique des rapports état/société dans la transition au capitalisme," in *Colonial Leviathan: State Formation in Mid-Nineteenth-Century Canada,* ed. Allan Greer and Ian Radforth (Toronto: University of Toronto Press, 1992), 134-62.

56 See Chapters 3 and 6 and my "Class and Community in Canadian Welfare Work, 1935-1960," *Journal of Canadian Studies* 32, 1 (1997): 63-92.

57 An example I noted while writing an early draft of this introduction was that newspaper columnist Margaret Wente, in arguing for the superiority of Toronto mayoral candidate John Tory, gave as one of her reasons that "he had also raised a record amount of money for the city's social services when he was chairman of the United Way, even after 9/11 devastated everybody's fundraising plans." Margaret Wente, "The Man Who Should Be Mayor," *Globe and Mail,* 9 September 2003, A17.

58 T. Lundstrom and F. Wykstrom, *The Non-Profit Sector in Sweden* (Manchester: Manchester University Press, 1997), 88, cited in Brooks, "Role of the Voluntary Sector," 210.

59 "Russian Love in a Cold Climate," *The Economist,* 13 August 1998, http://www.economist.com; Russian American Christian University, "Corporate Russia Reaches into Its Pockets," *News from Russia,* 4 August 2002, http://www.racu.org/newsfromrussia/04-Aug-02-RJ.html.

Chapter 1: The Citizenship of Contribution

1 For a discussion of some aspects of the wartime co-ordination of fundraising, see Desmond Morton, *Fight or Pay: Soldiers' Families in the Great War* (Vancouver: UBC Press, 2004), 174-200. The debate during and after the First World War about the state as an expression of the collective will is explained in Doug Owram, *The Government Generation* (Toronto: University of Toronto Press, 1986), Chapters 4 and 5.

2 James Struthers, *No Fault of Their Own: Unemployment and the Canadian Welfare State, 1914-1941* (Toronto: University of Toronto Press, 1983), 16-30; B.L. Vigod, "Ideology and Institutions in Quebec: The Public Charities Controversy, 1921-1926," *Histoire sociale* 11, 21 (1978): 167-82; Craig Heron and Myer Siemiatycki, "The Great War, the State, and Working Class Canada," in *The Workers' Revolt in Canada, 1917-1925,* ed. Craig Heron (Toronto: University of Toronto Press, 1998), 22; Desmond Morton and Glenn Wright, *Winning the Second Battle: Canadian Veterans and the Return to Civilian Life, 1915-1930* (Toronto: University of Toronto Press, 1987), 130-49; Katherine McCuaig, "From Social Reform to Social Service: The Changing Role of Volunteers: The Anti-Tuberculosis Campaign, 1900-1930,"

Canadian Historical Review 61, 4 (1980): 485-86. For some examples of special efforts required by charities in the postwar reconstruction crises, see P.G. Shallcross to Board of Trade, 15 June 1920, CVA, VBT, Add. Mss. 300, vol. 47, 173; minutes, 20 December 1921, NSARM, Rotary Club of Halifax (RH), MG 20, vol. 1976; Morton, *Fight or Pay*, 206-25; Janet Kitz, *Shattered City: The Halifax Explosion and the Road to Recovery* (Halifax: Nimbus, 1990); and Euclid Hérie, *Journey to Independence: Blindness, the Canadian Story* (Toronto: Dundurn, 2005), 55-60.

3 Directors' minutes, Report of Special Committee to Study the Community Chest System, 26 June 1923, CVA, VBT, Add. Mss. 300, 2, 4. On the first rationalization proposal, see Ottawa City Council minutes, 5 November 1923, 566; on the first proposal in Halifax, see minutes of a meeting of those interested in collecting and distributing charitable funds, 17 November 1921, NSARM, UWHD, MG 20.

4 J. Harvey Perry, *Taxes, Tariffs, and Subsidies: A History of Canadian Fiscal Development*, vol. 1 (Toronto: University of Toronto Press, 1955), 142-60; W. Irwin Gillespie, *Tax, Borrow, and Spend: Financing Federal Spending in Canada, 1867-1990* (Ottawa: Carleton University Press, 1991), 113-17, 306n27; J. Castell Hopkins, "Financial Policy of the Dominion Government: Sir Henry Drayton's Budget," *Canadian Annual Review, 1920* (*CAR*) (Toronto: Canadian Review Company, 1921), 47.

5 "Mandate of the Tariff Commission of Enquiry," *CAR, 1920*, 158.

6 "The Farmers and the Tariff Commission of 1920," *CAR, 1920*, 123-26.

7 Perry, *Taxes*, vol. 1, 128-36; Eleanor J. Stebner, "Young Man Knowles: Christianity, Politics, and the Making of a Better World," in *Religion and Public Life: Historical and Comparative Perspectives*, ed. Marguerite van Die (Toronto: University of Toronto Press, 2001), 224; Allen Mills, "Single Tax, Socialism, and the Independent Labour Party of Manitoba: The Political Ideas of F.J. Dixon and S.J. Farmer," *Labour/Le travail* 5 (1980): 33-56; minutes, 23 November 1920, NSARM, Halifax Board of Trade (HBT), MG 20.

8 "Financial Policy of the Dominion Government: Sir Henry Drayton's Budget," *CAR, 1920*, 50-56; minutes, 15 June 1920, NSARM, HBT, MG 20, 7.

9 Perry, *Taxes*, vol. 1, 210-11.

10 Ibid., 196.

11 Eric Hardy, "The Metropolitan Problem," in *Empire Club of Canada Speeches 1949-1950* (Toronto: Empire Club of Canada, 1950), 266.

12 See, for example, the directors listed in W.H. Wynne, *Special Study of Taxation and Public Expenditure in Canada: Report to Donors* (Toronto: Citizens' Research Institute of Canada, 1937), page H.

13 For a description of its membership and activities, see Royal Commission on Dominion Provincial Relations, Record of Proceedings, LAC, RG 33-23, 6633. For its role in the founding of the Toronto Federation for Community Service, see Wills, *Marriage of Convenience*, 40-43, 154n20. I have encountered pamphlets and correspondence from CRIC in a variety of collections, including those of political

organizers, Boards of Trade, and mayors: minutes, 1 March 1923 (proposal that the board take out a membership in CRIC to get its literature regularly), CVA, VBT, Add. Mss. 330, vol. 5; "There Are No Water-Tight Compartments in the Taxpayer's Pocket" (n.p.: Citizens' Research Institute of Canada, 1938), British Columbia Archives and Records Service (BCARS), J.A. Clark Papers, Add. mss. 815, box 30, file 4; "Municipal Indebtedness," *Commercial News* 1, 5 (1921): 5 (cites CRIC as its source of national data). I have also found correspondence or newsletters in some of the series of the Canadian Welfare Council: *Effective Government* (monthly newsletter of the Citizens' Research Council), 16 November 1951, LAC, Records of the Canadian Council on Social Development (CCSD), MG 28 I 10, vol. 115, file 840. Newspapers appear to have used their publications as the basis for news stories: for example, "Economy Urged on Cities by Municipal Bureau Head," *Brantford Expositor*, 30 January 1932, refers to a CRIC pamphlet called "Canadian Taxation: A Homely Statement of Fact."

14 See "Brittain, Horace L.," in *The Canadian Who's Who*, 1936-37 ed. (Toronto: Trans-Canada Press, 1936); "Brittain, Horace L.," in *Macmillan Dictionary of Canadian Biography*, 3rd ed., ed. W. Stewart Wallace (Toronto: Macmillan, 1963), 82; and Wills, *Marriage of Convenience*, 41.

15 Cited in "Financial Policy of the Dominion Government: Sir Henry Drayton's Budget," *CAR, 1920*, 53. For its continuing influence in the 1950s, see Hardy, "Metropolitan Problem," 266.

16 P.G. Shallcross to W.E. Payne (secretary of the board), 25 May 1920; minutes, 15 June 1920; report of the Social Welfare Societies Committee, 25 November 1920, CVA, VBT, Add. Mss. 300.

17 F.H. Bell, "Municipal Taxation in Nova Scotia," *Dalhousie Review* 1, 13 (1921): 265.

18 Ibid., 264-66; minutes, 11 September 1923 and 11 December 1923, CVA, VBT, Add. Mss. 300, vol. 48, 374, 361.

19 Bell, "Municipal Taxation," 269, describes the problems of income tax assessment and collection being such that the results were likely to be "meagre, unsatisfactory, and unjust."

20 Perry, *Taxes*, vol. 1, 249; John H. Taylor, *Ottawa: An Illustrated History* (Toronto: James Lorimer and Company, 1986), 186.

21 "Valuable Taxation Discussion Is Heard at the Annual Meeting of the Board of Trade," *Ottawa Journal*, 16 January 1923, 7.

22 "Exemptions from Municipal Taxation," *Commercial News* 1, 6 (1921): 6.

23 Eight of the fifty-five identifiable members of the Protestant and Roman Catholic boards of directors in the 1937 Ottawa Community Chests were residents of Rockliffe Park. So, too, was Dr. R.E. Wodehouse, the first chairman of Ottawa's Protestant chest's board of directors. *Ottawa City Directory, 1937* (Ottawa: Might Directories, 1937).

24 Minutes, 29 December 1919, NSARM, Halifax Local Council of Women (HLCW), MG 20, vol. 535.

25 Minutes, 15 September 1921, NSARM, HLCW, MG 20, vol. 535.

26 Minutes, 7 December 1920 and 29 May 1923, NSARM, RH, MG 20, vol. 1976.

27 Minutes, 24 June 1919, Halifax City Council Records (HCC), RG 35-102, reel 14, 110; "Exemptions from Municipal Taxation," *Commercial News* 1, 6 (1921): 6; Assistant City Engineer to T.S. Rogers of the Halifax Relief Commission, 31 October 1918, and City Clerk to Sir Thomas White, acting prime minister, 16 January 1919, NSARM, Halifax Relief Commission (HRC), MG 20, series A, Financial Relationship with City of Halifax, 1917-19.

28 Extra efforts for private unemployment relief fundraising were noted in minutes, 20 December 1921, NSARM, RH, MG 20, vol. 1976.

29 Minutes, 15 June 1920, NSARM, HBT, MG 20, 7.

30 "Financial Policy of the Dominion Government: Sir Henry Drayton's Budget," *CAR 1920*, 53; "Federal Taxation," *Commercial News* 1, 7 (1921): 2; "Municipal Indebtedness," *Commercial News* 1, 5 (1921): 5.

31 Bell, "Municipal Taxation," 267-68.

32 "Civic Taxation," *Commercial News* 1, 2 (1921): 6; on the nature of improvements, see "Report on Civic Taxation System," *Halifax Evening Echo*, 21 April 1920, 7.

33 Karl Marx is, of course, the origin of this view of the government: "The executive of the modern state is but a committee for managing the common affairs of the whole bourgeoisie" is the version he and Friedrich Engels offered in "Manifesto of the Communist Party," in *The Marx-Engels Reader*, ed. Robert C. Tucker (New York: W.W. Norton, 1972 [1872]), 337. The right to a vote in the electing of that management committee, according to Sir John A. Macdonald in his explanation of his proposed Dominion Franchise Act in 1870, was based on "whether or not [a man] has a sufficient interest at stake in the country to be entrusted with a share in its government." John A. Macdonald, quoted in W.L. Morton, "The Extension of the Franchise in Canada: A Study in Democratic Nationalism," *Canadian Historical Association Annual Report* 22, 1 (1943): 77n.

34 "Property Owners Re-Elect Board," 9 February 1934; "Rap Trustees for Increase," 4 May 1932; "City Finance Position Shows No Improvement," 20 July 1936, CVA, J.S. Matthews clippings files (JSM), fiche Associated Property Owners (APO) of Vancouver; APO of Vancouver, "Read, Mark, and Remember ... VOTE!" CVA, Pamphlets 1945-75, Taxation and Civic Elections 1945.

35 "Valuable Taxation Discussion Is Heard at the Annual Meeting of the Board of Trade," *Ottawa Journal*, 16 January 1923, 7.

36 "Municipal Indebtedness," *Commercial News* 1, 5 (1921): 5.

37 Perry, *Taxes*, vol. 1, 128-31; Ramsay Cook, *The Regenerators: Social Criticism in Late Victorian English Canada* (Toronto: University of Toronto Press, 1985), Chapter 7.

38 Minutes, 3 March 1921, NSARM, HCC, RG 35-102, reel 15, 753-55. This opposition, as well as being recognizable in its content, was identified at the time as the single-tax position in the Board of Trade minutes, 23 November 1920, NSARM, HBT, MG 20, 2.

39 See "Regan, John W.," and "Ritchie, G.E.," *Halifax City Directory, 1920* (Halifax: McAlpine's City Directories, 1920).

40 Minutes, 23 November 1920, NSARM, HBT, MG 20, 4.

41 The subject of businessmen's complaints about taxation was treated as a matter of humorous hyperbole in the Halifax labour paper: "How Does This Apply to Halifax Merchants?" *Halifax Citizen,* 10 December 1920, 8.

42 Minutes, 3 March 1921, NSARM, HCC, RG 35-102, reel 15, 755.

43 Minutes, 15 December 1921, NSARM, HLCW, MG 20, vol. 535.

44 Ibid., 16 February 1922.

45 Minutes, 3 March 1921, NSARM, HCC, RG 35-102, reel 15; minutes, 22 April 1920, NSARM, HLCW, MG 20, vol. 535.

46 Minutes, Annual General Meeting, 7 January 1926, NSARM, UWHD, MG 20, vol. 1713.

47 Chief Electoral Officer of Canada, *A History of the Vote in Canada* (Ottawa: Public Works Canada, 1997), 45-68. Sylvia Bashevkin, "Independence versus Partisanship: Dilemmas in the Political History of Women in English Canada," in *Rethinking Canada,* ed. Veronica Strong-Boag and Anita Clair Fellman (Toronto: Copp Clark Pitman, 1986), 250, summarizes in a useful table the "Legislative Changes Affecting the Political Status of Women in Canada"; House of Commons, *Debates,* 29 April 1920, 1813, 1815, 1816.

48 "Report of Halifax City Council Meeting," *Morning Chronicle,* 24 October 1863. I owe this reference to Janet Guildford, who touches on this question in her "Public School Reform and the Halifax Middle Class, 1850-1870" (PhD diss., Department of History, Dalhousie University, 1990), 154.

49 "Plan Series of Meetings," *Halifax Mail,* 7 November 1929, 13.

50 Bell, "Municipal Taxation," 272.

51 "Valuable Taxation Discussion Is Heard at the Annual Meeting of the Ottawa Board of Trade," *Ottawa Journal,* 16 January 1923, 7.

52 See "Whitman, Arthur Handfield," in *Canadian Who's Who,* 1936-37 ed. (Toronto: Trans-Canada Press, 1936); minutes, 8 December 1917 and 10 December 1917, NSARM, HRC, MG 20, vol. 525; and minutes, 17 November 1921, NSARM, UWHD, MG 20, vol. 1713. The description of the first group to attempt to organize management of the relief effort as the "big men" of Halifax comes from Samuel Henry Prince, *Catastrophe and Social Change: Based upon a Sociological Study of the Halifax Disaster* (New York: AMS Press, 1968 [1920]), 69. Prince further describes this group as "the men of prominence, the men of broad experience in

civic and philanthropic work, the men who knew the resources of the city and had the prestige to command them." The minutes of the early days of the committee show that the group included a number of the city's leading women as well, including Agnes Dennis and May Sexton.

An indication of how important the Halifax Welfare Bureau was is that its first president in 1914-15 was R.V. Harris, K.C. His entry in the 1936-37 *Canadian Who's Who* gives a vivid picture both of his family and professional connections in the Halifax elite and of his intense involvement in Halifax welfare work. See "Harris, Reginald Vanderbilt," *Canadian Who's Who,* 1936-37 ed. (Toronto: Trans-Canada Press, 1936). He also served on the national board of the Citizens' Research Institute of Canada. (See the list of directors given in W.H. Wynne, *Special Study of Taxation and Public Expenditure in Canada: Report to Donors* [Toronto: Citizens' Research Institute of Canada, 1937], page H.) Any organization that had Harris as its first president was ensured of prestige.

In Ottawa, the equivalent figure to Whitman was J.A. Machado, the president and general manager of the Canadian Bank Note Company. Active in the Board of Trade, the Rotary Club, and the Ottawa Welfare Bureau, Machado was one of the five people chosen by the city to study and recommend reforms to its Social Services Department in 1923. Machado again took a leading role in welfare questions, being one of the key actors in convoking and determining the constitution of the first Council of Social Agencies and the Community Chest. Minutes, Ottawa City Council, 15 January 1923, City of Ottawa Archives (COA), 40; see "Machado, Jose," in *Ottawa City Directory 1923* (Ottawa: Might Directories, 1923); minutes, meeting of the Ottawa Board of Trade (OBT), 27 February 1923, COA, MG 6, vol. 1, file 1; minutes, organizational meeting, Social Planning Council of Ottawa-Carleton (SPCOC), 12 September 1927, COA; minutes, meeting of representatives of charities, March 1928; Thelma Williams (Ottawa Welfare Bureau) to Charlotte Whitton, 18 April 1929, LAC, CCSD, MG 28 I 10, vol. 28, file 143; and minutes, meeting of the Protestant and general board of directors, United Way of Ottawa-Carleton (UWOC), 22 June 1933.

53 Minutes, 17 November 1921, 28 November 1922, 7 January 1923, 23 January 1923, 25 July 1923, 19 June 1924, 12 December 1924, and A.H. Whitman to R.B. Hayes, 8 December 1924, NSARM, UWHD, MG 20, vol. 1713; clipping, "Big Campaign for Budgets of Welfare Workers," 1926, NSARM, UWHD, MG 20, scrapbook, vol. 1715; minutes, 20 January 1920, 23 November 1920, 23 January 1923, NSARM, HBT, MG 20; minutes, 16 June 1920 and 21 November 1922, NSARM, RH, MG 20.

54 Gillespie, *Tax,* 179-80.

55 Martin J. Daunton, *Just Taxes: The Politics of Taxation in Britain, 1799-1914* (Cambridge, UK: Cambridge University Press, 2002), 22-23.

CHAPTER 2: THE TECHNOLOGIES OF CONTRIBUTION

1 A. Paul Pross, *Group Politics and Public Policy* (Toronto: Oxford University Press, 1992), Chapter 2.

2 Doug Owram, *The Government Generation* (Toronto: University of Toronto Press, 1986); Sara Z. Burke, *Seeking the Highest Good: Social Service and Gender at the University of Toronto, 1888-1937* (Toronto: University of Toronto Press, 1996), 91, 109, 114, 128; Roy Lubove, *The Professional Altruist: The Emergence of Social Work as a Career, 1880-1930* (Cambridge, MA: Harvard University Press, 1965), 47.

3 The development of industrial management technique, with its complex systems of data collecting and reporting, is described in Alfred D. Chandler, Jr., *The Visible Hand: The Managerial Revolution in American Business* (Cambridge, MA: Harvard University Press, 1977).

4 W. Irwin Gillespie, *Tax, Borrow, and Spend: Financing Federal Spending in Canada, 1867-1990* (Ottawa: Carleton University Press, 1991), 120; H.R. Kemp, "Dominion Taxation. 1. The Sales Tax," *Canadian Forum* 3 (1923): 298.

5 See the annual reports of the Department of National Revenue before 1945 and the department's *Taxation Statistics* in 1945 and thereafter.

6 Gwyneth MacGregor, *Employees' Deductions under the Income Tax* (Toronto: Canadian Tax Foundation, 1960), 19.

7 Citizens' Research Institute of Canada, *Submission to the Royal Commission on Dominion-Provincial Relations* (Toronto: Citizens' Research Institute of Canada, 1938), 60-62.

8 Stencilled canvasser training pamphlet for Vancouver Welfare Federation, 1937, CVA, Mayor's Office fonds, series 483, file 33-D-6-1.

9 This weight of British practice and principle was joined by the force of specifically economic competition from the United States in determining the shape of Canadian practice.

10 This is the general argument of Martin J. Daunton, *Trusting Leviathan: The Politics of Taxation in Britain, 1799-1914* (Cambridge, UK: Cambridge University Press, 2001).

11 The state of play in the British income tax in 1914 is summarized in the introduction to Martin J. Daunton, *Just Taxes: The Politics of Taxation in Britain, 1914-1979* (Cambridge, UK: Cambridge University Press, 2002), 5-9.

12 W.H. Wynne, *Special Study of Taxation and Public Expenditure in Canada: Report to Donors* (Toronto: Citizens' Research Institute of Canada, 1937), 50. The significance of this study has been pointed out by Jessica Squires in her study of the role of economic expertise in the Rowell-Sirois Commission. In the 1930s, Brittain's Citizens' Research Institute created a Taxation Enquiry Fund to finance the *Special Study of Taxation and Public Expenditure in Canada*. A study of the same title, apparently the same study, became CRIC's submission to the Rowell-Sirois

Commission in 1938, although Wynne is not credited as the author of the 1938 submission. Wynne was, however, described in the report of the Rowell-Sirois Commission as having helped with the economic research of the commission. Jessica Squires, "Ideological Formation and Liberal 'Consensus': Reading the Rowell-Sirois Commission" (MA thesis, Department of History, Dalhousie University, 2003), 9.

13 John H. Taylor, "Engineering, Audit, and Fire: Governance and Modernity in Depression Ottawa," in *Ottawa: Making a Capital,* ed. Jeff Keshen and Nicole St. Onge (Ottawa: University of Ottawa Press, 2001), 335-38.

14 The city tax collector in Halifax was fired in 1923 for peculation. City of Halifax, "City Collector Theakston, Suspension Of," reports submitted and read before council, 6 June 1923, NSARM, RG 35-102, vol. 35. In Vancouver in 1930, a relief officer was discovered taking kickbacks and was forced to resign. Todd McCallum, "'Still Raining, Market Still Rotten': Homeless Men and the Early Years of the Great Depression in Vancouver" (PhD diss., Department of History, Queen's University, 2004), 134-35.

15 Michael Piva, "Government Finance and the Development of the Canadian State," in *Colonial Leviathan: State Formation in Mid-Nineteenth Century Canada,* ed. A. Greer and I. Radforth (Toronto: University of Toronto Press, 1992), 265-67; Bruce Curtis, "Class Culture and Administration: Educational Inspection in Canada West," in *Colonial Leviathan: State Formation in Mid-Nineteenth Century Canada,* ed. A. Greer and I. Radforth (Toronto: University of Toronto Press, 1992), 116-19.

16 H.M. Cassidy to R.L. Maitland, 1 November 1939, BCARS, Maitland Family Papers, Add. Mss. 781, vol. 1, file 44.

17 Minutes, meeting of the board of directors, 18 September 1931, CVA, United Way of the Lower Mainland (UWLM), Add. Mss. 849.

18 Minutes of a special meeting of the Roman Catholic executive committee to discuss the Joan of Arc Institute, 8 June 1938, UWOC. In 1943, the chest director reported that chest staff had compiled budgets for the agency because agency staff had not supplied the obligatory budget when submitting their annual request for funding to the chest. Minutes of the Roman Catholic budget committee, 17 August 1943, UWOC.

19 The development of income tax assessment was in its infancy in Canada in the 1920s. Commissioner of Taxation R.W. Breadner explained his methods for identifying likely payers of income tax in a report to Members of Parliament in 1920; see "Net Tightens about Income Tax Dodgers," *Globe,* 8 May 1920, 1. Charlotte Whitton undertook a systematic estimation of giving capacity in 1932, the methods of which are described in "A Report on the Social Services and a Possible Basis of Financial Federation for the City and Area of Greater Ottawa" (typescript), 20 May 1932, CCSD, vol. 43, file 213, 109-11. In 1947, the CWC published a guide that summarized for fundraisers how to assess the donor capacity of their

communities; see Svanhuit Josie and Gordon H. Josie, *Facts for Fundraisers* (Ottawa: Canadian Welfare Council, 1947). Both the Josies and Breadner's staff used automobile ownership as an indicator of income high enough to be liable for income tax or to be likely to give to charity.

20 In Ottawa, an early member of the board and chairman of the joint executive committee of the Ottawa Community Chests, Dr. R.E. Wodehouse, was secretary of the Canadian Tuberculosis Association, 1921-33, and became deputy minister of pensions and national health, 1933-44. In these roles, Wodehouse was a frequent attender of the Canadian Life Insurance Officers Association. For Wodehouse's attendance at the Life Insurance meetings, see the listings of those present in the annual *Yearbook of the Canadian Life Insurance Officers Association;* also see reference to Wodehouse in J.G. Parker to E.S. Miller, 14 December 1932, LAC, CCSD, MG 28 I 10, vol. 44, file 215; for Wodehouse's positions in the Ottawa chests, see, for example UWOC, 10 October 1933; for biography, see "Wodehouse, Dr. Robert E.," in *Canadian Who's Who*, 1936-37 ed. (Toronto: Trans-Canada Press, 1936). Other insurance people connected with the Ottawa chests included Ottawa's paid publicity secretary from 1935 to 1954, Freda Fripp, who was an unmarried daughter of an insurance broker, H.D. Fripp, and may have worked in the family firm. See minutes, joint meeting of the Protestant and Roman Catholic federations, 30 April 1935, UWOC; "Report of the Committee on Special Retirement – Staff Separation Problems," http://www.Ottawabusinesscontacts.com/obhistory.htm, for the founding date of H.D. Fripp and Company; and entries for Freda Fripp and H.D. Fripp and Company in *Ottawa City Directory* (Ottawa: Might City Directories, 1933). A.L. Cawthorne-Page of Metropolitan Life was active as a volunteer leader in the 1930s, serving mainly in advertising and publicity. See minutes, meeting of the campaign committee, 18 July 1938, 1 August 1939, and 16 September 1940, UWOC.

In Halifax, insurance agent G. Raymond Smith was the campaign director of the Halifax chest from 1928 to the late 1930s and remained active as a volunteer in publicity matters during the war and into the postwar period. He was also a member of the Gyro Club, the service club that Whitman credited with providing the most important push for the chest. G.R. Smith, "Time Control and Work Habits," *Life Underwriters News* 33, 1 (1947): 13-14, 20; minutes, executive committee, 26 September 1928, 11 September 1930; minutes, campaign committee, 28 September 1928; minutes, council, 12 December 1944; special meeting, 8 March 1949, NSARM, UWHD, MG 20, vol. 1713.

In Vancouver, insurance man J.L. Noble was the author of a 1930 report on the chest method for the Board of Trade. Minutes, Board of Trade meeting, 19 October 1922 (for Noble's insurance industry occupation), and minutes, Board of Trade meeting, 16 April 1930 (for the report), CVA, VBT, Add. Mss. 300. Brenton S. Brown, manager of the BC division of Crown Life, was nominated to be campaign leader in the third campaign, and, although he did not accept the nomination, he was active in the Welfare Federation, as were a number of leading members of the Vancouver Liberal Party, through the 1930s. Minutes, special meeting of the executive committee of the Vancouver Welfare Federation, 13 July 1934, CVA, UWLM, Add. Mss. 849. On involvement in the Liberal Party, see BCARS, Patullo Papers, 11 September 1931, Add. Mss. 3, vol. 40, file 8; and Brenton S. Brown to Patullo, 1 April 1933, and Patullo to J.W.B. Farris, 23 December 1929, vol. 50, file 7. Victor Odlum and H.R. Glass in Vancouver (see Chapter 4) were both insurance executives.

21 Minutes, men's territorial division, 26 September 1941, UWOC; minutes, campaign committee, 29 November 1960, UWOC; "Is Organized Charity Really Charity?" episode of television program *Toronto File,* 3 November 1960 (insurance sales representative complains that he is required by his employer to participate in United Way canvassing), LAC, CBC TV fonds, item number 289670.

22 While we cannot know what these agents said in their fundraising interviews, the fear of having to rely on charity was one of the marketing angles used in the industry's general or "institutional" advertising, which began in Canada in 1921 – before it became a practice of American insurance firms. For the earliest date of institutional advertising in Canada, see the *Yearbook of the Canadian Life Insurance Officers Association, 1953,* 20. Readers of Canadian urban newspapers in the inter-war years will be familiar with this kind of advertising: see, for an example that emphasizes fear of needing charity, the Metropolitan Life ad in the *Vancouver Sun,* 23 February 1931, 2. "The insurance man's principle" that the value of insurance lies in being free of the fear of having to rely on charity was explicitly expressed in "Address by Stewart M. Scott, C.L.U.," in *Yearbook of the Canadian Life Insurance Officers Association, 1956-57,* 136. Also, the view that it is an act of kindness (charity) to others to ensure that one's dependants need not turn to others for help would have been a point of intersection between insurance sales and charitable fundraising. For an expression of that view at the Life Insurance Officers Association annual meeting, see Edgar Andrew Collard, "Are We Taking Advantage of Ourselves?" in *Yearbook of the Canadian Life Insurance Officers Association, 1954-55,* 168. More generally, we know that insurance sales methods entailed being alert to any and all opportunities to make personal connections with prospective customers. R.F. Mindell refers to such methods as "taking some of 'the cold' out of a cold canvass" in "Prospects and Prospecting," *Life Underwriters News* 33, 7 (1947): 5. It seems reasonable, then, to imagine that a canvasser for charitable funds might also canvass for business by using any available point of discursive connection between insurance and charity.

23 The description of canvassing methods and insurance agents' methods in this paragraph was developed from a wide variety of sources, such as the following: "Instruction pour soliciteurs," circa 1935, LAC, Records of the Fédération des

femmes canadiennes-françaises, MG 28 I 231, vol. 4, file "Fédération des œuvres d'Ottawa"; Lionel Brittle to Chairmen of the Executive Committees of the Ottawa Financial Federations, 1 June 1936, LAC, Bronson Family Papers, MG 28 III 26, vol. 747, file "Ottawa Community Chests," 5, 9, 7; G.B. Grant to M. Bradford, 18 December 1935, LAC, CCSD, MG 28 I 10, vol. 158, file 1935-37; minutes, meeting of members to discuss campaign plans, 9 March 1934, UWOC; minutes, luncheon meeting of division chairs and campaign committee, 9 December 1937, UWOC; minutes, joint executive committee of Protestant and Roman Catholic chests, July 1935, UWOC; minutes, campaign committee, 11 July 1938 and 8 August 1938, and publicity committee, 25 August 1938, UWOC; minutes, campaign committee, 6 September 1939, UWOC; clipping of full-page ad showing pledge card, 30 October 1950, NSARM, UWHD, MG 20, vol. 1718; clipping, "Is Not Authorized to Collect Funds," *Halifax Mail*, 6 November 1929, NSARM, UWHD, MG 20, vol. 1717.

On insurance agents' methods, see G.R. Smith, "Time Control and Work Habits," *Life Underwriters News*, January 1947, 13-14, 20; "Address by H.E. Lumsden," in *Yearbook of the Canadian Life Insurance Officers Association, 1956-57*, 125 (prospecting and answering objections); and minutes, meetings of the federated charities committee of the Board of Trade, 30 October 1933 and 3 November 1933, OBT, MG 6 1/3.

24 This goal was undoubtedly impossible to attain, but it was expressed as a rhetorical device in aid of the more reasonable goal of increasing the number of donors. Clipping, "Community Chest Grows in Favour: Figures Show It," 15 October 1926, NSARM, UWHD, MG 20, vol. 1717; "$350,000 – a Lot of Money," *Vancouver Sun*, 25 October 1935, 4. Post-campaign discussions in the first decade of a chest's life typically included some discussion of sectors (whether social, occupational, or geographical) that the canvass had failed to reach: the aspiration to complete coverage was implicit in these discussions. See, for example, executive director's report to board of directors, 22 November 1932, CVA, UWLM, Add. Mss. 849, 3-4.

25 Minutes, 19 June 1924, NSARM, UWHD, MG 20, vol. 1713; minutes, joint budget committee, 22 June 1936, UWOC; minutes, meeting to review unpaid pledges, 16 March 1938, UWOC; minutes, meeting of board of directors, 31 August 1943, CVA, UWLM, Add. Mss. 849, vol. 617-A-4.

26 "Community Chest Campaign off to Good Start Today," 22 February 1926, NSARM, UWHD, MG 20, vol. 1717; minutes and executive secretary's report, annual general meeting, 27 January 1930, NSARM, UWHD, MG 20, vol. 1713.

27 I have only one direct piece of evidence of this practice, for Vancouver. In that city, the use of the city directories as a list of those liable for poll tax began in 1925 and was still continuing in 1938. The city tax collector defended the use of this dubiously accurate instrument as a cheap and effective way of listing poll tax payers. Mayor [Telford] to Dr. L.W. MacNutt, 25 November 1938, and Mr. Corley

[city collector] to Dr. MacNutt, 15 December 1939, CVA, Mayor's Office fonds, series 483, file 33-F-1-4.

28 "Householders to Purge Lists Next Election," *Ottawa Journal*, 16 November 1937, 1.

29 "A Report on the Social Services and a Possible Basis of Financial Federation for the City and Area of Greater Ottawa" (typescript), 20 May 1932, LAC, CCSD, MG 28 I 10, vol. 43, file 213, 110-11; minutes, meeting to discuss the possibility of a combined financial drive in the children's field, 29 November 1932, LAC, CCSD, MG 28 I 10, vol. 43, file 214; clipping, "Halifax – Hold Up Your Head," 1932, NSARM, UWHD, MG 20, vol. 1717, uses both income tax payments and insurance sales as measures of donor capacity; "Summary of Report of Canadian Welfare Council Field Visit to Halifax Community Chest – May 15-19, 1950," LAC, CCSD, MG 28 I 10, vol. 228, file 228-17, bases assessment of donor capacity in part on the number of income tax returns that reported taxable income of greater than $10,000; "Towards a United Appeal," 1 May 1954, LAC, CCSD, MG 28 I 10, vol. 254, file 254-7, uses Department of National Revenue taxation statistics to estimate personal income in aggregate terms. See also Josie and Josie, *Facts for Fundraisers*.

30 "Only $55,687 Received Yet for Campaign," *Ottawa Journal*, 1 November 1933.

31 Minutes, meeting of the campaign committee and division chairmen, 19 October 1939, UWOC; minutes, meeting of the joint executive committee, 29 November 1937, UWOC; minutes, annual general meeting, 27 February 1936, NSARM, UWHD, MG 20, vol. 1713; "Report on Multiple Charitable Appeals," 19 July 1949, CVA, UWLM, Add. Mss. 849, vol. 617-B-1; *Annual Report 1950*, CVA, UWLM, Add. Mss. 849, vol. 618-B-2, 15.

32 L.H. Serene, "Organizing a Community Campaign: Some Suggestions for the Actual Organization of a Campaign for Voluntary Funds for Welfare Purposes, in a Community of Average Size in Canada," LAC, CCSD, MG 28 I 10, vol. 158, file "CWC Community Organization Division, 1940"; Charlotte Whitton to Major G.S. MacFarlane, 17 March 1932, and lists of prospective federation supporters in Ottawa, 12 May 1932, LAC, CCSD, MG 28 I 10, vol. 43, file 214; minutes, meeting to discuss the possibility of a combined financial drive in the children's field, 29 November 1932, LAC, CCSD, MG 28 I 10, vol. 43, file 214; minutes, meeting to discuss united appeal, 29 November 1932, LAC, CCSD, MG 28 I 10, vol. 43, file 214; "A Report on the Social Services and a Possible Basis of Financial Federation for the City and Area of Greater Ottawa" (typescript), 20 May 1932, LAC, CCSD, MG 28 I 10, vol. 43, file 213, part 2, 3. See Chapter 2 for a discussion of the relationship between contribution and decision-making rights.

33 For this general observation about the treatment of the Chinese-named donors and the treatment of "Orientals" in the city directories of the 1930s, I am indebted to my former research assistant, Russell Johnston. On the corporate mode of Chinese Canadians' contribution to the Vancouver Welfare Federation, see F.

Ivor Jackson, "History of the Community Chest and Council of the Greater Vancouver Area" (typescript), March 1960, CVA, UWLM, Add. Mss. 849, Social Planning and Research series, F. Ivor Jackson subseries, 37.

34 Minutes, meeting of campaign committee, division chairs, and advertising committee, 16 September 1937, UWOC; minutes, meeting of campaign committee, 26 September 1938, UWOC. These minutes show the examination of one small sector's response in relation to the presence or absence of a particular fundraising speaker.

35 Bruce Curtis, *The Politics of Population: State Formation, Statistics, and the Census of Canada, 1840-1875* (Toronto: University of Toronto Press, 2001), 38-44, Chapter 8.

36 The relationship between data gathering and administration is explored in James C. Scott, *Seeing like a State: How Certain Schemes to Improve the Human Condition Have Failed* (New Haven: Yale University Press, 1998).

37 Wellington Jeffers, "Finance at Large: Only Income Tax Can Be Increased for Social Services without Difficulty," *Globe and Mail,* 28 January 1938, 18. I thank Jessica Squires for the reference to this 1938 example, which is from Squires, "Ideological Formation," 152.

38 J. Harvey Perry, *Taxes, Tariffs, and Subsidies: A History of Canadian Fiscal Development,* vol. 2 (Toronto: University of Toronto Press, 1955), 696-98. Note especially 698n*a*.

39 Discussion of the income tax appears in House of Commons, *Debates,* on 4, 5, 9, 10, 15, 17, and 18 June 1931.

40 House of Commons, *Debates,* 9 June 1931, 2460.

41 This scale was used during Howard Falk's tenure as executive director, and Falk had been in on the design of federated fundraising appeals in Winnipeg and Montreal. Halifax also used such a scale, as described in "Constitution," Article 8, section 6, 20 January 1927, NSARM, UWHD, MG 20, vol. 1713.

42 Perry, *Taxes,* vol. 2, 698-99.

43 "Constitution," Article 8, section 6, 20 January 1927, NSARM, UWHD, MG 20, vol. 1713; minutes, meeting of subcommittee one, June 1938, UWOC; minutes, meeting of the board of directors, 26 June 1945, CVA, UWLM, Add. Mss. 849, file 617-A-5/1.

44 Stencilled canvasser training pamphlet for Vancouver Welfare Federation, 1937, CVA, Mayor's Office fonds, series 483, file 33-D-6-1.

45 A remarkably thorough inventory of objections to egalitarian redistribution by voluntary giving is provided by political philosopher G.A. Cohen in *If You Are an Egalitarian, How Come You Are So Rich?* (Cambridge, MA: Harvard University Press, 2000). While Cohen's goal in this work is to engage as a socialist in a debate with Rawlsian political theory, he has incidentally provided a kind of field guide to the bases on which people resist charitable giving. The practices developed by

fundraisers over the past seventy years respond to each of the objections that Cohen considers.

46 Minutes, meeting of the division chairmen and campaign committee, 9 December 1937, UWOC.

47 The number of families of male manufacturing employees numbered only 892. Include the stevedoring and shipbuilding workforces, and about 1,400 families would have been represented in Halifax's major and minor industries. Canada, Dominion Bureau of Statistics, *Census of Canada, 1921*, vol. 1, table 5. Preferring to work with the concept of a family budget, I used this table and not the one that listed all manufacturing workers. I have thus missed households headed by female industrial workers. In the context of women's wages and the general picture of women's labour force participation in this period, however, it seems justifiable to assume that such households would have been among the least likely to have money to spare, whether for charity or for any non-essential expense.

48 Published donor list, Halifax *Evening Mail*, 7 November 1929, 17. I chose a 1929 donor list to be sure that the recruitment of working-class donors in Halifax would have had a reasonable time to take effect. Occupations of donors were identified using the *Halifax City Directory 1929*. Daily earnings figures are derived from data presented in Catherine Ann Waite, "The Longshoremen of Halifax, 1900-1930: Their Living and Working Conditions" (MA thesis, Department of History, Dalhousie University, 1977), Table 2.5.

49 "Report of Gwladys Kennedy, Executive Secretary, Halifax Community Chest," 28 February 1938, LAC, CCSD, MG 28 I 10, vol. 228, file 228-16; minutes, meeting of the publicity committee, 25 August 1938, UWOC; "Analysis of Ottawa Chest Results," 1936, LAC, CCSD, MG 28 I 10, vol. 158, file 1935–37; George Davidson, "Interim Report of the Director," 23 March 1936, CVA, UWLM, Add. Mss. 849, file 617-A-3/2, 2.

50 "Report of the Joint Boards of Directors," 9 April 1937, UWOC; "Report of the Executive Director," 15 February 1937, CVA, UWLM, Add. Mss. 849, file 617-A-3-3, 1. In Halifax, the minutes of the 1936 and 1937 February annual meetings offer no sign that the chest leaders were willing to acknowledge any improvement or prospect of improvement in business conditions. Collections had risen from $57,070 in 1935 to $62,089 in 1936 – an unprecedented jump – but the president attributed this (at least in public) to the competence of the chest's fundraising efforts. Minutes, annual general meetings, 27 February 1936 and 18 February 1937, NSARM, UWHD, MG 20, vol. 1713.

51 Report of the joint boards of directors, 9 April 1937, UWOC; minutes, meeting of the executive committees and campaign chairs, 22 November 1936, UWOC; minutes, annual general meetings, 27 February 1936 and 18 February 1937, NSARM, UWHD, MG 20, vol. 1713; minutes, meeting of the board of directors, 10 February 1938, CVA, UWLM, Add. Mss. 849, file 617-A-3-4.

52 The Vancouver federation's analysis of its donor data for the years 1934 to 1936 indicated that, between 1935 and 1936, the increase in total collections had come from the increased number of donors in the category of twenty-five dollars or less. The director gave this information as a sign of progress in the federation's project of developing "community spirit" in the city. Clipping, "Welfare Body Grows but Is Still behind Records of Other Centres," *Vancouver Daily Province,* 6 February 1937, CVA, JSM.

53 Luke 10: 25–37. In the Bible, Jesus tells the story of the charitable Samaritan (someone from Samaria) in order to shame a lawyer figure who, when told to love his neighbour as himself, tries to escape responsibility by asking "who is my neighbour?" A fundraising film of the late 1940s uses this question as its title and answers with the collectivist wisdom that everyone is linked by bonds of neighbourly association. *Who Is My Neighbour?* 1946, LAC, National Film Board fonds, item 150637.

54 "The Privilege of Giving," *Vancouver Sun,* 16 October 1937; "The Good Citizen" (pamphlet), LAC, CCSD, MG 28 I 10, vol. 158, file 1935–37, 8.

55 Matthew 25: 40; "Be a Good Neighbour" (pamphlet), LAC, CCSD, MG 28 I 10, vol. 158, file 1935-37; "Inasmuch as Ye Have Done It unto One of the Least of These," *Halifax Mail,* 8 October 1937, 5.

56 "Does Ottawa Really Need a Community Chest Campaign?" *Ottawa Journal,* 17 November 1937, 15; Douglas J. den Uyl, "The Right to Welfare and the Virtue of Charity," *Social Philosophy and Policy* 10, 1 (1993). 207; speech by the archbishop of Quebec, LAC, CCSD, MG 28 I 10, vol. 13, file 59, Community Organization, 1933-34, Radio Broadcasts.

57 "An Appeal to You for $165,000" and "Why Should I Subscribe to the Community Chest," LAC, CCSD, MG 28 I 10, file 1935–37; "Community Chest Investment in Humanity," *Ottawa Journal,* 4 November 1937, 3.

58 Report of board of directors to annual meeting, 18 February, 1935, CVA, UWLM, Add. Mss. 849; clipping, "Race, Color, Creed No Bars in City Welfare Campaign," 10 November 1939, CVA, JSM, Vancouver Welfare Federation fiche.

59 Clipping, "Halifax Community Chest Will Open Financial Campaign October 12," 15 October 1937, NSARM, UWHD, MG 20, vol. 1717. The endorsement of both Protestant and Catholic leaders was also part of the Halifax chest tradition, but because there were not in Halifax separate sections for each, the celebration of their ecumenism was not standard in their rhetoric, as it was in Ottawa. Nonetheless, the fact of their joint endorsement was not trivial. Protestant-Catholic relations in Halifax were a source of stress and tension in fundraising and a venerable basis of division in the city's institutional life. The presence in the chest of institutions from both sides of this divide was tangible evidence of success, however strained, in the project of base broadening. For evidence of the strains in this relationship, see C.F. Curran (director of Catholic Charities) to Thomas O'Donnell

(archbishop of Halifax), 3 October 1932, Halifax Catholic Pastoral Centre Archives, O'Donnell Papers, vol. 2, #93. For this specific document, I thank Renée Lafferty. For a discussion of the role of denominational and sectarian divisions in Halifax child welfare services in the interwar years, see Renée Lafferty, "Child Welfare in Halifax, 1900-1960: Institutional Transformation, Denominationalism, and the Creation of a 'Public' Welfare System" (PhD diss., Department of History, Dalhousie University, 2003).

60 In eastern Canadian cities, this belief grew out of the poverty associated with the Irish famine immigration of the nineteenth century and was fuelled by larger international currents of anti-Catholicism, which linked Catholicism to deficiency in the preferred characteristics of capitalist competition. J.R. Miller, "Anti-Catholicism in Canada: From the British Conquest to the Great War," in *Creed and Culture*, ed. Terrence Murphy and Gerald Stortz (Montreal: McGill-Queen's University Press, 1993), 25-48. See Chapter 4 for the documentation of the view that Catholics were disproportionately users of welfare services and that the Catholic community gave less to the Community Chests in Ottawa, Halifax, and Toronto. In Vancouver, too, the inheritance of nineteenth-century anti-Catholicism was apparent in the accusation that "Catholic people generally were not contributing their fair proportion to the cause." Archbishop W.M. Duke to Howard T. Falk, 18 May 1935, CVA, UWLM, Add. Mss. 849, vol. 617-A-3, file 1, 2-3; C.T. McHattie to Reverend William Duke, 30 August 1935, item 7, paragraph 4.

61 Mark 12: 4–44. Typical examples include a story of an unemployed man who gives the chest a dollar, by "pinching" his own needs a bit, and the story of a newsboy (an urban figure of child poverty) giving his penny tips during the campaign week. "Brighter Air as Donations Reach $90,403," *Ottawa Journal*, 3 November 1933, 1; "Great Corporation and Newsboy Lead Chest Giving," *Vancouver Sun*, 24 February 1931, 9.

62 "Radio Broadcasts," 8 October 1933, LAC, CCSD, MG 28, I 10, vol. 13, file 59, 2; "You, Personally, Mr. Average Citizen," *Halifax Mail*, 5 October 1937, 7.

63 "Inasmuch as Ye Have Done It unto One of the Least of These," *Halifax Mail*, 8 October 1937, 5.

64 The exception was a depiction of the canvasser as a "friendly neighbour" to whom courtesy was owed. For the display ads, see *Vancouver Sun*, 13, 14, 16, 19, 21, and 23 October 1937. The *Vancouver Sun* prided itself, not quite accurately, as having been the main force in creating the Vancouver Welfare Federation through the work of the paper's founder and publisher, Robert Cromie. Whether or not Cromie was an absolutely pivotal figure, he was certainly an important one, and in the 1930s one has to look to the *Vancouver Sun*'s rival, the *Daily Province*, to find criticisms of the federation. On the former paper's self-congratulation, see "Fill the City's Community Chest," *Vancouver Sun*, 16 October 1938, 8.

65 "'Chest' Drive," *Vancouver Sun*, 18 October 1937, 2.

66 Shirley Tillotson, "Class and Community in Canadian Welfare Work, 1933-1960," *Journal of Canadian Studies* 32, 1 (1997): 63-92.

67 For a picture of the cook, see *Vancouver Sun*, 14 October 1937; the warehouse truck driver, 15 October; the business girl, 16 October; the milkman, 18 October; and the fireman, 20 October.

68 E.S. Roberts, "Our Whole Town's Working," *Vancouver Province*, 26 October 1935, CVA, JSM, subject "Vancouver Welfare Federation."

69 Another example of this theme can be found in newspaper coverage of the 1940 campaign in Vancouver. In a report of the campaign's progress, the increase in new donors was mentioned. To illustrate, the report quoted a woman who said, "until this year I never knew what Welfare meant but I know now because the Preventorium saved two of my children from tuberculosis." "Larger Donations Mark Services Fund Campaign," *Vancouver Sun*, 30 October 1940, 28.

70 The universalizing "everybody gives, everybody benefits," slogan and the salience of the citizen as consumer are documented and discussed in Chapter 7.

71 Not just fraternalism but also the life insurance industry's institutional ads used a commercial collectivism from which social insurance schemes would draw some of their cultural plausibility; see, for example, "Millions of Canadian Workers UNITED in one Great Co-Operative Enterprise" (ad), *Halifax Herald*, 6 October 1937, 6. In the insurance industry's rhetoric, the pooling of savings to protect against risk was not simply individual thriftiness but also a kind of mutual assistance. More concretely, life insurance not only provided protection for widows and fatherless children but also ensured a source of credit during times of breadwinner unemployment. By taking out a loan against the cash value of a life insurance policy, an unemployed worker had in his (or her) life insurance a kind of private (or commercial collectivist) unemployment insurance. The practice of using such loans is described in *Farm Women Asked Us ...* (Toronto: Canadian Life Insurance Officers Association, Women's Division, c. 1945), 15-17. A concrete example of the use of such loans may be found in minutes, meeting of the Vancouver City Council, 24 July 1933, CVA. The relief officer describes the case of a relief recipient who was discovered to have a life insurance policy with a loan value of approximately $600. The officer asked for, and got, permission from the councillors to require that the relief recipient borrow $300 of that $600, leaving the balance for the purpose of keeping the policy valid for another three years. The extent of the use of policy loans in the 1930s is noted in president's address, *Yearbook of the Canadian Life Insurance Officers Association, 1933*, 8-9.

Chapter 3: Social Advertising and Social Conflict

1 In December 1922, a meeting of fifty-three "welfare societies," convoked by the Board of Trade, decided to defer action on a chest plan and to ask a special committee of the board to study it further. In June 1923, a smaller group of welfare

organizations heard the report of the board committee and rejected a motion to launch a chest "as the societies have not yet shown definitely that they are prepared to accept the Community Chest idea." Minutes, meeting of organizations to discuss creating a Community Chest for Vancouver, 1 December 1922, CVA, VBT, Add. Mss. 300, vol. 48; minutes, meeting of organizations to receive a report on the Community Chest, 26 June 1923, and CVA, VBT, Add. Mss. 300, vol. 146. Although the Board of Trade venture failed to win assent in the early 1920s, Vancouver's Jewish community successfully launched a Jewish Community Chest in 1924. It combined an annual appeal with a fundraising bazaar and sought subscriptions within the Jewish community for health, education, and welfare organizations as far afield as Winnipeg, Palestine, and Los Angeles. While not confined to local charities or limited to the single annual appeal, the Jewish chest did, however, practise the same central auditing of member agency budgets that the federation method required. Vancouver's Jewish Community Chest joined the Vancouver Welfare Federation as a member agency in 1930. "Jewish Community Chest Organized in Vancouver in 1924," *Jewish Western Bulletin*, 30 June 1958, 58-60, reprinted from a 1929 souvenir book published by the Vancouver Jewish Community Chest. Concerning resistance to federation in Ottawa, see minutes, conference of children's agencies (Ottawa) re financial drive, 19 December 1932, LAC, CCSD, MG 28 I 10, vol. 43, file 214.

2 Among them were the Salvation Army, the Halifax Association for Improving the Conditions of the Poor, the YMCA, and the Red Cross. The Catholic Charities joined only in 1929, four years after the first campaign.

3 Roy Lubove, *The Professional Altruist: The Emergence of Social Work as a Career, 1880-1930* (Cambridge, MA: Harvard University Press, 1965), 203.

4 T.J. Jackson Lears, *Fables of Abundance: A Cultural History of Advertising in America* (New York: Basic Books, 1994), 215 and passim; Russell Johnston, *Selling Themselves: The Emergence of Canadian Advertising* (Toronto: University of Toronto Press, 2001), 174-77.

5 One of the supporters of the Vancouver Welfare Federation, Liberal and former provincial attorney general J.W.deB. Farris, was one of these, according to several members of the Vancouver Labour Council who wrote to Farris to challenge the assertions he had made in a speech entitled "What about Russia?" at the Board of Trade's annual banquet. Vancouver Labour Council delegates M. MacKinnon, P.C. Munro, and J. [or T?] Russell to J.W.deB. Farris, 28 January 1935, Special Collections, UBC Library, Farris Papers, box 8, file 8-2.

6 W. Peter Ward, *White Canada Forever: Popular Attitudes and Public Policy toward Orientals in British Columbia* (Montreal: McGill-Queen's University Press, 1978), 23-35; Patricia E. Roy, "British Columbia's Fear of Asians, 1900-1950," *Histoire sociale* 13, 25 (1980): 161-72; Chief Electoral Officer of Canada, *A History of the Vote in Canada* (Ottawa: Public Works Canada, 1997), 80.

7 Kay J. Anderson, *Vancouver's Chinatown: Racial Discourse in Canada, 1870-1980* (Montreal: McGill-Queen's University Press, 1991), Chapter 4; Masako Iino, "Japan's Reaction to the Vancouver Riot of 1907," *BC Studies* 60 (1983-84): 28-47.

8 Robert A. Campbell, *Demon Rum or Easy Money: Government Control of Liquor in British Columbia from Prohibition to Privatization* (Ottawa: Carleton University Press, 1991); Suzanne Morton, *At Odds: Gambling and Canadians, 1919-1969* (Toronto: University of Toronto Press, 2003), 123-24; Margaret J.H. Little, "Claiming a Unique Place: The Introduction of Mothers' Allowances in British Columbia," *BC Studies* 106 (1995): 80-102.

9 Iris Marion Young, *Justice and the Politics of Difference* (Princeton: Princeton University Press, 1990), Chapter 8.

10 For a discussion of postwar developments in these respects, see Chapter 7. Chief Electoral Officer, *History of the Vote,* 80-83. For the campaign against "the company vote" – a "personal" vote exercised by a corporation, see "Charter Provision Respecting Persons Entitled to Vote" and "CCF Program 1950," UBC Special Collections, Angus MacInnis Memorial Collection, box 22-10. A key episode indicating both the involvement of the chest in anti-racism work and the taken-for-granted leadership role of unionists is described in clipping, "Sikhs' Seven Neighbors Say: 'We Just Don't Want Them,'" *Vancouver Sun,* 29 September 1958, CVA, UWLM, Add. Mss. 849, Loc. 489-F-7, file 9.

11 The intentional use of such rivalries to give "coercive force" to a federation's appeals was frankly acknowledged as a valuable tool in a 1938 discussion among the Ottawa Protestant chest's board of directors. Comparing their own attempts to co-operate between linguistic and religious communities with Montreal's sectarian and linguistically separate chests, a member of that board suggested that "Montreal's success may be due to the fact that each of the Federations there has a minority group working toward a goal and, therefore, becomes a more coercive force." Minutes, meeting of the Protestant board of directors and budget committee, 18 January 1938, UWOC.

12 A good summary of the various sorts of symbiotic relationships that exist between apparently opposed sets of ideas may be found in Jonathan Dollimore, *Sexual Dissidence: Augustine to Wilde, Freud to Foucault* (New York: Oxford University Press, 1991), 225-27.

13 Clipping, "Englishman Who Contributed Much to Canada Was John Howard Falk," 2 May 1950, CVA, JSM, J.H.T. Falk fiche; clippings, "Welfare Campaign Official Chosen," 25 July 1934, and "Our Whole Town's Working," 26 October 1935, CVA, JSM, Vancouver Welfare Federation fiche; F. Ivor Jackson, "History of the Community Chest and Council of the Greater Vancouver Area" (typescript), March 1960, CVA, UWLM, Add. Mss. 849, Social Planning and Research series, F. Ivor Jackson subseries, 38; "Money to Clothe Needy," *Vancouver Sun,* 9 November 1932, 1; "Welfare Fund $40,000 Short," *Vancouver Sun,* 17 November 1933, 1,

3; "Welfare Campaign Who's Who," *Vancouver Sun,* 26 October 1935, 3; "Welfare Fund Reaches $270,000," *Vancouver Sun,* 7 November 1935, 3.

14 "1931 Budgets of the Agencies in the Welfare Federation" (ad), *Vancouver Sun,* 23 February 1931, 18.

15 "Report of Special Committee to Study the Community Chest System," 26 June 1923, CVA, VBT, Add. Mss. 300, vol. 146, 2, 4.

16 "Charity Sport Racket," *Vancouver Sun,* 26 October 1932, 1; "The Beaten Path for Beaten People," *Vancouver Sun,* 27 October 1931, 7. Reflecting on the decade just past, the Canadian Welfare Council community organization director spoke of Vancouver as particularly rife with "professional 'operators,'" often from the United States. Marjorie Bradford to Kathleen Gorrie, 7 October 1937, LAC, CCSD, MG 28 I 10, vol. 48, file 419. For a reference generally to the "unscrupulous promoter" as a problem for charitable giving, based on the experience of the 1930s, see "Memorandum from the Canadian Welfare Council re Possible Provincial and Municipal Provisions for the Registration of Charitable Appeals," LAC, CCSD, MG 28 I 10, vol. 47, file 418.

17 F. Ivor Jackson, "History of the Community Chest and Council of the Greater Vancouver Area" (typescript), March 1960, CVA, UWLM, Add. Mss. 849, Social Planning and Research series, F. Ivor Jackson subseries, 6-7.

18 See "Pennock, C.G.," in *Who's Who in British Columbia,* vol. 1 (Victoria: S.M. Carter, 1931).

19 "Mayne D. Hamilton Lauds Charity Chest," *Vancouver Sun,* 2 November 1935, 2.

20 "Charity Campaign," *Vancouver Sun,* 13 November 1933, 18.

21 "Welfare Fund $40,000 Short," *Vancouver Sun,* 17 November 1933, 3.

22 See http://www.boardoftrade.com/vbot_page.asp?pageid=82.

23 "Full Speed Ahead," *Vancouver Sun,* 29 October 1931, 22; "2800 Workers at Welfare Rally," *Vancouver Sun,* 28 October 1935, 13; Brenton S. Brown is mentioned as men's division chair in "$37,698 on 1st Day of Drive," *Vancouver Sun,* 27 October 1931, 1; W.C. "Billy" Woodward was also part of the Vancouver Liberals' inner circle; see various letters from J.W.B. Farris to "Billy" Woodward, UBC Special Collections, John Wallace deBeque Farris Papers, file 8-2.

24 Clipping, "Opposition to Welfare Drive Gross Treason," 12 October 1936, CVA, JSM, Vancouver Welfare Federation fiche.

25 "Conservative Party Organization, 1931-1942," list of candidates for membership in a Conservative Party club (the Macdonald Club) being organized by Clark, September 1935; minutes of a meeting to consider formation of the Macdonald Club of Vancouver, 1 May 1936; J.A. Clark to Reggie Tupper, 12 February 1936, BCARS, J.A. Clark Papers, Add. mss. 815, vol. 30, file 2; see "Kidd, George," and "Taylor, Austin C.," in *Canadian Who's Who,* 1936-37 ed. (Toronto: Trans-Canada Press, 1936). These sources also identify as active in the Conservative

Party participants in the Welfare Federation such as Chris Spencer, W.H. Malkin, C.H. McHattie, and Lyman Trumbull.

26 Margaret Ormsby, *British Columbia: A History* (Toronto: Macmillan, 1976), 446-48. The parallels between the much-mocked naïveté of the Kidd Commission and the ideals of the Community Chest movement are clear. Whether commenting on the public business or on the financing and management of charities, men such as Kidd and Taylor proposed efficiency and business methods as solutions to problems. Their perception of politics as a source of inefficiency is an echo of corporatist strains in interwar-year political culture nationally and internationally.

27 See http://www.discovervancouver.com/GVB/south-west-marine-drive.asp; and http://www.canadianhorseracinghalloffame.com/builders/1976/Austin_C_Taylor.htm.

28 "Anna Ethel Sprott," CVA, JSM, fiche 4039, 505-C-4, file 261.

29 According to a 1940 manual for chest organizers, the prestige of a Community Chest "for all time will depend upon the wise choice of its first sponsors." L.H. Serene, "Organizing a Community Campaign: Some Suggestions for the Actual Organization of a Campaign for Voluntary Funds for Welfare Purposes, in a Community of Average Size in Canada," LAC, CCSD, MG 28 I 10, vol. 158, file "CWC Community Organization Division, 1940." Minutes, meeting of the board of directors, July 1934, CVA, UWLM, Add. Mss. 849, recorded the work of a campaign advisory committee that had no duties except to lend "prestige" to the campaign. Halifax and Ottawa similarly relied on campaign leaders such as "business and professional men and women" who "enjoyed the confidence of the community." Report of the executive secretary, Halifax chest annual meeting, 28 Febuary 1938, LAC, CCSD, MG 28 I 10, vol. 228, file 228-16; minutes, meeting of the Protestant board of directors,. 27 May 1935, UWOC. In this use of community prestige, of course, the chests' strategy was much like that of a mainstream political party. In British Columbia in 1935, it is interesting to note, one Conservative's attempt to seek the support of businessmen for his party had to be justified by the observation that "their influence with the electorate is very often underestimated." This Conservative, J.A. "Art" Clark, was also a member of the board of the federation during the first campaign and might be expected to have held a similar view on the value of businessmen's influence in that setting. J.A. Clark to Dr. F.P. Patterson, 14 November 1935, BCARS, J.A. Clark Papers, Add. Mss. 815.

30 "Report of Special Committee to Study the Community Chest System," 26 June 1923, and "Report of the Executive re Community Chest," 8 November 1928, in minutes of a special meeting of the council of the Vancouver Board of Trade, CVA, VBT, Add. Mss. 300, vol. 146. For comparable initial reports in other cities, see also "A Report on the Social Services and on a Possible Basis of Financial

Federation for the City and Area of Greater Ottawa," May 1932, LAC, Charlotte Whitton Papers, MG 30 E 256, vol. 21; and "A Meeting of Those Interested in Collecting and Distributing Charitable Funds," 17 November 1921, NSARM, UWHD, MG 20, vol. 1713.

31 "Infants' Hospital Ball Grand Success Friday at Commodore," *Vancouver Sun*, 11 November 1933, 16.

32 Campbell, *Demon Rum or Easy Money*, 63; "Larger Subscriptions," *Vancouver Sun*, 17 November 1933, 3.

33 "What Club Women Are Doing?" *Vancouver Sun*, 30 October 1934, 9, and 8 November 1934, 9; "Season Opens for Charity, Bazaars, Teas, Bridges," *Vancouver Sun*, 26 October 1935, 17.

34 "Chest Fund Nears Objective," *Vancouver Sun*, 3 March 1931, 18; "Welfare Reaches $270,000," *Vancouver Sun*, 7 November 1931, 14.

35 "What Can We Tell Those 6000 Families?" *Vancouver Sun*, 7 November 1932, 5; "Welfare Rally," *Vancouver Sun*, 23 October 1935, 2; "$325,000 Raised in Welfare Drive," *Vancouver Sun*, 13 November 1935, 5.

36 "Society Rallying to Support of Welfare Federation," *Vancouver Sun*, 23 October 1935, 6.

37 "There Is Still Time to Help," *Vancouver Sun*, 4 November 1935, 1.

38 The use of "big man" in this sense is drawn from a Halifax ad in 1950. Clipping, "They're Two of the Biggest Men in Town!" 17 October 1950, NSARM, UWHD, MG 20, vol. 1718.

39 "There Is Still Time To Help" (editorial), *Vancouver Sun*, 6 November 1931.

40 In the *Vancouver Sun*, "Welfare Collectors Speed Up," 5 November 1931, 18; "Apathy of Public Affects Drive," 4 November 1932, 1; "Welfare Strives for Objective," 10 November 1932, 1; "$236,134 Charity TOTAL," 15 November 1933, 17; "The Job of Everyone" (editorial), 28 October 1935; "Bigger Gifts Too Slow," 4 November 1935, 1.

41 "$236,134 Charity TOTAL," *Vancouver Sun*, 15 November 1933, 17.

42 "Pay Your Bills" (editorial), *Vancouver Sun*, 28 October 1931.

43 See, for example, "What Should I Give?" (ad), *Vancouver Sun*, 19 February 1931, 20.

44 "Why Should I Give? What Should I Give?" (ad), *Vancouver Sun*, 25 October 1932, 13.

45 "Great Corporation and Newsboy Lead Chest Giving," *Vancouver Sun*, 24 February 1931, 9; "You Who Are Unselfish" (ad), *Vancouver Sun*, 31 October 1932, 4.

46 "Indifference?" (cartoon), *Vancouver Sun*, 5 November 1935, 1.

47 Carol Steedman, *Landscape for a Good Woman* (New Brunswick, NJ: Rutgers University Press, 1987), 123.

48 "Dear Jack" (ad), *Vancouver Sun*, 21 February 1931, 14.

49 Systematic proof that this form of women's sociability in this period appeared at various class strata, and not only in the middle class, awaits further research, but see references to class variations within Jewish women's charitable organizations in Halifax in the interwar years in Deborah Osmond, "Tzedekah: Jewish Women and Charity in Halifax, 1920-1945" (Honours thesis, Department of History, Dalhousie University, 1996); and report by Alice Trenchard of fundraising and sociability in women's auxiliary #303 of the Carpenters' Union in *The Carpenter* 59, 3 (1939): 46.

50 "Youth at the Crossroads" (ad), *Vancouver Sun*, 28 October 1935, 3.

51 "The Economics of a Welfare Fund" (editorial), *Vancouver Sun*, 2 November 1935.

52 F. Ivor Jackson, "History of the Community Chest and Council of the Greater Vancouver Area" (typescript), March 1960, CVA, UWLM, Add. Mss. 849, Social Planning and Research series, F. Ivor Jackson subseries, 25, 46; Sanford D. Horwitt, *Let Them Call Me Rebel: Saul Alinsky, His Life and Legacy* (New York: Alfred A. Knopf, 1989); James Struthers, "'Lord Give Us Men': Women and Social Work in English Canada, 1918-1953," in *The Benevolent State?* ed. A. Moscovitch and J. Albert (Toronto: Garamond Press, 1986), 126-43.

53 Howard Falk and YMCA general secretary Stanley Brent were both profiled in this series during campaign week. For the column on Falk, see 4 November 1931, 1; Brent is covered on 6 November 1931, 1.

54 "Business Romances of Successful B.C. Women: Ethelwyn Paterson (John Howard Society)," *Vancouver Sun*, 26 October 1931, 1.

55 "1000 Women Help in Drive," *Vancouver Sun*, 24 October 1931, 20.

56 Marlene Shore, *The Science of Social Redemption* (Toronto: University of Toronto Press, 1987), 56-57.

57 "Funds Sought in Welfare Drive," *Vancouver Sun*, 21 October 1931, 24.

58 Some examples may be found in the *Vancouver Sun* in "Welfare Fund over $200,000," 2 March 1931, 14; fairground strength test image used to display rising collections, 25 February 1931, 1; "How Much a Month Can You Give?" 29 October 1932, 17; "Welfare Drive Tops $40,000 in First Day," 30 October 1934, 1; "Welfare Support Shows Increase," 1 November 1934, 1, 14.

59 Clipping, "Welfare Campaign Official Chosen," 25 July 1934, CVA, JSM, Vancouver Welfare Federation fiche.

60 "$305,000 Needed: We Will Get It," *Vancouver Sun*, 24 October 1931, 20.

61 See the *Vancouver Sun*, 4 November 1931, 1; and 5 November 1931, 1.

62 "New Appeal for 'Chest,'" *Vancouver Sun*, 7 November 1932, 5.

63 A similar shaming logic may be seen in an editorial cartoon from the same year in which a little boy is shown being chivvied on by his big sister to do his bit for the federation. "Hurry! It Isn't Too Late to Give!" *Vancouver Sun*, 4 November 1931, 6.

64 "Welfare Drive May Continue," *Vancouver Sun*, 31 October 1931, 1, 29.

65 Clippings, "Welfare Campaign Official Chosen," 25 July 1934, and "Our Whole Town's Working," 26 October 1935, CVA, JSM, Vancouver Welfare Federation fiche.
66 See *Vancouver Sun* for 2 March 1931, 1; and 5 November 1932, 1.
67 "Nobody's Business," *Vancouver Sun,* 29 October 1934, 5.
68 For examples, see ads in *Vancouver Sun,* 30 October 1933, 7; and 3 November 1933, 11.
69 Compare the mother in the Welfare Federation publicity in the *Vancouver Sun,* 3 November 1932, 1, with similar 1930s ads in the newspaper for 28 October 1933, 3; 4 November 1933, 2; and 26 October 1935, magazine section, 5.
70 See *Vancouver Sun,* 26 October 1931, 11.
71 See, for example, *Vancouver Sun,* 31 October 1932, 4.
72 Bob Bouchette, "Lend Me Your Ears," *Vancouver Sun,* 8 November 1932, 6. For his Marxist socialism, see his column in the same newspaper on 19 November 1932, 6.
73 Ibid., 8 November 1932, 6.
74 Ibid.
75 "Radical Opposition," *Vancouver Sun,* 6 November 1935, 4.
76 Pat Conroy, typescript of letter to the editor of the *Ottawa Journal,* 13 May 1950, LAC, CCSD, MG 28 I 10, vol..77, file 564, "Labour – General, 1942-1951."
77 Minutes of CASW-organized panel discussion on social work and labour, 16 March 1944, LAC, Canadian Association of Social Workers (CASW) Papers, MG 28 I 441, vol. 35, file 14.
78 Wage cuts and layoffs in the mining industry in 1930 are briefly described in Ormsby, *British Columbia,* 443.
79 "How Big Is Your Heart?" (ad), *Vancouver Sun,* 28 October 1935, 3.
80 "Text of Broadcast by Robert Cromie on Behalf of the Community Chests of Canada" and J.H.T. Falk to Marjorie Bradford, 13 October 1934, LAC, CCSD, MG 28 I 10, vol. 13, file 59 – CWC Division Community Organization, "Publicity and Fundraising, 1934"; Robin Fisher, *Duff Patullo of British Columbia* (Toronto: University of Toronto Press, 1991), 208-9, 211-12. While there were clearly tensions between Cromie and Patullo, Cromie's appearance on John Lauchlan Farris' 1937 list of active Vancouver Liberals puts Cromie still in the Liberal camp. UBC Special Collections, John Wallace deBeque Farris Papers, box 66, file 66-2, "Young Liberal Association of Vancouver."
81 Report of the chairman of the budget committee to the annual meeting of the federation, 18 February 1935, cited in F. Ivor Jackson, "History of the Community Chest and Council of the Greater Vancouver Area" (typescript), March 1960, CVA, UWLM, Add. Mss. 849, Social Planning and Research series, F. Ivor Jackson subseries, 25.
82 "Welfare Drive on Second Lap," *Vancouver Sun,* 4 November 1935, 8.
83 Quoted in Fisher, *Duff Patullo,* 215.

84 Ibid., 234-35.

85 Marjorie Bradford to J.H.T. Falk, 18 October 1934, LAC, CCSD, MG 28 I 10, vol. 13, file 59, "Publicity and Fundraising, 1934."

86 H.R. MacMillan, cited in "Welfare Drive Tuesday," *Vancouver Sun,* 4 November 1933, 4.

87 Helen Gregory MacGill, "The Story of Vancouver Social Service" (1943), CVA, 54; Sylvia Bashevkin, "Independence versus Partisanship: Dilemmas in the Political History of Women in English Canada," in *Rethinking Canada,* 2nd ed., ed. V. Strong-Boag and A.C. Fellman, (Toronto: Copp Clark Pitman, 1991), 425-26.

88 Elsie Gregory MacGill, *My Mother the Judge: A Biography of Helen Gregory MacGill* (Toronto: PMA Books, 1981); biographical information on Glass is from "List of Names Submitted by Mr. Collins" for the Macdonald Club of Vancouver membership, BCARS, J.A. Clark Papers, Add. Mss. 815, vol. 30, file 2. He was a member of the federation board of directors in 1933 and was still serving in important board roles as late as 1943. Minutes, meetings of the board of directors, 1933-43, CVA, UWLM, Add. Mss. 849.

89 Veronica Strong-Boag, "'Wages for Housework': Mothers' Allowances and the Beginnings of Social Security in Canada," *Journal of Canadian Studies* 14, 1 (1979): 24-34; Little, "Claiming," 80-102.

90 Minutes, meeting of the board of directors, 5 September 1933, CVA, UWLM, Add. Mss. 849, 127.

91 MacGill, *Story,* 45-49; minutes, meetings of the board of directors, 8 July 1933 and 10 October 1933, and Mrs. Walter [Alma Gale] Mowatt, "History of the Community Chest and Councils of the Greater Vancouver Area" (typescript), 1951, CVA, UWLM, Add. Mss. 849, 30. The Mowatt typescript was with the records that I consulted when the current CVA Add. Mss. 849 materials were being held at the United Way offices. It is not listed at the series level in the finding aids for these materials at the CVA.

92 Clipping (probably from *Daily Province*), "City Demands Welfare Data," 22 March 1934, CVA, JSM, Vancouver Welfare Federation fiche; "Runs Again," *Vancouver Sun,* 6 November 1934, 2 (identifies Walter Deptford as a "Labor" candidate for council).

93 Minutes, meeting of the board of directors, 22 June 1934, CVA, UWLM, Add. Mss. 849, 238.

94 "New Era League Asks [for] Department of Public Welfare. Are Critical of City Organization under Mr. Falk," *Daily Province,* 20 June 1934, 11. Quotations in the following three paragraphs are from this source. It is easy to see here also an anticipation of later critiques of the income tax system: that is, the view that taxation of a low-income worker takes away money he or she can ill afford to lose and gives it into the hands of governments who spend it wastefully. In a

right-wing version of this critique, the wasteful spending is on people lacking the work ethic of the low-income taxpayer; in the left-wing critique, the moral fault lies in spending this money on corporate welfare bums.

95 "Welfare's Big Drive Opens Tuesday," *Vancouver Sun,* 28 October 1935, 13; UBC Special Collections, John Wallace deBeque Farris Papers, file 8-2.

96 In fact, Falk's listed salary seems not to have been his actual take-home pay. The listed salary was a combination of two salaries, one as executive director of the federation and the other as the same position of the Council of Social Agencies. In 1934 and 1935, Falk sent the board of directors letters saying that he waived "all claim to any moneys due to him and not drawn by him with respect to his salary" for the preceding years (1933 and 1934). These letters were submitted at the request of the VWF auditors, on 14 February 1934 (minutes binder, 175) and 28 January 1935 (minutes binder, 295). The total of cheques paid to Falk in 1935 as recorded in the VWF cheque register for the period was $3,300.34. My citation for these documents is based on the pagination of the minutes binders in which these records were held before they were transferred to the City of Vancouver Archives.

97 See Chapter 1.

98 "Visits Reveal Work of Social Agencies," *Vancouver Sun,* 31 October 1934, 5.

99 "Welfare Drive Speeds Up," *Vancouver Sun,* 6 November 1934, 7.

100 "Say Yes – and Say It with a Smile!" *Vancouver Sun,* 26 October 1935, magazine supplement, 5.

101 "Society Rallying to Support of Welfare Federation," *Vancouver Sun,* 23 October 1935, 6.

102 "Women Aid Fund Campaign," *Vancouver Sun,* 31 October 1931, 10.

103 "The Job of Everyone" (editorial), *Vancouver Sun,* 28 October 1935.

104 "Housewife's Anxiety to Aid Fund," *Vancouver Sun,* 2 November 1935, 8.

105 "Women's Poll Tax," *Vancouver Sun,* 25 October 1935, 12.

106 "$350,000 – a Lot of Money" (ad), *Vancouver Sun,* 25 October 1935, 4.

107 "Firemen, on Reduced Pay, Give $1100 to Welfare Fund," *Vancouver Sun,* 6 November 1935, 1, 4.

108 "$300,000 Reached by Welfare Fund," *Vancouver Sun,* 12 November 1935, 1.

109 A brief description of the longshoring conflicts of 1935 can be found in Michael Kevin Dooley, "'Our Mickey': The Story of Private James O'Rourke, VC.MM (CEF), 1879-1957," *Labour/Le travail* 47 (2001): 181.

110 Minutes, meeting of the board executive committee, 12 February 1935, CVA, UWLM, Add. Mss. 849.

111 Minutes, report of the executive director, meeting of the board of directors, 22 July 1937, CVA, UWLM, Add. Mss. 849, 3.

112 Clippings, "Welfare Men Back Report," 5 July 1939; "Welfare Federation Agencies under Fire at Trades Council," 5 July 1939; "Federation Is Not Surprised," 6 July

1939; "Welfare Head Is Surprised," 21 July 1939, CVA, JSM, Vancouver Welfare Federation fiche. The last article reported that the Vancouver Trades and Labour Council was going to seek institutional representation on the federation board, a move that the new executive director, Blair M. Clerk, met with apparent puzzlement, saying that there were already three labour men on the board. His response suggested that communication between the two organizations was imperfect and a bit touchy. His promise to take up the question at the next board meeting was apparently forgotten when the beginning of the war and its implications for fundraising intervened. For the invitation to participate, see "Vancouver Wins Laurels but Does Not Rest on Them," *Canadian Welfare* 16, 1 (1939): 34. For labour councils' fundraising, see minutes, meeting of the board of directors, 22 December 1942, CVA, UWLM, Add. Mss. 849; and clipping, "Labour Bodies Combine to Raise $50,000 Shortage for Welfare Federation," 12 December 1942, LAC, CCSD, MG 28 I 10, vol. 254, file 254-3. For E.A. Jamieson's role on the federation board, see minutes, meeting of the board of directors, 29 December 1942, CVA, UWLM, Add. Mss. 849; and Arthur Cowan to George Davidson, 16 February 1942, LAC, CCSD, MG 28 I 10, vol. 254, file 254-3.

113 "Give ..." (federation ad with illustration of Trades and Labour Congress of Canada president), *Vancouver Sun*, 11 November 1941, 2; minutes, meeting of the coordinating committee, 27 November 1942, CVA, UWLM, Add. Mss. 849. In 1942, unionist E.A. Jamieson was appointed to two of the federation's most important committees (budget and co-ordinating, the latter of which he chaired). Minutes, meeting of the board of directors, 2 October 1942; minutes, meeting of the coordinating committee, 10 April 1942, CVA, UWLM, Add. Mss. 849. George Davidson of the CWC worried that Jamieson was inadequate as a representative of labour, but even in expressing his worries to a leading federation volunteer he indicated that both of them thought adequate representation of labour was desirable. George Davidson to Arthur Cowan, 22 February 1942, LAC, CCSD, MG 28 I 10, vol. 254, file 254-3. For a retrospective view on the importance of labour participation, expressed in 1944 by the federation's wartime director, Marjorie Bradford, see clipping, "Activity of Labour in Social Work Stressed," circa 1944, LAC, CCSD, MG 28 I 10, vol. 77, file 564. On chronic objections from labour, voiced in 1942 by an avowed CCF supporter working at the federation office, see Edgar Brown to George Davidson, 18 October 1942, LAC, CCSD, MG 28 I 10, vol. 254, file 254-3. On controversial policies, see minutes, meeting of the board of directors, 30 November 1943, CVA, UWLM, Add. Mss. 849; and Chapter 5.

114 Minutes, meeting of the board of directors, 28 September 1943, CVA, UWLM, Add. Mss. 849; Edgar Brown to George Davidson, 18 October 1942, LAC, CCSD, MG 28 I 10, vol. 254, file 254-3.

115 Minutes, meetings of the board of directors, 4 January 1944, 1 February 1944, and 27 June 1944, CVA, UWLM, Add. Mss. 849.

116 For the inclusiveness claim, see board of directors, report to annual meeting, 18 February 1935, CVA, UWLM, Add. Mss. 849; and clipping, "Race, Color, Creed No Bars in City Welfare Campaign," unidentified Vancouver newspaper, 10 November 1939, CVA, JSM, Vancouver Welfare Federation fiche.

117 "Catholic Charities and the Welfare Federation," 14 October 1935, CVA, JSM, Vancouver Welfare Federation fiche.

118 For a summary of the issues in this relationship, see minutes, special meeting of the board of directors, 25 July 1935, CVA, UWLM, Add. Mss. 849. While I requested access to records of the Vancouver diocese to better understand the Catholic Church's views on the Welfare Federation, my request was refused.

119 Minutes, meetings of the board of directors, 7 December 1934 and 18 February 1935, CVA, UWLM, Add. Mss. 849.

120 "Welfare Collections up $4,000," *Vancouver Sun,* 30 October 1935, 1.

121 Alan Wolfe, *Whose Keeper? Social Science and Moral Obligation* (Berkeley: University of California Press, 1989), 112-13.

122 "The Job of Everyone" (editorial), *Vancouver Sun,* 28 October 1935; "You Who Are Unselfish" (ad), *Vancouver Sun,* 31 October 1932, 4.

123 I found only one instance of labour criticizing the chest in Halifax in the 1920s and 1930s. The Halifax Labour Council's newspaper, *The Citizen,* published some criticisms of the chest, not fundamental ones but questions about which organizations belonged or were excluded. The chest's response was to speak sternly to the paper's editor and to extract a promise that such ill-informed criticisms would not be made in the future. The chest also invited F.C. Craig, a sanitation inspector and Labour Council member, to join the chest board. He agreed to do so but did not become an active member. *The Citizen* published an editorial expressing satisfaction that its objections had been removed. Minutes, meeting of the executive committee, 7 and 10 October 1929, NSARM, UWHD, MG 20; Craig's occupation is from the *Halifax City Directory, 1929* (Halifax: McAlpine's City Directories, 1929), 100; "The Community Chest Drive" (editorial), *The Citizen,* 25 October 1929. I have been unable to find any evidence that the Ottawa Chests were aware of any labour criticism, and I note that Tom Moore of the Trades and Labour Congress of Canada appears in some early meetings of the Protestant board.

124 For a discussion of this conception of education in a common culture as an intrinsic element of nineteenth-century political liberalism, see David Lloyd and Paul Thomas, *Culture and the State* (London: Routledge, 1998), especially Chapter 4.

CHAPTER 4: RACE, CHARITY, AND DEMOCRACY

1 Shirley Tillotson, "Class and Community in Canadian Welfare Work, 1933-1960," *Journal of Canadian Studies* 32, 1 (1997): 77-83.

2 "L'honneur du service social a été sauvé," *Le Droit,* 23 March 1922, 10; "Report, He Says, on Social Dept. a Heartless One," *Ottawa Journal,* 19 March 1923, 1; "Requests Judicial Inquiry into City Social Services Office," *Ottawa Journal,* 20 March 1923, 1, 16; "Thirty Eight Applications for Assistant Commissioner and Relief Officer of Social Service Dept.," *Ottawa Citizen,* 18 April 1923, 12; "Labour Council Is Not to Take Part in Next Election," *Ottawa Citizen,* 21 April 1923, 7. The City Council committee struck in January 1923 to investigate the allegations of corruption included representatives from the Canadian Congress of Labour (J.A.P. Haydon), the Council of Women (Mrs. J.A. Wilson), the Fédération des femmes canadiennes-françaises (Mme P.E. [Almanda] Marchand), and the Board of Trade (J.A. Machado). Minutes, meeting of the board of control, Ottawa City Council, 15 January 1923. The committee also included representatives of the Rotary Club (T.H. Blair) and the anglophone Saint Vincent de Paul Society (T.H. Burns). The recommendations that flowed out of this crisis took ten years to unfold, but all of these individuals participated at some point in the subsequent efforts to organize private management of the city's relief distribution. The one exception, Haydon, was replaced by Tom Moore as a representative of his organization.

3 Judith C.M. Roberts-Moore, "Maximum Relief for Minimum Cost? Coping with Unemployment and Relief in Canada during the Depression, 1929-1939" (MA thesis, Department of History, Carleton University, 1980). In spite of its title, this thesis is exclusively concerned with Ottawa.

4 See, for example, Jan Nederveen Pieterse, "White Negroes," in *White on Black: Images of Africa and Blacks in Western Popular Culture* (New Haven: Yale University Press, 1992), 212-23; George M. Frederickson, "Understanding Racism," in *The Comparative Imagination: On the History of Racism, Nationalism, and Social Movements* (Berkeley: University of California Press, 1997), 77-97; and Elazar Barkan, *The Retreat of Scientific Racism: Changing Concepts of Race in Britain and the United States between the World Wars* (Cambridge, UK: Cambridge University Press, 1992), 16-55. I thank Amani Whitfield for his advice on this literature.

5 Frederickson, "Understanding Racism," 85.

6 A marker of the timing of change in the acceptability of this "race" language is that it appears in the order-in-council that established the Royal Commission on Bilingualism and Biculturalism (PC 1963-1106), but six years later, in 1969, the final report uses "francophone" and "anglophone," "persons of French mother tongue," and "French-speaking Canada" rather than "French Canada." A note in the introduction to Part 1 emphasizes the sensitivity of such matters of usage by commenting on the stylistic short form for "Canadians of French origin" and other parallel phrases: "In Part 1, the terms 'French,' 'British,' 'Germans,' 'Others,' etc. refer to the ethnic origin of Canadians, and *not* to nationality." *Report of the*

Royal Commission on Bilingualism and Biculturalism, volume 3A (Ottawa: Queen's Printer, 1969), 13 and passim.

7 From the relation of anxious suspicion described in the previous chapter, the chest moved in the late 1950s to the active engagement in administrative and leadership roles of a number of Asian Canadians. Clippings, "Well Known Chinese Citizens Talk at Tours," 15 January 1958, and "'Mixing' Feared by Old Chinese," 20 October 1960, CVA, UWLM, Add. Mss. 849, Loc. 589-F-7, file 9; interview by author, 25 January 1999, with Howard Naphtali, executive director of the federation in the 1950s and 1960s. In 1954, the Civic Unity League, an anti-discrimination organization, became one of the member agencies of the chest. See Chapter 7 for further description of its activities.

8 Robert Choquette, *Language and Religion: A History of English-French Conflict in Ontario* (Ottawa: University of Ottawa Press, 1975), sets this conflict in its larger context.

9 The "assessment" is quoted in "A Report on the Social Services and on a Possible Basis of Financial Federation for the City and Area of Greater Ottawa," May 1932, LAC, Charlotte Whitton Papers, MG 30 E 256, vol. 21, 1.

10 Robert Choquette, *La foi gardienne de la langue en Ontario, 1900–1950* (Montreal: Les Éditions Bellarmin, 1987), Chapter 8.

11 Renamed in 1918 with "nationale" removed from the title, this organization's history is briefly described at the website of the Centre de recherche en civilisation canadienne-française, http://www.uottawa.ca/academic/crccf/passeport/II/C/C1a/IIIC1a.html.

12 T. d'Arcy McGee, D'Arcy Scott, John P. Dunne, and Thomas Smith, quoted in F.A. Walker, *Catholic Education and Politics in Ontario* (Toronto: Thomas Nelson and Sons, 1964), 231.

13 This phrase comes from a chapter title in P.F. Morley, *Bridging the Chasm: A Study of the Ontario-Quebec Question* (Toronto: J.M. Dent and Sons, 1919). Morley was one voice of an emerging sympathetic view that sought to counter English race fears.

14 William Moore, *The Clash! A Study in Nationalities* (London: J.M. Dent, 1918), 74-75. Moore cites for his sources of English Canadians' holding of these views Madison Grant, *The Passing of the Great Race* (New York: C. Scribner, 1916).

15 Moore, *The Clash!* 125-26; *Toronto Mail*, 24 November 1886, from Walker, *Catholic Education*, 129, cited in Choquette, *Language and Religion*, 56. See also Choquette, *Language and Religion*, 58 and 60, for reference to beliefs about French Canadians being "backward" and "regressive."

16 "Survey of Greater Ottawa," June 1935, Charlotte Whitton Papers, LAC, MG 30 E 256, vol. 19.

17 "L'influence de la nationalité," *Le Droit*, 22 November 1921, 10.

18 On City Council, the francophone aldermen were the only voters in favour of a 1926 motion to overturn a new system of distributing relief that had been instituted in 1925. Coverage in *Le Droit* of the relevant council meeting was headlined "Beaucoup de gens se plaignent du présent système" and included the news that the Société Saint-Jean-Baptiste had written to City Council to protest the system as working to the disadvantage of "our element." Minutes, meeting of Ottawa City Council, 1 February 1926; "Beaucoup de gens se plaignent du présent système," *Le Droit,* 2 February 1926, 3.

19 Corresponding Secretary of the Federation of French Canadian Women to Colonel D.T. Irwin, President of the Children's Aid Society of Ottawa, 28 November 1922, LAC, Records of the Fédération des femmes canadiennes-françaises, MG 28 I 231, vol. 4, file "Children's Aid Society"; "Une saleté du 'Journal,'" *Le Droit,* 4 February 1926, 3 (author's translation of "le fanatisme de race, tellement développé chez le 'Journal' que, sciemment ou non, il regarde comme inférieur et corrompu tout ce qui ne lui ressemble pas").

20 George Thomas Daly, *Catholic Problems in Western Canada* (Toronto: Macmillan, 1921), 271.

21 The imprimateur of respectability the Orange Order enjoyed in interwar Ottawa came in large measure from its connection with Conservative premier Howard Ferguson, an Orange Order member and a vigorous supporter of Regulation 17. Peter Oliver, *G. Howard Ferguson, Ontario Tory* (Toronto: University of Toronto Press, 1977), 39-70. Those Protestant members of the Ottawa elite whom Charlotte Whitton identified in 1932 as essential to any fundraising effort included prominent Conservatives such as newspaper owner P.D. Ross, H.P. Hill, and Sir George Perley. Charlotte Whitton, "Confidential Memo re Ottawa Survey," 1929, LAC, CCSD, MG 28 I 10, vol. 28, file 143; Oliver, *G. Howard Ferguson,* 317; see "Hill, Hamnet Pinhey," and "Perley, Rt. Hon. Sir George Halsey," in *Who's Who in Canada,* 1930-31 ed. (Toronto: International Press, 1930). One of those on her 1932 list may have been the individual Dorothy Chunn describes in her discussion of the connections between family court judge John F. Mckinley and Ferguson's Conservatives in *From Punishment to Doing Good: Family Courts and Socialized Justice in Ontario* (Toronto: University of Toronto Press, 1992), 111-12, 125-26. In correspondence concerning the Child Welfare Survey in 1929, Whitton wrote to that "the most obstructive person on the Children's Aid [opposing a Council of Social Agencies] is one of the County Orange officials." Charlotte Whitton to J.H.T. Falk, 27 March 1929, LAC, CCSD, MG 28 I 10, vol. 28, file 143. On the persistence of the Orange Order's respectability, see John H. Taylor, *Ottawa: An Illustrated History* (Toronto: James Lorimer and Company, 1986), 182.

22 No comprehensive list exists of such agencies. From browsing contemporary issues of *Le Droit,* I have gleaned the following, no doubt incomplete, list: le Foyer,

Société Sainte-Élisabeth, Fédération des femmes canadiennes-française; l'Hospice Saint-Charles, Société Saint-Vincent-de-Paul, le Patronat, youth sports clubs in Lower Town.

23 Defeated in the 1926 provincial election, Séguin would win an Ottawa-area seat for the Conservative Party in 1929. *Canadian Parliamentary Guide* (Ottawa: Normandin, 1933), 493.

24 Charlotte Whitton, "Confidential Memo re Ottawa Survey," 1929, LAC, CCSD, MG 28 I 10, vol. 28, file 143.

25 For a description of such tensions as part of a larger pattern in Canadian society, see Robert Choquette, "English-French Relations in the Canadian Catholic Community," in *Creed and Culture: The Place of English-Speaking Catholics in Canadian Society, 1750-1930*, ed. Terence Murphy and Gerald Stortz (Montreal: McGill-Queen's University Press, 1993), 3-24.

26 "A Report on the Social Services and on a Possible Basis of Financial Federation for the City and Area of Greater Ottawa," May 1932, LAC, Charlotte Whitton Papers, MG 30 E 256, vol. 21, 9.

27 Minutes of open meeting to present welfare federation constitution, 23 October 1931; special meeting of the executive committee of the Council of Social Agencies, 6 November 1931; and public meeting on the constitution, 6 November 1931, COA, SPCOC. The records of the Social Planning Council of Ottawa-Carleton have not been archivally organized, so there are no volume or series references to documents in this collection of papers.

28 Minutes of a meeting to discuss the possibility of a combined financial drive in the children's field, 29 November 1932, LAC, CCSD, MG 28 I 10, vol. 43, file 214.

29 Ibid.

30 Gale Wills, *A Marriage of Convenience: Business and Social Work in Toronto, 1918-1957* (Toronto: University of Toronto Press, 1995), 53-55; F. Ivor Jackson, "History of the Community Chest and Council of the Greater Vancouver Area" (typescript), March 1960, CVA, UWLM, Add. Mss. 849, Social Planning and Research series, F. Ivor Jackson subseries, 188-89; "Protestant Community Service," *The Sentinel*, 15 September 1927, 1. My thanks to Robert Cupido for drawing my attention to this article in *The Sentinel*.

31 C.F. Curran (Director of Catholic Charities) to Thomas O'Donnell (Archbishop of Halifax), 3 October 1932, Halifax Catholic Pastoral Centre Archives, O'Donnell Papers, vol. 2, #93.

32 In a pamphlet written by Whitton in the 1930s, being revised in 1942, she wrote that "one of [the difficulties] most frequently encountered is that of whether money given by people of one faith, fervently held, is to be used to help people of another faith, which may not appeal to the donor." And "the fact to be faced in most cities is that a large number of people will not support or subscribe to causes – charitable or otherwise – of faiths other than their own." Joy Maines to

Eurith Goold, 7 January 1942, LAC, CCSD, MG 28 I 10, vol. 240, file 240-2. Maines urged the removal of the two sentences quoted above but accepted a continuing reference to earmarking – "a system of providing adequately for the social needs of all the population but, at the same time, ... restrict[ing] their actual support to charities of their own faith."

33 Charlotte Whitton to P.D. Ross, 19 November 1931, LAC, CCSD, MG 28 I 10, vol. 43, file 214.

34 Minutes of special meeting of the Council of Social Agencies, 8 December 1931, COA, SPCOC.

35 Charlotte Whitton to W.E. Weld (Secretary, Council of Social Agencies), 15 December 1931, COA, SPCOC, minutes file.

36 A reading of the issues of *Le Droit* from 19 November 1931 (the date of the public meeting to discuss the proposal) to 9 December 1931, by which time Whitton had enlisted the solid support of the two English-language papers, reveals no coverage of the federated charities proposals. There is no archival trace of consultation during this period, or before, between the Council of Social Agencies and the Fédération des femmes canadiennes-françaises, the organization that represented Ottawa's francophone women in welfare matters in the 1920s and 1930s. LAC, Records of the Fédération des femmes canadiennes-françaises, MG 28 I 231, vols. 4 and 5.

37 Charlotte Whitton to W.A. Gordon (Minister of Labour), 20 December 1932; correspondence among Whitton, E.A. Baker (CNIB), and F.E. Bronson (Chairman of the Citizens' Committee for the Emergency Relief Fund), December 1932; and resolution and memorandum by Whitton re disbursement of Emergency Relief Fund of $25,000, 9 December 1932, LAC, CCSD, MG 28 I 10, vol. 43, file 214. For an example of the direct impact of the early 1930s unemployment crisis on VON nurses' salaries, recalled in the late 1930s, see correspondence from VON read into minutes, meeting of the executive committee, 15 March 1938, NSARM, UWHD, MG 20.

38 Minutes of general meeting, 21 October 1932, OBT, MG 6, box 1, file council minutes; clipping, "News Note re: Citizens' Relief Fund," c. December 1932; Charlotte Whitton to W.A. Gordon (Minister of Labour), 20 December 1932; W.A. Gordon to Charlotte Whitton, 23 December 1932; two letters, over Bronson's signature, to presidents of the VON and Ottawa Day Nursery explaining the matching grant arrangments of the Relief Fund, 12 December 1932, LAC, CCSD, MG 28 I 10, vol. 43, file 214. That the text of these letters was actually composed by Whitton is documented in two other 12 December letters in this file: Whitton to Bronson and Whitton to City Relief Commissioner.

39 Laura Chartrand (Director of le Foyer) to Board of Control member Fulgence Charpentier, 13 December 1932 and 29 December 1932, LAC, CCSD, MG 28 I 10, vol. 44, file 214.

40 Thelma Williams (Director of Ottawa Welfare Bureau), memo "For Miss C. Williams," December 1932; Charlotte Whitton to F. Stapleford, 30 November 1932; Charlotte Whitton, "Memorandum re Control and Supervision of the Welfare Bureau," 2 December 1932; Dorothy King, Freda Held, and F. Stapleford, "Summary of Comment and Recommendations re Ottawa Welfare Bureau," 6 December 1932; and Charlotte Whitton to C. Russell (Ottawa Transportation Company), 16 December 1932, LAC, CCSD, MG 28 I 10, vol. 44, file 215.

41 Charlotte Whitton, "Memorandum re Control and Supervision of the Welfare Bureau," 2 December 1932; and Charlotte Whitton to F.N. Stapleford, 30 November and 13 December 1932, LAC, CCSD, MG 28 I 10, vol. 44, file 215.

42 Charlotte Whitton to E.W. Harrold (Editor of the *Ottawa Citizen*), 20 December 1932, LAC, CCSD, MG 28 I 10, vol. 43, file 214.

43 Author's translation of "il est d'importance nationale pour les contribuables de langue française d'avoir un interprète parmi les membres de la haute administration municipale." "Votez Charpentier au poste de Commissaire Municipal," *Le Droit,* 3 December 1931, 7.

44 "Le traitement des cancereux," *Le Droit,* 1 September 1927, 10; "Use Hopewell Hospital for Cancer Cases," *Ottawa Journal,* 1 September 1927, 11; "Une pétition en circulation," *Le Droit,* 2 September 1927, 12; "A Monstrous Suggestion," *Ottawa Journal,* 2 September 1927, 6; "Le projet n'est pas accuelli des citoyens," *Le Droit,* 14 September 1927, 10.

45 Elizabeth King (CCCW Survey Researcher) to Doctor Grant Fleming, 1929, describing sectarian issues in cancer care; and Charlotte Whitton, "Confidential Memo re: Ottawa Survey," 1929, LAC, CCSD, MG 28 I 10, vol. 28, file 143.

46 Charlotte Whitton to E.W. Harrold (Editor of the *Ottawa Citizen*), 20 December 1932; and Charlotte Whitton, memo "Re: The Organization of Social Services in the City of Ottawa," 20 December 1932, LAC, CCSD, MG 28 I 10, vol. 43, file 214.

47 See, for example, the foundational work of Richard Hofstadter, *The Age of Reform: From Bryan to F.D.R.* (New York: Vintage Books, 1960), 174-86; and, in the Canadian historiography, Paul Rutherford, "Tomorrow's Metropolis: The Urban Reform Movement in Canada, 1880-1920," in *The Canadian City: Essays in Urban and Social History,* ed. Gilbert A. Stelter and Alan F.J. Artibise (Ottawa: Carleton University Press, 1984), 442-45.

48 Dr. R.E. Wodehouse to J.G. Parker, 14 December 1932; Charlotte Whitton to C. Russell (Ottawa Transportation Company), 16 December 1932; Charlotte Whitton to Rev. Canon A.H. Whalley, 23 December 1932; and minutes of a meeting to discuss the developments between the city and the Ottawa Welfare Bureau, 29 December 1932, LAC, CCSD, MG 28 I 10, vol. 44, file 215; "Report of the Joint Committee on Ways and Means of Furthering the Plan of a System of Financial Federation of Charities in the City of Ottawa," 30 December 1932,

LAC, CCSD, MG 28 I 10, vol. 44, file 214. A relief scandal in 1923 prompted not only businessmen but also organized labour to complain about city aldermen and Board of Control members interfering in city relief administration to serve their personal business and political interests. "Thirty Eight Applications for Assistant Commissioner and Relief Officer of Social Service Dept.," *Ottawa Citizen,* 18 April 1923, 12; "Labour Council Is Not to Take Part in Next Election," *Ottawa Citizen,* 21 April 1923, 7.

49 Dr. R.E. Wodehouse to J.G. Parker, 14 December 1932, LAC, CCSD, MG 28 I 10, vol. 44, file 215. For Wodehouse's position in the Ottawa chests, see minutes, meeting of the joint executive committee, 10 October 1933, UWOC. For other details of his biography, see "Wodehouse, Dr. Robert E.," in *Canadian Who's Who,* 1936-37 ed. (Toronto: Trans-Canada Press, 1936).

50 Minutes of a meeting to discuss the developments between the city and the Ottawa Welfare Bureau, 29 December 1932, LAC, CCSD, MG 28 I 10, vol. 44, file 215.

51 Marjorie Thomson to F.N. Stapleford, 29 December 1932, LAC, CCSD, MG 28 I 10, vol. 44, file 215; clipping, "Are Setting Up a Public Board for City Relief," *Ottawa Journal,* 31 December 1932, LAC, CCSD, MG 28 I 10, vol. 44, file 215.

52 Roberts-Moore, "Maximum Relief for Minimum Cost?"

53 Whitton described the OWB in these terms in a letter seeking an endorsement of her campaign to reform the OWB. Charlotte Whitton to Rev. Canon A.H. Whalley, 23 December 1932, LAC, CCSD, MG 28 I 10, vol. 44, file 215.

54 "Report of the Joint Committee on Ways and Means of Furthering the Plan of a System of Financial Federation of Charities in the City of Ottawa," 30 December 1932, LAC, CCSD, MG 28 I 10, vol. 44, file 214.

55 Charlotte Whitton to J.H.T. Falk, 17 June 1933, LAC, CCSD, MG 28 I 10, vol. 44, file 214.

56 Minutes of a joint meeting of the Protestant and Catholic executive committees, 4 July 1933, UWOC.

57 Charlotte Whitton to J.H.T. Falk, 10 July 1933, LAC, CCSD, MG 28 I 10, vol. 44, file 214.

58 Minutes of a joint meeting of the Protestant and Catholic executive committees, 14 July 1933, UWOC.

59 "Un déficit à l'Orphélinat Saint-Joseph," *Le Droit,* 18 February 1935, 10; "Pourquoi l'Orphélinat Saint-Joseph a accusé un déficit de $4,640," *Le Droit,* 19 February 1935, 10.

60 Minutes, meeting of the Roman Catholic chest board of directors, 10 November 1936 and 17 November 1936; minutes, meeting of the Protestant board of directors, 13 November 1936; minutes, meeting of the campaign committee, 10 November 1939; minutes, meeting of the board of directors, honorary advisors,

and budget committee of the Roman Catholic chest, 16 November 1939; and minutes, meeting of the Roman Catholic chest board of directors, 5 April 1940, UWOC.

61 "Conference of Children's Agencies (Ottawa) re Financial Drive, Minutes of Meeting of December 19th, 1932," 20 December 1932, LAC, CCSD, MG 28 I 10, vol. 44, file 214.

62 Minutes, meeting of the campaign committee, 11 August 1939, UWOC.

63 Joy Maines to Eurith Goold (Canadian Welfare Council), 7 January 1942, LAC, CCSD, MG 28 I 10, vol. 240, file 240-2.

64 Report of the board of directors, annual meeting, 1947, UWOC.

65 Choquette, *La foi*, 242.

66 Minutes, annual meeting, 11 April 1951, UWOC. Racine offered the general thanks by the chests to the larger community. The first francophone to speak in French, A. Arvisais, had given the budget committee's thanks in 1950 to the participants in its deliberations. Minutes, annual meeting, 19 April 1950, UWOC.

67 Annual reports, 1933-65, UWOC.

68 For a description of these classical republican guardians, see Plato, *The Republic*, trans. B. Jowett (New York: Modern Library, n.d.), 121, 239-45. The guardians were to be "those who in their whole life show the greatest eagerness to do what is for the good of their country, and the greatest repugnance to do what is against her interests." On the shared interests of the guardians and their common feelings, see 189. For Plato's disparagement of popular democracy as inevitably producing envy, corruption, and revolt, see 308-10. J.G.A. Pocock summarizes the classical inheritance, emphasizing Aristotle's *Politics*, in "The Ideal of Citizenship since Classical Times," in *The Citizenship Debates*, ed. Gershon Shafir (Minneapolis: University of Minnesota Press, 1998), 31-42.

69 Emphasis added. Quoted from Jessica Squires, "Creating Hegemony: Consensus by Exclusion in the Rowell-Sirois Commission," paper presented at the Canadian Historical Association, June 2004, 16. This paper was based on Jessica Squires, "Ideological Formation and Liberal 'Consensus': Reading the Rowell-Sirois Commission" (MA thesis, Department of History, Dalhousie University, 2003).

70 Walter Lippmann, *An Inquiry into the Principles of the Good Society* (1943; reprint, Greenwood Press, 1973); Karl Popper, *The Open Society and Its Enemies* (London: Routledge and Kegan Paul, 1957). More recently, Michael Sandel has argued that, for obligation to be a part of liberal polities, citizens must cultivate "certain excellences – of character, judgment, and concern for the whole." In this view, a democratic welfare state must not be merely procedurally fair but also inspire "moral and civic engagement." In this view, as in the classical republican democracy, people who participate in civic affairs earn authority by way of their practice of civic virtue. Unlike the classical version, however, Sandel contemplates

multiple standards of virtue and varied routes to its achievement. Michael Sandel, *Democracy's Discontent: America in Search of a Public Philosophy* (Cambridge, MA: Belknap Press, 1996), 318-19 and passim.

71 Charlotte Whitton to Norman Smith (Managing Editor of the *Ottawa Journal*), 21 December 1932, LAC, CCSD, MG 28 I 10, vol. 44, file 215.

72 In a recent contribution to the discussion of civic republicanism, Adrian Oldfield echoes the notion that an active practice of service and fulfillment of community obligation is the essence of citizenship and not just the holding of rights. Adrian Oldfield, "Citizenship and Community: Civic Republicanism and the Modern World," in *The Citizenship Debates*, ed. Gershon Shafir (Minneapolis: University of Minnesota Press, 1998), 75-89.

73 George Davidson, interim report of the director, minutes of a meeting of the board of directors, 23 March 1936, CVA, UWLM, Add. Mss. 849, 2. No similar data analysis is available for the late 1930s in Halifax; however, if a similar ratio of donor numbers to percentage of funds collected existed, then the small donations in Halifax would have produced 11.9 percent of the total and in Ottawa 10.3 percent. "Summary of Report of Canadian Welfare Council Field Visit to Halifax Community Chest – May 15-19, 1950 [by Henry Stubbins]," LAC, CCSD, MG 28 I 10, vol. 228, file 228-17.

CHAPTER 5: HOW CHARITY SURVIVED THE BIRTH OF THE WELFARE STATE

1 "The Story of the Community Chest in 1944: Annual Report of the Board of Directors," CVA, UWLM, Add. Mss. 849, vol. 617-A-5, 2; and "Annual Report 1950, Community Chest and Council of Greater Vancouver," CVA, UWLM, Add. Mss. 849, vol. 617-B-2, 17; Dominion Bureau of Statistics, *The Canada Year Book, 1952-53* (Ottawa: Queen's Printer, 1953), 155. I used the 1951 Canadian census figure for Vancouver's population but, in the absence of 1951 donor numbers from Vancouver, used the 1950 donor count. If Vancouver's population grew between 1950 and 1951, then the participation rate in 1950 was probably slightly higher than 27 percent. For per capita income tax payers, see Canada, Department of National Revenue, *Taxation Statistics*, 1951, Table 3, 39. The percentage of the Canadian urban population aged twenty and over (79 percent) was drawn from F.H. Leacy, ed., *Historical Statistics of Canada* (Ottawa: Statistics Canada, 1983), series A94-109, and Vancouver, as one of Canada's largest urban centres, was assumed to have the same age distribution.

2 Kenneth Bryden summarizes these developments in *Old Age Pensions and Policy-Making in Canada* (Montreal: McGill-Queen's University Press, 1974), 112-13.

3 Donald Creighton, *The Forked Road: Canada 1939-1957* (Toronto: McClelland and Stewart, 1976), 88.

4 Clipping, "Gallup Poll Survey: 59 Percent Favor Voluntary Funds [to] Finance Social Service Work," *Edmonton Journal,* 22 May 1948, LAC, CCSD, MG 28 I 10, vol. 70, file 517.

5 Canadian Institute for Public Opinion polls in 1943 and 1944 showed 71 percent of adult Canadians in favour of many reforms after the war rather than a return to pre-war society. Hadley Cantril, *Public Opinion, 1935-46* (Princeton: Princeton University Press, 1951), 87.

6 J. Harvey Perry, *Taxes, Tariffs, and Subsidies: A History of Canadian Fiscal Development,* vol. 2 (Toronto: University of Toronto Press, 1955), 333-36, 367.

7 Minister of Finance, September 1939, as quoted in Perry, *Taxes,* vol. 2, 337. The somewhat peculiar punctuation is the original as recorded in *Hansard.*

8 Minutes, annual meeting, 27 February 1936; minutes, meeting of the executive committee, 13 December 1937; minutes, special meeting of the executive committee, 7 July 1938; and minutes, meeting of the executive committee, 11 December 1939, NSARM, UWHD, MG 20, vol. 1713. Minutes, meeting of the Protestant board of directors and budget committee, 18 January 1938; and minutes, annual meeting, 12 May 1938, UWOC, 1938 vol. Minutes, meeting of the joint budget committee, 22 January 1940, UWOC, 1940 vol. Charlotte Whitton to Joy Maines, 2 February 1938, LAC, CCSD, MG 28 I 10, vol. 240, file 240-42; and "It's Time to Act" (chest newsletter), July 1952, LAC, CCSD, MG 28 I 10, vol. 240, file 240-43. "Report of Executive Director," 15 February 1937, CVA, UWLM, Add. Mss. 849, vol. 617-A-3, file 3, front cover; "A Story of Achievement: Report of Executive Director," 21 February 1938, CVA, UWLM, Add. Mss. 849, vol. 617-A-3, file 4, 8; "Report of Executive Director," 20 February 1939, CVA, UWLM, Add. Mss. 849, vol. 617-A-3, file 4, 13. "Community Chest and Council of Greater Vancouver, History of Giving Related to Objectives, 1939-1954 Inclusive," LAC, CCSD, MG 28 I 10, vol. 254, file 254-57.

9 Annual reports, 1932-35; reports of the executive director, 1936-39; and especially report of the executive director, 20 February 1939, CVA, UWLM, Add. Mss. 849, vol. 617-A-3, 1-2, 5-6. Minutes, annual meetings, 27 January 1930; 20 February 1931; 22 February 1932; 21 February 1934; 14 February 1935; 27 February 1936; 18 February 1937; 28 February 1938; and 10 March 1939, NSARM, UWHD, MG 20, vol. 1713. Minutes, annual meetings, 3 April 1936; 12 May 1938; and 10 March 1939, UWOC.

10 Minutes, meeting of the Protestant board of directors and budget committee, 18 October 1938, UWOC.

11 For more detail on these funds, see Chapter 6.

12 Nova Scotia, *Journals of the House of Assembly,* Part 2, Appendix 23, 1930, 1934, and 1939, statistical reports of the Children's Aid Society of Halifax. I have calculated the number of wards requiring supervision by subtracting from the total number of wards whose "condition" was listed those who had died or reached

the age of majority or were in other categories where they were beyond the need of supervision.

13 Charlotte Whitton, memo to Miss Bradford re Halifax Community Chest, 11 October 1939, LAC, CCSD, MG 28 I 10, vol. 228, file 228-16; "They Built Better than They Knew" (obituary for S.R. Balcom), *Commercial News* (December 1963): 64.

14 Ottawa chest director Joy Maines described these sorts of problems vividly: "Unemployment figures went down; married women went to work; the Day Nursery was crowded, and private nurseries of doubtful standard[s] appeared. Housing became scarcer and scarcer for low income families, and evictions occurred frequently. At the urgent request of the city, the Children's Aid Society accepted for non-ward care large numbers of children for no other reason but lack of housing, and parents moved into rooms ... British children arrived to be taken care of for the duration. Foster homes in the city became very scarce, and more country homes had to be found." Joy Maines, "Notes re Development of Ottawa's Social Services," May 1966, COA, SPCOC, "Historical Files – Application to Canada Council for J. Laycock to Do History of Social Planning Council," 8.

15 On Halifax's normal donation limit, see Charlotte Whitton, memo to Miss Bradford re Halifax Community Chest, 11 January 1939, LAC, CCSD, MG 28 I 10, vol. 228, file 228-16; and minutes, special meeting of the executive committee, 28 July 1938, NSARM, UWHD, MG 20, vol. 1713. On the $200 increase, see minutes, special meeting to discuss an increase, 29 June 1942, NSARM, UWHD, MG 20, vol. 1713. On Farquhar's views on the chest budgeting practices, see George F. Davidson (CWC) to Lillian Farquhar of the Halifax Junior League, 30 April 1943; and Lillian Farquhar to George F. Davidson, 20 March 1944, LAC, CCSD, MG 28 I 10, vol. 228, file 228-16.

16 Minutes, annual meeting, 26 February 1945, NSARM, UWHD, MG 20, vol. 1713.

17 Nova Scotia, *Journals of the House of Assembly*, Part 2, Appendix 23, 1946, 8. This was F.R. MacKinnon's first report as the director of child welfare.

18 For fear of the takeover of a Children's Aid Society by a government agency, see minutes, 9 October 1951, 8 April 1952, and 7 May 1952, NSARM, Halifax-Dartmouth Welfare Council (HDWC), MG 20, vol. 415, file 9. For some of the reasons for this fear of takeover, see Chapter 4 and B.L. Vigod, "Ideology and Institutions in Quebec: The Public Charities Controversy, 1921-1926," *Histoire sociale* 11, 21 (1978): 178-79. Anti-statist arguments centred on curtailing the expenses of the state and on ensuring that personal services were delivered by private agencies. Robert Cromie to Duff Patullo, 30 January 1933, BCARS, Patullo Papers, Add. Mss. 3, vol. 50, file 12; "Text of Broadcast by Robert Cromie on Behalf of the Community Chests of Canada," LAC, CCSD, MG 28 I 10, vol. 13, file 59 – CWC Division Community Organization, "Publicity and Fundraising, 1934"; Dr. R.E. Wodehouse to J.G. Parker, 14 December 1932, LAC, CCSD, MG 28 I 10, vol. 44, file 215; Gwladys Kennedy, report of the executive secretary, 28

February 1938, LAC, CCSD, MG 28 I 10, vol. 228, file 228-16; *Yearbook of the Canadian Life Insurance Officers Association, 1932*, 41.

19 "Appeal to All Residents to Give Support," *Ottawa Journal*, 11 October 1934, 15.

20 Reverend Colwell was not the superintendent of the mission. That job was held by G(eorge?) Watson, an ex-policeman and a former "saloon keeper," who saw himself as a business manager. "But Times Are Better – Why Is the Need Not Less?" (canvassers' pamphlet), 1937, CVA, Mayor's Papers, series 483, vol. 33, file D-6-1; "The Central City Mission – Special Report Prepared by the Executive Director for Consideration by Group 'B' of the Budget Committee ... Aug. 7th, 1931," BCARS, GR 497, box 2, file 1; "1931 Budgets of the Agencies in the Welfare Federation" (ad), *Vancouver Sun*, 23 February 1931, 18; "Memorandum from Mr. Falk, Executive Director, ... in Respect to Attendance at the National Conference of Social Work in Montreal," July 1935, CVA, UWLM, Add. Mss. 849, 5; Vancouver Welfare Federation, *Annual Report 1933*, 8.

21 F. Ivor Jackson, "History of the Community Chest and Council of the Greater Vancouver Area" (typescript), March 1960, CVA, UWLM, Add. Mss. 849, Social Planning and Research series, F. Ivor Jackson subseries, Appendix E, 168, 171; "The Central City Mission – Special Report Prepared by the Executive Director for Consideration by Group 'B' of the Budget Committee ... Aug. 7th, 1931," BCARS, GR 497, box 2, file 1, 2-3. The concerns politely expressed in this report were given a sharper edge in allegations made by Vancouver communists. See Todd McCallum, "'Still Raining, Market Still Rotten': Homeless Men and the Early Years of the Great Depression in Vancouver" (PhD diss., Department of History, Queen's University, 2006), 427-33.

22 Minutes, meeting of the publicity committee, 25 August 1938, UWOC.

23 Ottawa Welfare Bureau, "Summary of Family Work from January to October 1932," LAC, CCSD, MG 28 I 10, vol. 44, file 215. Minutes, meeting of the joint budget committee, 13 June 1938; meeting of the men's territorial committee, 26 September 1941; and dinner meeting of agency representatives and division chairmen, 5 September 1946, UWOC. "Report of Dr. Murray Blair on St. Joseph's Hospital," 1942; and minutes, meeting of the board of directors, 29 June 1943, CVA, UWLM, Add. Mss. 849, vol. 617-A-4. Clippings, "Welfare Bureau Has Big Job," c. September 1946; and "Individual Tragedies" (editorial), 15 October 1949, NSARM, UWHD, MG 20, vol. 1718. Tom Moore script, LAC, CCSD, MG 28 I 10, vol. 13, file 59, "Radio Broadcasts 1933-34." Minutes, meeting of the budget committees of Protestant and Roman Catholic federations, 28 November 1934; and annual meeting, 6 September 1934, UWOC.

24 Gwladys Kennedy, annual report, 28 February 1938, LAC, CCSD, MG 28 I 10, vol. 228, file 228-16. Minutes, meeting of the executive committees of Protestant and Roman Catholic federations, 30 April 1935; budget committees of Protestant

and Roman Catholic federations, 26 February 1936; and executive committees and campaign division chairs, 22 November 1936, UWOC. Annual report, 1933, CVA, UWLM, Add. Mss. 849, 7; report of the executive director, 1938, CVA, UWLM, Add. Mss. 849, 6.

25 Minutes, luncheon meeting of division chairs and campaign committee, 9 December 1937, UWOC.

26 "City Hall Employees Turn Down Appeal from Welfare Federation," transcribed extract from *News/Herald,* October 1942, CVA, UWLM, Add. Mss. 849, war chest binder #1, 133.

27 Clipping, "Welfare Canvas Is Refused," 16 October 1942, LAC, CCSD, MG 28 I 10, vol. 254, file 254-3.

28 E. Brown to G. Davidson, 18 October 1942, LAC, CCSD, MG 28 I 10, vol. 254, file 254-3.

29 Charlotte Whitton to Marjorie Bradford, 14 January 1941; and G. Davidson to C.J. McNeely (Campaign Chairman), 22 September 1943, LAC, CCSD, MG 28 I 10, vol. 254, file 254-3; minutes, meeting of the board of directors, 28 September 1943, CVA, UWLM, Add. Mss. 849; André M. Guillemette, "Sentiment ... Charité ... Réalisme ...," *Canadian Welfare* 17, 8 (1942): 2-3; "And Off Relief!" *Canadian Welfare* 17, 4 (1941): 42.

30 G. Davidson to E. Brown (member of the publicity committee), 6 June 1942, LAC, CCSD, MG 28 I 10, vol. 254, file 254-3; report of the joint executive committee, 11 July 1942, UWOC.

31 Report of the joint executive committee, 2 May 1941, UWOC.

32 Halifax Community Fund "Information for Workers" pamphlet, 1945, LAC, CCSD, MG 28 I 10, vol. 228, file 228-16.

33 "A Soldier with Worries," *Canadian Welfare* 17, 4 (1941): 51-52.

34 This connection was explicit in the theme of Ottawa's 1942 campaign, based on a national agreement among chests: "It will help towards victory if we preserve the homes we fight for." In Ottawa, a shortened version was used, with an emphasis on soldiers: "Preserve the Homes They Fight For." Report of the Roman Catholic board of directors, 15 May 1942, UWOC.

35 "Leave Out the Decimal Point!" (ad), *Vancouver Sun,* 7 November 1941, 4.

36 An Ottawa fundraiser in 1945 expressed the view that this reaction had indeed begun to set in. Minutes, meeting of division chairmen of the United Welfare Campaign, 6 December 1945, UWOC. See Chapter 7 for a discussion of postwar fundraising.

37 Emphasis added. Report of the executive secretary (Maines), 10 March 1944, annual meeting minutes file; annual report of the children's division, 10 March 1944; and report of the executive secretary (Maines), 28 May 1945, COA, SPCOC, 4. For the use of this message in wartime Halifax, see "Information for Workers" (pamphlet), LAC, CCSD, MG 28 I 10, vol. 228, file 228-16.

38 Jeffrey Keshen, "Wartime Jitters over Juveniles: Canada's Delinquency Scare and Its Consequences, 1939-1945," in *Age of Contention*, ed. Jeffrey Keshen (Toronto: Harcourt Brace Canada, 1997), 364-86.

39 Marjorie Bradford, "The Personnel Deficit in British Columbia," December 1943, CVA, UWLM, Add. Mss. 849, vol. 617-A-4, file 1, 127.

40 Ibid.; F. Smelts (Chairman of the Vancouver Welfare Federation) to Charlotte Whitton, 30 June 1941, LAC, CCSD, MG 28 I 10, vol. 254, file 254-3; minutes, meeting of the chest council, 8 July 1943, NSARM, UWHD, MG 20. On the salary impacts of labour market competition, see minutes, meeting of the joint budget committee, 26 June 1941; meeting of the Protestant budget committee, 16 July 1941; meeting of the subcommittee of the joint executive committee, 6 August 1941; meeting of the Protestant board of directors, 27 August 1941; report of the Protestant budget committee, 19 December 1941; meeting of the joint budget committee, 9 June 1942; and conference of the budget committee with the Ottawa day nursery board, 29 May 1944, UWOC. Report of the budget committee, 9 March 1944, NSARM, UWHD, MG 20, vol. 1713; "Agency Budgets as at April 30th, 1942," CVA, UWLM, Add. Mss. 849, vol. 617-A-3, file 8.

41 See Chapter 3 for the salary issue in the 1934 criticism of the Vancouver Welfare Federation. For criticisms of social workers' salaries' contributing to the costs of private agencies, see Charlotte Whitton to F.N. Stapleford, 14 December 1932; and C. Russell to Charlotte Whitton, 15 December 1932, LAC, CCSD, MG 28 I 10, vol. 44, file 215; "War Chest Campaign" (letter to the editor), *Vancouver Sun*, 15 November 1939, 6. For the attack on social work salaries in postwar Toronto, see Gale Wills, *A Marriage of Convenience: Business and Social Work in Toronto, 1918-1957* (Toronto: University of Toronto Press, 1995), 113; clipping, "Unjust and Unfair" (editorial), *Toronto Star*, 17 June 1950, LAC, CCSD, MG 28 I 10, vol. 77, file 564, Labour – General. In Halifax, notorious for its badly paid social work staff, this criticism was not apparent. Clipping, "Meagre Financial Support Decried: Welfare Bureau Reports Take City Hall to Task for Lack of Assistance," c. October 1946, NSARM, UWHD, MG 20, vol. 1718.

42 Minutes, annual meeting, 14 February 1940, NSARM, UWHD, MG 20, vol. 1713. The new president was David R. Turnbull, the general manager of Acadia Sugar.

43 Minutes, meeting of the board of directors, 31 March 1942; and meetings of the co-ordinating committee, 10 April 1942, 14 April 1942, and 20 April 1942, CVA, UWLM, Add. Mss. 849; Edward A. Jamieson to F.W. Smelts (Chairman of the VWF Board), 30 April 1942, vol. 617-A-3, file 8; minutes, meeting of the executive finance committee, 25 June 1942, vol. 617-D-1, file 1, 110; "Report of the Committee on Coordination of Agency Work," 1942, vol. 617-A-4, file 1, 10; and "Budget Committee Comments on the Report of the Special Committee Referred by the Board of Directors," 21 August 1942, vol. 617-A-4, file 1, 11.

44 "Report of the Committee on Coordination of Agency Work," CVA, UWLM, Add. Mss. 849, vol. 617-A-4, file 1, 10, 2. I would have quoted the definition were it not soporifically verbose. Here is the original: "It should be the policy of private agencies, such as Vancouver Welfare Federation, to see a project through its experimental stages, endeavouring to prove during this period the worth of such a project. If, at the end of the determined period, the project has proven itself worthwhile, and a necessity, the government should be approached with a request to take it over. If the project proves unworthy of further financial support, or it is felt that the money could be diverted to some worthwhile need, then that particular project should be discontinued. Because an organization or an agency has survived over a period of years, this fact should not be accepted as conclusive proof that the work of that particular agency is either necessary, or in all cases desirable."

45 Ibid., 2 (and stapled attachment with amended version).

46 Ibid., 3; "Budget Committee Comments," CVA, UWLM, Add. Mss. 849, vol. 617-A-4, file 1, 5-8. For a similar mix of problems, in which decision making and funding contribution made policy setting complicated, see the Jamieson committee's discussion of the men's service bureau in "Report of the Committee on Coordination," 4; "Budget Committee Comments," 13-16.

47 "Report of the Committee on Coordination," 4; "Budget Committee Comments," 12; Kwannon Club to Executive Committee, 22 October 1946, CVA, UWLM, Add. Mss. 849, vol. 617-A-5, file 1, 93.

48 Clipping, "Community Chest Crows in Favor: Figures Show It," 15 October 1926, NSARM, UWHD, MG 20, vol. 1717; "They Spend Intelligently" (editorial), *Vancouver Sun*, 26 November 1941. An editorial from a Halifax paper, probably from the *Mail*, from May 1926, was unusually specific in describing the burden of contribution in racialized terms: "A Community Chest makes public support of charities a sure, continuous thing, not a gamble. It applies all the efficiency of organized business to the problem of the white man's burden." Clipping, NSARM, UWHD, MG 20, vol. 1717.

49 Halifax Community Fund, "Information for Workers" (pamphlet), 1945, LAC, CCSD, MG 28 I 10, vol. 228, file 228-16.

50 Minutes, meeting of directors, division chairs, team captains, and publicity committee, 28 November 1935; annual meeting, 3 April 1936; and meeting of the joint executive committee, 29 November 1937, UWOC. Clipping, "Halifax – Hold Up Your Head" (ad), c. October 1932, NSARM, UWHD, MG 20, vol. 1717; "Memo of Suggestions Made at Meeting of Generals and Captains in Community Chest Campaign," October 1936, vol. 1713; and minutes, special meeting of the publicity committee with the Council of Social Agencies, 18 April 1944, vol. 1713. Report of field visit by Henry Stubbins (CWC), 31 May 1950, LAC, CCSD, MG 28 I 10, vol. 228, file 228-17; and Harold Cribb (Vancouver Welfare Federation)

to G. Davidson (CWC), 27 May 1942, vol. 254, file 254-3. Isabel McElheran, "One National Agency and the Chest," *Canadian Welfare* 16, 4 (1940): 12. Report of the executive director, 15 February 1937, CVA, UWLM, Add. Mss. 849, vol. 617-A-3, file 3, 50; minutes, meeting of the board of directors, 28 September 1942; and "The Story of the Community Chest in 1944," vol. 617-A-5, file 1, 1-2.

51 This complaint was heard in Halifax as early as 1936, ten years into the chest's existence there. "Memo of Suggestions Made at Meeting of Generals and Captains in Community Chest Campaign," October 1936, NSARM, UWHD, HG 20, vol. 1713. It had become a familiar concern for the residential canvassers in Ottawa by 1961. Minutes, meeting of the campaign committee, 4 May 1961, UWOC.

52 Tom Moore, "Labour Policy in War-Time," *Public Affairs* 5, 1 (1941): 38.

53 George Davidson to Douglas Broome, 9 July 1942, LAC, CCSD, MG 28 I 10, vol. 254, file 254-3; "Laugh and Say 'No'" (editorial), *Vancouver Sun*, 18 October 1938. This editorial took aim at tag-days, in particular, whose "psychology [was] simply that of shaming every pedestrian into contributing," regardless of "financial ability to contribute or his preference in distributing whatever money he is able." Anyone who did not contribute was by virtue of his or her "untagged lapels proclaim[ed] a soured and miserly curmudgeon to all and sundry."

54 Minutes, meeting of the campaign committee, 19 September 1938, UWOC; Charlotte Whitton to A.W. Laver, 20 September 1940, LAC, CCSD, MG 28 I 10, vol. 48, file 419; and Douglas Broome to George Davidson, 13 July 1942, vol. 254, file 254-3.

55 Memorandum re Halifax chest, 8 April 1945, LAC, CCSD, MG 28 I 10, vol. 228, file 228-16. Similar tactics to collect overdue subscriptions were used in Ottawa and Vancouver. See minutes, meeting of the joint budget committee, 22 June 1936; meeting to review unpaid pledges for 1937 fund, 16 March 1938 and 6 April 1948; and meeting of the unpaid pledges committee, 1 February 1940, UWOC; also see leaflets geared toward the collection of overdue money included with minutes of the directors' meeting, CVA, UWLM, Add. Mss. 849, vol. 617-A-3, file 4, 77.

56 Minutes, meeting of the campaign committee, 26 September 1938, UWOC.

57 Douglas Broome to George Davidson, 13 July 1942, LAC, CCSD, MG 28 I 10, vol. 254, file 254-3. Perry, *Taxes*, vol. 2, 366, appears to date this innovation from 1943, but his phrasing is ambiguous enough to make the 1942 date mentioned in the Broome letter more plausible.

58 "Report on Organization of Campaign for 1945 Funds," 18 September 1945; and minutes, meeting of division chairmen of the United Welfare Campaign, 6 December 1945, UWOC. The record of minutes for the Ottawa chests breaks down in 1944, probably because of the pressures of war work. Unfortunately, this breakdown makes the reasons for the failure to organize the employee chest system in Ottawa difficult to discover.

59 Minutes, meeting of the board of directors, 2 October 1942, UWLM.

60 Clipping, "Advantages of Community Chest System Outlined," 13 September 1950, NSARM, UWHD, MG 20, vol. 1718; minutes, annual meeting, 24 January 1950, vol. 1713, 2-3; minutes, meeting of the chest council, 6 March 1951, vol. 1713; report of the budget committee, 21 June 1955, vol. 1713.

61 William P. Jenkins, "Why I'm Against the United Fund," *Maclean's* January 1957: 4. Jenkins was described as a "Toronto Scholar and Preacher [who] leads the largest Unitarian Congregation in Canada." See also reprint of "Labour Becomes a Big Giver," *Survey Graphic*, February 1943, LAC, CCSD, MG 28 I 10, vol. 177, file 564 – "Labour and Community Welfare"; and G. Davidson to E. Brown, 2 November 1942, vol. 254, file 254-3; Eugene Forsey, "Labour in the Post-War Period," *Canadian Welfare* 20, 1 (1944): 5-6.

62 G. Davidson to E. Brown, 2 November 1942, LAC, CCSD, MG 28 I 10, vol. 254, file 254-3.

63 Memo from Eurith Goold (Executive Assistant to the Executive Director) to George Davidson (Executive Director), 20 October 1942, with note by Goold summarizing Davidson's response, LAC, CCSD, MG 28 I 10, vol. 77, file 564 – "Labour – Relationships with and Attitude to Welfare Services, Community Planning, 1942-65."

64 Shirley Tillotson, "'When Our Membership Awakens': Welfare Work and Canadian Union Activism, 1950-1965," *Labour/Le travail* 40 (1997): 137-70; and Shirley Tillotson, "Class and Community in Canadian Welfare Work, 1933-1960," *Journal of Canadian Studies* 32, 1 (1997): 63-92. See also Chapter 7.

65 Audiotape of Red Feather campaign announcements produced by CBC Montreal and available for chests to broadcast in 1948 for the 1949 fund campaigns, LAC, C 8495(3), ISN 132568.

CHAPTER 6: RECONSTRUCTING CHARITY

1 Two sample interventions by social workers on these themes are Lieutenant Colonel H. Charles Tutte (Salvation Army), "Are Private Social Service Organizations Obsolete?" *Canadian Welfare* 21, 8 (1946): 24-26; and George F. Davidson, "Improving the Social Services," *Public Affairs* 6, 2 (1943): 74-77. Reflections on the relations of public welfare, the family allowances, and private charity (the chests) were offered by a rather differently positioned observer, John Heron, author of "Social Welfare," the Royal Bank of Canada Monthly Letter of May 1945, http://www.rbc.com/community/letter/may1945.html. A slightly later intervention by veteran social worker Bessie Touzel actually questioned whether the distinction between public and private agencies reflected real differences in function or funding and pointed to the variety of "quasi-public" agencies in existence. "Some Factors Affecting Public-Private Relationships in Social Work," reprinted from the *Proceedings of the Canadian Conference on Social Work*, Quebec City, 14-20 June 1952, LAC, CCSD, MG 28 I 10, vol. 79, file 591.

2 For example, the campaign chairman of the 1952 Vancouver appeal reported that contributions had more than doubled and that the number of donors had increased by 30 percent between 1945 and 1952, but he also expressed disappointment that the 1952 campaign had fallen $250,000 short of its target. Annual report of the Community Chest and Council of Vancouver, 1952 (February 1953), CVA, UWLM, Add. Mss. 849, vol. 617-3-2.

3 Minutes, meeting of the representatives of boards of directors, campaign committee, and budget committee, 8 June 1950, UWOC, 1950 vol. A concern was expressed about the problem raised when "campaign publicity during recent years had stated that in effect the Campaign goals were irreducible minima, but the Chests and agencies had been able to continue their services despite the Campaign reverses."

4 Gwendolen Lantz card, Dalhousie women graduates card file, Dalhousie University Archives, Judith Fingard Papers, MS-2-713; document 6.52, NSARM, HDWC, MG 20, vol. 411, file 6. Kennedy's age (one year older than Lantz) is from minutes, meeting of the chest council, 28 July 1953, NSARM, UWHD, MG 20, vol. 1713.

5 Shirley Tillotson, "Dollars, Democracy, and the Children's Aid Society: The Eclipse of Gwendolen Lantz," in *Mothers of the Municipality*, ed. Judith Fingard and Janet Guildford (Toronto: University of Toronto Press, 2004), 80; minutes, executive council meeting, 8 July 1943, NSARM, UWHD, MG 20; field report "Re: Halifax Chest," 8 April 1945, LAC, CCSD, MG 28 I 10, vol. 228, file 228-16. For Kennedy's marital status and childlessness, the evidence is the absence of any resident other than her husband in any of her city directory listings and the absence of any children among those people named in her obituary as surviving her. Clipping, "Founder of Community Chest Dies," 13 October 1960, NSARM, UWHD, MG 20, vol. 1725.

6 Lantz's 1928 salary is cited as an example of low salaries paid to social workers in Patricia Rooke and R.L. Schnell, *No Bleeding Heart* (Vancouver: UBC Press, 1987), 68. For the stagnation of Kennedy's salary between 1925 and 1943, and a modest wartime increase, see minutes, meeting of the chest council, 8 July 1943, NSARM, UWHD, MG 20, vol. 1713.

7 Field report "Re: Halifax Chest," 8 April 1945, LAC, CCSD, MG 28 I 10, vol. 228, file 228-16; Tillotson, "Dollars," 81-82.

8 Mrs. Charles Monroe (Association of the Junior Leagues of America, New York) to Nora Lea, 1 April 1943 (CWC cross-reference sheet 2 April 1943); Nan T. Pierpoint (Community Service Staff, Association of Junior Leagues) to Nora Lea, 16 February 1943; and Lillian M. Farquhar to George F. Davidson, 20 March 1944, LAC, CCSD, MG 28 I 10, vol. 228, file 228-16.

9 An international organization, created for women under forty-five years of age, the Junior League engaged in a wide array of community social and cultural work

with a novel twist. Unlike Rotarians or IODE members, for example, all Junior Leaguers were given a training course in social welfare and community planning called "Community Needs." The International Junior League, headquartered in New York, served as their consultants and advisors, sending out social workers to give lectures on agencies such as the juvenile courts, Children's Aid Societies, and welfare bureaus. They prided themselves on being a new breed of volunteer, demonstrating a professionalism in skill and standards, even if amateur in the strict sense. "Time to Look at 21 Years with the Junior League" (publicity pamphlet); and "Annual Reports from the President," a publication of the Halifax Junior League, NSARM; *V for Volunteers*, a 1951 film jointly produced by the CWC and the Junior League, LAC, item number 153656; Florence Bird, *Anne Francis: An Autobiography* (Toronto: Clarke, Irwin and Company, 1974), 149-50.

10 Lillian M. Farquhar to George F. Davidson, 4 May 1944, LAC, CCSD, MG 28 I 10, vol. 228, file 228-16. The CWC was an umbrella body for organizations engaged in social welfare work. Founded in 1920 as the Canadian Council on Child Welfare, by 1935 it had enlarged its scope of action and was renamed the CWC. Political scholar Rodney Haddow calls it the "leading non-governmental source of social policy innovation in Canada" before 1970. Rodney Haddow, *Poverty Reform in Canada, 1958-1978* (Montreal: McGill-Queen's University Press, 1993), 24.

11 Mrs. Charles Monroe (Association of the Junior Leagues of America, New York) to Nora Lea, 1 April 1943 (CWC cross-reference sheet 2 April 1943), LAC, CCSD, MG 28 I 10, vol. 228, file 228-16.

12 Eurith Goold, confidential memo to Dr. Davidson re Halifax, c. 1942, LAC, CCSD, MG 28 I 10, vol. 228, file 228-16; and Henry Stubbins, "Report of Field Trip to Halifax," 7 February 1952, vol. 228, file 228-17.

13 Lillian Farquhar to R.E.G. Davis, 6 June 1945, LAC, CCSD, MG 28 I 10, vol. 228, file 228-16; minutes, meeting of the chest council, 7 April 1949; and special meeting to discuss constitution, 14 December 1949, NSARM, UWHD, MG 20, vol. 1713.

14 For the report of this survey, see "Summary of Report of Canadian Welfare Council Field Visit to Halifax Community Chest – May 15-19, 1950," LAC, CCSD, MG 28 I 10, vol. 228, file 228-17. Biographical information on Wilson is based on the following sources. Halifax City Directory, 1950, gives Wilson's occupation. Clipping, "Seeks Labor's Aid to Solve Fund-Raising Problems," NSARM, UWHD, MG 20, vol. 1718, identifies Wilson as chest president; and minutes, meeting of the chest council, 17 May 1955, vol. 1713, identifies him as a Rotarian. Minutes, meeting of council, March 1953, NSARM, HDWC, MG 20, vol. 415, file 9, indicates his appointment as Welfare Council president; and document 6.85, vol. 411, file 6, notes that Wilson served as the vice president of the CWC board of governors circa 1957.

15 Document 6.5, NSARM, HDWC, MG 20, vol. 411, file 6; "An Acadia Love Story," http://ace.acadiau.ca/arts/Cycle%20of%20Opportunity/arts.htm. In a personal communication in 2007, George Hart gave me his correct age and corrected the date of his Acadia MA, which, from other sources, I had believed was conferred in 1947.

16 Minutes, meeting of the Child Welfare Division of Halifax Welfare Council, 29 May 1951, NSARM, HDWC, MG 20, vol. 408, file 10.

17 Minutes, meeting of the chest council, 27 October 1953, NSARM, UWHD, MG 20, vol. 1713.

18 Minutes, meeting of the chest council, 3 February 1954, NSARM, UWHD, MG 20, vol. 1713.

19 Minutes, meeting of the chest council, 7 July 1953, NSARM, UWHD, MG 20, vol. 1713. Her fundraising career was not over. She went on to serve as director of the Nova Scotia branch of the Canadian Arthritis and Rheumatism Society, a smaller organization where she once again would have had the kind of control she had enjoyed at the chest. Clipping, "Founder of Community Chest Dies," 13 October 1960, NSARM, UWHD, MG 20, vol. 1725.

20 Minutes, meeting of the chest council, 3 February 1954, NSARM, UWHD, MG 20, vol. 1713.

21 Campaign target in 1951 = $150,000; 1952 = $155,000; 1953 = $165,000; 1954 = $177,000. The year-to-year increases in these years were 3 percent, 6.45 percent, and 7.2 percent. *Canadian Welfare* 28, 3-4 (1952), 16, 30-31; 30, 2 (1954), 28-29; 31, 2 (1955): 94-95.

22 *Canadian Welfare* 23, 7 (1948): 10; 31, 2 (1955): 94-95.

23 Minutes, meetings of the chest council, 27 April 1955, 17 May 1955, 22 November 1955, 17 April 1956, 22 May 1956, 19 June 1956, 18 December 1956, 28 May 1957, and 27 June 1957, NSARM, UWHD, MG 20, vol. 1713; and clipping, "Name New Executive Director," 1 April 1958, vol. 1725. For M.A. Wilson's various positions, see note 13 above.

24 Document 10.15; report for the Committee of the Welfare Council of Halifax, 12 June 1951; Gwendolen Lantz, report from the Children's Aid Society, 29 May 1951, 7; and minutes, meeting of the Child Welfare Division of the Halifax Welfare Council, 29 May 1951, final page, NSARM, HDWC, HG 20, vol. 408, file 10. Minutes, meetings of the executive committee, 8 April 1952 and 9 October 1951; and meeting to discuss the Clarke Committee report, 9 October 1951, 3, vol. 415, file 9. Tillotson, "Dollars," 89-92.

25 Tillotson, "Dollars."

26 Tillotson, "Dollars"; minutes, meeting of the executive committee, 8 April 1952; and report of a meeting between Richard Donahoe and representatives from the chest and council, 7 May 1952, NSARM, HDWC, MG 20, vol. 415, file 9; minutes,

meeting of the executive committee, 28 May 1952, NSARM, UWHD, MG 20, vol. 1713.

27 Minutes, meetings of the executive committee, 8 April 1952 and 9 October 1951, NSARM, HDWC, MG 20, vol. 415, file 9.

28 Document 6.61, NSARM, HDWC, MG 20, vol. 411, file 6; Nova Scotia, *Journals of the House of Assembly,* 1954, Part 2, Appendix 23, CAS Halifax financial report, and 1952, Appendix 23, 10; document 10.15; and "Report for Committee of the Welfare Council of Halifax," 12 June 1951, 1, NSARM, HDWC, MG 20, vol. 408, file 10. This grading grant system had been in place in Ontario since the mid-1930s. See James Struthers, *Limits of Affluence: Welfare in Ontario, 1920-1970* (Toronto: University of Toronto Press, 1994), 130.

29 Gwladys Kennedy to Bessie Touzel, 6 August 1952, and Bessie Touzel to Gwladys Kennedy, 15 August 1952, LAC, CCSD, MG 28 I 10, vol. 227, file 25; minutes, meeting of the chest council, 21 June 1955, NSARM, UWHD, MG 20, vol. 1713.

30 Henry Stubbins to Gwladys Kennedy, 9 October 1952, LAC, CCSD, MG 28 I 10, vol. 70, file 517.

31 Miriam Jacobson, "A Better Deal for Children: An Historical Study of the Children's Aid Society of Halifax/a Half Century of Service, 1920-1970" (manuscript, 1971, NSARM), 99.

32 Minutes, meeting of the chest council, 16 March 1965, NSARM, UWHD, MG 20, vol. 1714.

33 Minutes, meeting of the chest council, 27 April 1965, NSARM, UWHD, MG 20, vol. 1714.

34 See Halifax case, described above. The amalgamation idea was also proposed in Ottawa and Vancouver. Minutes, meeting of the board of directors, 30 May 1962, UWOC; report of the executive director to the board of directors, 18 April 1947, CVA, UWLM, Add. Mss. 849.

35 Struthers, *Limits of Affluence,* 236-37; "Public-Private Relationships in Child Welfare," LAC, CCSD, MG 28 I 10, vol. 79, file 591; Fred R. MacKinnon, *Reflections: 55 Years in Public Service in Nova Scotia* (Halifax: Fernwood Publishing, 2004), 107-9; Haddow, *Poverty Reform,* 23-25. Struthers calls into question Haddow's claim about the influence of the CWC during the 1950s and early 1960s. The hostility that J.S. Band, Fred MacKinnon's Ontario counterpart, felt toward the CWC may indeed have particularly limited its influence in that province. Relations of influence between public welfare and private social work elsewhere may be better represented by MacKinnon and by the career of BC social worker Bert Iverson. He moved from the Vancouver chest (where he was budget director in Naphtali's early years), to positions in two provincial and municipal welfare administrations, and then to the CWC in 1962. He left the CWC to take a job administering the new National Welfare Grants program in the Department

of Health and Welfare. See LAC, CCSD, MG 28 I 10, vol. 266, file 266-2, Bert Iverson file.

36 Minutes, annual meeting, 24 February 1966, NSARM, UWHD, MG 20, vol. 1714; clipping, "Near-Misses Cause of Concern, United Appeal Members Told," 3 March 1966, vol. 1731; and main budget report, minutes, meeting of the chest council, 17 May 1966, vol. 1714.

37 Gwladys Kennedy to Henry Stubbins, 2 October 1952, LAC, CCSD, MG 28 I 10, vol. 70, file 517.

38 In Ottawa, a parallel case unfolded in which the two senior women in the Welfare Bureau, who had been on staff since the 1920s, were manoeuvred into retirement. The report by that city's welfare council referred obliquely to their perceived lack of fitness in the new welfare system: "The type of leadership required at one stage of development may not be effective at a later stage." "Interim Report on Personnel Practices at the Ottawa Welfare Bureau," 15 February 1954, UWOC.

39 Minutes, meeting of the board of directors, 28 October 1947, CVA, UWLM, Add. Mss. 849.

40 Minutes, special meeting concerning purchase of building at Pender and Hamilton, 16 January 1948, CVA, UWLM, Add. Mss. 849.

41 Minutes, meeting of the executive committee, 20 June 1958; and special meeting of the chest council, 25 April 1959, UWOC.

42 Minutes, annual meeting, 27 February 1936, NSARM, UWHD, MG 20, vol. 1713; various circular letters from chest to member agencies, soliciting publicity material, such as Gwladys Kennedy to President of Halifax Visiting Dispensary, 15 May 1948, Dalhousie University Archives, S.R. Balcom Papers, MSS-2-128, Halifax Community Chest file; minutes, meeting of the publicity committee, Council of Social Agencies, NSARM, HDWC, MG 20, vol. 411, passim; memo "Re: Halifax Chest," 8 April 1945, expressing Kennedy's unhappiness at CAS's refusal to participate in publicity work, LAC, CCSD, MG 28 I 10, vol. 228, file 228-16; "Visits Reveal Work of Social Agencies," *Vancouver Sun,* 31 October 1934, 5; J.H.T. Falk, memo on Vancouver Welfare Federation and Council, July 1935, CVA, UWLM, Add. Mss. 849, vol. 617-A-3, file 1; Mrs. Walter (Alma Gale) Mowatt, "History of the Community Chest and Councils of the Greater Vancouver Area" (typescript), description of agencies' role in public relations in the 1940s, CVA, UWLM, Add. Mss. 849, 48; minutes, luncheon meeting of division chairs and campaign committee, 9 December 1936; report of the joint board of directors, 12 May 1938; minutes, meeting of the joint executive committee, 4 September 1940; and minutes, meeting of the men's territorial division, 26 September 1941, UWOC.

43 On the effect of the Halifax Children's Hospital's attempts to manipulate the chest or to raise more money on its own by dropping out, see minutes, meetings of the executive committee, 13 September 1937, 13 December 1937, 23 June 1938, and

8 March 1949 (special meeting), NSARM, UWHD, MG 20, vol. 1713. For similar developments in relation to the Vancouver Children's Hospital, see report of the executive director, 30 April 1946, CVA, UWLM, Add. Mss. 849, vol. 617-A-5, 75. The threat of withdrawal became a bargaining chip for large "illness" charities when they became chest members in the 1950s. See, for example, the withdrawal of the Heart Fund from the Vancouver Welfare Federation in 1960 and the issues around it, described in Ross Wilson, president of the Community Chests and Councils of Greater Vancouver, "Dear Subscriber" (letter), LAC, CCSD, MG 28 I 10, vol. 254, file 254-9.

44 Document 3.5, "Information from Community Chests and Councils N.Y. January 1948," NSARM, HDWC, HG 20, vol. 416a. In spite of its title, this document is actually a commentary on information from the US organization and consists of a series of points about the strengths, weaknesses, and concerns of the Halifax Welfare Council.

45 Gale Wills, *A Marriage of Convenience: Business and Social Work in Toronto, 1918-1957* (Toronto: University of Toronto Press, 1995), 102-3, 108-9, 114, 119; minutes, meetings of the board of directors, 1 May 1945, 23 May 1946, 6 August 1951, and 31 March 1953, CVA, UWLM, Add. Mss. 849; "Interim Report on Personnel Practices at the Ottawa Welfare Bureau," 15 February 1954; and D. Longmire (Ottawa Welfare Bureau) to Board of Directors, 19 February 1954, UWOC.

46 A contemporary discussion of this issue can be found in Anne M. Angus, *The Children's Aid Society of Vancouver, 1901-1951* (Vancouver: Children's Aid Society), 35, 47. *V for Volunteers*, a 1951 film jointly produced by the CWC and the Junior League, was an attempt to represent respectful, complementary relations between volunteers and professionals in social work. LAC, item number 153656.

47 John Yerger's career at the Ottawa Community Chests illustrates this sort of bargaining power. When Yerger arrived in 1951, he assured the chests that he would stay for at least three years. In 1952, after a successful campaign, he persuaded the chests that his job must be divided into two paid jobs, with the social planning job done by someone else. His salary was increased in 1953, and the executive committee noted at the time that they were "anxious to keep [him]." And they did manage to keep him for just a bit more than three years, until the end of 1954. Minutes, meeting of the special committee on staff appointment, 10 May 1951; meeting of the joint executive committee, 4 November 1952; meeting of the executive committee, 2 December 1953; and meeting of the board of directors, 23 February 1955, UWOC.

48 Wills, *Marriage of Convenience*, 103, 124, 130; Gwendolyn Shand, "More or Less Confidential Material, 1948," NSARM, HDWC, MG 20, vol. 416a, file 3; minutes, annual meeting, 27 February 1950, CVA, UWLM, Add. Mss. 849; minutes, meeting of the executive committee, 10 April 1956, UWOC.

49 In the 1940s, CWC staffers considered Ottawa and Vancouver progressive chests because they combined chest and council under a joint director. Both had been set up by leading social workers (Whitton in Ottawa and Falk in Vancouver). Eurith Goold of the CWC wrote in 1946 to Vancouver chest board member C. Romer that "the closest possible integration between the Chest and Council ... is not only desirable, it is imperative if successful operation is to result." Eurith Goold to C. Romer, 4 March 1946, LAC, CCSD, MG 28 I 10, vol. 254, file 254-4. Wills cites an American expert report on Toronto from 1948 in support of a claim that separation of chest and council "was consistent with practice elsewhere in the Community Chest movement," providing that the Welfare Council had adequate administration, but this seems to be an overstatement. However, the cases of Vancouver, Halifax, and Ottawa certainly confirm Wills' observation, based on a fifty-city American survey, that chest-council relations "universally deteriorated after the war." Wills, *Marriage of Convenience,* 108, 124; Nora Lea to Hazeldine Bishop, 21 August 1946, describing tensions between council-agency social workers and chest fundraisers, referring to "dirty work at the crossroads" and the "unsocial process" by which chest and council relations had fallen into a bad state, LAC, CCSD, MG 28 I 10, vol. 254, file 254-6; Hugh Allan (Executive Director of the Vancouver Chest and Council) to Eurith Goold, 27 December 1945, commenting acerbically on the "theory" that needs should not be subordinated to budgetary constraints, LAC, CCSD, MG 28 I 10, vol. 254, file 254-4; Beverly Thorburn to John Yerger, June 1953, COA, SPCOC.

50 The terms of this debate are succinctly presented in M.J. Caldwell (CCF leader) and W. Gladstone Murray (former president of the Canadian Radio Broadcasting Corporation), "Monetary Debate for August: Should Canadian Industry be Socialized after the War?" undated magazine offprint from 1943, LAC, Bronson Papers, MG 28 III 26, file F.E. Bronson 1919-43. A detailed account of the Canadian debate about planning can be found in Peter S. McInnis, *Harnessing Labour Confrontation: Shaping the Postwar Settlement in Canada, 1943-1950* (Toronto: University of Toronto Press, 2002), Chapter 2.

51 William Lyon Mackenzie King, *Canada and the War: Victory, Reconstruction, and Peace* (Ottawa: National Liberal Association, 1945), 60.

52 Report of the executive director, 21 April 1943, UWOC.

53 See Chapter 7.

54 Minutes, meeting of the executive committee, 14 April 1936; and undated minutes from May 1936, UWOC.

55 Minutes, meeting of a special committee to consider the appointment of an executive director, 4 January 1946; meeting of a special committee on staff appointment, 7 March 1951; meeting of the Protestant board of directors, 26 February 1951; and biographical notes on John H. Yerger, 9 May 1951, UWOC; "Smith, Sidney T.," in *Ottawa City Directory,* 1952; Allan Moscovitch, *Seventy-Five Years of*

the *Social Planning Council* (Ottawa: Social Planning Council of Ottawa-Carleton, 2003), 22; Mrs. H.B. Thorburn to John Yerger, 2 June 1953, SPCOC.

56 Arthur Cowan to George Davidson, 2 February 1943 and 3 February 1943; Edgar Brown to George Davidson, 9 February 1943; and George Davidson to Arthur Cowan, 10 February 1943, LAC, CCSD, MG 28 I 10, vol. 254, file 254-3; biographical notes re Colonel Hugh Allan, 29 December 1945, organizational chart of the combined Community Chest and Council of Social Agencies in Vancouver, 1946, file 254-4; "Bradford, Marjorie," alphabetical biographical series, vol. 265; Hazeldine Bishop to Nora Lea, 18 August 1946; Nora Lea to Hazeldine Bishop, 21 August 1946; and Ivor Jackson to R.E.G. Davis, 15 November 1946, vol. 254, file 254-6; minutes, meeting of the board of directors, 21 July 1946, CVA, UWLM, Add. Mss. 849; Howard Naphtali, personal communication, January 1999.

57 Wills, *Marriage of Convenience*, 133; Struthers, "'Lord Give Us Men,'" 133-39; Judith Trolander, *Professionalism and Social Change* (New York: Columbia University Press, 1987), 51; Harold Wilensky, *Industrial Society and Social Welfare* (New York: Free Press, 1958), 323.

58 Gwen Shand and Alice Haverstock, "Social Status of Women in Nova Scotia," paper presented to the Provincial Council of Women of Nova Scotia, 26 April 1955, LAC, CCSD, MG 28 I 10, vol. 101, file 7-10-b. My thanks to Judith Fingard for drawing this document to my attention.

59 In her study of Halifax's denominationally organized children's institutions, Renée Lafferty demonstrates the active participation in the 1950s of other constituencies, particularly the volunteer leaders and religious staff of these institutions, in the remaking and survival of the private side of welfare work in the postwar period. Renée Nicole Lafferty, "Child Welfare in Halifax, 1900-1960: Institutional Transformation, Denominationalism, and the Creation of a 'Public' Welfare System" (PhD diss., Department of History, Dalhousie University, 2003).

60 In his history of fraternal organizations' welfare work, David Beito offers just such a doctrinaire libertarian interpretation of the fate of these agencies, describing them as having been the object of aggressive crowding-out tactics by ideologically motivated politicians seeking to destroy private welfare work. David Beito, *From Mutual Aid to the Welfare State: Fraternal Societies and Social Services, 1890-1967* (Chapel Hill: University of North Carolina Press, 2000).

61 James Struthers, "Shadows from the Thirties: The Federal Government and Unemployment Assistance, 1941-1956," in *The Canadian Welfare State: Evolution and Transition*, ed. Jacqueline S. Ismael (Edmonton: University of Alberta Press, 1987), especially 23-25.

62 Clipping, "County Relief Opposed," *Halifax Chronicle-Herald*, 4 April 1957, NSARM, UWHD, MG 20, vol. 1725; Charlotte Whitton to G.E. Beament (President of Ottawa Community Chests), 15 November 1954, LAC, Charlotte Whitton Papers, MG 30 E 256, vol. 43. As early as 1954, Whitton, as mayor of Ottawa

campaigning at Queen's Park for more provincial subsidies to certain social services, included the executive director of the Community Chest in the delegation she sent to Queen's Park to give authoritative weight to her claim that the prospect of further support from voluntary donations was negligible.

63 The extent of co-operation among the agencies, the social planning section, and the board of directors of the chest and council was remarkable given that the combined organization had been the creation of a "shotgun marriage" in 1946. Nora Lea to Hazeldine Bishop, 21 August 1946, LAC, CCSD, MG 28 I 10, vol. 254, file 254-6.

64 Minutes, meeting of the mobilization committee, 24 August 1945, CVA, UWLM, Add. Mss. 849, vol. 617-A-5, file 1; Nora Lea, "Inter-Office Memorandum. Hugh Allan June 12? [sic]," 15 June 1946, LAC, CCSD, MG 28 I 10, vol. 254, file 254-4; Nora Lea to Hazeldine Bishop, 21 August 1946; Nora Lea, field report on visit to Vancouver, March 1946; and Nora Lea to Mrs. Buttar (chest volunteer), 6 April 1946, file 254-6.

65 Angus, *Children's Aid Society,* 34-36, 42; CVA Library, Ann Margaret Angus Fonds, Add. Mss. 351, finding aid and file 550-B-5; Henry Forbes Angus, "My First Seventy-Five Years," CVA Library, Ann Margaret Angus Fonds, Add. Mss. 351, 12; minutes, annual meeting of the UWLM, 28 February 1949; and Mrs. Alex Eastwood, "Referral Centre," 18 June 1951, CVA, UWLM, Add. Mss. 849, vol. 617-F-6, file 1, 2. My inference about the way in which being married to Henry Forbes Angus would have made Ann Angus familiar with public policy is based mainly on his description of her in his "My First Seventy-Five Years." In reading work by both of the Anguses, I was also reminded of the Telfords of Saskatchewan and the Skeltons of Ontario. Ann Leger-Anderson, "Marriage, Family, and the Cooperative Ideal in Saskatchewan," in *Telling Tales: Essays in Western Women's History,* ed. Catherine A. Cavanaugh and Randi R. Warne (Vancouver: UBC Press, 2000), 281-334; Terence Crowley, *Marriage of Minds: Isabel and Oscar Skelton Reinventing Canada* (Toronto: University of Toronto Press, 2003).

66 Report of the executive secretary of the social planning committee, 18 March 1947, CVA, UWLM, Add. Mss. 849, vol. 617-F-6, file 1. In his 1952 history of the Vancouver Welfare Federation, Jackson contrasted appropriate charity work in relief (entailing counselling, referral, and policy advocacy) with "primitive" practice. He reserved this disparaging term for the giving of relief in kind ("old clothes and food"), dispensed in ways designed to emphasize recipients' dependency and disbursed without any records kept of "services to their clients." See F. Ivor Jackson, "History of the Community Chest and Council of the Greater Vancouver Area" (typescript), March 1960, CVA, UWLM, Add. Mss. 849, Social Planning and Research series, F. Ivor Jackson subseries, 25-26, 170. On Jackson's postwar opposition to the chest agencies engaging in relief work, see report of the executive

secretary to the social planning committee, 17 December 1946, vol. 617-F-6, file 1. On his involvement in social service innovation, see report of the executive secretary to the social planning committee, 29 October 1946, vol. 617-F-6; minutes, meeting of the board of directors, 30 December 1947; report of the executive director, 31 January 1950, vol. 617-B-1; report of the social planning committee, 27 May 1952, vol. 617-B-2; and Ivor Jackson to R.E.G. Davis, 15 November 1946, LAC, CCSD, MG 28 I 10, vol. 254, file 254-6.

67 Donald Creighton, *The Forked Road: Canada 1939-1957* (Toronto: McClelland and Stewart, 1976), 206-7; Douglas Weatherbee Fowler, "The Unemployment Assistance Act (1956): Its Implications for Social Security and Public Welfare Administration in Canada" (MSW thesis, Department of Social Work, University of British Columbia, 1958), 27, 31; James Struthers, "Shadows from the Thirties: The Federal Government and Unemployment Assistance, 1941-56," in *The Canadian Welfare State: Evolution and Transition,* ed. Jacqueline S. Ismael (Edmonton: University of Alberta Press, 1987), 3-32.

68 Struthers, *Limits of Affluence,* 131-32; Janet Guildford, "The End of the Poor Law: Public Welfare Reform in Nova Scotia before the Canada Assistance Plan," in *Mothers of the Municipality: Women, Work, and Social Policy in Post-1945 Halifax,* ed. Judith Fingard and Janet Guildford (Toronto: University of Toronto Press, 2005), 50-51, 57-58; Goldenberg report, 1947, CVA, Mayor's Office Fonds, Add. Mss. 483, vol. 34-C-6, file 17.

69 David Gagan and Rosemary Gagan, *For Patients of Moderate Means: A Social History of the Voluntary Public General Hospital in Canada, 1890-1950* (Montreal: McGill-Queen's University Press, 2002); Jeff Keshen, "Getting It Right the Second Time Around: The Reintegration of Canadian Veterans of World War II," in *The Veterans' Charter and Post World War II Canada,* ed. Peter Neary and J.L. Granatstein (Montreal: McGill-Queen's University Press, 1998), 62-84; Struthers, *Limits of Affluence,* 142-45; Dennis Guest, *The Emergence of Social Security in Canada,* 3rd ed. (Vancouver: UBC Press, 1997), 122-23, 304; Lafferty, "Child Welfare in Halifax," 293. Local awareness of the increase in child welfare work was noted in the minutes of a meeting of the division chairmen of the United Welfare Campaign, 6 December 1945, UWOC.

70 A sample of the tone may be found in a letter from George S. Pearson (Provincial Secretary) to Frank Kelly (President, Greater Vancouver Unemployment [sic] Organization), 13 February 1946, UBC Library Special Collections, Angus MacInnis Memorial Collection, box 33, folder 2.

71 J.I. Chambers (Administrator) to Alderman R.K. Gervin, 17 February 1947, CVA, Department of Social Services records, series 450, file 106-D-5-8.

72 British Columbia, Department of Health and Welfare, Social Welfare Branch, *Annual Report,* 1947, 7; report of a committee of the Family and Child Welfare

Division, 18 April 1947; and Family Welfare Bureau of Greater Vancouver, "Summary of Unemployment, 15 Cases Described," 1947, CVA, UWLM, Add. Mss. 849, vol. 617-F-7, file 6.

73 G.J. to George Pearson, n.d., UBC Library Special Collections, Angus MacInnis Memorial Collection, box 33, folder 2. The original text of his note illustrates the challenge posed for a non-native speaker of English by these kinds of bureaucratic arguments and suggests the courage and persistence that G.J. demonstrated in struggling to make his case: "If S.S. [the National Employment Service, which was linked with UI] will not give you any work, because 'You don't able for work' ('unemployable') you will be in position: 'My neighbours give me some eat and some clothes.' Because the [municipal] Relief office will not gives you the relief, because you able for work. Many workers are between Sel. Serv. and the Relief office now ... If they are work, they are not unemployable. Therefore they don't able to get relief."

74 George S. Pearson to Frank Kelly, 13 February 1946, UBC Library Special Collections, Angus MacInnis Memorial Collection, box 33, folder 2.

75 Report of a committee of the Family and Child Welfare Division, 18 April 1947, CVA, UWLM, Add. Mss. 849, vol. 617-F-7, file 6.

76 Gwendolyn Shand (Halifax Welfare Council) to Hugh Allan, 3 May 1947, re national circular question from Vancouver on unemployed employables, CVA, UWLM, Add. Mss. 849, vol. 617-F-7, file 6.

77 "Vagrants from Necessity," *Vancouver Sun,* 13 January 1948, 4. Thanks to Mark Leier for his transcontinental assistance in locating this editorial.

78 Report to the social planning committee on correspondence regarding the need for assistance to unemployed employable persons, identifiable as 1948 on the basis of the content of the document, CVA, UWLM, Add. Mss. 849, vol. 617-F-7, file 6.

79 Community Chest and Council of Greater Vancouver, memo on regulations under the Unemployment Insurance Act, February 1948, CVA, UWLM, Add. Mss. 849, vol. 617-F-7, file 6.

80 Summary of correspondence etc. re homeless men's committee, 1948; report to the social planning committee on correspondence regarding the need for assistance to unemployed employable persons; Community Chest and Council of Greater Vancouver, memo on regulations under the Unemployment Insurance Act, February 1948; and Mary MacPhedran to Ivor Jackson, 3 March 1948 and 24 March 1948, CVA, UWLM, Add. Mss. 849, vol. 617-F-7, file 6; "The Victoria Cross and Lt-Col Cecil Merritt, V.C. (November 1908–July 2000)," http://www.civilization.ca/cwm/media/bg_merritt_e.html.

81 Minutes, meetings of the board of directors, 4 January 1949 and 25 January 1949; meeting of the committee on the employable unemployed, 1949; joint meeting of the board of directors and the executive committee, 19 December 1950, CVA,

UWLM, Add. Mss. 849, vol. 617-B-1. Minutes, meeting of the social planning committee, 22 September 1952, 20 October 1952, and 15 February 1954, vol. 617-G-6. Minutes, meeting of the board of directors, executive director's report, 31 January 1950, vol. 617-B-1. Minutes, meetings of the board of directors, 25 March 1952 and 26 May 1953; and *Annual Report 1952,* vol. 617-B-2. Minutes, meetings of the board of directors, 27 March 1956 and 25 November 1958; recommendations concerning social assistance rates, 28 January 1958 and 25 November 1958; and report of the executive committee, 24 June 1958, vol. 617-B-3. Mrs. Alex Eastwood, "Referral Centre," 18 June 1951, vol. 617-F-6. Clippings, "Govt. Gives 'Raw Deal' on Jobless Aid: Miller," *Vancouver Herald,* 11 May 1948; and "Strong Language" (editorial), *Vancouver Herald,* 12 May 1948, vol. 617-F-7.

82 Minutes, meeting of the board of directors, 31 January 1950, CVA, UWLM, Add. Mss. 849.

83 Minutes, meeting of the board of directors, executive director's report, 31 January 1950, CVA, UWLM, Add. Mss. 849.

84 *Annual Report 1952,* CVA, UWLM, Add. Mss. 849, vol. 617-B-2, 6; *Canadian Parliamentary Guide* (Ottawa: Normandin), *1934,* 363; *1939,* 413; *1943,* 399, 417; *1946,* 426; *1952,* 458; *1953.*

85 Minutes, meeting of the committee on the employable unemployed, 1949; and Mrs. Alex Eastwood, "Referral Centre," 18 June 1951, CVA, UWLM, Add. Mss. 849, vol. 617-B-1, 3.

86 Family Welfare Bureau of Greater Vancouver, study of unemployment relief applicants, January 1948, CVA, UWLM, Add. Mss. 849, vol. 617-F-7.

87 Board of directors, report of the executive director, 28 March 1950; and report of the chair of the council section reporting on the social planning committee, 25 April 1950, CVA, UWLM, Add. Mss. 849, vol. 617-B-1.

88 Minutes, annual meeting, 28 February 1949, CVA, UWLM, Add. Mss. 849.

89 Minutes, meeting of the board of directors, report on multiple appeals, 19 July 1949, CVA, UWLM, Add. Mss. 849, vol. 617-B-1.

90 Report of the campaign chair, 31 May 1949 and 30 August 1949, CVA, UWLM, Add. Mss. 849, vol. 617-B-1, 49; "Conservative Party Organization, 1931-1942," BCARS, J.A. Clark Papers, Add. Mss. 815, vol. 30, file 2.

91 *Canadian Welfare* 25, 5 (1950): 24; 26, 8 (1951): 24-25.

92 Minutes, meeting of the board of directors, report of the executive director, 29 November 1949, CVA, UWLM, Add. Mss. 849, vol. 617-B-1.

93 Minutes, special meeting of the agency representatives and Community Chest and Council, 8 December 1949, CVA, UWLM, Add. Mss. 849, vol. 617-B-1.

94 "Red Feather Appeal – 1950, Revenue and Expenditure Account," in *Annual Report 1950,* CVA, UWLM, Add. Mss. 849, 22.

95 "Unavoidable emergencies may be experienced by some agencies during the year, which will necessitate making supplementary grants, but agencies have been

warned that this year some emergencies which the Chest has been able to meet in the past, will have to be met from the regular budget, even though it may entail drastic readjustments in programme and policy." In *Annual Report 1950*, CVA, UWLM, Add. Mss. 849, vol. 617-B-2, 12.

96 Report of the executive secretary to the social planning committee, 21 October 1947, CVA, UWLM, Add. Mss. 849, vol. 617-F-6.

97 Absences are notoriously hard to prove. To test whether or not the chests continued to use appeals for material relief, I surveyed for one sample year, 1957, every ad used during the campaigns in the three cities in this study. I selected 1957 because it was the first year after the implementation of UA in most Canadian provinces and because, for comparative purposes, I had made equally close studies of the chest advertising used in 1947, 1937, and 1927. While the Ottawa campaign did list "the destitute" among those whom the chest helped, it also itemized five other categories of need. In the same year's campaign, the Halifax ads carefully listed the kinds of care their agencies offered and nowhere mentioned unemployment or poverty. (This is especially remarkable given that Nova Scotia was one of the provinces that had not yet been able to draw on the federal UA program to bolster the provincial social assistance budget.) Of Vancouver's twenty-two agency ads in 1957, only four described even part of an agency's purpose as enabling its clients to work and earn their own support. Ads for the Canadian National Institute for the Blind, foster day care association (children of single working mothers), BC Borstal Association (juvenile delinquents), and Harbour Light mission (homeless men), in *Vancouver Sun,* respectively, 2 October 1957, 5; 4 October 1957, 5; 8 October 1957, 5; and 18 October 1957, 5. The remaining eighteen ads emphasized efforts to end discrimination, to build community relationships, and to support families (and especially children) suffering from a variety of health and personal problems. See Chapter 7 for further description and discussion of the place in or absence of relief in the chests' 1950s advertising strategies.

98 Clippings, "Govt. Gives 'Raw Deal' on Jobless Aid: Miller," *Vancouver Herald,* 11 May 1948; and "Strong Language" (editorial, *Vancouver Herald,* 12 May 1948, CVA, UWLM, Add. Mss. 849, vol. 617-F-7.

99 Nora Lea to Hazeldine Bishop, 21 August 1946, LAC, CCSD, MG 28 I 10, vol. 254, file 254-6.

100 Struthers, "Shadows," 19.

101 Charlotte Whitton to G.E. Beament, President, Ottawa Community Chests, 15 November 1954, LAC, Charlotte Whitton Papers, MG 30 E 256, vol. 43. Whitton outlined the scope by which Ottawa's social service spending was exceeding the municipal budget in "Report to the Board of Control re: Welfare Disbursements," 25 October 1954, LAC, Charlotte Whitton Papers, MG 30 E 256, vol. 50, file Social Service Dept. 1954-55.

102 Struthers, "Shadows," 20-21.

103 For a mention of this connection, see Irving Abella and Harold Troper, *None Is Too Many: Canada and the Jews of Europe* (Toronto: Lester and Orpen Dennys, 1986), 183. For particular references by King to the Freimans' place as Liberals, see LAC, Diaries of William Lyon Mackenzie King, 26 October 1927, 226, and 14 February 1930, 38.

104 Henry Stubbins, report on a field trip to Vancouver, 18-21 March 1952, LAC, CCSD, MG 28 I 10, vol. 254, file 254-7.

Chapter 7: Justice, Inclusion, and the Emotions of Obligation in 1950s Charity

1 For an overview of the literature on the ethic of care and its place in relation to Rawlsian liberalism and particular matters of Canadian social policy, see Olena Hankivsky, *Social Policy and the Ethic of Care* (Vancouver: UBC Press, 2004). My summary in this paragraph also draws on a special issue of *Hypatia* 10, 2 (1995) and in particular on two essays in that issue: Monique Deveaux, "Shifting Paradigms: Theorizing Care and Justice in Political Theory," 115-19, and Joan C. Tronto, "Care as a Basis for Radical Political Judgements," 141-49. I thank Janet Guildford, of Nova Scotia's Feminists for Just and Equal Public Policy, for introducing me to social impact assessment methods.

2 Linda Gordon, "Social Insurance and Public Assistance: The Influence of Gender in Welfare Thought in the United States, 1890-1935," *American Historical Review* 97, 1 (1992): 27-31; Shirley Tillotson, "Dollars, Democracy, and the Children's Aid Society: The Eclipse of Gwendolen Lantz," in *Mothers of the Municipality*, ed. Judith Fingard and Janet Guildford (Toronto: University of Toronto Press, 2004), 88-89. For a labour leader's view that only a male social worker could be successful in persuading labour councils to give financial support to the Canadian Welfare Council, see minutes of a meeting between R.E.G. Davis, David Crawley (CWC), Gordon Cushing (TLCC), and Leslie Wismer (TLCC), 30 January 1952, LAC, CCSD, MG 28 I 10, vol. 77, file 564, file "Labour General, 1952-62."

3 Nancy Christie has persuasively argued that the development of universalist income support policies after the Great Depression was closely associated with an emphasis on the obligations and needs of male breadwinners. Nancy Christie, *Engendering the State: Family, Work, and Welfare in Canada* (Toronto: University of Toronto Press, 2000).

4 *The Call* 1, 4 (1945): 7; *Labour Statesman*, April 1950, 16.

5 J. Harvey Perry, *Taxes, Tariffs, and Subsidies: A History of Canadian Fiscal Development*, vol. 2 (Toronto: University of Toronto Press, 1955), 392-95; Canadian Tax Foundation, *Report on the Proceedings of a Conference on the Income Tax Bill, 8-9 December 1947* (Ottawa: Canadian Tax Foundation, n.d.), 21-22; William Anderson, "Economic Security for Older Canadians," *Canadian Welfare* 25, 5 (1950): 6;

William Anderson, "Some Reflections on Personal Taxation in Relation to Social Security Benefits and Contributions," address given to the Third Tax Conference of the Canadian Tax Foundation, Montreal, 6 December 1947, 2-3, 5. Anderson, a life insurance executive, was involved in the wartime Ontario nutrition committee during the war, and in the mid-1950s he would be a member of the CWC's committee on public-private relations and chair the executive committee of the new Social Planning Council of Toronto. Gale Wills, *A Marriage of Convenience: Business and Social Work in Toronto, 1918-1957* (Toronto: University of Toronto Press, 1995), 100, 129; minutes, meeting of a committee to make recommendations about a study of public-private relationships, 11 November 1955, LAC, CCSD, MG 28 I 10, vol. 79, file 591; Eurith Goold to Eugene Forsey, 25 January 1944, vol. 77, file 564 "Labour – General"; and "Information for Workers," 1945, vol. 228, file 228-16; confidential memo to directors general, directors, and chief intelligence officers, 14 November 1949, LAC, Records of the Department of National Revenue, RG 16, vol. 1017, item 65; "And off Relief!" *Canadian Welfare* 17, 4 (1941): 42; minutes, meeting of the campaign committee, 10 July 1951, UWOC.

6 Clippings, "Multiple Charity Drives Condemned," *Vancouver Sun*, 7 June 1950; and "Says Charity Groups Growing like Weeds," *Ottawa Journal*, 13 June 1950; telegram from Betty Govan to Miss Gould [sic], 13 June 1950; Eurith Goold to R.E.G. Davis, 14 June 1950; and memo from Eurith Goold to Henry [Stubbins], 14 June 1950, LAC, CCSD, MG 28 I 10, vol. 77, file 564 "Labour – General"; minutes, meeting of 6 June 1950, CVA, Records of the Vancouver, New Westminster, and District Trades and Labor Council, Add. Mss. 307, 269; Board of directors, executive director's report, 25 July 1950, CVA, UWLM, Add. Mss. 849, vol. 617-B-1.

7 Memo from Eurith Goold to Henry [Stubbins], 14 June 1950, LAC, CCSD, MG 28 I 10, vol. 77, file 564 "Labour – General."

8 Clipping, "Community Chests Hinting Libel in Pat Conroy's 'Racket' Charge," *Ottawa Journal*, 12 May 1950, LAC, CCSD, MG 28 I 10, vol. 77, file 564 "Labour – General."

9 A typescript copy of Conroy's letter, dated 13 May 1950, is in LAC, CCSD, MG 28 I 10, vol. 77, file 564 "1942-1951 Labour – General."

10 Shirley Tillotson, "Class and Community in Canadian Welfare Work, 1933-1960," *Journal of Canadian Studies* 32, 1 (1997): 63-92.

11 I thank Sue Campbell of the Dalhousie Department of Philosophy for prompting me to note the high emotions in Conroy's critique of charitable emotion.

12 Clippings, "Says Charity Groups Growing like Weeds," *Ottawa Journal*, 13 June 1950; and "Unjust and Unfair" (editorial), *Toronto Star*, 17 June 1950; Henry Stubbins, report of field visit to Community Chest of Greater Toronto, 29 June 1950, LAC, CCSD, MG 28 I 10, vol. 77, file 564 "Labour – General"; Ronald Williams, "Is Charity Campaigning Getting out of Hand?" *Financial Post*, 5 August 1950, 1.

13 Sidney Katz, "The Unholy Mess of Our Charity Appeals," *Maclean's*, 15 November 1953, 20, 95-99; George Hart to Henry Stubbins, 1 December 1943, LAC, CCSD, MG 28 I 10, vol. 228, file 228-17. Two weeks after the article appeared, and immediately after George Hart took over the Halifax chest in 1953, he requested from the CWC 1,000 copies of the article to distribute to "our local firms and our [volunteer] workers." He went on to say that "this article has had quite an impact on the thinking of readers of *MacLean's* in Halifax, and I would like to make sure that everyone will have the opportunity to read it." I have added "volunteer" before "workers" to make clear that, when chest leaders used this term, they were typically referring to volunteers in the chest campaigns. If they were talking about wage earners in their communities, they used the term "employees."

14 Katz, "Unholy Mess," 20.

15 Ibid., 95, 97. Although Katz did not indicate his source of statistics on campaign failure, it was most likely the annual tabulation of campaign results published in *Canadian Welfare*.

16 Ibid., 97.

17 Corporate opinion on this question was well documented in Shea's study. Separate or combined business and labour donor organizations designed to constrain fundraising were afoot in each of the cities discussed here and elsewhere in Canada. Between 1950 and 1953, Vancouver's Board of Trade made at least two efforts to clean up the mess of multiple appeals, striking a Citizens' Committee and including a representative of at least one of Vancouver's Labour Councils. (That representative, CCF activist Tom Alsbury, would become mayor of Vancouver in 1959.) In 1951, Ottawa's chest learned that the local Board of Trade was also taking charity organization into its own hands by setting up a Public Appeals Commission. In response to such pressure, Halifax's chest adopted as its 1952 slogan "Too Many Campaigns" and offered "the United Way" as the solution. And in 1956 the Halifax Board of Trade's *Commercial News* celebrated the success of the Detroit United Fund and asserted that the same method was "inevitable" in Halifax. Minutes, meeting of the board of directors, 15 December 1953, CVA, UWLM, Add. Mss. 849; minutes, meeting of the Vancouver, New Westminster, and District Trades and Labor Council, 6 June 1950, CVA, Add. Mss. 307, series M-5, reel 3; minutes, meeting of the campaign committee, 16 January 1951, UWOC; John McVittie to Henry Stubbins, 29 September 1952, LAC, CCSD, MG 28 I 10, vol. 228, file 228-17; "More Appeals," *Commercial News*, June 1956, 21.

18 Katz, "Unholy Mess," 96-97.

19 Ibid., 20.

20 Ibid. It is worth noting that neither he nor the commentators whom he chose to quote had anything to say about free enterprise versus communism or the importance of private welfare to "our way of life" or "the free world." Indeed,

the only argument in the article that might be construed as anti-statist is Katz's rueful acknowledgment that tax expenditure by way of increased corporate charitable deductions might simply be balanced by the imposition of some other higher or new tax to counteract the cost of the deductions to overall government revenues. But this observation could easily be read as skepticism about the value of the charitable deduction as a fundraising technique and thus be a criticism of naive fundraisers and short-sighted corporations as much as or more than a disparaging of the rapacious state.

21 Ibid., 95.

22 Ibid., 98. The reasons I give here were not expressly stated in the Katz article. They are clearly expressed, however, in other places: minutes, meeting of the joint executive committee and the Salvation Army advisory board, 28 March 1946; and meeting of the joint executive committee with other agencies, 27 January 1953, UWOC; Salvation Army position cited in William P. Jenkins, "Why I'm Against the United Fund," *Maclean's,* 19 January 1957, 4; Henry Stubbins, report on a field trip to Vancouver, 18-21 March 1952, LAC, CCSD, MG 28 I 10, vol. 254, file 254-7. The minutes of a meeting of Canadian Cancer Society representatives to discuss their joining, 19 January 1953, UWOC, refer to the end of "the old Chest policy that all the money should stay in the city where it was raised." This policy had been cited in the 1920s and 1930s as the reason why national and international organizations such as the Red Cross and the Salvation Army were not appropriate as chest agencies.

23 Clippings, "Multiple Charity Drives Condemned," *Vancouver Sun,* 7 June 1950; and "Says Charity Groups Growing like Weeds," *Ottawa Journal,* 13 June 1950, LAC, CCSD, MG 28 I 10, vol. 77, file 564 "Labour – General"; report of the campaign chair, annual meeting, 24 January 1950; and clipping, "Red Feather Drive $15,000 Short: Seek Labor's Aid to Solve Fund-Raising Problems," *Halifax Chronicle-Herald,* 28 November 1950, NSARM, UWHD, MG 20; minutes, meeting of the social planning committee, 16 November 1953, CVA, UWLM, Add. Mss. 849, vol. 617-G-6; Board of directors, "Report on Labour Representation," 22 June 1955; minutes, meeting of the nominating committee, 20 January 1956; and minutes, campaign committee postmortem, 21 November 1956, UWOC.

24 Henry Stubbins, presentation to the joint meeting of the Halifax Community Chest and Council, minutes by Gwendolyn Shand, 6 February 1952, NSARM, UWHD, MG 20, vol. 1713; minutes, meeting of the campaign committee, 26 January 1960; and Community Chests and Councils division of the CWC to Community Chests, 1 December 1953, UWOC; *Annual Report 1950,* CVA, UWLM, Add. Mss. 849, vol. 617-B-2, 9; memo to Commissioner G. Sutton-Brown from Chief Licence Inspector re charity appeals and proposed regulations, 6 September 1961, CVA, Mayor's Papers, series 483, file 36-d-3-38.

25 Ross Wilson, "Dear Subscriber" (circular letter), 15 February 1960, LAC, CCSD, MG 28 I 10, vol. 254, file 254-9.

26 Memo from Henry Stubbins to R.E.G. Davis, November 1951, LAC, CCSD, MG 28 I 10, vol. 254, file 254-7; minutes of a special meeting to discuss open door policy, 8 March 1949, NSARM, UWHD, MG 20, vol. 1713; minutes, meeting of the social planning committee, 17 May 1954, CVA, UWLM, Add. Mss. 849, vol. 617-G-6; report of the budget subcommittees to the budget committee, 30 November 1954, UWOC.

27 The two systems are compared in detail in Ralph Albrant's memo summarizing his discussion with staff of the Vancouver Community Chest and Council in which they defended their preference for the former method. Ralph Albrant, draft report of field trip, 31 May 1956, LAC, CCSD, MG 28 I 10, vol. 254, file 254-8. For the negotiation of terms with national agencies, see minutes, meeting with Canadian Cancer Society representatives to discuss their joining the chest, 19 January 1953; special meeting of Roman Catholic and non-sectarian chests to consider the application of Les scouts catholiques for membership, 28 July 1950; and meeting of the joint executive committee with other agencies, 27 January 1953, UWOC.

28 Minutes, meeting with Canadian Cancer Society representatives to discuss their joining the chest, 19 January 1953; meeting of the joint executive committee with other agencies, 27 January 1953; R.S.W. Fordham to G.H. Burland, 13 December 1952; and meeting of the executive committee, 18 February 1960 and 21 April 1960, UWOC.

29 George Hart to Henry Stubbins, 2 August 1954, LAC, CCSD, MG 28 I 10, vol. 228, file 228-17.

30 George Hart to Ralph Albrant, 7 February 1956, LAC, CCSD, MG 28 I 10, vol. 228, file 228-17; minutes, meeting of the chest council, 7 April 1949, NSARM, UWHD, MG 20, vol. 1713; minutes, meeting of the executive committee, 8 May 1956, UWOC; campaign ads showing Red Cross logo, *Halifax Chronicle-Herald*, October 1957, NSARM, UWHD, MG 20, vol. 1713; minutes, annual meeting, 26 February 1958, NSARM, UWHD, MG 20, vol. 1713.

31 Ralph Albrant, draft report of field trip, 31 May 1956, LAC, CCSD, MG 28 I 10, vol. 254, file 254-8.

32 Ross Wilson, "Dear Subscriber" (circular letter), 15 February 1960; and Hugh H. Harvey (Director of Public Relations) to George Hart (CWC), 11 March 1960, LAC, CCSD, MG 28 I 10, vol. 254, file 254-9; minutes, meeting of the board of directors, 29 November 1955; clipping, "Chest between Two Fires: President Predicts Crisis," 1960; and clipping, "Six Named to Chest Probe," 31 March 1960, CVA, UWLM, Add. Mss. 849, Loc. 589-F-7, file 10. Members included a former cabinet minister, a development officer for UBC, an executive of the BC Medical Society, the president of the BC Lumbermen's Association, a labour

representative, a delegate of the Council of Women, and one from the Junior League; clipping of editorial cartoon showing the Community Chest as a knight riding a "United Way" steed against a hail of arrows, 22 September 1960, CVA, UWLM, Add. Mss. 849, Loc. 589-F-7, file 10. In Ottawa in 1952, the director used the fear of agencies withdrawing to spur his campaign team on to greater effort: "It's Time to Act" (newsletter), July 1952, LAC, CCSD, MG 28 I 10, vol. 240, file 240-3. Whether or not this threat was real, it formed part of the chests' available incentives in the 1950s. The withdrawal of agencies, along with the multiplicity of appeals, was what was meant by the Chests' "failing" as much as, if not more than, their inadequately funded services.

33 John Yerger, "Some Important Facts for Your Study Based on 40 Years of Federation in North America," 21 June 1954, UWOC. It's worth noting that Ottawa's Elizabeth Fry Society, a small agency dealing with a rather unpopular clientele, had some difficulty getting admitted to the chest in 1964. Assessing the quality of its service was the apparent reason for the delay. Minutes, meeting of the executive committee, 8 October 1964, UWOC. It is clear, however, that the pressure to accept this new agency was slight, because the minutes show that the chest was aware the society's fundraising outside the chest would pose little threat to the size of the chest's donor pool.

34 Minutes, meeting of the board of directors, 24 October 1955, CVA, UWLM, Add. Mss. 849; minutes, meeting of the board of directors, 22 September 1954; meetings of the executive committee, July and August 1955; and meeting of the committee on the Community Chests' boundaries, 17 April 1956, UWOC; minutes, annual meeting, 26 February 1958, NSARM, UWHD, MG 20, vol. 1713; "Decisive Steps Taken towards United Appeal," *Halifax Mail-Star,* 27 June 1957, 6.

35 For Eastview attitudes, I draw on Franco-Ontarian Michel Gratton's *The French Canadians: An Outsider's Inside Look at Quebec* (Toronto: Key Porter, 1992), 1-18, in which Gratton describes the Eastview of his childhood in the 1950s.

36 Report of a Conference on Community Chest Possibilities in Eastview, 9 October 1952, LAC, CCSD, MG 28 I 10, vol. 240, file 240-3. I infer that Mayor Lavergne hoped to save or supplement tax money because, as the Eastview situation developed, the Ottawa chest officials specifically warned the mayor's group that, although the creation of a chest might relieve Eastview of some of the tax-funded grants that it would have to make to agencies, the town would not be relieved of all of its responsibilities to subsidize agencies. Minutes, meeting of the executive committee with officials of the Eastview Community Chest, 22 October 1954, UWOC.

37 Report of a Conference on Community Chest Possibilities in Eastview, 9 October 1952, LAC, CCSD, MG 28 I 10, vol. 240, file 240-3.

38 Memo to Miss Touzel and Mr. Davis re Ottawa Community Chests' relationship with French-speaking groups of Ottawa, 23 May 1952, LAC, CCSD, MG 28 I 10, vol. 240, file 240-3.

39 Memo to Mr. Davis and Miss Touzel re French problems of Ottawa Community Chests, 12 June 1952, LAC, CCSD, MG 28 I 10, vol. 240, file 240-3.

40 John Yerger to R.E.G. Davis, 7 November 1952, LAC, CCSD, MG 28 I 10, vol. 240, file 240-3.

41 Minutes, meeting of the Protestant chest and the Roman Catholic chest to revise the bylaws, 18 June 1956; and meeting of the committee on community chests' boundaries, 17 April 1956, UWOC; "Why the Community Chest?" (ad), *Ottawa Journal*, 28 September 1957, 9.

42 Société Radio-Canada, "La passion de nos 40 ans," 1994 [1955], LAC, MIKAN no. 87254; minutes, meeting of the executive committee, 24 July 1957; job description for secretary of French services and assistant public relations director, 1960; and minutes, meeting of the board of directors, 25 February 1959, UWOC.

43 Minutes, meeting of the campaign committee, 18 August 1959, 29 November 1960, 22 September 1961, 1 December 1961 (located in the 1964 minutes binder), 19 March 1962, and 10 July 1962, UWOC.

44 Minutes, meeting of the campaign committee, 1 February 1961, 25 July 1961, 8 September 1961, and 22 September 1961; minutes, meeting of the campaign cabinet, 24 January 1963; and minutes, meeting of the board of directors, 26 September 1962, UWOC. I thank Brad Miller, who took time from his research at Library and Archives Canada to research Filion's occupation in the Ottawa City Directory.

45 Minutes, meeting of the special committee on Community Chest bylaws, 1961 (located in the 1964 minutes binder); annual meeting, April 1962; and meeting of the executive committee, 22 June 1964, UWOC.

46 Chief Electoral Officer of Canada, *A History of the Vote in Canada* (Ottawa: Public Works Canada, 1997), 83.

47 Clipping, "Well Done, Friends!" (editorial), 15 October 1949, NSARM, UWHD, MG 20, vol. 1718.

48 Clipping, "34th Annual Report" (ad), 1960, NSARM, UWHD, MG 20, vol. 1725.

49 Clipping, photograph of Miss Edith Sparks, Mrs. Lalia Grant, and Mrs. Laura Tynes, *Halifax Mail-Star*, 30 September 1957, NSARM, UWHD, MG 20, vol. 1724. The caption for this photo concluded that "the three will head a canvass of the area bounded by Cogswell, Robie, and North Streets, and the harbour, making the United Appeal a united citizens' effort." The neighbourhood specified included two streets described as "a deteriorating mixed-race area where the majority of the city's Black population resided [in the late 1950s]." Wanda Thomas-Bernard and Judith Fingard, "Black Women at Work: Race, Family, and Community in Greater Halifax," in *Mothers of the Municipality*, ed. Judith Fingard and Janet Guildford (Toronto: University of Toronto Press, 2004), 192.

50 This is not to say that only events in 1958 were included. The interest continued, for example, in the chest's record of its support in 1960 for a cross-cultural event,

where Chinese Canadian social worker Douglas Nann explained the reasons behind Chinatown residents' opposition to redevelopment, based on fear of being criticized for such basic daily things as "the pungent odor of Chinese food and cooking." Clipping, "'Mixing' Feared by Old Chinese," 20 October 1960, CVA, UWLM, Add. Mss. 849, Loc. 589-F-7, file 10.

51 Clippings, "You're Chinese? Apartment Refused," 12 December 1958; and "Sikhs' Seven Neighbours Say: 'We Just Don't Want Them,'" *Vancouver Sun,* 29 September 1958, CVA, UWLM, Add. Mss. 849, Loc. 589-F-7, file 9.

52 "Construction and Building Workers" (ad), *Halifax Chronicle-Herald,* 21 September 1956, 21.

53 "$264,318 Raised in Chest Drive," *Halifax Chronicle-Herald,* 22 December 1956.

54 Bessie Touzel, field report, 21 January 1956, LAC, CCSD, MG 28 I 10, vol. 77, file 564 "Labour – General, 1952-1962"; memo to Miss P. Godfrey from L. Smith, 3 May 1957; and statement from CIO liaison officer, Labor [sic] Participation Department, Community Chests and Councils of America, August 1950, LAC, CCSD, MG 28 I 10, vol. 77, file 564 "Labour and Welfare Services, 1946-59"; Community Chest and Council of Greater Vancouver, annual report, 1950, CVA, UWLM, Add. Mss. 849, vol. 617-B-2, 11.

55 In conversation with me in the late 1990s, a recently retired United Way director, social worker Bill Zimmerman, used this turn of phrase to describe labour participation arrangements in Ottawa. Another of the costs of doing business was the use of union printers to produce publicity material. In Ottawa in 1954, Gordon Cushing of the TLC advised the Ottawa chests' board of directors that, even though Ottawa's two union shops did not have sufficient capacity to produce all of the necessary material, the board of directors should avoid pointing that out in their response to the local Labour Council's concerns about union printing until after the 1954 campaign for funds was over, or some members of the Labour Council would make public criticisms of the chests. Minutes, meeting of the board of directors, 27 October 1954, UWOC.

56 Minutes, meeting of the social planning committee, 22 September 1952, CVA, UWLM, Add. Mss. 849, vol. 617-G-6, file 7.

57 Memo to Miss P. Godfrey from L. Smith, 3 May 1957; and Bud Neville to Laton Smith, 1 May 1957, LAC, CCSD, MG 28 I 10, vol. 77, file 564 "Labour and Welfare Services, 1946-59"; minutes, meeting of the chest council, 6 March 1951, NSARM, UWHD, MG 20, vol. 1713; Peter C. Newman, "Is the United Appeal Too Big – or Big Enough?" *Maclean's,* 27 September 1958, 69.

58 *United Appeal Labour Reports* 1, 5 (1957): 1, LAC, MG 28 I 44, Labour Council of Metro Toronto Papers, vol. 7.

59 For an explicit use of that analogy by a labour leader, see Donald MacDonald, "Labour Participation in Community Chests," *Canadian Labour* 1, 7 (1956): 28.

60 Not only a campaign strategy, the notion that working-class people had an interest in the federated charities because they were potential consumers of the member agencies services was also part of the call for workers' organizations to have a voice in the administration of charities. Toronto and Lakeshore Labour Council, report of the special committee on welfare, 12 February 1951, LAC, CCSD, MG 28 I 10, vol. 77, file 564 "Labour and Welfare Services, 1946-1959"; minutes, meeting of the campaign committee, 11 June 1956, UWOC.

61 For the slogan's use in the late-1940s campaign advertising, see *Ottawa Journal,* 7 October 1947, 18, and 19 October 1957, 9; clippings, Robert Simpson Company-sponsored chest ad, 19 October 1948; chest display ad, 1 October 1949; and "Labor Backs the Chest" (ad), from the *Herald* and the *Mail,* c. 17 October 1950, NSARM, UWHD, MG 20, vol. 1718; Wayne and Shuster skit, fall 1948 (for 1949 funds), LAC, CBC Radio fonds, Montreal collection, Red Feather Campaign – Announcements, ISN 132568. For its use in the CCL endorsement, see text of CCL's endorsement, 25 June 1948, LAC, CCSD, MG 28 I 10, vol. 77, file 564 "Labour and Welfare Services, 1946-1959." For an example of the logo, see Ralph Blanchard to John Yerger, 21 September 1953, UWOC; re the Vancouver fundraiser, minutes, meeting of the board of directors, 27 October 1953, CVA, UWLM, Add. Mss. 849; re national publicity materials after 1953, commercial featuring Alex Barris of "The Barris Beat," LAC, ISN 236411; speech by Florence Philpott (consultant to the United Community Fund and the Community Chest report of the Fourteenth Ontario Recreation Association conference, 1959), Archives of Ontario, RG 65, series C3, box 38, file 1137.

62 Minutes, meeting of the campaign committee, 25 March 1957, UWOC; minutes, meeting of board of directors, report of the public relations committee, 28 June 1949, CVA, UWLM, Add. Mss. 849; United Way referral service pamphlet, 1954, CVA, Mayor's Papers, series 483, file 35-b-6-11; National Council of Women endorsement, fall 1948 (for 1949 funds), LAC, CBC Radio fonds, Montreal collection, Red Feather Campaign – Announcements, ISN 132568; reprint, "How Chest Money Works," *Globe and Mail,* 20 February 1952, LAC, CCSD, MG 28 I 10, vol. 77, file 564 "Labour – General, 1952-62."

63 "Let's All Join Hands" (ad), *Halifax Herald,* 11 October 1950, 13. It would have been easy to include one African Nova Scotian hand, but they did not.

64 "19 Campaigns in One" (ad), *Halifax Herald,* 4 October 1950, 17.

65 See note 71 in Chapter 2. Another example of this conception of the insurance consumer may be found in a life insurance ad in *Vancouver Sun,* 21 October 1940, 3: "'United and Resolved' symbolizes the spirit of nearly four million Canadians banded together for mutual protection through the great co-operative enterprise of life insurance." For the industry's deliberate emphasis on advertising insurance as co-operation, see *Yearbook of the Canadian Life Insurance Officers Association,*

1943, 32. A sample of the "personal responsibility as social service rhetoric" may be found in the 1954-55 edition of this yearbook, 170, address by Edgar Andrew Collard, editor, *Montreal Gazette*, "Are We Taking Advantage of Ourselves?" – "the importance of people serving their fellowmen by carrying their own burdens."

66 "The Red Feather Show," 2 October 1951, LAC, CBC Radio fonds, Miscellaneous Discs, ISN 148202. See also on these themes LAC, Saskatchewan Archives Board fonds, Canadian Welfare Council spots (1958-62), ISN 36653; "800 Volunteers Start Working for *You* Today" (ad), *Halifax Herald*, 10 October 1950; governor general's endorsement, fall 1948 (for 1949 funds), LAC, CBC Radio fonds, Montreal collection, Red Feather Campaign – Announcements, ISN 132568.

67 Sue Campbell, *Interpreting the Personal: Expression and the Formation of Feelings* (Ithaca: Cornell University Press, 1997). I appreciated the comments of my research assistant in 1999, Paul Jackson, on this question of how one's life circumstances affect the reading of emotional rhetoric.

68 Stanley C. Allyn, "Responsibility of Industry in Community Welfare" (excerpts from speech), reprinted by the Canadian Welfare Council, 1950, LAC, CCSD, MG 28 I 10, vol. 53, file 531 1946-50.

69 Michael Stocker, "The Schizophrenia of Modern Ethical Theories," *Journal of Philosophy* 73, 14 (1976): 453-66. Critiquing the ethical reasoning behind social legislation as too narrowly preoccupied with "duty, rightness, and obligation," Stocker argues that an integrated basis for moral action necessarily includes moral emotions such as love and fellow-feeling. In this view, "enlightened self-interest" fails as an adequate ground for creating community, just as an inability to care for and act for a supposedly beloved person for his or her own sake makes love impossible. Extrapolating the question of motive to political ethics, Adrian Oldfield similarly underscores that a certain motivation is an intrinsic part of citizenship: "No amount of political participation and economic democracy, no level of civic education or national service, will suffice for the practice of citizenship in a political community – unless and until the external covenant becomes an internal one." Adrian Oldfield, "Citizenship and Community: Civic Republicanism and the Modern World," in *The Citizenship Debates*, ed. Gershon Shafir (Minneapolis: University of Minnesota Press, 1998), 79, 82-83, 87-89.

70 For a biography of William Jenkins and evidence of the membership of social work professor John H. Morgan in his congregation, see http://firstunitariantoronto.org/history.htm and http://firstunitariantoronto.org/Sermons/At_the_Crossroads_Again.htm; *Maclean's*, 19 January 1957, 4, 32; Newman, "United Appeal," 14, 66; minutes, meeting of the executive committee, 17 March 1960; and meeting of the campaign committee, 1 December 1961 (1964 binder), UWOC; clipping, "Community Chest Needs Overhaul, Say Panelists," 10 February 1960, CVA, UWLM, Add. Mss. 849, Loc. 589-F-7, file 10; "Mailbag," *Maclean's*, 2 March 1957, 55;

Katz, "Unholy Mess," 97; "Is Organized Charity Really Charity?" episode of television program *Toronto File,* 3 November 1960, LAC, CBC Television fonds, Kines from PARC, ISN 289670. George Davidson of the CWC (and formerly of the Vancouver Welfare Federation) was aware early that federation militated against the sort of real engagement in social service that independent private agencies afforded and hoped that democratic organizational methods could counteract this tendency. George Davidson to Edgar Brown, 2 November 1942, LAC, CCSD, MG 28 I 10, vol. 254, file 254-3. Neither the minutes of the Halifax chest in the 1950s nor its correspondence with the CWC reveals this line of concern about impersonality and coercion. This absence may be an artifact of the sources I used in my research, or it may reflect some real difference in the relation between the Halifax chest and its community.

71 Newman, "United Appeal," passim; "Is Organized Charity Really Charity?"; minutes, meeting of the campaign committee, reference to "attacks made on [the united appeals] by Pierre Berton and others in Toronto," 14 April 1961, UWOC.

72 Minutes, meeting of the campaign committee, 10 March 1959; meeting of the board of directors, 28 October 1959; meeting of the agency directors, 17 February 1960; and meeting of the executive committee, 17 March 1960, UWOC.

73 Minutes, meeting of the executive committee, 17 March 1960; meeting of the campaign committee, 1 December 1961 (in 1964 vol.); and meeting of the campaign cabinet, 6 March 1962, UWOC.

74 Minutes, meeting of the agency directors, 17 February 1960, and meeting of the press committee, 11 June 1958, UWOC; C.H. Naphtali to C.F. Harrington, 18 January 1960, LAC, CCSD, MG 28 I 10, vol. 254, file 254-9.

75 Newman, "United Appeal," 14, 67; minutes, annual meeting, April 1962, UWOC.

76 Minutes, meeting of the campaign committee, 6 September 1951, UWOC; Mayor Fred Hume to Mayor G.E. Sharpe (Winnipeg), 28 September 1955, CVA, Mayor's Papers, series 483, file 35-e-3-10; clipping, "Big Take for Chest at Races," 17 May 1958, CVA, UWLM, Add. Mss. 849, Loc. 589-F-7, file 9; "United Appeal Launched at Centre of Bridge," *Halifax Mail-Star,* 8 October 1957, 3; Wayne and Shuster skit, fall 1948 (for 1949 funds), LAC, CBC Radio fonds, Montreal collection, Red Feather Campaign – Announcements, ISN 132568; clipping, "'No Danger of Collapse,' Says Chest President," 4 December 1962 (reports 1959 campaign, most successful ever, as exceptional in its "showmanship and razzle-dazzle"), CVA, UWLM, Add. Mss. 849, series Loc. 589-F-7, file 11.

77 Minutes, meeting of the campaign committee, 12 June 1958, UWOC.

78 Suzanne Morton, *At Odds: Gambling and Canadians, 1919-1969* (Toronto: University of Toronto Press, 2003), 172-75; minutes, meeting of the chest council, 29 March 1951, NSARM, UWHD, MG 20, vol. 1713; R.E.G. Davis to Rev. J.R. Mutchmor, 7 August 1959, LAC, CCSD, MG 28 I 10, vol. 70, file 517.

79 Lynne Marks, *Revivals and Roller Rinks: Religion, Leisure, and Identity in Late-Nineteenth-Century Small-Town Ontario* (Toronto: University of Toronto Press), 77-78.

80 T.J. Jackson Lears, *Fables of Abundance: A Cultural History of Advertising in America* (New York: Basic Books, 1994), 215 and passim.

81 Nancy Fraser and Linda Gordon, "Dependency Demystified: Inscriptions of Power in a Keyword of the Welfare State," *Social Politics* 1, 1 (1994): 4-31. A 1955 survey of Vancouver family agencies shows the emphasis on psychological origins of dependency. "Report of the Pilot Survey of 34 Agencies sponsored by the Family and Child Welfare Division of the Community Chest and Council," LAC, CCSD, MG 28 I 10, vol. 254, file 254-8.

82 Raymond Labarge (assistant deputy minister of national revenue), quoted in "Red Feather Drive Passes Half-Way Mark," *Ottawa Journal*, 9 October 1957, 19.

83 Ralph Blanchard to Marjorie Bradford, 7 April 1936, LAC, CCSD, MG 28 I 10, vol. 158, file "CWC Divisions – Community Organization 1935-37."

84 I chose the 1957 campaign somewhat arbitrarily as falling twenty years after the 1937 campaigns, for which I had also done a close analysis of all the campaign advertising in each city. It seemed likely to me that the 1957 campaign strategies might also show the effect on the fundraisers' strategies of the recent implementation of unemployment assistance, at least in Vancouver and Ottawa. Nova Scotia was not fully integrated into the national social assistance system until after 1958.

85 I thank Jim Struthers for pointing out to me the parallels in the purposes served by representations of the old and the young.

86 Canadian Welfare Council radio advertisements for the United Way campaign, c. 1960, LAC, C04699. This compilation includes two series, one based on celebrity endorsements, such as the Messer ad, and another, apparently later series based on a creative use of "mystery" sound clips – the creak of a porch swing and the sound of a cigarette being smoked, for example, lead into an appeal based on the loneliness of the elderly.

87 For an example from each of Vancouver and Ottawa, see "The Need Is There, Give Your Share!" (ad), *Ottawa Journal*, 23 September 1957, 26; and illustration for "Lend a Hand – the United Way," *Vancouver Sun*, 28 September 1957, 1.

88 Ads for the Canadian National Institute for the Blind, foster day care association (children of single working mothers), BC Borstal Association (juvenile delinquents), and Harbour Light mission (homeless men), in *Vancouver Sun* on, respectively, 2 October 1957, 5; 4 October 1957, 5; 8 October 1957, 5; and 18 October 1957, 5.

89 Minutes, meeting of the campaign committee, 7 September 1950; T.E. Moore of St. Mary's Home to J.H. Yerger, 23 July 1953; D. Longmire of Ottawa Welfare Bureau to the board of directors of the Ottawa Community Chests, 19 February 1954; minutes, meeting of the board of directors, 22 September 1954; and report

of the budget committee to the board of directors, 30 November 1955, UWOC. *Annual Report 1946*, 6; minutes, meeting of the board of directors, 6 August 1951; memo on some principles of budgeting, 20 March 1952; minutes, meeting of board of directors, 25 March 1952 and 29 September 1953, CVA, UWLM, Add. Mss. 849, vol. 617-A-5. Minutes, meetings of the chest council, 6 June 1946, 29 March 1951, and 21 June 1955, NSARM, UWHD, MG 20, vol. 1713.

90 Clippings, "Mr. O'Neal's Statements" (editorial), *Vancouver Sun*, 7 October 1964; "Good for You, Pat O'Neal!" (editorial), n.d.; and Vancouver *Labour Statesman*, October 1964, LAC, Canadian Labour Congress Papers, MG 28 I 103, reel H223.

CONCLUSION: SIMILARITIES, DIFFERENCES, AND HISTORICAL CHANGE

1 George Davidson to Edgar Brown, 2 November 1942, LAC, CCSD, MG 28 I 10, vol. 254, file 254-3.

2 "The National Committee was developing material to defend federation in a positive way with a view to neutralizing attacks made on it by Pierre Berton and others in Toronto." Minutes, meeting of the campaign committee, 14 April 1961, UWOC.

3 Goal-setting manual, 10 May 1965, UWOC; interview with Toronto United Way board member William Ingram, in "The Way Things Are," episode of *Compass*, 12 September 1965, LAC, CBC TV Fonds, item number 96432.

4 Clipping, "United Appeal a Sham," *Vancouver Sun*, 1 October 1969, CVA, UWLM, Add. Mss. 849, Loc. 589-F-7, vol. 1, file 14.

5 Interview with SUPA member Liora Proctor, in "The Way Things Are," episode of *Compass*, 12 September 1965, LAC, CBC TV Fonds, item number 96432.

6 Clipping, "UCS Kick-Off Marred by Blast," *Vancouver Province*, 6 October 1970; and "Appeal Leaders Fire Back at Barrett," *Vancouver Province*, 22 October 1969, CVA, UWLM, Add. Mss. 849, Loc. 589-F-7, file 14. Minutes, annual meeting, 24 February 1966, NSARM, UWHD, MG 20, vol. 1714; and clipping, "Near-Misses Cause of Concern, United Appeal Members Told," 3 March 1966, vol. 1731. George Hart (CWC) to Tom Ward (CLC), 16 August 1962, LAC, Canadian Labour Congress Papers, MG 28 I 103, reel H223. In Vancouver, in particular, the chest's claim to be an advocate for improved public services was warranted by its work through the 1950s and early 1960s in documenting the inadequacy of social assistance rates in the Greater Vancouver area. Copies of its reports may be found in CVA, Department of Social Services Fonds, in, for example, "The Adequacy of Social Assistance Allowances in Greater Vancouver," 24 November 1966, series 450, file 106-D-5-9.

7 F. Ivor Jackson, "History of the Community Chest and Council of the Greater Vancouver Area" (typescript), March 1960, CVA, UWLM, Add. Mss. 849, Social Planning and Research series, F. Ivor Jackson subseries, 25-26.

8 Gwen Archibald, Wolfville, NS, personal communication, 2005.

9 An unnamed American tax commission, quoted in F.H. Bell, *Principles of Civic Taxation* (Saint John: Sun Printing Company, 1899[?]), 13. This study and Bell's "Municipal Taxation in Nova Scotia," *Dalhousie Review* 1, 13 (1921): 264-80, indicate that Bell was a well-known authority on tax issues in the first decades of the twentieth century.

10 In 2007, I embarked on research in this area.

Bibliography

NOTE ON ARCHIVAL REFERENCES

The records of the United Way of Ottawa-Carleton consist of a series of annual minutes books or binders that, during my research, were held at the offices of the United Way. Unless otherwise noted, the documents referred to in this collection are located in the volume for the year of the date of the document. Similarly, the records of the Social Planning Council of Ottawa-Carleton were, at the time I consulted them, not arranged archivally. Held at the City of Ottawa Archives, they were organized loosely in files usually labelled by type and date. I have therefore identified them by type and date.

The references to documents in the records of the United Way of the Lower Mainland are of two different types because my research in these archives was conducted in two stages. In the first stage, the records were held in the offices of the Lower Mainland and were not organized archivally. In the second stage, my assistants and I were able to consult these records at the City of Vancouver Archives (CVA), where the records had been deposited and arranged. References to the board of directors minutes and to the annual reports consulted in the first stage of my research do not have the CVA archival references. They are consistently identified by date, however, so that researchers who consult the chronologically arranged CVA collection will be able to locate these sources.

ARCHIVAL SOURCES

British Columbia Archives and Records Service (BCARS)

J.A. Clark Papers
Maitland Family Papers
Patullo Papers

City of Ottawa Archives (COA)

Ottawa Board of Trade (OBT) Papers
Ottawa Local Council of Women
Rotary Club of Ottawa
Social Planning Council of Ottawa-Carleton (SPCOC) Records

City of Vancouver Archives (CVA)

Ann Margaret Angus Papers
Annual reports of the Vancouver Children's Aid Society
Imperial Order of Daughters of the Empire Papers
J.S. Matthews (JSM) Collection
Jewish Historical Society
Kiwanis Club of Vancouver Papers
Rotary Club of Vancouver Papers
United Way of the Lower Mainland (UWLM) Papers
Vancouver Board of Trade (VBT) Papers
Vancouver, New Westminster, and District Trades and Labor Council

Library and Archives Canada (LAC)

Bronson Family Papers
Canadian Council on Social Development (CCSD) Papers
Canadian Labour Congress Papers
Charlotte Whitton Papers
Fédération des femmes canadiennes-françaises fonds

Nova Scotia Archives and Records Management (NSARM)

Angus L. Macdonald Papers
Halifax Board of Trade (HBT)
Halifax City Council (HCC) Records
Halifax Club of Business and Professional Women
Halifax-Dartmouth Welfare Council (HDWC)
Halifax Local Council of Women (HLCW)
Halifax-Dartmouth District Labour Council Papers
Halifax Relief Commission (HRC)
Rotary Club of Halifax (RH)
United Way of Halifax-Dartmouth (UWHD)

University of British Columbia Rare Books and Special Collections

Angus MacInnis Memorial Collection
John Wallace deBeque Farris Papers
UBC School of Social Work Records

Other Repositories

Federation of Jewish Philanthropies Papers, Canadian Jewish Congress Archives
United Way of Ottawa-Carleton (UWOC) Papers, held at its own office

BOOKS AND ARTICLES

Alexander, Jeffrey C. "The Binary Discourse of Civil Society." In *The New Social Theory Reader: Contemporary Debates*, ed. Jeffrey C. Alexander and Steven Seidman, 193-201. New York: Routledge, 2001.

Anderson, W.M. "Some Reflections on Personal Taxation in Relation to Social Security Benefits and Contributions." Address to the Third Tax Conference of the Canadian Tax Foundation, Montreal, 6 December 1949.

Angus, Anne Margaret. *The Children's Aid Society of Vancouver, B.C. 1901-1951*. Vancouver: Children's Aid Society, 1951.

Anonymous. *L'École de Charité Ozanam*. Montreal: La société Saint-Vincent de Paul, n.d. [1964?].

Armstrong, Pat. "The Welfare State as History." In *The Welfare State in Canada: Past, Present, and Future*, ed. Raymond B. Blake, Penny E. Bryden, and J. Frank Strain, 52-73. Toronto: Irwin Publishing, 1997.

Barkan, Elazar. *The Retreat of Scientific Racism: Changing Concepts of Race in Britain and the United States between the World Wars*. Cambridge, UK: Cambridge University Press, 1992.

Beito, David. *From Mutual Aid to the Welfare State: Fraternal Societies and Social Services, 1890-1967*. Chapel Hill: University of North Carolina Press, 2000.

Bell, F.H. "Municipal Taxation in Nova Scotia." *Dalhousie Review* 1, 13 (1921): 264-80.

Berton, Pierre. *The Great Depression, 1929-1939*. Toronto: McClelland and Stewart, 1990.

Bremner, Robert. *American Philanthropy*. Chicago: University of Chicago Press, 1960.

Brilliant, Eleanor L. *The United Way: Dilemmas of Organized Charity*. New York: Columbia University Press, 1990.

Brooks, Neil. "The Role of the Voluntary Sector in a Modern Welfare State." In *Between State and Market: Essays on Charities Law and Policy in Canada*, ed. Jim Phillips, Bruce Chapman, and David Stevens, 166-216. Montreal: McGill-Queen's University Press, 2001.

Burke, Sara Z. *Seeking the Highest Good: Social Service and Gender at the University of Toronto, 1888-1937*. Toronto: University of Toronto Press, 1996.

Campbell, Robert A. *Demon Rum or Easy Money: Government Control of Liquor in British Columbia from Prohibition to Privatization*. Ottawa: Carleton University Press, 1991.

Campbell, Sue. *Interpreting the Personal: Expression and the Formation of Feelings*. Ithaca: Cornell University Press, 1997.

Canadian Life Insurance Officers Association. *Submission Made to the Royal Commission on Dominion-Provincial Relations at Ottawa, Canada, January 18th, 1938*. Toronto: Canadian Life Insurance Officers Association.

–. Women's Division. *Farm Women Asked Us* ... Toronto: Canadian Life Insurance Officers Association, n.d.

–. *Yearbook of the Canadian Life Insurance Officers Association*. Toronto: Canadian Life Insurance Officers Association, 1930-58.

Canadian Tax Foundation. Report on Proceedings of the Conference on the Income Tax Bill, 8-9 December 1947.

Caritas-Canada. Section française. *Rapports annuels des congrès généraux.*

Cassidy, Harry M. *Public Health and Welfare Reorganization: The Postwar Problem in the Canadian Provinces.* Toronto: Ryerson Press, 1945.

Choquette, Robert. "English-French Relations in the Canadian Catholic Community." In *Creed and Culture: The Place of English-Speaking Catholics in Canadian Society, 1750-1930*, ed. Terence Murphy and Gerald Stortz, 3-24. Montreal: McGill-Queen's University Press, 1993.

–. *La foi gardienne de la langue en Ontario, 1900-1950.* Montreal: Les Éditions Bellarmin, 1987.

–. *Language and Religion: A History of English-French Conflict in Ontario.* Ottawa: University of Ottawa Press, 1975.

Christie, Nancy. *Engendering the State: Family, Work, and Welfare in Canada.* Toronto: University of Toronto Press, 2000.

Chunn, Dorothy. *From Punishment to Doing Good: Family Courts and Socialized Justice in Ontario, 1880-1940.* Toronto: University of Toronto Press, 1992.

Citizens' Research Institute of Canada. *Special Study of Taxation and Public Expenditure in Canada: Report to Donors.* Toronto: Citizens' Research Institute of Canada, 1937.

Clarke, Brian. *Piety and Nationalism: Lay Voluntary Associations and the Creation of an Irish-Catholic Community in Toronto, 1850-1895.* Montreal: McGill-Queen's University Press, 1993.

Cohen, G.A. *If You Are an Egalitarian, How Come You Are So Rich?* Cambridge, MA: Harvard University Press, 2000.

Cohen, Lizabeth. *Making a New Deal: Industrial Workers in Chicago, 1919-1939.* New York: Cambridge University Press, 1990.

Cook, Ramsay. *The Regenerators: Social Criticism in Late Victorian English Canada.* Toronto: University of Toronto Press, 1985.

Creighton, Donald. *The Forked Road: Canada 1939-1957.* Toronto: McClelland and Stewart, 1976.

Critchlow, Donald T., and Charles H. Parker, eds. *With Us Always: A History of Private Charity and Public Welfare.* New York: Rowman and Littlefield, 1998.

Crocker, Ruth. "From Gift to Foundation: The Philanthropic Lives of Mrs. Russell Sage." In *Charity, Philanthropy, and Civility in American History*, ed. Lawrence J. Friedman and Mark D. McGarvie, 199-216. New York: Cambridge University Press, 2003.

Curtis, Bruce. "Class Culture and Administration: Educational Inspection in Canada West." In *Colonial Leviathan: State Formation in Mid-Nineteenth Century Canada*, ed. A. Greer and I. Radforth, 116-19. Toronto: University of Toronto Press, 1992.

–. *The Politics of Population: State Formation, Statistics, and the Census of Canada, 1840-1875.* Toronto: University of Toronto Press, 2001.

Daunton, Martin J. *Charity, Self-Interest, and Welfare in the English Past.* New York: St. Martin's Press, 1996.

–. *Just Taxes: The Politics of Taxation in Britain, 1914-1979.* Cambridge, UK: Cambridge University Press, 2002.

–. *Trusting Leviathan: The Politics of Taxation in Britain, 1799-1914.* Cambridge, UK: Cambridge University Press, 2001.

Davies, Stephen. "Two Conceptions of Welfare: Voluntarism and Incorporationism." In *The Welfare State,* ed. Ellen Frankel Paul, Fred D. Miller, Jr., and Jeffrey Paul, 39-68. New York: Cambridge University Press, 1997.

Deveaux, Monique. "Shifting Paradigms: Theorizing Care and Justice in Political Theory." *Hypatia* 10, 2 (1995): 115-19.

Dollimore, Jonathan. *Sexual Dissidence: Augustine to Wilde, Freud to Foucault.* Oxford: Clarendon Press, 1991.

Duff, David G. "Charitable Contributions and the Personal Income Tax: Evaluating the Canadian Credit." In *Between State and Market: Essays on Charities Law and Policy in Canada,* ed. Jim Phillips, Bruce Chapman, and David Stevens, 407-56. Montreal: McGill-Queen's University Press, 2001.

Fahrni, Magda. *Household Politics: Montreal Families and Postwar Reconstruction.* Toronto: University of Toronto Press, 2006.

Fecteau, Jean-Marie. "État et associationnisme au XIXe siècle québécois: Éléments pour une problématique des rapports état/société dans la transition au capitalisme." In *Colonial Leviathan: State Formation in Mid-Nineteenth-Century Canada,* ed. Allan Greer and Ian Radforth, 134-62. Toronto: University of Toronto Press, 1992.

Feldman, Lawrence C. "Redistribution, Recognition, and the State: The Irreducibly Political Dimension of Injustice." *Political Theory* 30, 3 (2002): 410-40.

Ferretti, Lucia. *Entre voisins: La société paroissiale en milieu urbain: Saint-Pierre-Apôtre de Montréal, 1848-1930.* Montreal: Boréal, 1992.

Fingard, Judith. *The Dark Side of Life in Victorian Halifax.* Porter's Lake, NS: Pottersfield Press, 1989.

Fingard, Judith, and Janet Guildford, eds. *Mothers of the Municipality: Women, Work, and Social Policy in Post-1945 Halifax.* Toronto: University of Toronto Press, 2005.

Finlayson, Geoffrey. *Citizen, State, and Social Welfare in Britain, 1830-1990.* Oxford: Clarendon Press, 1994.

Fish, Stanley. "Interpreting the *Variorum.*" In *Is There a Text in This Class? The Authority of Interpretive Communities,* 147-73. Cambridge, MA: Harvard University Press, 1980.

Fisher, Robin. *Duff Patullo of British Columbia.* Toronto: University of Toronto Press, 1991.

Fowler, Douglas Weatherbee. "The Unemployment Assistance Act, 1956: Its Implications for Social Security and Public Welfare Administration in Canada." MA thesis, Department of Social Work, University of British Columbia, 1958.

Fraser, Nancy. *Justice Interruptus: Critical Reflections on the "Post-Socialist" Condition.* New York: Routledge, 1997.

Frederickson, George M. *The Comparative Imagination: On the History of Racism, Nationalism, and Social Movements.* Berkeley: University of California Press, 1997.

Friedman, Lawrence J., and Mark D. McGarvie, eds. *Charity, Philanthropy, and Civility in American History.* New York: Cambridge University Press, 2003.

Gillespie, W. Irwin. *Tax, Borrow, and Spend: Financing Federal Spending in Canada, 1867-1990.* Ottawa: Carleton University Press, 1991.

Gordon, Linda. "Social Insurance and Public Assistance: The Influence of Gender in Welfare Thought in the United States, 1890-1935." *American Historical* Review 97, 1 (1992): 19-54.

Guest, Dennis. *The Emergence of Social Security in Canada.* 3rd ed. Vancouver: UBC Press, 1997.

Guildford, Janet. "The End of the Poor Law: Public Welfare Reform in Nova Scotia before the Canada Assistance Plan." In *Mothers of the Municipality: Women, Work, and Social Policy in Post-1945 Halifax,* ed. Judith Fingard and Janet Guildford, 49-75. Toronto: University of Toronto Press, 2005.

Haddow, Rodney. *Poverty Reform in Canada, 1958-1978.* Montreal: McGill-Queen's University Press, 1993.

Hall, Stuart. "Gramsci's Relevance for the Study of Race and Ethnicity." In *Stuart Hall: Critical Dialogues in Cultural Studies,* ed. David Morley and Kuan-Hsing Chen, 411-40. New York: Routledge, 1996.

Hammack, David C. "Failure and Resilience: Pushing the Limits in Depression and Wartime." In *Charity, Philanthropy, and Civility in American History,* ed. Lawrence J. Friedman and Mark D. McGarvie, 263-80. New York: Cambridge University Press, 2003.

Hankivsky, Olena. *Social Policy and the Ethic of Care.* Vancouver: UBC Press, 2004.

Hawley, Ellis W. "Herbert Hoover, Associationalism, and the Great Depression Relief Crisis of 1930-1933." In *With Us Always: A History of Private Charity and Public Welfare,* ed. Donald T. Critchlow and Charles H. Parker, 161-90. New York: Rowman and Littlefield, 1998.

Irving, Allan, and Patricia Daenzer. "Unemployment and Social Work Practice: An Historical Overview – 1929-1987." In *Unemployment and Welfare: Social Policy and the Work of Social Work,* ed. Graham Riches and Gordon W. Ternowetsky, 271-88. Toronto: Garamond Press, 1990.

Johnston, Russell. *Selling Themselves: The Emergence of Canadian Advertising.* Toronto: University of Toronto Pres, 2001.

Jones, Andrew, and Leonard Rutman. *In the Children's Aid: J.J. Kelso and Child Welfare in Ontario.* Toronto: University of Toronto Press, 1981.

Lafferty, Renée. "Child Welfare in Halifax, 1900-1960: Institutional Transformation, Denominationalism, and the Creation of a 'Public' Welfare System." PhD diss., Department of History, Dalhousie University, 2003.

Latour, Bruno. *Pandora's Hope: Essays on the Reality of Science Studies.* Cambridge, MA: Harvard University Press, 1999.

Lears, T.J. Jackson. *Fables of Abundance: A Cultural History of Advertising in America.* New York: Basic Books, 1994.

Lewis, Jane. *The Voluntary Sector, the State, and Social Work in Britain: The Charity Organisation Society/Family Welfare Association since 1869.* Aldershot: E. Elgar, 1995.

Little, Margaret J.H. "Charity and the Moral Regulation of Motherhood." *Studies in Political Economy* 47 (1995): 89-109.

–. "Claiming a Unique Place: The Introduction of Mothers' Allowances in British Columbia." *BC Studies* 106 (1995): 80-102.

–. *"No Car, No Radio, No Liquor Permit": The Moral Regulation of Single Mothers in Ontario, 1992-1997.* Toronto: Oxford University Press, 1998.

Lloyd, David, and Paul Thomas. *Culture and the State.* London: Routledge, 1998.

Lubove, Roy. *The Professional Altruist: The Emergence of Social Work as a Career, 1880-1930.* Cambridge, MA: Harvard University Press, 1965.

MacLennan, Anne. *Red Feather in Montreal: A History.* Montreal: Red Feather Foundation, 1996.

Marks, Lynne. "Personal Ties and Poor Relief in Small Town Ontario." *Studies in Political Economy* 47 (1995): 61-87.

–. *Revivals and Roller Rinks: Religion, Leisure, and Identity in Late-Nineteenth-Century Small-Town Ontario.* Toronto: University of Toronto Press, 1996.

Martin, Samuel A. *An Essential Grace: Funding Canada's Health Care, Education, Welfare, Religion, and Culture.* Toronto: McClelland and Stewart, 1985.

Maurutto, Paula. *Governing Charities: Church and State in Toronto's Catholic Archdiocese, 1850-1950.* Montreal: McGill-Queen's University Press, 2003.

McCallum, Todd. "'Still Raining, Market Still Rotten': Homeless Men and the Early Years of the Great Depression in Vancouver." PhD diss., Department of History, Queen's University, 2004.

McCarthy, Kathleen D. "Women and Political Culture." In *Charity, Philanthropy, and Civility in American History,* ed. Lawrence J. Friedman and Mark D. McGarvie, 179-98. New York: Cambridge University Press, 2003.

McClintock, Anne. *Imperial Leather: Race, Gender, and Sexuality in the Colonial Contest.* New York: Routledge, 1995.

McGarvie, Mark D. "The *Dartmouth College* Case and the Legal Design of Civil Society." In *Charity, Philanthropy, and Civility in American History,* ed. Lawrence J. Friedman and Mark D. McGarvie, 91-106. New York: Cambridge University Press, 2003.

McInnis, Peter S. *Harnessing Labour Confrontation: Shaping the Postwar Settlement in Canada, 1943-1950.* Toronto: University of Toronto Press, 2002.

Meyers, Diana T. "Decentralizing Autonomy: Five Faces of Selfhood." Paper presented at Dalhousie University, Department of Philosophy, 20 August 1999.

–. *Self, Society, and Personal Choice.* New York: Columbia University Press, 1989.

Miller, J.R. "Anti-Catholicism in Canada: From the British Conquest to the Great War." In *Creed and Culture: The Place of English-Speaking Catholics in Canadian Society, 1750-1930*, ed. Terence Murphy and Gerald Stortz, 25-48. Montreal: McGill-Queen's University Press, 1993.

Mitchinson, Wendy. "Canadian Women and Church Missionary Societies in the 19th Century: A Step towards Independence." *Atlantis* 2, 2, part 2 (1977): 57-75.

Moore, William. *The Clash! A Study in Nationalities.* London: J.M. Dent and Sons, 1918.

Morley, P.F. *Bridging the Chasm: A Study of the Ontario-Quebec Question.* Toronto: J.M. Dent and Sons, 1919.

Morton, Desmond. *Fight or Pay: Soldiers' Families in the Great War.* Vancouver: UBC Press, 2004.

Morton, Suzanne. *At Odds: Gambling and Canadians, 1919-1969.* Toronto: University of Toronto Press, 2003.

Moscovitch, Allan. *Seventy-Five Years of the Social Planning Council.* Ottawa: Social Planning Council of Ottawa-Carleton, 2003.

Murphy, Terence, and Gerald Stortz, eds. *Creed and Culture: The Place of English-Speaking Catholics in Canadian Society, 1750-1930.* Montreal: McGill-Queen's University Press, 1993.

Oldfield, Adrian. "Citizenship and Community: Civic Republicanism and the Modern World." In *The Citizenship Debates*, ed. Gershon Shafir, 75-91. Minneapolis: University of Minnesota Press, 1998.

Oliver, Peter. *G. Howard Ferguson, Ontario Tory.* Toronto: University of Toronto Press, 1977.

O'Malley, Pat. "Risk and Responsibility." In *Foucault and Political Reason: Liberalism, Neo-Liberalism, and Rationalities of Government*, ed. Andrew Barry, Thomas Osborne, and Nikolas Rose, 189-208. Chicago: University of Chicago Press, 1996.

Ormsby, Margaret. *British Columbia: A History.* Toronto: Macmillan, 1976.

Owram, Doug. *The Government Generation.* Toronto: University of Toronto Press, 1986.

Paul, Ellen Frankel, Fred D. Miller, Jr., and Jeffrey Paul, eds. *The Welfare State.* New York: Cambridge University Press, 1997.

Perry, J. Harvey. *Taxes, Tariffs, and Subsidies: A History of Canadian Fiscal Development.* Vols. 1 and 2. Toronto: University of Toronto Press, 1955.

Phillips, Jim, Bruce Chapman, and David Stevens, eds. *Between State and Market: Essays on Charities Law and Policy in Canada.* Montreal: McGill-Queen's University Press, 2001.

Pierson, Ruth Roach. "Gender and the Unemployment Insurance Debates in Canada, 1934-1940." *Labour/Le travail* 25 (1990): 77-103.

Pieterse, Jan Nederveen. *White on Black: Images of Africa and Blacks in Western Popular Culture.* New Haven: Yale University Press, 1992.

Piva, Michael. "Government Finance and the Development of the Canadian State." In *Colonial Leviathan: State Formation in Mid-Nineteenth-Century Canada*, ed. A. Greer and I. Radforth, 257-83. Toronto: University of Toronto Press, 1992.

Pocock, J.G.A. "The Ideal of Citizenship since Classical Times." In *The Citizenship Debates*, ed. Gershon Shafir, 31-42. Minneapolis: University of Minnesota Press, 1998.

Poovey, Mary. *Uneven Developments: The Ideological Work of Gender in Victorian England.* Chicago: University of Chicago Press, 1988.

Prochaska, Frank. *The Voluntary Impulse: Philanthropy in Modern Britain.* London: Faber and Faber, 1988.

Pross, A. Paul. *Group Politics and Public Policy.* Toronto: Oxford University Press, 1992.

Roberts-Moore, Judith C.M. "Maximum Relief for Minimum Cost? Coping with Unemployment and Relief in Canada during the Depression, 1929-1939." MA thesis, Department of History, Carleton University, 1980.

Rodgers, Daniel T. *Atlantic Crossings: Social Politics in a Progressive Age.* Cambridge, MA: Belknap Press, 1998.

Rooke, Patricia, and R.L. Schnell. *No Bleeding Heart: Charlotte Whitton, a Feminist on the Right.* Vancouver: UBC Press, 1987.

Rorty, Richard. *Contingency, Irony, and Solidarity.* Cambridge, UK: Cambridge University Press, 1989.

Rose, Nikolas. "Governing 'Advanced' Liberal Democracies." In *Foucault and Political Reason: Liberalism, Neo-Liberalism, and Rationalities of Government*, ed. Andrew Barry, Thomas Osborne, and Nikolas Rose, 37-64. Chicago: University of Chicago Press, 1996.

Ross, Aileen D. "Organized Philanthropy in an Urban Community." *Canadian Journal of Economics and Political Science* 18, 4 (1952): 474-86.

Salamon, Lester M. *Partners in Public Service: Government-Nonprofit Relations in the Modern Welfare State.* Baltimore: Johns Hopkins University Press, 1995.

Sandel, Michael. *Democracy's Discontent: America in Search of a Public Philosophy.* Cambridge, MA: Belknap Press, 1996.

Schmidtz, David. "Guarantees." In *The Welfare State*, ed. Ellen Frankel Paul, Fred D. Miller, Jr., and Jeffrey Paul, 1-19. New York: Cambridge University Press, 1997.

Scott, James C. *Seeing Like a State: How Certain Schemes to Improve the Human Condition Have Failed.* New Haven: Yale University Press, 1998.

Scott, Joan W. "Gender: A Useful Category of Historical Analysis." *American Historical Review* 91, 5 (1986): 1053-75.

Seeley, John R., et al. *Community Chest: A Case Study in Philanthropy.* Toronto: University of Toronto Press, 1970.

Shore, Marlene. *The Science of Social Redemption.* Toronto: University of Toronto Press, 1987.

Skinner, Quentin. "Language and Social Change." In *Meaning and Context: Quentin Skinner and His Critics*, ed. James Tully, 119-32. Cambridge, UK: Polity Press, 1988.

Speisman, Stephen. *The Jews of Toronto.* Toronto: McClelland and Stewart, 1979.

Squires, Jessica. "Ideological Formation and Liberal 'Consensus': Reading the Rowell-Sirois Commission." MA thesis, Department of History, Dalhousie University, 2003.

Stocker, Michael. "The Schizophrenia of Modern Ethical Theories." *Journal of Philosophy* 73, 14 (1976): 453-66.

Struthers, James. *The Limits of Affluence: Welfare in Ontario: 1920-1970.* Toronto: University of Toronto Press, 1994.

–. "'Lord Give Us Men': Women and Social Work in English Canada." In *The "Benevolent" State: The Growth of Welfare in Canada,* ed. Allan Moscovitch and Jim Albert, 111-25. Toronto: Garamond, 1987.

–. *No Fault of Their Own: Unemployment and the Canadian Welfare State, 1914-1941.* Toronto: University of Toronto Press, 1983.

–. "Shadows from the Thirties: The Federal Government and Unemployment Assistance, 1941-1956." In *The Canadian Welfare State: Evolution and Transition,* ed. Jacqueline S. Ismael, 3-32. Edmonton: University of Alberta Press, 1987.

Taylor, John H. "Engineering, Audit, and Fire: Governance and Modernity in Depression Ottawa." In *Ottawa: Making a Capital,* ed. Jeff Keshen and Nicole St. Onge, 333-48. Ottawa: University of Ottawa Press, 2001.

–. *Ottawa: An Illustrated History.* Toronto: James Lorimer and Company, 1986.

–. "Sources of Political Conflict in the Thirties: Welfare Policy and a Geography of Need." In *The "Benevolent" State: The Growth of Welfare in Canada,* ed. Allan Moscovitch and Jim Albert, 144-54. Toronto: Garamond, 1987.

Thomas-Bernard, Wanda, and Judith Fingard. "Black Women at Work: Race, Family, and Community in Greater Halifax." In *Mothers of the Municipality: Women, Work, and Social Policy in Post-1945 Halifax,* ed. Judith Fingard and Janet Guildford, 189-225. Toronto: University of Toronto Press, 2005.

Tillotson, Shirley. "Class and Community in Canadian Welfare Work, 1933-1960." *Journal of Canadian Studies* 32, 1 (1997): 63-92.

–. "Dollars, Democracy, and the Children's Aid Society." In *Mothers of the Municipality: Women, Work, and Social Policy in Post-1945 Halifax,* ed. Judith Fingard and Janet Guildford, 76-109. Toronto: University of Toronto Press, 2005.

–. *The Public at Play: Gender and the Politics of Recreation in Postwar Ontario.* Toronto: University of Toronto Press, 2000.

–. "'When Our Membership Awakens': Welfare Work and Canadian Union Activism, 1950-1965." *Labour/Le travail* 40 (1997): 137-70.

Trattner, Walter. *From Poor Law to Welfare State: A History of Social Welfare in America.* New York: Free Press, 1974.

Trolander, Judith Ann. *Professionalism and Social Change: From the Settlement House Movement to Neighborhood Centers, 1886 to the Present.* New York: Columbia University Press, 1987.

Tronto, Joan C. "Care as a Basis for Radical Political Judgements." *Hypatia* 10, 2 (1995): 141-49.

Tuennerman-Kaplan, Laura. *Helping Ourselves: Power, Giving, and Community Identity in Cleveland, Ohio, 1880-1930.* Kent: Kent State University Press, 2001.

Ursel, Jane. *Private Lives, Public Policy: 100 Years of State Intervention in the Family.* Toronto: Women's Press, 1992.

Valverde, Mariana. *The Age of Light, Soap, and Water: Moral Reform in English Canada, 1885-1925.* Toronto: McClelland and Stewart, 1991.

–. "The Mixed Social Economy as a Canadian Tradition." *Studies in Political Economy* 47 (1995): 33-60.

Varty, Carmen Nielsen. "The City and the Ladies: Politics, Religion, and Female Benevolence in Mid-Nineteenth-Century Hamilton, Canada West." *Journal of Canadian Studies* 38, 2 (2004): 151-71.

Vigod, B.L. "Ideology and Institutions in Quebec: The Public Charities Controversy, 1921-1926." *Histoire sociale* 11, 21 (1978): 167-82.

Walkowitz, Daniel J. *Working with Class: Social Workers and the Politics of Middle-Class Identity.* Chapel Hill: University of North Carolina Press, 1999.

Wills, Gale. *A Marriage of Convenience: Business and Social Work in Toronto, 1918-1957.* Toronto: University of Toronto Press, 1995.

Wolfe, Alan. *Whose Keeper? Social Science and Moral Obligation.* Berkeley: University of California Press, 1989.

Young, Iris Marion. *Justice and the Politics of Difference.* Princeton: Princeton University Press, 1990.

Index

Note: (f) after a page number indicates a figure or an illustration, (t) a table

Printed and bound in Canada by Friesens

Set in Giovanni Book and Scala Sans by Artegraphica Design Co. Ltd.

Copy editor: Dallas Harrison

Proofreader: James Leahy

Indexer: Samantha Bissix